FUTURE
ISRAEL

OTHER BOOKS IN THIS SERIES:

NAC STUDIES IN BIBLE & THEOLOGY

FUTURE ISRAEL

WHY CHRISTIAN ANTI-JUDAISM MUST BE CHALLENGED

BARRY E. HORNER

SERIES EDITOR: E. RAY CLENDENEN

ACADEMIC

NASHVILLE, TENNESSEE

Future Israel: Why Christian Anti-Judaism Must Be Challenged
by Barry E. Horner

Copyright © Barry E. Horner
All rights reserved.
ISBN 13: 978–0–8054–4627–2

Dewey Decimal Classification: 261.26
Subject Heading: JUDAISM \ ESCHATOLOGY \
CHRISTIANITY—RELATIONS—JUDAISM

Printed in the United States of America

1 2 3 4 5 6 7 • 10 09 08 07
LB

Dedication

My wife Ann and editor Ray,
also Moishe, David, John, Ron, Carolyn, Kay, Eddie,
all encouragers after the spirit of Barnabas.

The God of Abraham praise, Who reigns enthroned above;
Ancient of everlasting days, and God of Love;
Jehovah, great I AM! by earth and Heav'n confessed;
I bow and bless the sacred Name forever blessed.

The God of Abraham praise, Whose all sufficient grace
Shall guide me all my happy days, in all my ways.
He calls a worm His friend, He calls Himself my God!
And He shall save me to the end, thro' Jesus' blood.

He by Himself has sworn; I on His oath depend,
I shall, on eagle wings upborne, to Heav'n ascend.
I shall behold His face; I shall His power adore,
And sing the wonders of His grace forevermore.

The goodly land I see, with peace and plenty bless'd;
A land of sacred liberty, and endless rest.
There milk and honey flow, and oil and wine abound,
And trees of life forever grow with mercy crowned.

There dwells the Lord our King, the Lord our righteousness,
Triumphant o'er the world and sin, the Prince of peace;
On Sion's sacred height His kingdom still maintains,
And glorious with His saints in light forever reigns.

The God Who reigns on high the great archangels sing,
And "Holy, holy, holy!" cry, "Almighty King!
Who was, and is, the same, and evermore shall be:
Jehovah—Father—great I AM, we worship Thee!"

Before the Savior's face the ransomed nations bow;
O'erwhelmed at His almighty grace, forever new:
He shows His prints of love—they kindle to a flame!
And sound thro' all the worlds above the slaughtered Lamb.

The whole triumphant host give thanks to God on high;
"Hail, Father, Son, and Holy Ghost," they ever cry.
Hail, Abraham's God, and mine! (I join the heav'nly lays,)
All might and majesty are Thine, and endless praise.

Thomas Olivers

TABLE OF CONTENTS

LIST OF ABBREVIATIONS

CH	*Church History*
GTJ	*Grace Theological Journal*
ICC	International Critical Commentary
ISBE	*International Standard Bible Encyclopedia*
MSJ	*The Master's Seminary Journal*
NAC	New American Commentary
NACSBT	NAC Studies in Bible and Theology
NT	New Testament
OT	Old Testament
TDNT	G. Kittel and G. Friedrich, eds., *Theological Dictionary of the NT*
WTJ	*Westminster Theological Journal*

SERIES PREFACE

We live in an exciting era of evangelical scholarship. Many fine educational institutions committed to the inerrancy of Scripture are training men and women to serve Christ in the church and to advance the gospel in the world. Many church leaders and professors are skillfully and fearlessly applying God's Word to critical issues, asking new questions and developing new tools to answer those questions from Scripture. They are producing valuable new resources to thoroughly equip current and future generations of Christ's servants.

The Bible is an amazing source of truth and an amazing tool when wielded by God's Spirit for God's glory and our good. It is a bottomless well of living water, a treasure house of endless proportions. Like an ancient tell, exciting discoveries can be made on the surface, but even more exciting are those to be found by digging. The books in this series, NAC Studies in Bible and Theology, often take a biblical difficulty as their point of entry, remembering B. F. Westcott's point that "unless all past experience is worthless, the difficulties of the Bible are the most fruitful guides to its divine depths."

This new series is to be a medium through which the work of evangelical scholars can effectively reach the church. It will include detailed exegetical-theological studies of key pericopes such as the Sermon on the Mount and also fresh examinations of topics in biblical theology and systematic theology. It is intended to supplement the New American Commentary, whose exegetical and theological discussions so many have found helpful. These resources are aimed primarily at church leaders and those who are preparing for such leadership. We trust that individual Christians will find them to be an encouragement to greater progress and joy in the faith. More important, our prayer is that they will help the church proclaim Christ more accurately and effectively and that they will bring praise and glory to our great God.

It is a tremendous privilege to be partners in God's grace with the fine scholars writing for this new series as well as with those who will be helped by it. When Christ returns, may He find us "standing firm in one spirit, with one mind, working side by side for the faith of the gospel" (Phil 1:27, HCSB).

E. Ray Clendenen
B&H Publishing Group

FOREWORD

by Moishe Rosen

To be perfectly blunt: I must say the Christians have robbed the Jews! And perhaps what is worse is that this thievery has been encouraged by theologians, pastors, and even Sunday School teachers, where small children are taught to sing the song, "Every promise in the book is mine, every chapter, every verse, every line."

Every promise in Scripture in some way benefits Christians, but it is not all promised to Christians. Sometimes the thievery has been inadvertent and unintentional. It's like thinking that the raincoat hanging in the office closet is yours for wearing home because of unexpected showers. Hopefully, you will discover the raincoat belongs to a fellow worker and you will restore it. It is not as if Christians do not have the greatest promise of God, which is I John 2:25: "And this is the promise that He hath promised us, even eternal life."

Barry Horner is a theologian who furnishes evidence of this identity theft and the false claim that the Church inherited all the promises of Israel. Not only that, he demonstrates how by restoring the election of God or chosenness to the Jewish people, the Church is even more blessed.

He shows that the Jewish people represent current historical evidence of the Bible's complete trustworthiness. Every living Jewish person, no matter what he believes, no matter what he observes, no matter whether or not he cares, is evidence that the God of the Bible *is*, and that He keeps His Word.

Israel may be blinded in part, yet there is a glorious destiny to be fulfilled. That glorious destiny is a light and a blessing to the Church of today and tomorrow.

Horner's scholarship is impeccable, his reasoning is profound, his revelation of theological anti-Semitism is astounding. His proposal for the solution is based on the integrity of Scripture and the sovereignty of God. I can't imagine a more useful book for those who take theology seriously.

PERSONAL INTRODUCTION

In the pilgrimage of a Christian, significant junctures are encountered that bring about a radical change of direction, particularly in the realm of doctrinal course correction, that may be regarded as near-revolutionary. Such was the case when I came to a knowledge of a more Reformed doctrinal emphasis, that is, exegetical Calvinism. I will never forget the change of perspective that came about with the reading of Martin Luther's *Bondage of the Will*; a whole gospel worldview was turned around, even though appreciation still remained for an earlier evangelical heritage that did not agree with the German Reformer's understanding of human corruption and the sovereign grace of God. Furthermore, having been raised in Methodism, this new doctrinal allegiance became more sympathetic with the Calvinistic foundation of George Whitefield rather than John Wesley's Arminianism, and as a result fellowship tilted toward those of a more Reformed persuasion. There further came appreciative acquaintance with John Owen, C. H. Spurgeon, Charles Hodge, B. B. Warfield, Loraine Boettner, J. I. Packer, Martyn Lloyd-Jones, and others, by means of *The Banner of Truth Trust* and other similar publishers. Consequently, there also developed a more heartfelt understanding of the grace of God in the light of man's thorough sinful pollution, which led to expanding familiarity with Calvinism, more euphemistically referred to as "the doctrines of grace."

This whole new environment, although incorporating Anglican, Presbyterian, Congregational, and Baptist legacies, has presented an admirable unified front. With this aura there has been fervent endorsement of the major historic strands of the Reformation with regard to God, man, sin, and the gospel, and to a lesser degree with regard to the doctrine of the church. The area of eschatology, however, has also revealed a lesser degree of unity, except that it would be true to say that Augustinian amillennialism has appeared to be the predominant school of prophetic thought, with postmillennialism ranking a respectable second, and premillennialism being relegated to a tolerable third place, provided that it was purged of that much maligned subset, dispensationalism. Certainly amillennialism has been paraded, in the main, as the most historically viable scheme of eschatology, having been rooted in the esteemed, fourth-century Bishop of Hippo, as well as the subsequent revered Reformers, and to a lesser and yet more variegated degree, their Puritan successors.

Following this awakening, I continued to maintain interest in the prophetic schools of thought while retaining premillennial convictions, even though pressure was experienced, especially from amillennialists, to advance to purer Reformed heights that abandoned a carnal, Zionist system that clung to Jewish "weak and bankrupt elemental forces" (Gal 4:9). Yet while there was firm conviction that biblical Calvinism rested on solid exegetical grounds, there was never the same strength of belief that one's prophetic convictions needed overturning as well. Certainly many challenging arguments were offered to convince me that the premillennial perspective was not in the mainstream of Reformation thought. After all, Augustine had surely dealt chiliasm or millennialism, which he had earlier affirmed, such a crippling blow. There was also the suggestion that as the sixteenth and seventeenth centuries had certainly witnessed the recovery of the Pauline gospel, so this awakening was to be heeded in terms of a parallel and more reliable scheme of eschatology. In addition there was the inference that since premillennialism was more aligned with the popular tide of Arminianism, this provided further proof for Calvinists of its lack of validity.

Yet the gnawing conviction remained that the persuasive exegesis that led to biblical, soteriological Calvinism did not necessarily lead to the companion scheme of amillennialism. The reason for this was that such a system was inclined to rely too heavily on lauded historical currents of belief, the result being that a questionable hermeneutical framework was imposed on the plain meaning of the biblical text. In other words, historic tradition—especially that allied with Wittenberg in Germany, Geneva in Switzerland, and Westminster in England—tended to strongly influence exegesis. After all, Martin Luther, John Calvin, or John Owen could not possibly be wrong!

More recently, a closer study of four books of the Bible has led me now to more firmly assert that the basic premillennial model of biblical prophecy, and especially as it relates to ethnic and national Israel, is closest to the truth of Scripture. First, there was a study of Zechariah, so permeated with the ultimate triumph of the Messiah and the nation of Israel. The prophet speaks of God's vindication on earth when He "will become king over all the earth—Yahweh alone, and His name alone" (Zech 14:9).[1] I will never forget the study of David Baron's commentary on this book, which seemed

---

[1] Amillennialist V. S. Poythress has made a significant comment when, in dialogue with dispensationalists under the auspices of the *Evangelical Theological Society*: "Zechariah 14, if read in a straightforward manner, is particularly difficult for an amillennialist. In fact, if I were to defend premillennialism in a debate, I would probably choose Zechariah 14 as a main text" ("Response to Robert L. Saucy's Paper," *GTJ* 10.2 [Fall 1989]: 159).

so much more illuminating to the text than Calvin's. Then a close study of Romans over several years, and particularly chaps. 9–11, resulted in an indelible impression that for Paul, the converted Hebrew rabbi, Israel has an ongoing national identity, its unbelief notwithstanding. On the other hand, it seemed as if Reformed exegesis, at least on a prima facie reading of the text, was attempting to avoid the obvious.

One particular comment has helped me to grasp better Paul's Jewish thrust within Romans at this juncture. John McRay, Professor of Old Testament and Archaeology at Wheaton College Graduate School, in the introduction to his significant volume, *Paul: His Life and Teaching*, wrote:

> I have tried to 'put on my first-century glasses,' look at Paul in his Jewish and Hellenistic world of the Mediterranean, and see him not as a fourth-century church father, a sixteenth-century Protestant reformer, or a twenty-first century evangelical missionary, but as what he was, a first-century Jewish rabbi who accepted Jesus as his Messiah and became an ardent, dedicated Messianic Jew. In this volume I have tried to emphasize that Paul was not the founder of Christianity, that he never ceased to be a Jew, and that Christianity is not a Gentile religion. There has never been a greater advocate of the universal composition of the Christian faith than Paul, who emphatically asserted that in Christ "there is neither Jew nor Greek, there is neither slave nor free, there is neither male not female; for you are all one in Christ Jesus" (Gal. 3:28). This means that when people place their trust in Jesus, neither Jews nor Gentiles have to abandon their ancestry, neither males nor females have to abandon their gender, and neither slaves nor free people have to abandon their sociological status. Paul's central focus in his preaching was that Gentiles do not have to become Jews any more than Jews have to become Gentiles, for as he went on to say, "If you are Christ's, then you are Abraham's offspring, heirs according to the promise" (Gal 3:29).[2]

This comment has struck a chord that is still resonating.

At the same time, a study of Hosea for a series of Sunday evening messages, especially the repeated emphases on the mercy of God triumphing over a persistently adulterous Israel, only confirmed what the other three books were declaring. At that time a man of amillennial convictions recommended to me the commentary of Jeremiah Burroughs on Hosea that I believe he had not studied too closely. How delightful it was to discover the clear premillennial convictions of this seventeenth-century Puritan, including his belief in a glorious future for national Israel. Then a study of Ezekiel, especially chaps. 36–39, led to the conclusion that this is also a

[2] J. McRay, *Paul: His Life and Teaching* (Grand Rapids: Baker, 2003), 11–12.

pivotal passage showing God's plan for Israel's national future. In particular, my understanding of Judeo-centric eschatology owes much to the inability of supercessionism (or replacement theology, the view that the church has replaced Israel in God's plan of redemption) to deal satisfactorily with the details of the text. This is despite supercessionism's broad abstraction on account of supposedly superseded old covenant terms and apocalyptic genre. To treat these chapters as providing no more than general and idealistic instruction on regeneration and resurrection, as is done by Patrick Fairbairn and O. Palmer Robertson, is quite unsatisfactory.

In the nineteenth century Horatius Bonar published his *Prophetic Landmarks: Containing Data for Helping to Determine the Question of Christ's Pre-millenial Advent*, which is a solid and judicious premillennial apology. This upholder of the doctrines of sovereign grace considered the pivotal issue regarding a right perception of prophetic revelation to be the primacy of the nature and destiny of the Jewish people in the whole eschatological scheme of things. He wrote,

> The prophecies concerning Israel are the key to all the rest. True principles of interpretation, in regard to them, will aid us in disentangling and illustrating all prophecy together. False principles as to them will most thoroughly perplex and overcloud the whole Word of God.[3]

This significant point will be recommended quite frequently throughout this book. Indeed at this juncture we coin the term "Judeo-centric Eschatology" since it offers such a cohesive basis for the integration of various elements of biblical prophecy, and even more so than the common premillennial recourse to Revelation 20. Given a right understanding of Israel in relation to the Christian Church, an eschatology will nevertheless result that incorporates an essentially premillennial understanding of Revelation 20.

[3] H. Bonar, *Prophetical Landmarks: Containing Data for Helping to Determine the Question of Christ's Pre-millenial Advent* (5th ed.; London: J. Nisbet, 1876), 228. It is accessible (with the revised title *Judeo-centric Premillennialism: Concerning Christ's Pre-Millennial Advent*) on the internet at http://www.bunyanministries.org. E. Sandeen makes a related point when in his *The Roots Of Fundamentalism: British and American Millenarianism, 1800–1930* (Chicago: University of Chicago Press, 1970), 11: "The restoration of the Jews to Palestine—the return of the promised people to the promised land—became firmly established as a plank in the millenarian creed." Also see W. A. VanGemeren, "Israel as the Hermeneutical Crux in the Interpretation of Prophecy," *WTJ* 45 (1983): 132–44; 46 (1984): 254–97. Also Bonar's opponent, Samuel Waldegrave, *New Testament Millenarianism*, Bampton Lectures (London: Hamilton, Adams, 1855), 547, who confesses that the topic of "literal Israel" is the most prominent subject in his published discourse.

Of course, someone is bound to suggest, as if trumping any of the historic prophetic approaches, that when all has been said and done with regard to the three major schools of eschatology, the real, overshadowing central issue concerns the person of Jesus Christ. It is the new covenant which He has established by His blood, and His present reign at the right hand of the Father, that should dominate our thinking and not some distinctive scheme of prophecy. So Reformed amillennialist George Murray commented, "It is Christ, rather than the Hebrew people, Who is the subject of the Old Testament prophets."[4] And of course, all the major schools of prophecy would heartily agree at this point, so that nothing in fact would have been trumped at all. The reason for this is simply that amillennialism, postmillennialism, and premillennialism are all based on their future perspective of history as it will be climaxed at the second coming or parousia of Jesus Christ that crowns the redemptive work of His first coming. In this sense, Jesus Christ is clearly central to all three perspectives, whatever their disagreements might involve. However, this being said, it must be borne in mind that the Lord Jesus Christ remains the quintessential Jew. We would even dare to say that He has lost none of His essential Jewishness. However, Murray continues, "To be sure, the nation was sovereignly chosen by God as the channel through which His oracles might be given to the world; but God no longer deals with them as a chosen nation."[5] How incomplete is the allusion here to Rom 3:2 that ignores Rom 9:4 concerning those who "are [present tense] Israelites, and to them belong the adoption, the glory, the covenants, the giving of the law, the temple service, and the promises." For a professing Calvinist such as Murray to suggest that Israel has lost its election is not only astonishing, but it also flies in the face of Paul's further explanation that "regarding the gospel, they [unbelieving national Israel, not the remnant] are enemies for your [the Gentiles'] advantage, but regarding election [the election, *tēn eklogēn*], they [unbelieving national Israel] are loved because of their forefathers [Abraham, Isaac, and Jacob]" (Rom 11:28). How then can Jesus Christ be exalted when He, "the King of the Jews" (John 19:19), who declared that "salvation is from the Jews" (John 4:22), has His Jewish brethren permanently and nationally defrocked?

Of course, the great difficulty here in dealing with this subject is to maintain a calm spirit that is respectful of opposing points of view while unashamedly pressing home the truth without apology. I do not hesitate to confess my disturbance at that opinion, held by many Calvinists (though

---

[4] G. L. Murray, *Millennial Studies* (Grand Rapids: Baker, 1948), 57.
[5] Ibid.

by no means all), which declares that the Jew today, on account of stubborn unbelief, is covenantally and eternally *persona non grata* in the sight of God. Perhaps most disturbing of all in this regard has been an evident form of theological anti-Judaism among a considerable number of those holding to Reformed convictions. This matter will be documented and addressed with some detail. In conversation, quite a few by their derogatory manner have inferred that they would be delighted if the Arabs would push Israel into the Mediterranean Sea, repossess Palestine, and thus vindicate their eschatology![6] I strongly believe that a true child of God will have a distinctive, persistent (though often anguished) love for the Jewish people notwithstanding their unbelief. Such an attitude follows the example of the apostle Paul, whose fervor endured repeated suffering at the hands of their hard-heartedness and obstinacy. It is significant that when Paul deals with his "countrymen by physical descent" in Romans 9–11, this subject, involving such ultimate national glory, stimulates his passions as do few others.

Many years ago I asked a representative of a leading Reformed publisher why they had not published any volume in sympathy with premillennialism, even though amillennialism and postmillennialism had been well represented. The response was that the reprint of a premillennial volume by J. C. Ryle was being considered, and so some hope was raised though subsequent years saw it diminish. Later, in correspondence with that same person, further enquiry was made but no encouragement was received that a book from a premillennial perspective might arise. Hence, this volume is dedicated to the elucidation of the premillennial perspective, especially as it focuses on national Israel, that has been ignored, belittled, and distorted in Calvinistic, Reformed, and Sovereign Grace circles.

A most important matter that needs to be clarified at this juncture concerns the crucial distinction that must be appreciated between the overriding significance of Israel in the Word of God and relatively lesser matters

---

[6] For instance, S. Sizer has disparagingly stated that "the present brutal, repressive racist policies of the State of Israel would suggest another exile on the horizon rather than a restoration." *Whose Promised Land: Israel and Biblical Prophecy Debate between Neil Cornell (CMJ & ITAC) and Stephen Sizer,* Guildford Diocesan Evangelical Fellowship, St. John's, Woking. Surrey, 18th March, 1997 (http://www.cc-vw.org/articles/ debate.html); Internet accessed May 2007. Also consider the haunting intimation of Chapman: "I *don't* believe that the State of Israel is 'of God' in the sense that it is the fulfillment (or even the preliminary stage in the fulfillment) of all that God promised and predicted in the Old Testament about the future of the land and its people. I would go further and suggest that for Christians to interpret these events simply as the fulfillment of prophecy represents a kind of regression." C. Chapman, *Whose Promised Land?* (Tring, Herts, England: Lion Publishing, 1983), 227.

of eschatological concern, as with regard to the antichrist, the great tribulation, the rapture, etc. The nature and role of Israel in the Bible, in both Testaments, is transcendently more important than the aforementioned details, though they may necessarily call for serious consideration of lesser proportions. Furthermore, with regard to Israel we are not dealing with a doctrinal emphasis that has little relationship with significant Christian ethics. Quite the contrary, as our study will unquestionably prove, the wrong perception of Israel and the Jews by Christians, biblically speaking, has produced consequences of horrific proportions during the history of the Christian Church in all its strands. Such a shameful legacy, perpetuated during the illustrious Reformation and onwards, is still prevalent in substantial degrees in many Calvinist, Reformed, and Sovereign Grace environments. The reader who is disturbed by such a charge is simply asked to hold back judgment until the following evidence is weighed. This unethical consequence will be pressed home in succeeding chapters. While the process may be painful, nevertheless it is hoped that the end result will be the fruit of genuine repentance evidenced by heartfelt love for God's beloved "enemies" (Rom 11:28), they being every Christian's kinsmen through faith in Abraham's God (Gal 3:29).

If a Christian's eschatology produces an indifference, detachment, or even antagonism towards things Jewish, though there continues to be manifest unbelief within national Israel, there is most likely something fundamentally wrong with that eschatological expression. True doctrine, rightly comprehended, does not produce bad attitudes, especially that which is so obviously un-Pauline. It ought to be a shame for any professing Christian to lack that apostolic compassion for the Jews which never diminished, even when Paul eventually reached Rome (Acts 28:17–22). Hence, where this unsavory attitude prevails, even with a mere facade of token respect for the Jewish people, there is need for a return with freshness to the only final source that can resolve an issue having such profound moral implications, that is to the objective, truthful, inscribed Word of God. The major part of this book contends for the present and future hope of national Israel according to theological synthesis based on biblical exegesis that receives particular focus in chapter 10. Here exposition deals with Rom 11:1–32, Gal 6:16, Eph 2:11–22, Phil 3:2–3, Heb 8:7–13, and 1 Pet 2:9–10. Chapters 9 and 11 also deal with Scripture in some detail. In addition, a number of appendices are included that underpin the overall theological argument.

Concerning terminology, a word of explanation is necessary. Instead of the common emotive term of "anti-Semitism" being employed, which is often qualified as either racial or theological, the more specific "anti-Judaism" is mainly used. Nevertheless, even anti-Judaism needs explication. Here it is intended to refer to classic anti-Judaism, which involves opposition to the biblical legacy of Torah mediated through Abraham and Moses rather than opposition to the Rabbinic and Talmudic accretions that Jesus Christ so vigorously opposed, though doubtless some overlap will nevertheless be involved. The use of "anti-Zionism" will more narrowly focus on opposition to the recent establishment of the nation of modern Israel. With regard to the Augustinian legacy of Israel's displacement by the Christian church as the new spiritual Israel, the accepted terms of "replacement theology" and "supercessionism" will be used interchangeably. Some authors vigorously renounce association with these designations and often attempt to argue against their validity. Nevertheless, for all such verbal ducking and weaving by those who in reality are supercessionists, they are unable to obscure obvious identification with the same essential anti-Judaic spirit that substitutes concepts such as "progression," "transference," and "fulfillment."

In a nutshell then, the issue here concerns whether Israel, incorporating individuality, nationality, and territory, has a future according to the mind of Abraham's God. It is certain that great ethical consequences are at stake here, and not mere eschatological speculation. Consider the comment of Reformed theologian Herman Ridderbos.

> The church, then, as the people of the New Covenant has taken the place of Israel, and national Israel is nothing other than the empty shell from which the pearl has been removed and which has lost its function in the history of redemption.[7]

I suggest that the illustration here, in being representative of much Reformed opinion, is quite inappropriate in that it alludes to Judaism and national Israel as a matter only worthy of being discarded. So the issue of supercessionism is not something to be taken lightly or merely academically. When a scholar and exegete of the stature of C. E. B. Cranfield so movingly and publicly repents of his former belief that the church has replaced Israel,[8] then none ought to exclude themselves from hearing the call to seriously

---

[7] H. Ridderbos, *Paul: An Outline of His Theology* (trans. J. R. De Witt; Grand Rapids: Eerdmans, 1975), 354–55.

[8] "And I confess with shame to having also myself used in print on more than one occasion this language of the replacement of Israel by the Church" (C. E. B. Cranfield, *The Epistle to the Romans*. ICC [Edinburgh: T&T Clark, 1979], 448, n. 2)..

review this matter and the vital issues that are involved. He also wrote in his commentary concerning Romans 9–11,

> It is only where the church persists in refusing to learn this message [of Romans 9–11], where it secretly—perhaps unconsciously—believes that its own existence is based on human achievement, and so fails to understand God's mercy to itself, that it is unable to believe in God's mercy for still unbelieving Israel, and so entertains the ugly and unscriptural notion that God has cast off His people Israel and simply replaced it by the Christian Church. These three chapters emphatically forbid us to speak of the Church as having once and for all taken the place of the Jewish people.[9]

Yes, longstanding historic error dies hard. However, let us Scripturally, prayerfully, and soberly reason together.

[9] Ibid., 448.

Chapter 1

ISRAEL AND CHRISTIAN ANTI-JUDAISM IN CONTRAST

That Paul, the apostle to the Gentiles, was decidedly pro-Israel in his ministry is often neglected. This should not surprise us since the Lord declared to Ananias that Paul would be "My chosen instrument to carry My name before the Gentiles, kings, and the sons of Israel" (Acts 9:15). Furthermore, it is clear from Romans 9–11 that the present status and future destiny of unbelieving national Israel in general, apart from a remnant of Jewish Christians, was a matter of passionate, unrelenting, even primary concern for Paul (Rom 1:16). He especially seems to have considered it necessary that Gentile Christians at Rome should be addressed, not simply on account of their predominance, but more particularly because of their tendency to be arrogant toward Jewish believers (Rom 11:18–20). Paul's concerns included the need to clarify whether the promises of God to national Israel have now been nullified. In other words, has national Israel sinned away the grace of God so that it is, now and forever, persona non grata in His sight? Hence, is there a future destiny for national Israel, as perhaps a minority of Jewish believers at Rome might talk about with persistence? Or is Jewishness now a matter of receding concern in the present since it will certainly have no future validity? Do believing Gentiles have any ongoing responsibilities toward unbelieving national Israel that include acknowledgement of a distinct covenantal future? To these questions the apostle responds that "the promises" still "belong" to Israel (9:4), that "the Word of God" has not "failed" to the promised seed of Abraham (9:6–8), that "God has not rejected His people" (11:1–2), that Israel has not "stumbled so as to fall" (i.e., to be beyond divine recovery, 11:11), that Gentile Christians are to humbly and respectfully regard unbelieving Jews with fear (11:20), so that, as a consequence, eventually "all Israel will be saved" (11:26).

It is unfortunately true that over 1900 years of church history have not witnessed the eventual resolution of these problems as proposed by Paul, and especially at a practical level, however clarifying he may have intended to be. In the same vein then, it might well be asked, "Has the Christian Church learned anything in this regard, but especially in ethical terms, concerning its treatment of unbelieving Jews over many centuries according to Paul's injunction (Rom 11:18–20)?" In spite of voluminous Christian study of these questions, the evidence culled from past centuries would tend to indicate abysmal failure, particularly in terms of the shameful record of Christianity's consistently disgraceful treatment of the Jews. And further, this well attested reputation cannot possibly be divorced from the horrific record of anti-Judaism that erupted during the twentieth century.

However, even in this twenty-first century, the controversy still rages, seemingly afresh. The establishment of the State of Israel in 1948, as well as the reclamation of Old Jerusalem by the Jews in 1967, has only appeared to exacerbate the conflict whereby such terms as "Zionism" and "a Palestinian State" have become highly emotive epithets for fiercely opposing causes. While there has been substantial support for the nation of Israel within conservative evangelical Christendom, according to biblical presuppositions and identification as Christian Zionism, nevertheless a vociferous segment has opposed any acknowledgment whereby God continues to have present covenantal interest in His ancient people, especially in a national and territorial sense. Along with this reaction there has usually been the expression of sympathy for the beleaguered Palestinian people, particularly in terms of their being deprived of land and respect by the rapacious Israelis. As a result, a growing literary response from some Christians has challenged the very legitimacy of Israel's existence, but particularly at a biblical and societal level. Much of this has suggested that the complex issues revolve around the need of justice for the Palestinians on account of their suffering at the hands of Jewish injustice. Allied to this belief has been the conviction that a compromise resolution must be brokered for the parties in conflict. Thus a Palestinian State must be established alongside or within Israel (perhaps by means of a "Road Map" proposal), that would establish the relative social peace that has so far eluded the Middle East over the centuries.

As a result, opposition to Christian Zionism in biblical and covenantal terms has elicited the counter-charge of "theological anti-Judaism" from those who support the cause of national Israel, even though the Jews remain in general unbelief. Hence, the polarizing result has been a defensive loyalty expressed by Christian Zionists in the face of harsh criticism of national Israel by Christian sympathizers with the Palestinian and Arab cause. These anti-Zionist Christians usually espouse an Augustinian, homogenous eschatology that would absorb and supplant all former Jewish distinctions. Furthermore, this conflict has particularly manifested itself within much of conservative evangelical Christendom. Thus, some Christians maintain that Israel has a national and territorial eschatological future according to

God's covenantal purposes, and in particular a mass conversion at the end of this age. However, many others hold to an anti-Judaic belief denying that modern Israel has any eschatological future in national and territorial terms. This book proposes that the former of these two theses is the more biblically and morally correct. Further, I believe that such a difference is not merely a theological one that we can calmly agree to disagree over, as if divorced from any behavioral accountability. The reason is that the pro-Judaic perspective involves a vital ethical element, sharply contrasting with unethical anti-Judaism throughout church history, which is inextricably bound to the theological construct that we hope to demonstrate both exegetically and historically. However, we will first consider these two opposing eschatological perspectives from the viewpoint of specific historic examples concerning biblical interpretation.

National Israel with No Distinctive Eschatological Hope

I offer here two examples of at best a cool toleration of the Jews and certainly an absence of that Pauline passion that the apostle maintained throughout his missionary endeavors. Whatever the terminology that is used concerning this perspective, whether replacement theology, supercessionism, fulfillment theology, transference theology, or absorptionism, they all amount to the same basic denigration of the Jews and ultimately of national Israel in the present Christian dispensation. More evidence in this regard will follow in subsequent chapters.

Aurelius Augustine

The monumental contribution of this fourth-century church father of North Africa in the realm of eschatology cannot be exaggerated. It is not simply a question of his prevailing dominance over millennialism whereby the church in his present world was esteemed as the true earthly representation of the heavenly city of God in anticipation of heavenly consummation; it is the fact that his teaching concerning the future of the Jews, in relation to the church triumphant on earth, both saved them from total decimation and preserved them for intentional humiliation. This was a major feature of Augustine's famous, yet obviously mistaken, interpretation of Ps 59:11, "Do not kill them [the Jews]; otherwise, my people will forget. / By Your power, make them homeless wanderers." So he concluded,

Therefore God has shown the Church in her enemies the Jews the grace of His compassion, since, as saith the apostle, "their offence is the salvation of the Gentiles." And therefore He has not slain them, that is, He has not let the knowledge that they are Jews be lost in them, although they have been conquered by the Romans, lest they should forget the law of God, and their testimony should be of no avail in this matter of which we treat. But it was not enough that he [God] should say, "Slay them not, lest they should at last forget Thy law," unless he had also added, "Disperse them;" because if they had only been in their own land with that testimony of the Scriptures, and not everywhere, certainly the Church which is everywhere could not have had them as witnesses among all nations to the prophecies which were sent before concerning Christ.[1]

So by way of imposition upon the text, David's enemies are interpreted as the Jews, being enemies of the church. Unlike the ferocity of some earlier church fathers, Augustine's influential attitude appears more temperate so that, with enforced humiliation, the vagabond Jews might be a testimony of God's dealings in judgment on them according to Scripture. However, the result of his seeming tolerant exposition here was what James Carroll described as a double-edged sword:

On one side, against Chrysostom and even Ambrose, it requires an end to all violent assaults against synagogues, Jewish property, and Jewish persons. . . . On the other side, Augustine's relatively benign attitude toward Jews is rooted still in assumptions of supercessionism that would prove to be deadly. The "Witness" prescription attributed to him—Let them survive but not thrive!—would underlie the destructive ambivalence that marked Catholic attitudes toward Jews from then on. Ultimately history would show that such double-edged ambivalence is impossible to maintain without disastrous consequences. For a thousand years, the compulsively repeated pattern of that ambivalence would show in bishops and popes protecting Jews—but from expressly Christian mobs that wanted to kill Jews because of what bishops and popes had taught about Jews. Such a teaching which wants it both ways was bound to fail, as would become evident at every point in history when Jews presumed, whether economically or culturally or both, to even think of thriving. This is the legacy that haunts the Catholic Church into the twenty-first century, a perverse legacy from which, despite the twentieth century's jolts, the Church is not yet free.[2]

---

[1] Augustine, *The City of God*, 18.46. It is tragic that such obvious misinterpretation of this passage should have become so influential over the centuries that followed. Plainly, in Ps 59:11, David the Jew is interceding for his enemies, and not especially the Jews, when he declares, "Do not kill them; . . . By Your power, make them homeless wanderers."

[2] J. Carroll. *Constantine's Sword: the Church and the Jews: A History* (Boston: Houghton Mifflin, 2001), 218–19.

Consequently, the Augustinian legacy kept the Jews dispersed, disgraced, and depressed—except for the hope of their individual conversion, or until their national conversion at the end of this age when they would then become absorbed into the one true, holy, catholic, apostolic church. Hence, such a scattered preservation in no way anticipated any distinctive eschatological hope for the Jews. Rather for Augustine, in Romans 11,

> Some Jews have believed in Christ, and they are the remnant of the natural olive and fulfillment of the divine promises to historical Israel. . . . The "Israel" that will ultimately be saved are the predestined elect, drawn into a unity out of Jews and Gentiles. . . . Judaism is simply relegated to the latter [non-elect] category, and its status in salvation-history assigned to the pre-Christian past.[3]

So the Christian can take to himself the name of Israelite since it has been forfeited by the Jews who, having lost their birthright, are now to be named Esau. Augustine commented on Ps 114:3,

> For if we hold with a firm heart the grace of God which hath been given us, we are Israel, the seed of Abraham. . . . Let therefore no Christian consider himself alien to the name of Israel. . . . The Christian people then is rather Israel. . . . But that multitude of Jews, which was deservedly reprobated for its perfidy, for the pleasures of the flesh sold their birthright, so that they belonged not to Jacob, but rather to Esau.[4]

The effect then of this supercessionist teaching upon subsequent centuries was profound, as Carroll has pointed out. So Jeremy Cohen confirmed,

> Augustine of Hippo bequeathed so much to western civilization that one need hardly wonder if this bequest included his ideas on Jews and Judaism. Indeed, modern students of Jewish-Christian relations typically attribute the theological foundations of the medieval church's Jewish policy to Augustine, referring as a matter of course to the legacies and principles of Augustinian anti-Judaism.[5]

---

[3] Peter Gorday, *Principles Of Patristic Exegesis: Romans 9–11 in Origen, John Chrysostom, and Augustine* (New York: E. Mellen Press, 1983), 171, 333.

[4] Augustine, *Expositions on the Book of Psalms by Saint Augustine*, Vol. 5 (Oxford: John Henry Parker, 1853), 114.3.

[5] Jeremy Cohen, *Living Letters of the Law: Ideas of the Jew in Medieval Christianity* (Berkeley: University of California Press, 1999), 19. This is a significant study of not only Augustine's foundational contribution toward theological anti-Judaism, but also the widespread embrace in varying degrees of this legacy, through to the thirteenth century, by means of Gregory the Great, Isidore of Seville, Agobard of Lyon, Anselm of Canterbury, Bernard of Clairvaux, and Thomas Aquinas.

Hence, Augustine's eschatology regarding Israel, as having played out over centuries of church history, is not something that any Christian ought to boast in thoughtlessly. This legacy is certainly unbiblical in its exegetical, theological and ethical outworking, and thus is un-Pauline. Consequently, it rightly justifies repudiating that basic supercessionist theology which has flowed from these historic beginnings. A better and more pro-Judaic eschatology is needed, and this we believe to be rooted in the full canvas of Scripture when rightly exegeted.

John Calvin

The contribution of this sixteenth-century reformer of Geneva to the emergence of western civilization in Europe, as well as the Reformed movement within Christianity, was truly monumental. His indebtedness to Augustine, like that of Luther, was substantial, as the abundance of al-most adoring references in his *Institutes Of The Christian Religion* indicates. According to the editor of the Battles edition of this work, "Calvin may be said to stand at the culmination of the later Augustinianism. He actually incorporates in his treatment of man and of salvation so many typical pas-sages from Augustine that his doctrine seems here entirely continuous with that of his great African predecessor."[6]

With regard to the Jews and Israel, there is an attitude of tolerance, similar to Augustine's that is void of any distinctive, covenantal, passionate eschatological acknowledgment. As Paul Johnson explained,

> Jean Calvin . . . was more well disposed towards Jews [than Luther], partly because he tended to agree with them on the question of lending at interest; he reported Jewish arguments objectively in his writings and was even ac-cused by his Lutheran enemies of being a Judaizer. Nonetheless, Jews were expelled from Calvinist cities and the Calvinist Palatinate.[7]

Like Augustine, Calvin taught that the Christian Church had become the new spiritual Israel, the amalgam of Jew and Gentile, whereby past ethnic identity had become null and void. He commented on Rom 11:26, where Paul declares, "And in this way all Israel will be saved":

---

[6] J. Calvin, *Institutes Of The Christian Religion* (ed. J. T. McNeill; trans. F. L. Battles; Philadel-phia, Westminster, 1960), 1.lviii.

[7] P. Johnson, *A History Of The Jews* (New York: Harper & Row, 1988), 242–43. Also refer to M. J. Vlach, *The Church as a Replacement of Israel: An Analysis of Supercessionism* (Ph.D. diss., Southeastern Baptist Theological Seminary, 2004), 56–59.

Many understand this of the Jewish people, as though Paul had said, that religion would again be restored among them as before: but I extend the word *Israel* to all the people of God, according to this meaning, "When the Gentiles shall come in, the Jews also shall return [as an accumulating remnant] from their defection to the obedience of faith; and thus shall be completed the salvation of the whole Israel of God, which must be gathered from both; and yet in such a way that the Jews shall obtain the first place [at the commencement of the Church], being as it were the first-born in God's family." This interpretation seems to me the most suitable, because Paul intended here to set forth the completion of the kingdom of Christ, which is by no means to be confined to the Jews, but is to include the whole world. The same manner of speaking we find in Galatians 6:16. The Israel of God is what he calls the Church, gathered alike from Jews and Gentiles.[8]

Calvin's understanding of the future of national Israel can also be observed in his comments on Hos 1:10–11:

For so long a time has passed away since their [the sons of Israel's] exile, and . . . since there has been no restoration of this people, it is certain that this prophecy ought not to be restricted to seed according to the flesh. For there was a prescribed time for the Jews, when the Lord purposed to restore them to their country; and, at the end of seventy years, a free return was granted them by Cyrus. Then Hosea speaks not here of the kingdom of Israel, but of the Church, which was to be restored by a return, composed both of Jews and of Gentiles.[9]

Also consider Calvin's explanation of the Lord's promise in Jer 32:37–41 of an "everlasting covenant" with those whom He would "gather . . . from all the lands where I have banished them" and "plant them faithfully in this land":

We now then understand what the Prophet means when he compares to a plantation the restoration of the people after their return from exile. We know, indeed, that the people from that time had not been banished, and that the Temple had ever stood, though the faithful had been pressed down with many troubles; but this was only a type of a plantation. We must therefore necessarily pass on to Christ, in order to have a complete fulfillment of this promise. . . . Let us then know that the Church was planted in Judea, for it remained to the time of Christ. And as Christ has pulled down the wall of partition, so that there is now no difference between Jews and Gentiles, God plants us now in the holy land, when he grafts us into the body of Christ.[10]

---

[8] J. Calvin, *The Epistle of Paul the Apostle to the Romans* (Edinburgh: Calvin Translation Society, 1849), 437.

[9] J. Calvin, *The Book of the Prophet Hosea* (Edinburgh: Calvin Translation Society, 1847), 64.

[10] J. Calvin, *The Book of the Prophet Jeremiah* (Edinburgh: Calvin Translation Society, 1854), 220–21.

These instances clearly display the fruit of a subjective, impositional hermeneutic that appears to be more presuppositionally than exegetically driven. It is as if Calvin leapt from the plain meaning of the text right into Augustine's supercessionist lap. Our chief concern in this regard is that such a course is historically shown to be fraught with shameful results concerning the treatment of the Jews. This being the case, according to history and exegesis, we seriously question the validity of the eschatology that undergirds this legacy.

National Israel
with a Distinctive Eschatological Hope

Both individuals discussed here exhibit a passionate concern for the Jews much more after the manner of the apostle Paul's. Here is warm-hearted, Judeo-centric eschatology at its best. More evidence in this regard will follow in subsequent chapters.

Horatius Bonar

While Horatius Bonar (1808–1889) is better known today as a nine-teenth-century hymn writer, his overall ministry in Scotland was of far greater dimensions, both practically and scholarly, especially with regard to his preaching and writing. He participated in a remarkable moving of the Spirit of God in Scotland that involved Thomas Chalmers, William C. Burns and Robert Murray M'Cheyne. He also joined a Mission of Enquiry to the Jews in 1839 in which he, along with his brother Andrew and M'Cheyne, toured the Holy Land for the purpose of reporting their findings back to the Church of Scotland.[11] Another related concern of Bonar, which is also reflected in his prolific hymn writing, was a considerable interest in prophetic events, particularly from a premillennial perspective. He founded and edited *The Quarterly Journal of Prophecy* from 1849 to 1873. In 1847 he published *Prophetical Landmarks, Containing Data for Helping to Determine the Question of Christ's Premillennial Advent*, which went to at least five editions. Here then are some pertinent comments from his Judeo-centric writings that concern such a heartfelt love for the Jewish people.

---

[11] See A. A. Bonar and R. M. McCheyne, *Narrative of a mission of inquiry to the Jews from the Church of Scotland in 1839* (Presbyterian Board of Publication, n.d.; repr. ed. A. M. Harman, *Mission of Discovery: the Beginnings of Modern Jewish Evangelism*, Christian Focus, 1996).

To begin with Bonar declared:

Let us speak reverently of the Jew. Let us not misjudge him by present appearances. He is not what he once was, nor what he yet shall be.

Let us speak reverently of the Jew. We have much cause to do so. What, though all Christendom, both of the East and West, has for nearly eighteen centuries treated him as the offscouring of the race? What though Mohammad has taught his followers to revile and persecute the sons of Abraham? . . .

Nay, what though he [the Jew] may have a grasping hand, and a soul shut up against the world,—a world that has done nothing but wrong and revile him? What though he may inherit the crookedness of his father Jacob, instead of the nobility of Abraham, or the simple gentleness of Isaac?

Still let us speak reverently of the Jew,—if not for what he is, at least for what he was, and what he shall be, when the Redeemer shall come to Zion and turn away ungodliness from Jacob [Isa 59:20; see. Rom 11:26].

In him we see the development of God's great purpose as to the woman's seed, the representative of a long line of kings and prophets, the kinsmen of Him who is the Word made flesh. It was a Jew who sat on one of the most exalted thrones of the earth; it is a Jew who now sits upon the throne of heaven. It was a Jew who wrought such miracles once on our earth, who spoke such gracious words. It was a Jew who said, "Come unto me and I will give you rest;" and a Jew who said, "Behold I come quickly, and my reward is with me." It was Jewish blood that was shed on Calvary; it was a Jew who bore our sins in His own body on the tree. It was a Jew who died, and was buried, and rose again. It is a Jew who liveth to intercede for us, who is to come in glory and majesty as earthly judge and monarch. It is a Jew who is our Prophet, our Priest, our King.

Let us, then, speak reverently of the Jew, whatever his present degradation may be. Just as we tread reverently the level platform of Moriah, where once stood the holy house where Jehovah was worshipped; so let us tread the ground where they dwell whose are the adoption, and the glory, and the covenants, and of whom, concerning the flesh, Christ came. That temple hill is not what it was. The beautiful house is gone, and not one stone is left upon another. The seventeen sieges of Jerusalem, like so many storms rolling the waves of every sea over it, have left few memorials of the old magnificence. The Mosque of the Moslems covers the spot of the altar of burnt-offering; the foot of the Moslem defiles the sacred courts . . . . But still the ground is felt to be sacred; the bare rock on which you tread is not common rock; the massive stones built here and there into the wall are witnesses of other days; and the whole scene gathers round it such associations as, in spite of the rubbish, and desolation, and ruin, and pollution, fill you irresistibly with awe. . . .

So it is with the Jew,—I mean the whole Jewish nation. There are indelible memories connected with them, which will ever, to anyone who believes in the Bible, prevent them from being contemned; nay, will cast around them a nobility and a dignity which no other nation has possessed or can attain to. To Him in whose purposes they occupy so large a space, they are still "beloved for their fathers' sake" [Rom 11:28]. Of them, as concerning the flesh, Christ came, who is over all, God blessed forever. [12]

Later Bonar boldly confessed:

I am one of those who believe in Israel's restoration and conversion; who receive it as a future certainty, that all Israel shall be gathered, and that all Israel shall be saved. As I believe in Israel's present degradation, so do I believe in Israel's coming glory and preeminence. I believe that God's purpose regarding our world can only be understood by understanding God's purpose as to Israel. I believe that all human calculations as to the earth's future, whether political or scientific, or philosophical or religious, must be failures, if not taking for their data or basis God's great purpose regarding the latter-day standing of Israel. I believe that it is not possible to enter God's mind regarding the destiny of man, without taking as our key or our guide His mind regarding the ancient nation—that nation whose history, so far from being ended, or nearly ended, is only about to begin. And if any one may superciliously ask, What can the Jews have to do with the world's history?—may we not correctly philosophize on that coming history, and take the bearing of the world's course, leaving Israel out of the consideration altogether? We say, nay; but O man, who art thou that repliest against God? Art thou the framer of the earth's strange annals, either past or future? Art thou the creator of those events which make up these annals, or the producer of those latent springs or seeds of which these arise?

He only to whom the future belongs can reveal it. He only can announce the principles on which that future is to be developed. And if He set Israel as the great nation of the future, and Jerusalem as the great metropolis of earth, who are we, that, with our philosophy of science, we should set aside the divine arrangements, and substitute for them a theory of man? . . .

I believe that the sons of Abraham are to re-inherit Palestine, and that the forfeited fertility will yet return to that land; that the wilderness and the solitary places shall be glad for them, and the desert will rejoice and blossom as the rose. I believe that, meanwhile, Israel shall not only be wanderers, but that everywhere only a remnant, a small remnant, shall be saved; and that it is for the gathering in of this remnant that our missionaries go forth. I believe that these times of ours (as also all the times of the four monarchies [Dan 2]) are the times of the Gentiles; and that Jerusalem and Israel shall be trodden down of the Gentiles, till the times of the Gentiles be fulfilled. I believe that, with the filling up of these times of the Gentile pre-eminence, and the completion of what the apostle calls the fullness of the Gentiles, will be the signal for the judgments which are to usher in the crisis of earth's history, and the deliverance of Israel, and the long-expected kingdom.

[12] H. Bonar, "The Jew," *The Quarterly Journal of Prophecy* (July, 1870): 209–11.

. . . How Jewish history shall once more emerge into its old place of grandeur and miracle, and how it shall unwind from itself the bright future of all nations, I know not. But so it is fore-written, "What shall be the reconciling of them be, but life from the dead?" [Rom 11:15] "Israel shall blossom and bud, and fill the face of the world with fruit" [Isa 27:6].[13]

How refreshingly different is the attitude here from that of Augustine and Calvin. Undergirding this teaching is not the eschatological blending of national Israel into mere shadowy insignificance and obscurity, but rather the acknowledgment that while grace has blessed the Gentiles in a grand manner, so too will that same grace of God, according to the same sovereign purpose, ultimately bless the Jewish people in a most climactic and triumphant sense. This is something to rejoice about, and not surprisingly Bonar has penned a hymn in this vein.

> Forgotten! No; that cannot be,
>   All other names may pass away;
> But thine, My Israel, shall remain
>   In everlasting memory.
> Forgotten! No; that cannot be,
>   The oath of Him who cannot lie
> Is on thy city and thy land,
>   An oath to all eternity.
> Forgotten of the Lord thy God!
>   No, Israel, no, that cannot be,
> He chose thee in the days of old
>   And still His favor rests on thee.[14]

C. H. Spurgeon

Although like Bonar, his contemporary, he held Augustine and Calvin in high esteem, this pastor of the Metropolitan Tabernacle in London did not embrace their essentially Catholic eschatology. Rather, Spurgeon maintained a fervent interest in the Jewish people and particularly their being reached with the gospel. Preaching on Ezek 24:26 in 1855, just prior to the rise of modern Zionism, he plainly declared,

Not long shall it be ere they [the Jews] shall come—shall come from distant lands, where'er they rest or roam; and she who has been the off-scouring of all things, whose name has been a proverb and a bye-word, shall become the glory of all lands. Dejected Zion shall raise her head, shaking herself

---

[13] Ibid., 214–15.

[14] *Lamp & Light Hymns* (Hitchin, Hertfordshire, England: The Society for Distributing Hebrew Scriptures, 2000), 64.

from dust, and darkness, and the dead. Then shall the Lord feed his people, and make them and the places round about his hill a blessing. I think we do not attach sufficient importance to the restoration of the Jews. We do not think enough of it. But certainly, if there is anything promised in the Bible it is this. I imagine that you cannot read the Bible without seeing clearly that there is to be an actual restoration of the children of Israel. "Thither they shall go up; they shall come with weeping unto Zion, and with supplications unto Jerusalem." May that happy day soon come! For when the Jews are restored, then the fullness of the Gentiles shall be gathered in; and as soon as they return, then Jesus will come upon Mount Zion to reign with his ancients gloriously, and the halcyon days of the Millennium shall then dawn; we shall then know every man to be a brother and a friend; Christ shall rule with universal sway.[15]

Speaking on Ezek 37:1–10 in 1864 at the Metropolitan Tabernacle in aid of funds for the British Society for the Propagation of the Gospel amongst the Jews, Spurgeon declared,

This vision has been used, from the time of Jerome onwards, as a description of the resurrection, and certainly it may be so accommodated with much effect. . . . But while this interpretation of the vision may be very proper as an accommodation, it must be quite evident to any thinking person that this is not the meaning of the passage. There is no allusion made by Ezekiel to the resurrection, and such topic would have been quite apart from the design of the prophet's speech. I believe he was no more thinking of the resurrection of the dead than of the building of St. Peter's at Rome, or the emigration of the Pilgrim Fathers. . . .

The meaning of our text, as opened up by the context, is most evidently, if words mean anything, first, that there shall be a political restoration of the Jews to their own land and to their own nationality; and then, secondly, there is in the text, and in the context, a most plain declaration, that there shall be a spiritual restoration, a conversion in fact, of the tribes of Israel. . . . Her sons, though they can never forget the sacred dust of Palestine, yet die at a hopeless distance from her consecrated shores. But it shall not be so forever. . . . They shall again walk upon her mountains, shall once more sit under her vines and rejoice under her fig-trees. And they are also to be re-united. There shall not be two, nor ten, nor twelve, but one— one Israel praising one God, serving one king, and that one king the Son of David, the descended Messiah. They are to have a national prosperity which shall make them famous; nay, so glorious shall they be that Egypt, and Tyre, and Greece, and Rome, shall all forget their glory in the greater splendor of the throne of David. . . .

If there be meaning in words this must be the meaning of this chapter. I wish never to learn the art of tearing God's meaning out of his own words.

[15] C. H. Spurgeon, *The C. H. Spurgeon Collection, Metropolitan Tabernacle Pulpit,* I, no. 28, 1855 (Albany, Oregon: Ages Software, 1998), 382.

If there be anything clear and plain, the literal sense and meaning of this passage–a meaning not to be spirited or spiritualized away–must be evident that both the two and the ten tribes of Israel are to be restored to their own land, and that a king is to rule over them.[16]

Spurgeon derived a very different meaning from the OT with regard to national Israel than that of Augustine and Calvin. Indeed, when we return to Jer 32:41, it is obvious that Spurgeon's understanding of this passage is fundamentally different from that of Calvin which we previously referenced. So in 1887 he declared,

We cannot help looking for the restoration of the scattered Israelites to the land which God has given to them by a covenant of salt: we also look for the time when they shall believe in the Messiah whom they have rejected, and shall rejoice in Jesus of Nazareth, whom today they despise. There is great encouragement in prophecy to those who work among the seed of Israel; and it is greatly needed, for of all mission fields it has been commonly represented to be one of the most barren, and upon the work the utmost ridicule has been poured. God has, therefore, supplied our faith with encouragements larger than we have in almost any other direction of service. Let those who believe work on! Those who believe not may give it up. They shall not have the honor of having helped to gather together the ancient nation to which our Lord himself belonged; for be it never forgotten that Jesus was a Jew.[17]

Here then we especially draw attention to the more literal interpretation by Bonar and Spurgeon when compared with Augustine and Calvin. But also, with the aid of centuries of hindsight along with the present state of the Middle East at our fingertips, we frankly declare the approach of Bonar and Spurgeon toward the sacred text to be much closer to the truth, that this is the intended meaning of God's inspired Word. Augustine's renowned allegorical hermeneutic was not entirely followed by Calvin, and in this eschatological scenario Calvin did far more consistently and accurately exegete the sacred text as a whole than did his mentor.

I reiterate, however, that the doctrines deduced by these opposing schools of eschatology, the one being Judeo-centric, the other Judeo-eccentric, have profound ethical consequences. On the one hand, Judeo-centricity, as represented by Bonar and Spurgeon, exults in the national seed of Abraham and its promised, fulfilled, territorial glory through sovereign covenant grace. Consequently, it esteems that seed, according to Paul's exhortation in Rom 11:18–20, because it remains "loved because of their

[16] Ibid., X, 1864, no. 582: 533, 536–37.
[17] Ibid., XXXIV, 1887, no. 2036: 545.

ancestors" (Rom 11:28). On the other hand, Judeo-eccentricity, as represented by Augustine and Calvin, dismisses the national seed of Abraham
beyond the perimeter of the kingdom of God, except for the condescending
inclusion of "a remnant chosen by grace" (Rom 11:5), that has no ultimate,
divine, national, territorial validity. Augustine and Calvin were at best tolerant of the Jews; Bonar and Spurgeon were deeply affectionate toward the
Jews. Which of these parties approximates the attitude of Paul toward his
"kinsmen according to the flesh" (Rom 9:3, ESV), and what is it about the
doctrine they embrace that produces their kindly disposition? The answers
to these questions are abundantly clear and are especially significant with
regard to the prosperity of Jewish evangelism in this present age.

Chapter 2

ISRAEL AND CENTURIES OF CHRISTIAN ANTI-JUDAISM

W hile Augustine and Calvin represent a predominant Catholic and Reformed heritage of Jewish/Christian relations that spans seventeen centuries of church history, a more detailed panorama of this era now needs to be surveyed. An astonishing ignorance abides today concerning the legacy of Christian anti-Judaism, and works of church history frequently fail to discuss it.[1] Here we have the record of a conflict fraught with uncomfortable truth, especially with regard to the violation of Christian ethics. We ask all who might be skeptical at such a claim to reserve judgment and remain open to a concert of opinion coming from both Christian and non-Christian sources. They may also refer to Appendix E. A broad spectrum of writings will provide a better understanding of how Christians have treated Jews throughout church history, particularly with regard to the underlying, driving eschatology. This vital matter needs to be not only acknowledged but also studied so that a genuine attitude of repentance might result.

I have encountered numerous Christians who simply do not want to face this unsavory historic record. Certainly they have offered token acknowledgment of the problem while at the same time retaining a firm commitment to Augustinian eschatology in this regard. Further they have frequently retreated to the claim that Scripture alone is the basis of their eschatology, and as a consequence they have strenuously asserted a willingness to contend strictly according to the biblical text. Now this we have gladly assented to do, but only provided it is agreed that our derived doctrine, being "sound" (2 Tim 4:3), that is, spiritually nourishing and fruitful, is also expected to be productive of a godly Christian lifestyle. We insist that there is a necessary connection here whereby sound doctrine or teaching ought to "promote godliness" (1 Tim 6:3). We discover the practical outworking of Christian doctrine by resorting to a comprehensive study

---

[1] A recent volume by R. E. Olson, *The Story of Christian Theology: Twenty Centuries of Tradition & Reform* (Downers Grove, Ill.: InterVarsity, 1999), does not even mention "Israel," "Judaism," or "Jews" in its subject index. The same is true for older works such as O. W. Heick, *A History of Christian Thought*, 2 vols. (Philadelphia: Fortress, 1965–1966), and W. Cunningham, *Historical Theology*, 2 vols. (London: Banner of Truth, 1969).

of church history, for here is the real expression of Christian truth in its resultant behavior, warts and all.

Certainly the ethical fruit of the eighteenth-century evangelical awakening in England and America under Whitefield, Wesley, and Edwards resulted from the holy root of faithful gospel proclamation. So Bready has concluded in his doctoral research that here, in contrast with bloody revolution in France, "was the true nursing mother of the spirit and character values that have created and sustained Free Institutions throughout the English-speaking world."[2] With this principle in mind, I believe that the unsavory fruit of much anti-Judaism is rooted in supercessionist. The following critique, in the form of a historical survey, will make this point abundantly clear. This is in no way meant to convey a lack of delight in so much that God accomplished through many human instruments discussed here. We praise their courageous and sound proclamation of the gospel; we so admire their teaching of vital biblical truth. However, good doctrine produces good fruit, not bad fruit, and bad doctrine produces bad fruit (Matt 7:17–20). Consequently the historic outworking of supercessionist cannot be neglected. The overwhelming testimony which follows will inevitably lead to questioning of the viability of the underlying eschatology. In a real sense, history is the proving ground of revealed truth. Those who neglect this relationship between doctrinal truth and ethics end up conferring on mankind error and its unethical consequences.

The Early Church to 135

When Jesus Christ declared to Peter, "I will build My church [assembly]" (Matt 16:18), this quintessential Jew appointed twelve Jews as foundation blocks for His new spiritual edifice or church (Eph 2:19–22). In the upper room, these Jews listened to Jesus' promise of the new covenant (Luke 22:20), which was established the following day by means of His crucifixion before a Jerusalem multitude that also was essentially Jewish. At Pentecost these same foundation stones were supernaturally identified before a Jewish throng (Acts 1:26–2:4), after which thousands of Jews were added to the new covenant fellowship. As a result, this Jerusalem assembly of Christian believers became the mother congregation that increasingly gathered around her a host of Jewish spiritual children. Immediate tension then developed between the Jewish Synagogue and the expanding Jewish Church, the result being "severe persecution [that] broke out against the

---

[2] J. W. Bready, *England: Before and After Wesley* (London: Hodder and Stoughton, 1938), 13, 205.

church in Jerusalem [by the likes of Saul], and all except the apostles were scattered throughout the land of Judea and Samaria" (Acts 8:1).

Then with the inclusion of hybrid Jewish Christians from Samaria (Acts 8:4–17) and Gentile Christians from Caesarea (Acts 10:1–48) the seeds of dissension were sown even within Christ's own disciples, that is, until Peter made explanation at Jerusalem of God's new revelation to him. What joy resulted from the decision of the Council of Jerusalem in c. 50 when it was concluded, with the full agreement of Peter and Paul, that the Gentile Christians of Antioch in the north did not have to submit to the distinctive Judaism that the Jewish Christians conformed to in Jerusalem (Acts 15:1–31). However, while this concord between Jewish and Gentile Christians continued for approximately 85 years, it did not last. Eusebius tells us that the fifteen succeeding bishops of Jerusalem were all Jewish, that is, up to 135.[3] Up to this point, the mother church was revered by her children; then the tide began to turn, bringing about devastating results. To begin with, the essentially Jewish church at Jerusalem had suffered withering persecution, dispersal, and impoverishment at the hands of militant Judaism. Nevertheless, the daughter fellowship at Antioch thrived under Paul and Barnabas with the accomplishment of far reaching missionary expansion in the Gentile world.

On the other hand, in rebelling against Rome, Jerusalem Judaism suffered considerable destruction, hence humiliation, under Titus in 69–70. After the temple was desecrated, burned, and leveled, many hundreds of thousands of Jews who had gathered for the Passover season were slaughtered, while a remnant fled to Babylonia, Egypt, North Africa, and relatives in the Diaspora. Surely Christ's prophetic declaration would have been called to mind by the Christians of that time, namely, that "Jerusalem will be trampled under foot by the Gentiles until the times of the Gentiles are fulfilled" (Luke 21:24). Here this divine role reversal had now begun to play out in a manner that ought not to be opposed. Now the mother Jewish church would be trodden down for an indefinite period, and her latter Gentile children would begin to assert themselves to the point of maternal neglect, even denigration of their Jewish parentage. Then in AD 135 the messianic claims of Bar Kokhba resulted in climactic humiliation, whereby Emperor Hadrian destroyed 985 towns, slaughtered a further 580,000 Jews, expelled the remainder from Jerusalem, prohibited circumcision and Sabbath observance, erected a temple to Jupiter on the temple mount, and

---

[3] Eusebius, *Ecclesiastical History*, 4.5.

renamed the city as Aelia Capitolina (after himself) and the land as Syria Palestina, that is, Palestine or Philistia.[4] As a result, now the mother church became thoroughly scattered abroad and humiliated. Now she was associated with national Israel's desolation and judgment while prominent centers of Gentile Christianity, such as at Alexandria, Caesarea, Ephesus, and Rome—inclusive of a Jewish remnant—were thriving. The stage was now set for the arrogant self-assertion of the reconciled Gentile prodigal children of the far country over the weakened seed of the impoverished Jewish elder brethren. So,

> for Christianity in its early stages, the real debate was never between Christians and Jews but among Christians. Eventually the anti-Jewish side won. Its ideology became normative, not just for subsequent Christianity and Western culture but, through the formation of the New Testament, for our perception of earlier Christianity as well. The voice of the losing side fell silent.[5]

The Patristic Period

Because of Bar Kokhba's messianic claims, Christianity offered no support for the Judaism inherent in this uprising. At the same time, the expulsion of Jews from Jerusalem by Hadrian necessitated the appointment of the first Gentile bishop over the mother church. Consequently, the scene was set to increase Gentile dominance. Hence subsequent to Judaism's demise through Roman oppression and the shame ascribed to them for putting to death their Messiah, Gentile Christianity increasingly asserted itself, especially in the midst of a necessary apologetic environment. Whereas the Gentiles had originally understood themselves as grafted into the blessings of Abrahamic Judaism, now they asserted the church to be the new, superseding, spiritual Israel. As James Parkes indicated,

> Little by little the Church was read back into the whole of Old Testament history, and Christian history was shown to be older than Jewish history in that it dated from the creation, and not from Sinai, or even Abraham.[6]

---

[4] P. Johnson, *A History of the Jews* (New York: Harper & Row, 1988), 141–43.

[5] J. G. Gager, *The Origins of Anti-Semitism* (New York: Oxford, 1983), 269. I reject the idea of anti-Judaism as being inherent in the formation of the canon, although the NT was certainly misused in the promotion of anti-Judaism.

[6] J. Parkes, *The Conflict of the Church and the Synagogue* (New York: Atheneum, 1969), 100. The attitude described here is not unlike the contemporary supercessionist claim that, according to the prototype of Eden, the land of Israel, as promised to Abraham, is now transcended by the more encompassing land of the whole earth. Refer to O. P. Robertson, *The Israel of God* (Phil-

The hermeneutical shift from the more literal Palestinian Judaic tradition to dominant allegorical interpretation, as thought to be more "spiritual" according to Origen of Alexandria and Justin Martyr,[7] resulted in the repudiation of supposed carnal, Judaistic conclusions, and thus of any future national identity. Hence, following years of development, it was eventually believed that Israel had been replaced or superseded; this emerging emphasis was formally recognized as a "capstone,"[8] by Justin Martyr at Ephesus in his *Dialogue with Trypho c.* AD 160. Here for the first time in extant literature, the church was plainly described as the new spiritual Israel, as well as the new custodian of Scripture.[9]

The Pre-Constantinian Era

While the status of Judaism was receding within Christianity, Judaizing groups similar to those Paul had opposed (Acts 15:1–5; Gal. 5:2–4,12), remained a serious irritant. There were radical and conservative groups of Jewish Christians, such as the pro-Judaic Elkasaites, Ebionites, and Cerinthians,[10] which aroused vigorous orthodox apologetic responses that consequently took on a strong anti-Judaic tone. For Irenaeus of Lyons, the Jews had been disinherited from the grace of God.[11] With Tertullian of Carthage, anti-Judaism permeated every aspect of his thought; the Jews were the very anti-type of true virtue and so embodied the principle of obsolescence.[12] For Hippolytus of Rome, Jewish exile and judgment would not be limited to 430 years of servitude in Egypt or 70 years in Babylonia, for their plight would last forever.[13] Along the same lines, Cyprian of Carthage argued that the Jews had been replaced by the Christians[14] and should all be expelled from his diocese at the point of the sword.[15] Parkes considers

lipsburg, N.J.: P&R, 2000) 3–31; S. Sizer, *Christian Zionism* (Leicester, England: Inter-Varsity, 2004), 164, 260–61.

[7] L. M. McDonald, "Anti-Judaism in the Early Church Fathers," in *Anti-Semitism and Early Christianity* (ed. C. A. Evans and D. A. Hager; Minneapolis: Fortress, 1993), 230–32.

[8] R. L. Saucy, *The Case for Progressive Dispensationalism* (Grand Rapids: Zondervan, 1993), 212.

[9] P. Richardson, *Israel in the Apostolic Church* (London: Cambridge Univ. Press, 1969), 1.

[10] T. Callan, *Forgetting the Root* (New York: Paulist, 1986), 44–47.

[11] Parkes, *Conflict of the Church and Synagogue*, 106.

[12] Gager, *The Origins of Anti-Semitism*, 163–64, referencing D. Efroymsen, "The Patristic Connection," in *Antisemitism and the Foundations of Christianity* (ed. A. Davies; New York: Paulist, 1979), 98–117.

[13] D. Cohn-Sherbok, *Anti-Semitism: A History* (Stroud, Gloucestershire: Sutton, 2002), 41.

[14] Callan, *Forgetting the Root*, 95.

[15] P. E. Grosser and E. G. Halperin, *The Causes and Effects of Anti-Semitism* (New York: Philosophical Library, 1978), 48.

that Justin, Tertullian, Hippolytus, Cyprian, and Origen deserve special
mention at this juncture, that is, prior to the infamous fourth century:

> They thus represent not only geographically but also in their trainings an
> astonishingly varied range of interests. Their different writings are of capi-
> tal importance for the development throughout the Church of the absolute
> condemnation of the Jews which is characteristic of the patristic literature
> as a whole.[16]

The Constantinian Era

The development of anti-Judaism further intensified in the fourth century.
As Parkes explained, "The Jew as he is encountered in the pages of fourth-
century writers is not a human being at all. He is a 'monster,' a theological
abstraction, of superhuman cunning and malice, and more than superhuman blindness."[17] We enter this century via Eusebius, a follower of Origen
and the acknowledged Father of Church History, who in c. 315 became
Bishop of Caesarea. Not surprisingly he also believed that the Church was
the "new Israel" that replaced the Jews. Further, he so lionized the Emperor
Constantine over the union of empire and Church that his biographical
writing in this regard became more adulation and eulogy than objective,
factual record.[18] Most significant was the legislation that Constantine ef-
fected concerning the Jews, making it a crime to convert to Judaism. A Jew
who circumcised his non-Jewish slave was subject to the death penalty, as
was also the case if he married a Christian woman employed in the imperial
factories.[19] Thus the Christian state more militantly than ever asserted itself
against the synagogue. Not only did anti-Judaism became the established
teaching of the Christian Empire, but an even more virulent strain was cultivated by means of four pillars of the church whose legacy remains with us
today: Ambrose, Jerome, Chrysostom, and Augustine, all contemporaries.

Ambrose of Milan, eloquent preacher and opponent of Arianism, had
declared that the Jewish synagogue was "a house of impiety, a recepta-
cle of folly, which God himself has condemned." Not surprisingly, he orchestrated and praised the burning of a synagogue. When the Emperor
Theodosius commanded that the bishop rebuild the synagogue, Ambrose

---

[16] Parkes, *Conflict of the Church and Synagogue*, 72.

[17] Ibid., 158.

[18] J. Carroll, *Constantine's Sword* (Boston: Houghton Mifflin, 2001) 173–74; D. Gruber, *The Church and the Jews* (Hannover, N.H.: Elijah, 1997), 14–16.

[19] Parkes, *Conflict of the Church and Synagogue*, 179–80.

defiantly remonstrated against this judgment and caused the civil ruler to back down.[20]

The most notable achievement of Jerome of Bethlehem was the Vulgate, his Latin translation of the Bible, which dominated the church until modern times. He was the only church father really conversant with Hebrew and rabbinic thought. But tragically this knowledge better enabled him to express both ridicule and disgust concerning the behavior of the Jews. Jerome had as much contempt for Judeo-Christians as did the Jews themselves.[21] Influenced by asceticism, he was convinced that "there was no place for Jews," whom he always referred to as the "carnal," "lewd," and "materialistic Jew."[22]

Chrysostom, the "golden-mouthed" expositor, nevertheless became the most notorious and rabid proponent of anti-Judaism in his generation. In a series of eight *Homilies Against the Jews*, his tirade knew no limits. James Parkes wrote,

> There is no sneer too mean, no gibe too bitter for him to fling at the Jewish people. No text is too remote to be able to be twisted to their confu-
> sion, no argument is too casuistical, no blasphemy too startling for him to employ. . . . On the strength of Psalm 106:37, he states that they "sacrificed their sons and daughters to devils: they outraged nature; and overthrew from their foundations the laws of relationship. They are become worse than the wild beasts, and for no reason at all, with their own hands they murder their own offspring, to worship the avenging devils who are the foes of our life. . . . The synagogues of the Jews are the homes of idolatry and devils, even though they have no images in them. They are worse even than heathen circuses. . . . I hate the Jews for they have the law and they insult it."[23]

Thus Daniel Goldhagen's definitive study of the Holocaust, especially in terms of focus on "ordinary Germans," is painfully correct in its conclusion:

> John Chrysostom, a pivotal Church Father whose theology and teachings had lasting import, preached about Jews in terms that would become the stock-in-trade of Christian anti-Jewish teachings and rhetoric, which would condemn the Jews to live in a Christian Europe that despised and feared them. . . . John, an influential theologian, is but an early example of the Christian world's essential relationship to Jews, which was to endure well into modernity. . . . The very definition of what it meant to be a Christian

---

[20] M. Hay, *Thy Brother's Blood* (New York: Hart, 1975), 25–26; Parkes, *Conflict of the Church and Synagogue*, 166–68.

[21] Parkes, *Conflict of the Church and Synagogue*, 153–54.

[22] F. Heer, *God's First Love* (London: Phoenix, 1999) 39.

[23] Parkes, *Conflict of the Church and Synagogue*, 163–64, 166.

entailed a thoroughgoing and visceral hostility to Jews, just as it did to evil, and to the devil. It is no surprise that medieval Christians came to see Jews as agents of both.[24]

Augustine of Hippo, although seemingly more temperate than his mentor Ambrose, nevertheless, as we have already seen, bequeathed a supremely dominant and enduring anti-Judaic legacy. This was divine consignment of the Jews to universal abandonment through the mediation of the church, the result being a wandering, homeless, rejected and accursed race, incurably carnal, blind to spiritual truth, perfidious, faithless and apostate. Their crime of deicide was one of cosmic proportions that merited permanent exile and subordination to Christianity. Israel, the older son, must be made to "serve" the Church, the younger son (Gen 25:23), which is the true heir and rightful owner of the divine promises enunciated in the OT. Not only Cain, but also Hagar, Ishmael, and Esau denote the Jews who have been rejected, while their contrasting pairs, Abel, Sarah, Isaac, and Jacob, represent the election of the Church.[25]

Not surprisingly, the church councils of this period reflected the consensus of the church fathers. In AD 306 the Council of Elvira in Spain banned all community contact between Spanish Christians and the "evil" Hebrews. Especially prohibited was marriage between Christians and Jews, except where the Jew was willing to be converted. The Council of Nicea in 325, called by Constantine to settle the controversy over Arianism, continued the efforts of the early Church to dissociate Christianity from Judaism by deciding that Easter would no longer be determined by or celebrated during Passover. It declared that "it is unbecoming beyond measure that on this holiest of festivals we should follow the customs of the Jews. Henceforth let us have nothing in common with this odious people."[26]

The Medieval Period

The subsequent thousand years was not without its times when the Jews, notwithstanding their unbelief, were protected and tolerated, if not respected, by civil and religious Christian leaders. Nevertheless, as the Reformation period drew near, the overall attitude of Christendom increasingly hardened.

---

[24] D. J. Goldhagen, *Hitler's Willing Executioners* (New York: Vintage, 1997), 50–51.

[25] R. S. Wistrich, *Antisemitism, The Longest Hatred* (New York: Pantheon, 1991), 19.

[26] Grosser and Halperin, *Causes and Effects of Anti-Semitism*, 58, 77.

The Old Catholic Early Period

Whereas the Old Catholic Church had been led by a plurality of bishops, in the fifth century the bishop of Rome had primacy over an established imperial church, while the civil rulership of the empire had been moved to Constantinople. Thus Pope Gregory the Great (540–604) became the revered agent of consolidation, who following in the steps of Augustine[27] established the theological foundation of the Middle Ages until Thomas Aquinas bequeathed his *Summa Theologica*. Although expressly forbidding the forced conversion of Jews, Gregory sanctioned Augustine's tolerance requiring subjection with misery. On the one hand, there were his flowery denunciations of the Jews' diabolical perversity and detestable characteristics; on the other hand, he could rebuke a bishop, who had been physically carrying out these denunciations by calling for love, charity, and justice in winning them to Christianity. Thus, while Gregory attempted to forge a balanced policy, nevertheless he harbored no love for the Jews.[28]

The Monastic Middle Period

Occupied with barbarian assaults on Europe, the pope of Rome strengthened his influence through the conversion and devotion of Clovis, the Germanic king (496), and his conquest of Gaul. In Spain, the industrious Isidore, Archbishop of Seville (560–636), castigated the Jews more harshly than did his mentor Augustine. Zealous for their conversion, he believed they did not belong in a properly integrated Christian kingdom. Such a belief became influential during the centuries to come.[29] The conquest of Spain and Portugal by the Arab Moors (711) resulted in a relatively improved situation for the Jews in that region where they received better treatment under non-Christian governments. Muslim expulsion from Spain, following Charles Martel's victory at Tours (732), paved the way for the reign of Charlemagne (768–814), in which the status of Jews again improved.[30] Agobard, Archbishop of Lyon (779–840), however, subsequently attacked the Jews with vigor similar to that of Chrysostom, proposing that Christians should not fraternize with the unclean and corrupt synagogue,

---

[27] J. B. Y. Hood asserts that concerning the Jews and Judaism, Augustine's ideas on these matters "dominated the medieval debate." *Aquinas and the Jews* (Philadelphia: University of Pennsylvania Press, 1995), 10.

[28] Carroll, *Constantine's Sword*, 248; J. Cohn, *Living Letters of the Law* (Berkeley, Calif.: University of California Press, 1999), 79; Parkes, *Conflict of the Church and Synagogue*, 220–21.

[29] Cohn, *Living Letters of the Law*, 96, 122.

[30] Cohn-Sherbok, *Anti-Semitism: A History*, 64.

as if seated with a whore.[31] In England, the scholastic Anselm, Archbishop of Canterbury (1033–1109), was a saint whose love for humanity did not exclude the children of Israel, even though he appeared to regard them as pagan. Such genuine concern was rare in those times. His moderation, however, never extended to renouncing the Augustinian regard for the Jews as a biblical witness of divinely imposed degradation.[32] Then in AD 1095, Pope Urban II initiated the first Crusade and an era of eight campaigns concluding in 1270. The Holy Land and sacred sites were to be delivered from pagan infidels. En route through Europe, the barbarous crusaders, incited by priests such as Peter the Hermit, offered Jews baptism or death. At Mainz several hundred Jews were killed followed by a service of thanksgiving. The capture of Jerusalem in 1099 resulted in the burning of a synagogue filled with Jews.[33] Abelard of Paris (1079–1142), a father of dawning scholasticism and a follower of Jewish and Arabic learning, became a lone defender of the Jews. He was the only leader in the Middle Ages who ventured to attack openly the anti-Jewish tradition of Christendom.[34] Bernard of Clairvaux (1090–1153) encouraged a second Crusade. Although critical of the killing of Jews during the first Crusade, he characterized them as bestial descendants of the Devil and murderers from the beginning of time.[35] Because of supposed unorthodoxy and the minimizing of Jewish culpability, Abelard was ruined by the persecutions of Bernard, who also sought the assistance of Pope Innocent II in this pursuit, though they were eventually reconciled.[36]

When Thomas Aquinas (1225–1274) entered the religious stage of Europe, he "served as a major conduit of the traditional Christian view of the Jews for some seven hundred years."[37] Like Augustine he believed in a future salvation of the Jews, according to Romans 11, that would lead to absorption into the Christian Church. This was a period when the Catholic Church and Christian state reached the peak of their united power. Yet the Jewish people were to be plunged into new depths of oppression and misery by the scourge of anti-Semitic hysteria.[38] It should be understood

---

[31] Heer, *God's First Love*, 61–62; C. M. Williamson, *Has God Rejected His People?* (Nashville: Abingdon, 1982), 113.

[32] Cohn, *Living Letters of the Law*, 167–80; Hay, *Thy Brother's Blood*, 39–40.

[33] Williamson, *Has God Rejected His People?* 113–14.

[34] Hay, *Thy Brothers Blood*, 67; Heer, *God's First Love*, 68, 76.

[35] Grosser and Halperin, *Causes and Effects of Anti-Semitism*, 106.

[36] Carroll, *Constantine's Sword*, 290–300; Cohn, *Living Letters of the Law*, 287–89.

[37] Hood, *Aquinas and the Jews*, xii.

[38] Wistrich, *Antisemitism, The Longest Hatred*, 28.

that at the Fourth Lateran Council (1215), at which the dogma of transubstantiation was canonized, baptized Jews were forbidden to practice Jewish customs; Jews were forbidden to appear in public at Easter time and were barred from public office. They were even required to wear a distinguishing badge. The Council of Canterbury in England (1222) affirmed these same prohibitions.[39] In responding to an enquiry from a duchess as to compliance with these church decrees, we are told of Aquinas:

> In the matter of distinctive Jewish dress, however, Thomas deemed the issue an easy one (*plana est responsio*); the recent decision of the Fourth Lateran Council that the Jews wear an identifying sign must be observed, especially because biblical law itself commands them to place distinctive fringes on their cloaks. . . . [Thus] the provisions of *De regimine Iudaeorum* [the enquiry of the Duchess] proceed directly from the two basic premises of Augustinian doctrine and its applications in canon law: First, the sin of the Jews has resulted in their consignment to perpetual servitude in Christendom; second, no Christian ruler may deprive them of that which they require to live as Jews under his rule.[40]

How tragic that such a history was to repeat itself from 1941 onwards during the German Nazi occupation of Europe, when Jews were forced to wear the degrading yellow stars and badges.[41]

The Renaissance Late Period

The three hundred years that preceded the Reformation saw a scholastic, artistic, and literary revival as reflected in Colet, Moore, Bacon, Chaucer, and Caxton in Britain, along with Aquinas, Boccaccio, Dante, Leonardo da Vinci, Machiavelli, Michaelangelo, Raphael, Erasmus, and Guttenberg in Europe. Nevertheless, at the same time the Jewish community became increasingly oppressed through several movements. Monasticism, at the forefront of this trend, had always known zealotry. But with the increasing influence of the more recently formed mendicant Dominican and Franciscan orders, which focused on preaching for conversion, they became the most implacable religious adversaries of the Jews in the late Middle Ages. This ferocity became inquisitorial and included book burnings, especially of the Talmud.[42]

[39] Grosser and Halperin, *Causes and Effects of Anti-Semitism*, 110.

[40] Cohn, *Living Letters of the Law*, 366.

[41] Goldhagen, *Hitler's Willing Executioners*, 138–39.

[42] Carroll, *Constantine's Sword*, 304–10; Cohn, *Living Letters of the Law*, 317–89; Johnson, *A History of the Jews*, 215–16; Wistrich, *Antisemitism, The Longest Hatred*, 34–36.

Then such suppression and humiliation of the Jews was extended to mass expulsion, just one step away from extermination. Britain initiated this move when Edward I, having first confiscated Jewish assets, expelled them all in 1290. Only after more than 350 years were they able to return under Oliver Cromwell, though even then with qualified scrutiny.[43] Not until the middle of the nineteenth century would they obtain full citizenship in Great Britain. Jews were also expelled from France in 1306 and again in 1394. Having become prosperous in Spain, after the Inquisition they were all expelled in 1492, but they met the same fate in Portugal where they fled. Justification for this racial eviction of the Jews was their deicide and obduracy in unbelief.[44]

Furthermore, new forms of vilification were injected. The blood libel accusation, originating in Norwich, England in 1144, charged the Jews with infanticide in using a slain child's blood to make *matzos*, the unleavened bread consumed at Passover. Perpetuation of this horrendous accusation, although repudiated by emperor and pope, led to many centuries of such slander that resulted in numerous efforts at extermination. There was also the charge of wafer desecration, which is abuse of Christ as present in the offering of the Mass. This was claimed to be a recapitulation of Jewish abusive treatment of Christ as recorded in Scripture. For this, many Jews were hounded to death, undoubtedly with the encouragement of a zealous priesthood.[45]

By the sixteenth century we can easily identify a pervasive, smoldering anti-Judaic legacy throughout Britain and Europe. Hence the great question concerns whether the religious awakening about to erupt at that time, the laying of the very foundation of western society, would be able to cleanse the emerging modern world of this dark, insidious, shameful inheritance.

The Reformation Period

The fact that Martin Luther was a devoted Augustinian monk should help us appreciate the antecedents of his blatant anti-Judaic tirades that climaxed his momentous life. His last sermon, preached several days before his death, pleaded that all Jews should be expelled from Germany.[46]

---

[43] Johnson, *A History of the Jews*, 213; Wistrich, *Anrisemitism, The Longest Hatred*, 101; Grosser and Halperin, *Causes and Effects of Anti-Semitism*, 183.

[44] Williamson, *Has God Rejected His People?* 117–18.

[45] Ibid., 114–17.

[46] E. H. Flannery, *The Anguish of the Jews* (New York: Paulist, 1985), 152; also S. W. Baron, "John Calvin and the Jews," in *Essential Papers on Judaism and Christianity in Conflict* (ed. J. Cohen; New York: New York University Press, 1991), 380–400.

Notwithstanding Luther's earlier hopes that the Jews would believe in Jesus as the Christ and become incorporated within the church, his later vitriolic denunciations of their obstinate unbelief are such that Lutheran scholar Jaroslav Pelikan has frankly declared that "the time has come for those who study Luther and admire him to acknowledge, more unequivocally and less pugnaciously than they have, that on this issue Luther's [anti-Judaic] thought and language are simply beyond defense."[47]

Yes, as difficult as it is to digest, spiritual giants to whom we become eternally indebted can nevertheless act in a pigmy manner! John Calvin, despite being more moderate than Luther on this point, nevertheless was rooted in the same essential Augustinian legacy. Although not going out of his way to harass Jews, he was content to keep them out of Geneva and repeat traditional anti-Judaic statements.[48]

Reformation Europe certainly experienced gospel and ecclesiastical emancipation at this time, which was undoubtedly stimulated by the surging printed page of the Bible; yet the synagogue continued to experience vigorous anti-Judaism. Furthermore, Spanish Marranos or "pigs," those Jews forced to "convert" to Christianity by the Inquisition, continued to be hounded. This was especially the case in Spain, so many sought refuge in Portugal, Salonica, and Turkey. Poland also offered a degree of protection in Eastern Europe in attracting emigrants streaming away from oppression in the west, yet with the result that anti-Judaism also began to erupt there as well.[49] In 1562 the Polish Diet (Legislative Assembly) confirmed previous anti-Jewish legislation. Jews were to dress differently from Christians; they were prohibited from owning Christian serfs or domestics and from holding public office.[50] However, it is well to remember that this development was more a matter of resurgence within awakened Europe, of recapitulation with a modern flair, than the beginning of a movement. As Heiko Oberman has pointed out in his definitive analysis,

> Hatred of the Jews was not an invention of the sixteenth century. It was an inherited assumption. Far from acquitting the age of Renaissance and Reformation, we should recognize that this same age which so consciously scrutinized the medieval traditions, simultaneously passed on, with new strength, whatever withstood the test of inspection.[51]

---

[47] Cited by F. H. Littell, *The Crucifixion of the Jews* (New York: Harper & Row, 1975), 105..

[48] Williamson, *Has God Rejected His People?* 102–103.

[49] Heer, *God's First Love*, 134–38.

[50] Grosser and Halperin, *Causes and Effects of Anti-Semitism*, 167.

[51] H. A. Oberman, *The Roots of Anti-Semitism* (Philadelphia: Fortress, 1984), xi.

With the ideological thrust of the Counter Reformation waning, however, the expanding mercantile and financial character of Europe at this time provided opportunity for initiative to thrive. Thus the Jews were thrust into the very center of the European economy in which capitalism began to displace feudalism and cash became the accepted currency rather than produce. In this new atmosphere, sophisticated Jews were welcomed on their merits, at least until anti-Judaic reaction fomented again, especially in Eastern Europe.[52]

The Seventeenth-Century Puritan Period

The growing influence of Protestantism appeared to bode well for European Jews in terms of much greater esteem being offered than Augustinian tolerance normally allowed. Furthermore, the Puritanism of England in particular, at the advent of freedom for popular publishing that the interregnum government of Cromwell allowed, suddenly deluged the country with eschatological speculation.[53] This inevitably raised the specter of the salvation of the Jews and their future national destiny. At the same time a series of events originating from Eastern Europe gave further impetus to the arousal of Judaism in Britain. In 1648 savage slaughter of many Ukranian Jews was instigated by Russian Cossacks upon their refusal to convert to the Orthodox faith.

> Killing was accompanied by barbarous tortures; the victims were flayed alive, split asunder, clubbed to death, roasted on coals, or scalded with boiling water. Even infants at the breast were not spared. . . . Scrolls of the Law were taken out of the synagogues by the Cossacks who danced on them while drinking whiskey. After this Jews were laid upon them and butchered without mercy.[54]

The result was the flight of refugees seeking safety in the west. This surge troubled a Jewish scholar in Amsterdam, Manasseh ben Israel, who feared Dutch reprisals at such an influx. Consequently, taking advantage of the more sympathetic parliament of Cromwell that had displaced the English royalists, in 1655 he personally visited London and petitioned the Lord Protector for a repeal of long standing laws forbidding Jewish entry into England. Following characteristic English delay and subtlety, citizen-

---

[52] Johnson, *History of the Jews*, 249–52.

[53] C. Gribben, *The Puritan Millennium* (Dublin, Ireland: Four Courts, 2000), 39–40, 47, 108, 194–95.

[54] Grosser and Halperin, *Causes and Effects of Anti-Semitism*, 181.

ship for Jews was in time allowed, eventually resulting in Prime Minister Benjamin Disraeli. A further consequence was the enabling of immigration as well to America by means of which American Jewry was born.[55] The ramifications of this more open policy was an England with increasingly awakened eschatological interest, which would eventually take the lead among the nations of the world in the establishment of the modern State of Israel.

As the seventeenth century closed, however, emerging modernity did not bring about a reduction in overall Judaphobia. Certainly some Reformers, such as Philipp Melanchthon, Justas Jonas, Andreas Osiander, and Theodore Beza, toned down Luther's shrill emphasis. The Lutheran Pietistic movement, originating with Jacob Spener (1635–1705) in reaction to sterile dogmatic orthodoxy, resulted in a mild millenarian eschatology that aligned with a more kindly attitude toward the Jews. From this there developed a pro-Semitic premillennial Lutheran strain that continued through Bengel, Zahn, Delitzsch, Godet, Auberlen, and on to America through Seiss, Schmucker, and Peters. These convictions were not widely shared, however, especially in mainstream Lutheranism. Throughout Europe Jews were viewed with contempt and hostility.[56] Many with a Reformed heritage, along with numerous Puritans, did express a heartfelt interest in the conversion of the Jews, even a climactic ingathering in a more national sense. Yet this hope usually envisaged incorporation into the church with the loss of individual, national, and territorial identity. Cohn-Sherbok puts the matter quite plainly,

> The early modern period thus witnessed the continuation of the long tradition of Christian anti-Semitism alongside a growing awareness of the need to improve the position of Jewry. Voices were ranging on different sides of this debate by leading figures of the Reformation. Yet even those Reformers who encouraged their coreligionists to adopt a more positive attitude towards the Jewish community shared many of the prejudices of previous ages. Basing themselves on Scripture, they prayed for the Jews' eventual conversion to the true faith. In this way, they hoped for the eventual elimination of the Jewish race, an aspiration shared centuries later by the Nazis, who sought to accomplish the same end but through very different means.[57]

[55] Cohn-Sherbok, *Anti-Semitism: A History*, 87–88; Johnson, *History of the Jews*, 275–80.
[56] Cohn-Sherbok, *Anti-Semitism: A History*, 158–59, 161.
[57] Ibid., 162.

This approach was not unlike that which Napoleon later proposed, namely, that the remedy concerning these objectionable people lay in the abolition of Jewry by dissolving it into Christianity.[58]

The Eighteenth-Century Evangelical Period

While Britain experienced the Evangelical Awakening under Whitefield and Wesley, America experienced the Great Awakening under Whitefield and Edwards. Also Germany experienced the Pietistic and Moravian revival under Spener, Francke, and Zinzendorf, while France endured bloody revolution along with "rational enlightenment"! A scientific awakening was also under way, launched by Newtonian physics, which had paved the way for the coming industrial revolution. On the other hand, Jewish intelligentsia had been made to seem backward and obscurantist. Jews appeared to educated and even uneducated Christians as figures of contempt and derision, dressed in funny clothes, imprisoned in ancient and ludicrous superstitions, as remote and isolated from modern society as one of the lost tribes. The Gentiles knew and cared nothing about Jewish scholarship. Even Moses Mendelssohn's argument for the existence of God was alleged to have been demolished by Immanuel Kant,[59] who denigrated Jewish religion and derided the Jews as a nation of usurers.[60]

In 1740 the Russians wanted either to convert the Jews or to expel them. The threat of expulsion was thought of as an incentive for the Jews to embrace the Greek Orthodox faith. In 1747 Pope Benedict XIV issued a papal bull which asserted that Jewish children over the age of seven could be baptized against the will of their parents.[61] Then at the commencement of his reign the anti-Semitic Pope Pius VI (1775–1799) published his *Edict on the Jews* that led directly to forced baptisms as well as abductions from Jewish parents. Jews were also obliged by law to listen to contemptuous and insulting sermons. In 1787 an Austrian law compelled Jews to adopt German-sounding first and family names, many of which translated into insults.[62]

A significant step in Jewish emancipation was taken when in 1791, over one hundred years after the emancipation established in England, the French National Assembly abrogated all anti-Jewish laws, the result being

---

[58] Ibid., 182.

[59] Johnson, *History of the Jews*, 294, 299, 302.

[60] Cohn-Sherbok, *Anti-Semitism: A History*, 171–72.

[61] Grosser and Halperin, *Causes and Effects of Anti-Semitism*, 193.

[62] Johnson, *History of the Jews*, 304–305.

that Louis XVI also proclaimed full equality for the Jews. The preceding debate had suggested that, not unlike the rationale of much twentieth-century anti-Judaic eschatology, "The Jews should be denied everything as a nation but granted everything as individuals."[63] That is, they should be allowed individuality without nationality or territory.

Even so, this legislative ideal did not become permanently established in societal expression within France, or indeed Europe as a whole. Once Napoleon was defeated at Waterloo in 1815, there came a vehement reaction against Jewish emancipation. In Italy Jews would be forced to live in ghettos and deprived of their rights. German Jewry would be treated similarly. In Frankfurt Jews would also be forced to live in the ghetto, and in Lübeck a total expulsion did take place. Hence, paradoxically, the French quest to emancipate the Jews eventually led to regression toward previous attitudes concerning both Jewry and the Jewish faith.[64]

The Nineteenth-Century Gentile Missionary Period

If the dismal clouds of Jewish oppression during the early eighteenth century had then briefly parted for a period to let in the light of emancipation through legislative enlightenment and democratic ideals, the nineteenth century eventually saw a pall of darkness roll in once again, initially in ideological terms. This gathering gloom over Europe foreshadowed a horrendous storm upon the eye of which the Jews would find themselves impaled, with their oppressors first being called the proponents of "anti-Semitism" by Wilhelm Marr in Hamburg in 1879. The ideological mix of this period, which tended to avow both humanistic and eschatological optimism, included emerging social Darwinism, socialism, fascism, free market capitalism, liberal Christianity, along with the inherited legacies of deism and rationalism. Even evangelical Christianity, especially within Anglicanism, with its great missionary thrust emanating through the vast resources of the British Empire, expressed considerable eschatological hope, except that popular, optimistic postmillennialism began to be eclipsed by apocalyptic premillennialism, from which there emerged new and enthusiastic support for Jewish projects and belief in the restoration of the Jews to their own land.[65]

[63] Ibid., 306.

[64] Cohn-Sherbok, *Anti-Semitism: A History*, 183–84.

[65] N. A. D. Scotland, *Evangelical Anglicans in a Revolutionary Age, 1789–1901* (Carlisle: Paternoster, 2004), 172–78.

However, in the world of literature, politics, philosophy, theology, and music, opposition to Jewry became identified with much of high European culture. For Voltaire, Jews are "our masters and our enemies . . . whom we detest [and are] the most abominable people in the world." Fichte (a disciple of Kant) believed that the expulsion of the Jews was the only means of protecting the German nation. Goethe poetically caricatured the Jews' shabby commercial dealings. Feuerbach considered the Jews to be crassly materialistic. Nietzsche believed that "the extinction of many types of people is just as desirable as any form of reproduction." Wagner warned the King of Bavaria: "I regard the Jewish race as the born enemy of pure humanity and everything that is noble in it."[66] Thus the intellectual tone of Europe gave anti-Judaism a new respectability. As religion lost ground to science, anti-Judaism became in part scientific. No longer based solely on religious belief, this new version of anti-Judaism became respectable and acceptable to the center of the western world. Even a story from Grimm's German *Fairy Tales* titled "The Jew in the Bush" has as its main character a cheating, thieving Jew who winds up on the gallows. In 1823 Pope Leo XII reestablished the Jewish ghetto in Rome, which had been opened by the Napoleonic armies during the occupation of Italy, and ordered the revival of forced conversion sermons on the Sabbath. In 1870, despite the opposition of Pope Pius IX, this same Roman ghetto was formally and finally abolished so that Jews were granted equal rights in Italy.

In 1844 Karl Marx published his *On the Jewish Question*, in which he wrote, "Out of its entrails bourgeois society continually creates Jews. . . . Emancipation from huckstering and from money, and consequently from practical, real Judaism, would be the self-emancipation of our era." In 1880 a new anti-Judaic campaign was launched in Berlin that gathered 250,000 signatures on a petition submitted to Chancellor Bismarck.[67] A complex anti-Judaic movement developed in Germany, indeed in Europe, involving an intensely rabid ideology that gathered support from pseudo-intellectual commitment to eugenics. Based on the arrogant belief that all high cultures were created by Aryans, it was deemed desirable that the state should uphold purity in this regard. Thus the impurity of Judaism must necessarily be removed. Here the philosophic foundation of the Holocaust became entrenched a generation before its actual outworking in German history.[68] The religious community did not exclude itself from participa-

---

[66] Cohn-Sherbok, *Anti-Semitism: A History*, 149, 168, 172, 206, 208, 212.

[67] Grosser and Halperin, *Causes and Effects of Anti-Semitism*, 208–9, 212, 215, 218, 222.

[68] Cohn-Sherbok, *Anti-Semitism: A History*, 204–13.

tion in this burgeoning movement. In the 1780s, Adolf Stoecker, chaplain to the imperial court in Berlin, founded the Christian Socialist Workers' Party, which adopted anti-Judaism as a central feature of its platform.[69] As an influential church historian and theologian at this time, Adolf Harnack's Marcionite rejection of the OT was a primary instance of classical anti-Jewish theology. Then later Gerhard Kittel, first editor of the highly re-garded *Theological Dictionary of the New Testament*, in attempting to deal with the Jewish question, not only rejected assimilation and mixed mar-riage, but also chose the alternative of the ghetto for separated, non-par-ticipatory national "guests."[70]

Of course, this heightening of anti-Judaism was not confined to Germany, even if it seemed primarily to incubate there. In 1890 the National Anti-Semitic League of France was formed in Paris under the presidency of Edouard Drumont, a Catholic socialist. In stridently taking to the streets, Nazi style, this movement sought the support of the masses. In November 1891 a bill ordering the expulsion of the Jews from France received 32 votes in the Chamber of Deputies. Then in 1892 the Dreyfus Affair erupted as an international incident in which a Jewish Captain Dreyfus was charged with treason due to his alleged betrayal of a secret French memo to a German Colonel. Found guilty and exiled to Devil's Island, Dreyfus was eventu-ally pardoned, then exonerated, though not before much exacerbation of the whole anti-Judaic conflict. Hence, with the further uprising of anti-Judaism in Russia and Poland, it was not so surprising that Theodor Herzl was moved to publish his monumental *Der Judenstaat* (*The Jewish State*) in 1896. He had personally witnessed the outcry of a mob shouting "Death to the Jews," when Dreyfus was stripped of his rank. Having become dis-tressed at the European cauldron of anti-Judaism that continued to boil, he came to the conclusion that the only solution for the wandering Jews would be the establishment of a Jewish homeland.[71]

The Jewish Missionary Period

It may seem paradoxical that the period that saw anti-Judaism reach an unprecedented climax, from the mid-nineteenth to the mid-twentieth century, was the same period that also witnessed the most energetic effort since Pentecost for the proclamation of the Christian gospel to the Jewish

[69] Ibid., 215.
[70] Williamson, *Has God Rejected His People?* 128–31.
[71] Cohn-Sherbok, *Anti-Semitism: A History*, 218–20.

people through numerous missionary agencies. However, our concern at this juncture remains the attitude of Christianity in central Europe toward this rising tide of Jewish hatred that reached immense proportions by 1933 and subsequently engulfed the western world in unspeakable and degrading horror. On January 30, 1933, Hitler assumed the office of German Chancellor. By this means he was enabled, through the agency of the Nazis, to employ national aversion to Jewry as a catalyst in his campaign for racial cleansing. From then on, no public institutionalized support existed in Germany for any view of Jews other than the one long dominant in Germany, now given extreme expression in a relentless and obsessive Nazi campaign for Jewish elimination.[72]

Even more horrifying was the manifest, extensive, and moral bankruptcy of the German churches, Protestant and Catholic alike. During the Weimar Republic from 1919 onwards, 70 to 80 percent of Protestant pastors had allied themselves with the anti-Judaic German National People's Party, and their hostile anti-Judaism had permeated the Protestant press, with its millions of readers, even before the Nazis were voted into power. These religious weeklies, which were devoted to the edification of their readers and to the cultivation of Christian piety, preached that the Jews were "the natural enemies of the Christian-national tradition." Of course, this religious thrust could only arise through the authorization of the church's religious leadership. One such Lutheran pastor, Bishop Otto Dibelius, wrote in a letter in 1933 that he had been "always an anti-Semite. One cannot fail to appreciate that in all the corrosive manifestations of modern civilization Jewry plays a leading role." A German evangelical pastor and historian observed that Bishop Dibelius' anti-Semitic sentiments were "well nigh representative of German Christendom in the beginning of 1933." Although at the highest levels of the German Catholic Church there was private dissent from aspects of Nazi doctrine, the Catholic Church as an institution remained thoroughly and publicly anti-Semitic. While some church leaders in German-occupied Denmark, the Netherlands, Norway, and France, openly condemned the Jewish persecution and slaughter, the German religious leadership left the Jews to their fates, or even contributed to the horror. By way of contrast, Dietrich Bonhoeffer, protestant theologian (and eventual martyr), had written to a friend just before Hitler came to power that, concerning

---

[72] Goldhagen, *Hitler's Willing Executioners*, 87, 106.

the treatment of the Jews, "the most sensible people have lost their heads and their entire Bible."[73]

If Germany was the crucible centered on the tableau of western and eastern Europe when the most vile racial atrocity in human history was perpetrated on the Jewish people, then other nations—especially France, Poland, and Russia—intimately nestled close to this decadent Teutonic ideology and consequently fomented the same evil agenda. As we have already pointed out, the thread of this problem is traceable through the main corridors of Christian history, both Catholic and Protestant, to the second century when Justin Martyr, then Ambrose, Chrysostom, Augustine, Jerome, and on through Gregory the Great, established dominant supercessionist theology. This is no extreme claim, but simply the stark unsavory reality of church history. Clark Williamson put it this way:

> All the literature one reads on the final solution leaves the clear impression that the pervasiveness of classical Christian anti-Jewish theology was a significant factor in the success of Hitler's program. Where it did not directly contribute to support for Hitler's policies—and it often did—it created an apathy toward Jews that was equally decisive in permitting the Holocaust. The great majority of the German people did not actively support or actively oppose Hitler; they were merely indifferent.[74]

Perhaps no better contemporary proof of this disastrous theological heritage being still with us could be found than in the astonishing awakening that dawned on Melanie Phillips, a Jewish columnist with the *London Daily Mail*, in 2002. She reported attending a discussion group of Jews and Christians concerning the churches' increasing hostility toward Israel. The surprise came when it was openly confessed by Christians present that

> the Churches' hostility had nothing to do with Israel's behavior towards the Palestinians. This was merely an excuse. The real reason for the growing antipathy, according to the Christians at that meeting, was the ancient hatred of Jews rooted deep in Christian theology and now on widespread display once again. A doctrine going back to the early Church fathers, suppressed after the Holocaust, had been revived under the influence of the Middle East conflict. This doctrine is called replacement theology. In essence, it says that the Jews have been replaced by the Christians in God's favor, and

[73] Ibid., 107–9, 111.
[74] Williamson, *Has God Rejected His People?* 134.

so all God's promises to the Jews, including the land of Israel, have been inherited by Christianity.[75]

If the preceding panoramic thrust of history has not been sufficiently grasped, and there is hesitation in embracing this report by Melanie Phillips, then the reader is now simply invited to consider the evidence in chapters 3 and 4 that follow.

---

[75] M. Phillips, "Christians Who Hate Jews," *The Spectator* (16 February, 2002). An expanded consideration of the context of this quotation can be found in Appendix D: "Melanie Phillips on Replacement Theology."

Chapter 3

ISRAEL AND CONTEMPORARY EXAMPLES OF CHRISTIAN ANTI-JUDAISM IN THE US

Introduction

This chapter and the next seek to warn the reader about anti-Judaism that exists today at a scholarly level within conservative Christianity, especially that which is Reformed in character, in the United States and the United Kingdom. My purpose is not to disrupt the unity of the Spirit or to engage in unfruitful "arguments over words" (1 Tim 6:4; cp. 2 Tim 2:14). Rather my goal is "warning and teaching with all wisdom." With Paul, "I labor for this, striving with His strength that works powerfully in me" (Col 1:28–29). Jesus could not have more strongly urged unity, yet it had to be based on the sanctifying work of the truth of God's word (John 17:11, 17–23). Although Paul adamantly advocated Christian unity (Eph 4:3; Col 3:13–14), he was just as zealous in maintaining "the sound teaching of our Lord Jesus Christ . . . that promotes godliness" (1 Tim. 6:3). Therefore while maintaining the "common salvation" that binds us, we must also "contend for the faith that was delivered to the saints once for all" (Jude 3).

Albertus Pieters

Albertus Pieters (1897–1987), former Professor of Bible and Missions at Western Theological Seminary in Holland, Michigan (Reformed Church in America), is undoubtedly an esteemed and widely quoted representative of classic Reformed theology, especially its European formulation. He is often quoted by Calvinists who espouse an Augustinian eschatology, especially his volume, *The Seed of Abraham*. The following quotations are mostly drawn from this work and plainly indicate an outspoken, anti-Judaic spirit.

> God willed that after the institution of the New Covenant there should no longer be any Jewish people in the world—yet here they are! That is a fact—a very sad fact, brought about by their wicked rebellion against God.[1]

What a nuisance, what a worldly impediment the Jew currently presents for Pieters! While the centuries-old vitriolic charge that they were

---

[1] A. Pieters, *The Seed of Abraham* (Grand Rapids: Eerdmans, 1950), 123.

"Christ-killers" is not directly expressed, the tone of this racist slander, both here and following, remains. Of course, Gentile guilt need not be mentioned since it is of a far lesser rank!

> But is it not monstrous to hold that by reason of this wickedness the said undesired and undesirable group are now heirs to the many exceedingly precious promises of God? Shall we be accused of anti-Semitism, because we speak thus of the Jews? We have not spoken so harshly as the apostle Paul, who knew them intimately and loved them passionately. . . . [Pieters quotes here 1 Thess 2:14–16]. How is it possible to believe that there are still prophecies of divine grace to be fulfilled in a group upon which the wrath of God has come "to the uttermost"?[2]

The HCSB better translates v. 16, "They [the Jews] are always adding to the number of their sins, and wrath has overtaken them completely." The assumption here that such condemnation by Paul was irrevocably applicable to ethnic Israel as a nation, is erroneous. The context, and especially I Thess 2:14, indicate that what the apostle had in mind concerned that distinctive Jewish opposition which he had encountered in Judea, but particularly Jerusalem, and now was reportedly in Thessalonica. When Paul found it necessary to leave Thessalonica due to violent Jewish opposition, after his first visit there, on moving south to Berea he immediately commenced to witness, as was his pattern, at the local synagogue (Acts 17:1–12), hardly evidencing ethnic Jewish abandonment. The same generalization with regard to Israel as a "synagogue of Satan" (Rev. 2:9; 3:9) also fails to acknowledge that these charges concerned the localities of Smyrna and Philadelphia rather than a comprehensive ethnic application.[3]

> Some years ago, in a conference, I heard a brother minister say: "God is through with the Jews." At the time, this statement startled me, and I thought it extreme, but the more I study the Scriptures the more it seems to me he certainly was right. And, after all, was he saying anything more than the Lord Jesus Christ said, addressing the unbelieving Jewish people through the symbolism of the barren fig tree: "Let there be no fruit from thee henceforward forever?" (Matthew 21:19).[4]

The cursing of the fig tree that had only leaves and no fruit, representative of prospective judgment on Israel (Jer 5:15–17; Joel 1:5–7,12), took place on the Monday morning of Passion Week following Palm Sunday.

---

[2] Ibid., 123–24.

[3] See D. A. Hagner, "Paul's Quarrel with Judaism," in *Anti-Semitism and Early Christianity* (ed. C. A. Evans and D. A. Hagner; Minneapolis: Fortress, 1993), 130–36.

[4] Pieters, *The Seed of Abraham,* 124.

The curse did not point to the nation itself as a total ethnic entity, but to the present and subsequent corrupt generations, as Matt 21:42–43 confirms. In Matt 23:37–39 Jesus indicates that an eventual change of heart will come to Jerusalem, hence national Israel. The same point is made in Deut 31:14–22 and Josh 23:16 concerning Israel's future disobedience and dispersal in judgment. Yet Deut 30:1–10 gives assurance that after this dispersal the Lord will bring about Israel's return to the land and regeneration.

> There are at present people in the world who are called, and who call themselves, "The Jews". They claim that they are the continuation of ancient Israel, and are the "Seed of Abraham" to whom the divine promises were made, and to whom they are to be fulfilled. The claim is conceded by many earnest Christian people who believe that they find in the Bible very important prophecies that must some day be fulfilled in this company who are called "The Jews", who worship in the synagogue and adhere to the Talmud. . . . How could the Jews be held together and continue to be a "peculiar people" [without a temple, a country, a government]? Only by preserving in all possible rigidity the ordinances handed down from the fathers, with regard to eating and drinking, trimming or shaving the beard, observing fasts and feasts, circumcision, Sabbath keeping on the seventh day of the week, synagogue worship, prohibition of intermarriage, etc., etc. These things must henceforth be their life; for if these were lost all was lost, and they must expect speedily to be absorbed in the mass of the population around them.[5]

Yet Hosea made it plain that "the Israelites must live many days without king or prince, without sacrifice or sacred pillar, and without ephod or household idols. Afterwards, the people of Israel will return and seek the LORD their God and David their king. They will come with awe to the LORD and to His goodness in the last days" (Hos 3:4–5). So as is well confirmed throughout many centuries, stripped of much of their distinctive heritage, the Israelites have remained and will remain as Israelites. However, Pieters continued,

> Ignorant that their separateness from the rest of the world was in the divine purpose temporary, they strove to render it permanent. Thus that which had been in itself good and holy became through their error a source of poison in the life of the world; and "The Jew" became the great persistent international problem.[6]

This is nothing short of despicable language that reflects the anti-Judaic vehemence of shameful, early twentieth-century Europe. There is something

---

[5] Ibid., 132, 134.
[6] Ibid., 134.

fundamentally wrong here with a professed Christian mentality that is so objectionably racist in character. However, this rabid example of replacement theology continues.

> The Visible Christian Church being now the New Covenant Israel, those whom we call "The Jews" are outsiders, cut off branches, having no more connection with either promises or prophecies than any Gentile group.[7]
>
> Those now called "Jews," . . . have . . . no prophetic destiny, except a continuance of their present sad and bitter state, so long as they continue disobedient and unbelieving. They will not always so continue. St. Paul assures us that in time to come they will again be grafted into the olive tree. That, however, will give them no prophetic future as a separate group. They will then also lose their distinct existence by absorption into the Christian Church. The closed book of Israel's history will not be reopened.[8]

Pieters expresses his belief in the eventual salvation of the Jews, though with the result that all taint of Jewishness will be lost. It is to come about through absorption into the Christian church, the result being the loss of Jewish identity and at the same time purification through Gentile identification. This is not unlike Augustine, Vos, John Murray, and a host of Reformed commentators, all of whom, while deftly describing a mass conversion of the Jews at the climax of the church age, are careful to avoid associating this with the perpetuation of national and territorial Judaism.[9] Pieters tolerates a token, nominal individuality while vehemently repudiating ethnic individuality, nationality, and territory in covenantal terms.

How utterly un-Pauline is this theologically anti-Judaic diatribe. It savors of being bitter, not just tart. One almost senses here a degree of delight at the prospect of the alleged coming extinction of Judaism. The whole tone here is so unworthy of any Christian who glories in being saved by a Jew (John 4:22). Can such an obviously so unsavory emphasis be the fruit of a sound eschatology?

Loraine Boettner

Loraine Boettner (1901–1990), a graduate of Princeton Theological Seminary and a member of the Orthodox Presbyterian Church, was a twen-

---

[7] Ibid., 137–38..

[8] A. Pieters, *The Ten Tribes in History and Prophecy* (Grand Rapids: Eerdmans, 1934), 109.

[9] In John Murray's commentary on Rom 11:11–32, whereas he writes of "ethnic Israel" and "the restoration of Israel" and the "conversion" and "fullness" and "recovery" and "blessing" and "the salvation of Israel" in relation to "the mass of Israel," he nowhere refers to the "nation of Israel" or the likes of Ezekiel 36–37 since these would then implicate the "land" as being integral to such terminology (*The Epistle to the Romans* [Grand Rapids: Eerdmans, 1965], 2.75–103).

tieth-century scholar of classic Reformed convictions. His influential volume, *The Reformed Doctrine of Predestination,* has had considerable influence and is an excellent presentation of the doctrines of sovereign grace. His book, *The Millennium,*[10] however, contains not only the most emphatic and categorical expressions of supercessionism, but also declarations on the destiny of the Jews that reflect theological anti-Judaism.

> While the Jews no longer occupy a place of special favor in the divine plan, this does not mean that God has cast them off. *Nothing has been taken from the Jews as individuals.* Only the external forms have been abolished. The blessings and privileges of salvation which they enjoyed during the Old Testament dispensation have been magnified and heightened and extended to all nations and races alike. After the Jews had forfeited their rights as a chosen nation, or, to put it more accurately, after God had completed His purpose with the Jews as a separate people, they continued to have the privileges of full and free salvation individually.[11]

Franklin Littell expressed considerable dismay about this portion of Boettner's replacement theology:

> At first blush, this looks like a simple dehydrated statement of the displacement myth. The revealing phrase is, however, this: "Nothing has been taken from the Jews as individuals." This formula does not derive from ancient teachers and synods of the church; it is precisely the dogma of the Enlightenment. "Everything to the Jew as an individual; nothing to the Jews as a people."[12]

Littell was absolutely correct, but perhaps we might add a modification: "Everything to the Jew as an individual under humiliation; nothing to the Jew with regard to Israel as a territorial nation."

Boettner continued his harangue,

> With the establishment of the Christian Church Judaism should have made a smooth and willing transition into Christianity, and should thereby have disappeared as the flower falls away before the developing fruit. Its continued existence as a bitter rival and enemy of the Christian Church after the time of Christ, and particularly its revival after the judgment of God had fallen on it so heavily in the destruction of Jerusalem and the dispersal of the people in 70 A.D., was sinful.[13]

[10] L. Boettner, *The Millennium* (Philadelphia: Presbyterian and Reformed, 1958). The author openly upholds his postmillennial views in 103 pages; he critiques amillennialism in 28 pages and premillennialism in 237 pages. The tilt of Boettner's criticism is quite obvious.

[11] Ibid., 312.

[12] F. H. Littell, *The Crucifixion of the Jews* (New York: Harper & Row, 1975), 33.

[13] Boettner, *The Millennium,* 313.

The overall tenor here is antithetical to that of Paul. Particularly objectionable is the suggestion, seemingly without compassion, that the Jews were responsible for the misery they have endured over the centuries. One would expect at least mention of widespread anti-Judaism throughout the centuries of the Christian Church and western society that calls for shameful confession. The problem is chiefly that of the Jew; he has become a blot on society. There is even the intimation that Christians in particular were, to a considerable extent, justified in their campaigns of ostracism concerning the perfidious, Christ-killing Jew. Arnold Fruchtenbaum, a Jewish Christian, rightly expresses his distress:

> According to Boettner, the Jews are totally to blame for their history of persecution. The problem is not with the Gentiles' attitude toward the Jews, but with the Jews failure to disappear. The solution is that the Jews should cease to be Jews, and by so doing will make a great contribution to the world. It is the Jewish failure to assimilate that has produced tragic results, both for the Jews and "for the world at large." This is theological anti-Semitism with a vengeance![14]

To support his overall contention here concerning Israel, Boettner quoted at length from *The Seed of Abraham* by Albertus Pieters, previously referenced in this chapter. For a professing Christian, such an attitude is quite outrageous. It is full of Gentile arrogance, namely, that the problems of the suffering Jew are essentially those of his own making. If this deplorable attitude is the fruit of a certain doctrinal system, then there must be something fundamentally wrong with the originating body of teaching.

Boettner's contemptible attitude is further evidenced as follows:

> The continuance of this bitterly anti-Christian racial Group has brought no good to themselves, and there has been strife and antagonism in practically every nation where they have gone. They have not been a happy people. One only need think of the pogroms in Russia, the ghettos of eastern Europe, the many restrictions and persecutions that they have suffered in Italy, Spain, Poland, and other countries, and in our own day the campaign of extermination waged against them in Germany by Hitler. At the present time we see this problem in a particularly aggravated form in the Near East, where the recently established nation of Israel has ruthlessly displaced an Arab population and seeks to expand further into surrounding regions, some 900,000 Arabs in refugee camps around the borders of Israel being one of the chief continuing causes of bitterness. . . . Israel is not a self-sustaining nation, and her existence to date has been heavily subsidized by

---

[14] A. Fruchtenbaum, *Israelology* (Tustin, California: Ariel Ministries, 1996), 49. The reference here is to Boettner, *Millennium*, 315.

American money and equipment—much of it undoubtedly having been given for the purpose of influencing the Jewish vote in this country. . . . The mere fact that these people are Jews does not in itself give them any more moral or legal right to Palestine than to the United States or any other part of the world.[15]

The language here is loaded with anti-Jewish innuendo. Furthermore, avoidance of mentioning culpability on the part of the Gentiles concerning European persecution is astounding, while the nuanced blame of the Jews for their sufferings is extremely shameful. Hence the Jews have only themselves to blame for their troubles, as well as a hopeless future. Qualification in no way takes away from the essential disparagement.

> It may seem harsh to say that, "God is through with the Jews." But the fact of the matter is that He is through with them as a unified national group. . . . This does not mean, of course, that the Jews will never go back to Palestine—as indeed some of them have already established the nation of Israel, a little less than 2 million out of an estimated world Jewish population of 12 million now being in that country. But it does mean that as any of them go back they do so entirely on their own, apart from any covenanted purpose to that end and entirely outside of Scripture prophecy. No Scripture blessing is promised for a project of that kind.[16]

Here then is the unveiling of a common form of duplicity among a number of Reformed Christian scholars, and indeed evangelicals more broadly speaking. On the one hand, they will declare that in this Christian dispensation there is "a remnant according to God's gracious choice" (Rom 11:5), that is, Christians who are to be designated as Jewish, without national and territorial claims. They will also confess that there are individual non-Christians today who are to be designated "Jews" in some worldly social sense. On the other hand, as with Pieters, Boettner, and as we shall also see with Gary Burge, O. Palmer Robertson and the signatories of *An Open Letter to Evangelicals*, there is yet for these "Jews" no nation, no land, no covenant relationship in any sense that abides according to the original promise made to Abraham. That, they claim, has been permanently done away with. In other words, for authors such as Boettner, the use of the term "Jew" is really a hoax. He is quite frank in this regard, even though he continues to speak of "Jews" in the parlance of modern society.

> We should point out further that those who today popularly are called "Jews" are in reality not Jews at all. Legitimate Judaism as it existed in the

---

[15] Boettner, *The Millennium*, 314.
[16] Ibid., 319, 321.

Old Testament era was of divine origin and had a very definite content of religious and civil laws, priesthood, ritual, sacrifices, temple, Sabbath, etc. But
with the destruction of Jerusalem and the dispersion of the people in A.D.
70, that system was effectively destroyed. It has since not been practiced
anywhere in the world.[17]

There is an honesty here that is breathtaking, even chilling, and unfortunately lacking in the writings of others who obviously hold the same
doctrinal convictions that are inherent in replacement theology. In other
words, some, like Boettner, confess their belief at this point quite can-
didly, while many others, in holding an identical point of view, declare
it with a more subtle touch. Even so, they are essentially all saying the
same thing. We might even ask them if this alleged ethnic deception adds
any degree of justification for the mistreatment of the Jews. So I strenuously maintain that this shameful attitude, so blatantly confessed, clearly
betrays a most un-Pauline disposition. It also causes us to see this as history tragically repeating itself after centuries of Jewish disqualification by
arrogant Gentiles.

Our resultant practical concern here is with regard to the contemporary
Jew who is alleged to have no status in the sight of God, that is, according to Pieters and Boettner, apart from the more subtle terminology in the
same vein on the part of many others. Consequently, will such a conviction
with regard to the "Jew" be productive of a certain biblical ethical behavior
toward him, especially if this "Jew" nevertheless claims a national identity
that includes an historic claim to Palestine? The answer is obvious, particularly as centuries of church history up to the present have plainly illustrated. The preceding quotations very much parallel that doctrine which
resulted in the shameful behavior of the past. The conclusion here is inescapable. Therefore, do devotees of replacement theology, as representa-
tively set forth thus far, enthusiastically involve themselves in distinctive
missionary outreach toward the Jews, according to the Pauline model? In
witnessing to the "Jew," would they present to them the declarations of
Boettner and Pieters? Further, would they encourage the establishment
in Israel of Christian churches that proclaim this teaching concerning the
"poisonous" influence of Judaism?

---

[17] Ibid., 381. Of course Paul continued to maintain his Jewishness (Acts 21:39; 22:3; Rom
11:1), though Boettner might respond that these affirmations were before AD 70. But there is not
the slightest indication, as in Luke 21:24, that such a disqualification took place; in fact, Rom
11:25–28 declares quite the opposite on account of the Israelites' "forefathers."

Gary Burge

Gary Burge, professor of NT at Wheaton College Graduate School, has aligned himself with the pro-Palestinian and anti-Judaic movement that vociferously opposes the modern State of Israel, derided as unjust, carnal Zionism. Along with Don Wagner and Stephen Sizer, he spoke at the 2004 *Friends of Sabeel-North America, Voice of the Palestinian Christians* conference (www.fosna.org) having the theme, *Challenging Christian Zionism*. Liberation theology was dominant, and the presence of terrorist Yasar Arafat was ominous. Burge is also on the board of *Evangelicals for Middle East Understanding* (www.emeu.net), which notwithstanding it name tilts toward non-evangelical ecumenism, especially that which is eastern, supercessionist, and anti-Judaic. On the web site of *Challenging Christian Zionism, Christians committed to Biblical Justice* (www.christianzionism.org) Burge wrote this comment on *Christian Zionism, Evangelicals, and Israel*:

> But the most important critique—and here I think we discover the Achilles' heel—is that Christian Zionism is committed to what I term a "territorial religion." It assumes that God's interests are focused on a land, a locale, a place. From a NT perspective, the land is holy by reference to what transpired there in history. But it no longer has an intrinsic part to play in God's program for the world. This is what Stephen pointed to in his speech in Acts 7. The land and the temple are now secondary. God wishes to reveal himself to the entire world. And this insight cost Stephen his life.[18]

There may be a tendency here toward a more Gnostic form of spirituality that so abhors the inclusion of materiality and the alleged inferiority of carnal territory. Be this as it may, biblical Christianity and consummate redemption is founded on spiritual materiality in space, time, and history on planet earth (Zech 14:9–11; John 1:14; Acts 3:20–21; 1 John 1:1–3), and Christians rejoice in this divine condescension. Stephen's concern was not the need to "de-materialize," "spiritualize," or "universalize" the promise to Abraham concerning the land, but rather to focus on the coming of Messiah whose presence would certainly transcend the interim "holy place and the law; . . . this place [the Temple] and . . . the customs that Moses handed down" (Acts 6:13–14). The land and the temple are not abrogated in parallel as Burge suggests. It is the old covenant that Stephen challenged,

---

[18] G. Burge, *Christian Zionism, Evangelicals and Israel*, (www.christian-zionism. org/article-sN.asp); cited May 2007. Further pro-Palestinian and anti-Israel indications concerning Burge are his being on the Advisory Board of *The Holy Land Christian Ecumenical Foundation* (www. hcef.org), as well as his favorable review of Sizer's *Christian Zionism: Road Map to Armageddon?* on *Friends of Al-Aqsa*, www.aqsa.org.uk.

not the land promise intrinsic to the Abrahamic covenant (see chapter 9 of this book).

Burge's most significant writing concerning the issue at hand is his *Whose Land? Whose Promise? What Christians Are Not Being Told about Israel and the Palestinians*. While the style is temperate, the overall thrust is uncompromisingly supercessionist, anti-Judaic, and pro-Palestinian. From a graphic point of view, the front cover photograph says it all. Here is a young Palestinian boy, David-like, about to throw a stone at a gargantuan, Goliath-like Israeli tank that is armed to the teeth. In ignoring centuries of the wandering, down-trodden, despised Jew, the pitiable Palestinians are portrayed as the unjustly treated underdogs in the face of such a rapacious, heartless, and devouring foe. In his preface Burge presents his thesis:

> I will argue that even if Christian theologians reject the position that modern Israel inherits the land promised to Abraham (thanks to a new covenant that abrogates the old), this should not diminish the church's respect for Judaism nor the rights of the Jewish people to live in the land of Israel.[19]

Let us look at four aspects of this statement that the subsequent text considers in detail.

Abrogation of the Abrahamic Land Promise

Burge subscribes to the view that although the land was promised to Abraham in such clear, repeated, unilateral, and covenantal terms, the advent of the Christian era means that this truth no longer has any validity. This is a difficult position to maintain in view of the weight of biblical evidence to the contrary. First, there is God's initial promise to Abraham:

> The LORD said to Abram: Go out from your land, your relatives, and your father's house to the land that I will show you. . . . He took his wife Sarai, his nephew Lot, all the possessions they had accumulated, and the people he had acquired in Haran, and they set out for the land of Canaan. When they came to the land of Canaan, Abram passed through the land to the site of Shechem, at the oak of Moreh. At that time the Canaanites were in the land. Then the LORD appeared to Abram and said, "I will give this land to your offspring." So he built an altar there to the LORD who had appeared to him (Gen 12:1,5–7).

Numerous biblical references also incorporate confidence in the inviolate character of the land promise made to Abraham.[20] In light of such

---

[19] G. Burge, *Whose Land? Whose Promise?* (Cleveland, Ohio: Pilgrim, 2003), xviii.
[20] See 13:14–15,17; 15:7,18; 17:8; 24:7; 26:3; 28:4,13–15; 35:12; 48:3–4,21; 50:24; Exod

weighty evidence, Burge's comment concerning Genesis 12:1–3 is astonishing: "Strikingly, this promise fails to mention the land. Virtually every
scholar who studies the passage notes that this omission is peculiar."[21]
Nevertheless he admits to the clear promise of the land in 13:14–17, then
suggests again that the promise is omitted in 15:1–6, and finally affirms
that the land is formally covenanted in 15:18–21. Significantly the emphatic unilateral character of this last reference, in which God alone passed
between the cut animal pieces while Abraham slept, is totally ignored.
According to Burge, however, the fundamental reason for the abrogation
of the land covenant with Abraham is its alleged conditionality. There is
nothing new here since this is the most common reason given for such land
nullification by supercessionists. But it is especially surprising when found
in the Calvinist argumentation of Boettner, Fairbairn, Hendriksen, Mauro,
Pieters, Riddlebarger and others. Consequently, the inevitable question that
must be asked is this: If the land promise in the Abrahamic covenant was
conditional (that is, based on an unspecified degree of obedience), then
does the same principle of conditionality equally apply to the fulfillment
of other aspects of the Abrahamic covenant, and particularly the resultant
new covenant? If it is claimed in response that the Abrahamic covenant
has distinctive conditional and unconditional elements, I would reply that
such an attempted covenantal bifurcation is exegetically untenable, especially where a Calvinist understanding of Scripture is concerned, and indicates a fundamental doctrinal weakness.

Nevertheless Burge claims that in the NT record, the land is to be newly
focused through the advent of Jesus, the result being redefinition and
reinterpretation.

> Christ is the reality behind all earthbound promises. . . . land is rejected as
> the aim of faith; . . . land is *spiritualized* as meaning something else; . . . the
> promise is historicized in Jesus, a man who lives in the land. . . . Whatever
> the "land" meant in the Old Testament, whatever the promise contained,

3:15–17; 6:3–4,8; 13:5,11; 32:13; 33:1; Lev 26:42; Num 11:12; 14:23; 32:11; Deut 1:8,21,35;
4:1; 6:3,10,18,23; 9:5,27–28; 10:11; 11:9,21; 12:1; 19:8; 26:3,15; 27:3; 28:11; 30:5,20; 31:7,20;
34:4; Josh 1:6; 18:3; 21:43–44; Judg 2:1; 1 Kgs 8:34,40,48; 14:15; 1 Chr 16:15–18; 2 Chr 20:7;
Neh 9:7–8; Ps 105:8–11,42–44; Ezek 33:24.

[21] Ibid., 69. Von Rad is referenced as one example. The fine point being made is that in 12:1
the land is to be "shown" to Abraham, but is not here promised. *The Jewish Study Bible* does not
describe this point as if a curiosity. Rather it comments concerning 12:1–3, "The twin themes of
land and progeny inform the rest of the Torah." Concerning 15:1–6,7–20, "This ch. falls into two
sections, the first (vv. 1–6) focused on God's promise to provide Abram with an heir who will be
his own son, and the second (vv. 7–20) on God's covenanted pledge to redeem Abram's descendants from enslavement abroad and to give them a land" (New York: Oxford, 2004), 30, 35.

this now belongs to Christians. . . . The land was a metaphor, a symbol of a greater place beyond the soil of Canaan.[22]

Primary support for this subjective extrapolation is acknowledged to be W. D. Davies, considered in more detail in chapter 9 of this book. However repetition of the following acknowledgment of this author is sufficient to indicate the uncertain ground, especially argument based on alleged silence, which such a speculative edifice rests on. Davies wrote,

> Because the logic of Paul's understanding of Abraham and his personalization of the fulfillment of the promise "in Christ" demanded the deterritorializing of the promise, salvation was not now bound to the Jewish people centered in the land and living according to the Law: it was "located" not in a place, but in persons in whom grace and faith had their writ. By personalizing the promise "in Christ" Paul universalized it. For Paul, Christ had gathered up the promise into the singularity of his own person. In this way, "the territory" promised was transformed into and fulfilled by the life "in Christ." *All this is not made explicit, because Paul did not directly apply himself to the question of the land, but it is implied* [emphasis added]. In the Christological logic of Paul, the land, like the Law, particular and provisional, had become irrelevant."[23]

Here is Gentile exegesis come to full bloom that at the same time excludes any Jewish Christian perspective such as is surely inherent in the writings of converted rabbi Paul (Rom 8:18–21; 11:26). Surely this same Jewish Christian perspective was in Peter's mind when he preached eschatologically of the return of Jesus Christ to inaugurate "the times of the restoration of all things, which God spoke about by the mouth of His holy prophets from the beginning" (Acts 3:21). For Davies and Burge, however, belief that the land of Abrahamic Judaism should find recognition in Christianity is demeaned in terms of territorial "irrelevance." Thus by means of a Gentile, spiritualizing hermeneutic, anti-Judaism is inevitably cultivated in principle, and history has repeatedly, shamefully demonstrated the outworking of this process by means of the disenfranchisement of the Jew. I suggest that for the Apostles, however, especially in consultation at the Council of Jerusalem (Acts 15), such "deterritorialization" was unthinkable. The reason it was not foremost in their writings was preoccupation with a divinely appointed evangelistic mandate within the window of the "times of the Gentiles" (Luke 21:24).

---

[22] Ibid., 176–177, 179.
[23] W. D. Davies, *The Gospel And The Land* (Sheffield: JSOT, 1994), 179.

New Covenant Supplanting the Old

Here Burge makes an assertion with regard to the new covenant that I believe is fundamentally in error. With many theologians he rejects the belief "that modern Israel inherits the land promised to Abraham," and he bases this on "a new covenant that abrogates the old." But the new covenant obviously abrogates the old Mosaic covenant, *not* the Abrahamic covenant (Jer 31:31–34; Heb 8:7–13). Certainly the Mosaic covenant, as an interim administration, was imposed on the ongoing Abrahamic administration that had already been established for 430 years. Just prior to the institution of the Mosaic covenant, Moses was instructed, "I will bring you to the land that I swore to give to Abraham, Isaac, and Jacob, and I will give it to you as a possession. I am the LORD" (Exod 6:8). Until the actual establishment of the Mosaic covenant, including its renewal because of Israel's disobedience, possession of the promised land remained as a certain hope (Exod 12:23–25; 13:11; 20:12; 33:1). With this in mind, Paul affirmed, as a fundamental gospel principle, that "the law, which came 430 years later, does not revoke a covenant that was previously ratified by God and cancel the promise" (Gal 3:17).

An especially egregious example of how this principle of nullification of the Abrahamic covenant plays out in Burge's supercessionism concerns his questioning of Father George Makhlouf, a parish priest of St. George's Greek Orthodox Church in Ramallah, Israel.

> I asked . . . , "How can you argue with the Israeli claim to own this land since God gave it to the Jews in the Old Testament? Israeli Jews have inherited the promises to Abraham, have they not?" . . . "The church," he began, "has inherited the promises of Israel. The church is actually the new Israel. What Abraham was promised, Christians now possess because they are Abraham's true spiritual children just as the New Testament teaches."[24]

Burge then makes a most revealing comment that appears to be utterly void of a sense of church history, warts and all.

> The Greek Orthodox tradition of Father George has been consistent in defending this view throughout the centuries. From the earliest years, the Middle Eastern churches have claimed the promises of the Old Testament for their own. This concept shows up in Orthodox icons. Churches display beautiful pictures (or icons) of Old Testament stories whose truths have now been swept up by the Christian tradition and "baptized" with new meaning.[25]

[24] Burge, *Whose Land? Whose Promise?* 167.
[25] Ibid., 168.

What fails to be acknowledged here, in all its shameful ugliness, is that this "sweeping" process involved an Augustinian anti-Judaic heritage that later enveloped both the eastern church and the western church. Such an appeal to church tradition here, as if this might provide added weight of argument, only heightens the degree of disgrace caused by this supercessionist tradition that flowed through subsequent centuries.

One chapter of Burge's book is devoted to twelve biographical vignettes of Palestinian or Arab Christians under the title "Living Stones in the Land." A number of these individuals align with Eastern Orthodoxy, and there is every indication that all are committed to supercessionist, anti-Judaic theology.

One more instance may be offered of this anti-Judaic spirit that evacuates the Abrahamic covenant of its Jewish essence and works out as a theology of Jewish disenfranchisement:

> Jesus' emphasis on the kingdom of God gave him every opportunity to talk about land and inheritance, but he refused. *The kingdom of Israel did not capture his interest* [emphasis his]. He preferred to talk about "the kingdom of God" or the "kingdom of heaven." . . . [His disciples'] minds were on political restoration, but for Jesus, God's kingdom was fundamentally God's reign over the lives of men and women—not an empire, not a political kingdom with borders and armies. The kingdom was fundamentally a spiritual idea, a spiritual experience that transcended any particular place or time or land. People who took pride in their possession of land or city as the trophy of their spirituality would find themselves in opposition to Jesus' message.[26]

While agreeing in principle with the final comment that ignores the biblical concept of spiritual materiality, the simple answer to this overall voiding of Jewish national significance in Jesus' ministry is a consideration of His most clearly expressed Jewishness (Matt 10:5–7; 15:24; John 4:22). All the exegetical juggling in the world cannot evade the Judeo-centric eschatological significance of Jesus' words of encouragement to His disciples: "I assure you: In the Messianic age [see Acts 3:20–21], . . . you who have followed Me will also sit on 12 thrones, judging the 12 tribes of Israel" (Matt 19:28). The new Jerusalem also upholds this perpetuated Jewishness (Rev 21:10–14).

To also imply, however, that the terms "kingdom of God" and "kingdom of heaven" are somehow purposely employed in the NT so as to circumvent consideration of Jewish nationalism is strange indeed, especially if these terms are traced to their OT Hebrew roots. Undoubtedly Jesus repudiated

---

[26] Ibid., 172–73.

much of the perverse Jewish nationalism of His time. But I reject the suggestion that He also renounced the Jewish eschatological vision of the OT by means of neo-Platonic dualism, reinterpretation, and supercession (see chapter 8 of this book). I agree that the salvation and sanctification of the human soul is more important than the salvation and sanctification of the land of Israel. But on the other hand, the NT emphatically repudiates as heresy the concept that the salvation and sanctification of the soul nullifies the importance of the salvation and sanctification of the human body. Hence we must reject the implied Gnostic spirit whereby the land is regarded as eschatologically insignificant.

Christian Respect for Judaism

In rejecting the land promise of the Abrahamic covenant, somehow Burge wants to soften the clear implications of supercessationism by means of a subtle linguistic accommodation. He maintains that, "this [nullification of the land promise given to Abraham] should not diminish the church's respect for Judaism." While Burge believes that the land in which Israel presently dwells has no biblical, covenantal significance, he thinks this should not diminish the church's respect for contemporary Judaism, and even its national and territorial manifestation. Of course, the key question here that Burge needs to answer concerns his definition of "Judaism." And it seems quite clear that for him, being a Jew today is not a genuine, divine, covenantal relationship even in the flesh, but more the employment of accepted social nomenclature that fits within the worldly national parameters of our time. Burge acknowledges on the basis of Rom 11:28–29 that

> if Judaism remains—even in its brokenness—a people with a unique future, a people still to be redeemed, then it follows that they currently have a place of honor even in their unbelief. . . . Judaism has rejected the new covenant. Nevertheless, even in this disobedience, these broken branches still possess an incomparable place in history. . . . For the sake of their history, for the sake of the promises made to their ancestors [Abraham, Isaac, and Jacob], God will retain a place for Jews in history. In their present condition of unbelief, they deserve honor. And when they accept Christ, be it now or in the future, their brokenness will be restored.[27]

Although this may appear to be a commendable explanation, even Augustine could align himself with such plasticity of expression. Burge's statement of "honor" for Judaism must be interpreted against his belief that the land

[27] Ibid., 187.

promise, repeatedly confirmed to Abraham, Isaac, and Jacob, has been nullified. Fortunately, he summarizes his actual meaning:

> Some Christians think that unbelieving Israel still lives today as heirs to Abraham's promises, that Christ's new covenant did not bring about an epoch-changing shift among God's people. But as we have seen, this view neglects much of Paul's teaching in Galatians and Romans about Christians as Abraham's heirs. . . . Father George of Ramallah would tell us [see above] that the question "Who owns the land?" is not so simple. The answer is not just a matter of pointing to the promises of Abraham, identifying modern Israel as heirs to those promises, and then theologically justifying the Israeli land claim. On the contrary, Christian theology demands that the true recipients of these promises will be found in the Christian church. Perhaps the church alone receives these promises![28]

Here is the reason why it is hardly to be expected that the Jew of today would respond at this juncture, "Thank you very much, Mr. Burge!" The reason is that he would quickly appreciate the shallow patronage that is being employed to obfuscate supercessionist anti-Judaism. This is simply that Augustinian tolerance of the Jew that in reality is a foil for temporal sufferance.

Jewish Rights to the Land of Israel

In the same vein we are told that the Christian church should also uphold "the rights of the Jewish people to live in the land of Israel [Palestine]." Hence another vital question arises concerning the exact nature of these stated "rights" that he appears to uphold. In light of the author's confessed belief in the invalidation of the Abrahamic covenant insofar as the land promise is concerned, it can only be concluded that some more secular judicial standard is intended, and not divine decree. He appears to be simply making a concession to the status quo. Should he have written a century ago, there would have been no encouragement whatsoever concerning the Zionist hope of that time concerning a return to the land of Israel. Most likely the United Nations mandate of 1948 is in Burge's mind, and of course the borders stipulated at that time, or perhaps some similar definitions. But there is absolutely no reason for believing that an inviolate biblical covenant is understood to be the basis of such a territorial hope. So the inhabitation of Israel in the land today would simply be at the mercy of worldly pragmatism, the tempestuous forum of the nations, a most ungodly assembly if ever there was one, and not the Word of God. But further, Burge seems to

[28] Ibid., 188.

suggest, this agenda ought also to be swayed by the counsel of the mainline Christian churches, hardly a proven ally of the Jews in centuries past!

Surprisingly, on the one hand Burge condescendingly admits, "By comparison with other states in the Middle East, . . . Israel is an exemplar of moderation, civility, and freedom." He admits that in comparison with a specific instance of savage Syrian brutality that drew little dissent, "Israel has not participated in this sort of wholesale massacre."[29] Nevertheless, there then follows an extensive litany of accusations against Israel concerning apartheid, discrimination, land and water seizure, village and home destruction, abuse of human rights, and religious compromise. Doubtless some of these charges may be justified, and some may find new light shed on them through explanation by the Israelis. However, there is not the slightest mention here of complicity in the Palestinian cause by the Arab states, so stridently anti-Judaic, nor the vehement Palestinian opposition to Israel's very existence, and even the concerted supercessionism of the mainstream Palestinian Christians. I agree with Burge when he writes:

> I am convinced that if the prophets of the Old Testament were to visit Tel Aviv or Jerusalem today, their words would be harsh and unremitting. Strangely enough, just as in the Bible, their authority would likely go unrecognized, and like Jeremiah, they would be imprisoned by the Israeli Defense Forces as a security risk.[30]

Yes, Christian missionary agencies that focus on the Hebrew people are also well aware of frequent, aggressive opposition by the Jews, even as Paul experienced. However, they also continue to wondrously see the hand of God hovering over this disobedient people and thus agree with the apostle that, notwithstanding centuries of rebellion and related suffering, they remain "loved because of their forefathers" (Rom 11:28). God's present covenantal interest is rooted in the original promise given to Abraham that included the land (Gen 12:1–3,7; 13:14–17; 15:18–21). But in light of Israel's incessant unbelief how could this forbearance of God be possible? The answer is simply in terms of the glorious truth of sovereign covenant grace that Burge, as well as Chapman and Sizer, would doubtless claim for themselves after the manner of Eph 2:8–9, and yet deny for Israel since, as Burge erroneously proposes, "Possession of the land is tied to obedience to the covenant."[31] In other words, Israel lost its inheritance because of

---

[29] Ibid., 132.
[30] Ibid., 136.
[31] Ibid., 163.

disobedience while Christians gain this inheritance, spiritually speaking, strictly by grace through faith alone in Jesus Christ.

This conditional perspective, common among Christian supercessionists, calls for possession of the land based on obedience and dispossession based on disobedience, obviously recalling the Mosaic promise of either blessing or cursing for Israel based on obedience or disobedience to the law (Deut 11:26–28). So Burge references a number of OT passages that certainly detail the promise of severe discipline for Israel, in relation to the land, on account of various forms of ungodliness. He strongly suggests that for these repeated transgressions, Israel has been disinherited from its blessings while the Christian church has inherited these same essential blessings by way of supercession or transference. The only problem here is that so many other passages in the OT promise God's ultimate triumph, through grace, over Israel's sins, even as is the case in the saving of *any* sinner. So Burge either ignores or minimizes or relegates to past fulfillment these Bible passages. Consider the following Scriptural references that are said to condemn the nation of Israel's present ungodliness, causing it permanently to have become *person non grata* in God's sight:

> Deut 4:25–27—yet reference to vv. 28–31 is omitted.[32]
> Deut 8:17–19—[33]yet reference to 30:1–14 (esp. v. 6) is omitted.[34]
> Isa 1:16–17; 5:1–7—yet references to 2:2–4; 11:1–16; 27:2–13; 35:1–10; 41:8–16; 43:1–7; 49:14–26; 62:1–5 are omitted.[35]
> Jer 3:19–20; 7:5–7—yet references to 30:1–31:40; 33:1–26; Ezekiel 36–37, are omitted.[36]
> Hos 9:2–3—yet references to 3:4–5; 11:8–11; 14:1–17 are omitted.[37]
> Amos 4:1–2—yet reference to 9:11–15 is omitted.[38]
> Micah 2:1–3—yet references to 4:1–8; 7:7–20 are omitted.[39]

The reader is strongly encouraged to read the additional references included here that Burge does not draw attention to in the main. Time after time they indicate the triumph of sovereign grace over the sins of Israel, even as Paul describes with regard to the Christian in Rom 5:20. Yes, the sins of Israel bring severe punishment, but *not* covenantal abandonment. Of

[32] Ibid., 74.
[33] Ibid., 99–100.
[34] Ibid.
[35] Ibid., 101–2.
[36] Ibid., 101.
[37] Ibid., 100.
[38] Ibid.
[39] Ibid., 99–100.

course Burge is all too aware of these references, some of which he merely footnotes.[40] However, unlike the prophets who often portray these passages so climactically and triumphantly, he treats them as almost bothersome and outmoded. Notwithstanding the eschatological glory that stands out here, Burge's opinion is that "of course, these predictions did come true."[41] In other words, it is the period of the post-exilic return of Israel to the first coming of Christ that swallows up and nullifies the eschatological glory which appears to be so plain here (see Ezek 36–37; Zech 14).

To sum up then, and with reference to Ezek 47:22–23 where the eschatological temple is concerned, Burge rightly references the necessity here for Israel to provide an inheritance for an alien remnant.[42] However, it is clearly and contextually the responsibility of that same alien remnant to acknowledge that the land of Israel does covenantally belong to Israel. If today the Palestinians were to acknowledge this and the Israelis were to hear it and be convinced that it is true, there is every possibility that, upon sitting down in conference, a peaceable resolution to present problems might emerge. Yet even if the Palestinians were genuinely so inclined, is it conceivable that the surrounding Arab/Moslem states would readily invest their cooperation?

O. Palmer Robertson

O. Palmer Robertson is Principal of African Bible College, Uganda, Professor of Theology at African Bible College, Malawi, and Visiting Professor at Knox Theological Seminary, Florida. His significant volume, *The Christ of the Covenants*, is a contemporary presentation of Reformed covenant theology from a conservative perspective. More recently (2000) he authored *The Israel of God: Yesterday, Today, and Tomorrow*, which also provides a contemporary Reformed perspective that is essentially updated Augustinianism. While Robertson's tone is to some degree more moderate than that of Pieters and Boettner, nevertheless his overall regard for national Israel could hardly be called friendly, that is in a Pauline manner. Even the tokenism offered is sparse indeed when compared with his more frequent harsh regard for the Jews and the modern State of Israel. For instance, he states, "Clearly the plight of the Jews after the horrors of the Holocaust must be fully appreciated. Yet the tragic circumstances of the residents of the land displaced during the

[40] Ibid., 103, n.12.
[41] Ibid., 104.
[42] Ibid.

twentieth century must also be appreciated."[43] Then is attached a near half page footnote that focuses on an instance of alleged Jewish brutality toward Palestinians in 1948 according to Naim Ateek in his *A Palestinian Theology of Liberation*.[44] But there is no mention of the savage assault by the surrounding Arab states on Israel the day following the establishment of the State of Israel according to the United Nations charter, also in 1948. The tilt of sympathy, here and elsewhere, cannot be avoided. Further antipathy by this author toward the modern Jewish state and sympathy for the Palestinians are found in a series of depreciative references to Golda Meir, Theodor Herzl, David Ben-Gurion, and Joseph Weitz, all drawn from Colin Chapman's anti-Judaic *Whose Promised Land?*[45]

The title that Robertson employs, *The Israel of God: Yesterday, Today, and Tomorrow,* is followed by chapter titles that are all prefaced with "The Israel of God." Hence, like an edifice built on an inverted pyramid, the author indicates that his case is based on one major text, namely Galatians 6:16, for this is the only reference where the expression "Israel of God" is found in the NT. Therefore, Robertson's substantial study of this verse occupies considerably more space than most other Scripture passages referenced in his book[46] since it is made to be the essential proof of Robertson's case—that the Christian Church, that is, the NT people of God, are described here as the spiritual "Israel of God." But if his interpretation is shown to be in error, as I believe it is, then so much of his book is seriously brought into question. Nevertheless, in spite of the contrary opinions of F. F. Bruce, G. C. Berkouwer, Hans Dieter Betz, James Dunn, Ernest De Witt Burton, A. T. Hanson, and others, he bravely states,

> The only explanation of Paul's phrase "the Israel of God" that satisfies the context as well as the grammar of the passage [is that it describes] . . . the new community within humanity brought into existence by the cross of Christ in its uniting of Jews and Gentiles into one new people of God."[47]

In response, simply let the reader consider more detailed evidence of the tenuousness of Robertson's opinion as explained in chapter 10 of this book.

On the one hand, the author asserts that the Christian Church is the new spiritual Israel whereby former national and territorial identity, ac-

---

[43] O. P. Robertson, *The Israel of God* (Phillipsburg, New Jersey: P&R, 2000), 27–28.
[44] Ibid., 28.
[45] Ibid., 47–48. For further consideration of Chapman in this regard, refer to chapter 4.
[46] Ibid., 39–45.
[47] Ibid., 43.

cording to covenantal determination, has been eliminated. But on the other hand, he disclaims belief in "replacement theology" when defined as bare substitution with little connectedness.

> [Jesus] is not, as some suppose, replacing Israel with the church. But he is reconstituting Israel in a way that makes it suitable for the new covenant. From this point on, it is not that the church takes the place of Israel, but that a renewed Israel of God is being formed by the shaping of the church. This kingdom will reach beyond the limits of the Israel of the old covenant.[48]

How shall this come about? Concerning national Israel, it occurs as a result of Israel's rejection of the Messiah.

> The solemn consequences of this rejection find expression in the words of Jesus: "The kingdom shall be taken away from you and given to a people bearing the fruit of it" (Matt. 21:43). Israel as a nation would no more be able to claim that they possessed the kingdom of God in a way that was distinct from other nations. Yet the people of the new covenant would still be designated as Israel, "the Israel of God." This new covenant people would be formed around the core of twelve Israelites who were chosen to constitute the ongoing Israel of God.[49]

How discouraging this is for the inquiring Jew! The Christian Church takes the name of Israel and leaves everything else behind as worthless Jewish fables and shadows. This is not reconstitution; it is the prodigal son attempting to disinherit the elder brother and claim his title. To suggest that old Israel, having Jewish individuality, nationality, and territory is "reconstituted" so that the original distinctive Jewishness is reformed but not replaced, is to play with words while at the same time retaining an eliminationist agenda. It is to subtly deal with the "Jewish problem," even as Napoleon suggested, through "the abolition of Jewry by dissolving it into Christianity" (see chapter 2 of this book). The reality is that such absorption into a homogenous body in fact results in the elimination of distinctive Jewish individuality, nationality, and territory. That this is so is proved by Robertson's dismissive attitude when he gets down to the reality concerning the Jew, the nation, and the land of Israel today. For instance, he states,

---

[48] Ibid., 118.

[49] Ibid., 121. Here is yet another instance of the misuse of Matt 21:43 that ignores Christ's subsequent lament turning to hope (Matt 23:37–39).

Only two references to "Jews" and three references to "Israel" are found
in the book of Revelation. Though few in number, these references shed
some light on the role of Israel in the coming of the kingdom. . . . This
absence of a distinctive role for Israel in the coming of the consummate
kingdom of Messiah characterizes the whole book of Revelation. Nowhere
in this book are the Jewish people described as having a distinctive part in
this kingdom. . . . The land of the Bible . . . is not to be regarded as having
continuing significance in the realm of redemption other than its function as a teaching model. . . . The future manifestations of the messianic
kingdom of Christ cannot include a distinctively Jewish aspect that would
distinguish the peoples and practices of Jewish believers from their Gentile
counterparts. . . . The future messianic kingdom will embrace equally
the whole of the newly created cosmos, and will not experience a special
manifestation of any sort in the region of the "promised land." . . . [A] day
should not be anticipated in which Christ's kingdom will manifest Jewish
distinctives either by its location in "the land," or by its constituency, or by
its distinctively Jewish practices.[50]

Robertson's repudiation of replacement theology is not believable, while a
simmering anti-Judaism is quite apparent. With due regard for the absur-
dity of the above comment concerning Revelation, how strange it is that
the new Jerusalem descending from heaven gives prominent recognition to
24 descendants of Abraham, "the 12 tribes of the sons of Israel" and "the
Lamb's 12 apostles" (Rev 21:2,12,14)!

Nevertheless, an area in which I would agree with Robertson concerns
his statement that "this new covenant people would be formed around the
core of twelve Israelites who were chosen to constitute the ongoing Israel
of God." However, I would also maintain that those twelve apostles, in
retaining their historic Jewishness, constituted "a [Jewish] remnant chosen by grace" (Rom 11:5) that passionately anticipated the restoration and
regeneration of national Israel. Peter, one of these apostles, declared to
the Jewish Sanhedrin and high priest concerning Jesus Christ that "God
exalted this man to His right hand as ruler and Savior, to grant repentance
to Israel, and forgiveness of sins" (Acts 5:31). Now the meaning of "Israel"
here does not need to be reinterpreted, as C. H. Spurgeon made plain.

Israel as a nation will yet acknowledge her blessed Prince and Savior.
During many centuries, the chosen people, who were of old so highly favored above all other nations on the face of the earth, have been scattered
and peeled, oppressed and persecuted, until sometimes it seemed as if they
must be utterly destroyed; yet they shall be restored to their own land,
which again shall be a land flowing with milk and honey. Then, when their

[50] Ibid., 153, 165, 194, 195.

hearts are turned to Messiah the Prince, and they look upon him whom they have pierced, and mourn over their sin in so long rejecting him, the fullness of the Gentiles shall also come, and Jew and Gentile alike shall rejoice in Christ their Savior. In taking such a text as this, I think it is right always to give first the actual meaning of the passage before using it in any other way.[51]

How then does Robertson understand national Israel's permanent disqualification from the land? He refers to Christ's words, "the kingdom of God will be taken away from you and given to a nation producing its fruit" (Matt 21:43), even though there is no mention here of permanent divine abandonment, as is subsequently proved (Matt 23:37–39). However, Robertson frequently identifies the land with the temporary, conditional old Mosaic covenant and consequently with their mutual abrogation at the advent of the new covenant. Thus he writes,

> The possession of the land under the old covenant was not an end in itself, but fit instead among the shadows, types, and prophecies that were characteristic of the old covenant in its presentation of redemptive truth. Just as the tabernacle was never intended to be a settled item in the plan of redemption but was to point to Christ's tabernacling among his people (cf. John 1:14), and just as the sacrificial system could never atone for sins but could only foreshadow the offering of the Son of God (Heb. 9:23–26), so in a similar manner Abraham received the promise of the land but never experienced the blessing of its full possession. In this way, the patriarch learned to look forward to "the city with foundations, whose architect and builder is God" (Heb. 11:10).[52]

Another fundamental error of this author is evidenced here: his incorporation of the land promise into the conditional, temporal Mosaic covenant. There is great confusion here.[53] Certainly the whole tabernacle order was merely a temporal shadow of the substance yet to be embodied in Christ. However, the promise of the land was according to the unconditional, everlasting terms of the Abrahamic covenant (Gen 15:1–21) that were revealed 430 years before the giving of the law, and thus cannot be annulled. (Gal 3:17). The land of Israel was not a mere shadow. When Abraham first entered Canaan from Haran, the land was thoroughly pagan. For this reason,

[51] C. H. Spurgeon, "The Royal Savior," Acts 5:31, *Metropolitan Tabernacle Pulpit*, 56:3229, 790–791, Ages Software.

[52] Robertson, *Israel of God*, 13.

[53] Robertson makes the same mistake when he writes that circumcision was also "an old covenant institution," and incorrectly invokes Gal 5:2, which was in fact addressed to Gentile Christians concerning Judaizers, to suggest that what was in reality an Abrahamic covenant rite is now invalid, even for the Jewish Christian. Ibid., 31.

his hope was in the cleansing and regeneration of the land that would eventually result when the holiness of heaven would descend on it, including Messiah, subsequent to its possession by the 12 tribes of Israel. For further evidence of the abiding nature of the land, see chapter 9 of this book.

In a concluding summary of Robertson's theology of Israel, 12 propositions are set forth that attempt to repudiate, with considerable emphasis, the common premillennial belief in a distinctive, eschatological future for ethnic and national Israel.[54] It will be noted that the wording of these propositions needs careful consideration since often there is a lack of clarification, a subtle turn of expression, as well as the avoidance of some pertinent issues. I select the most significant of these for more detailed analysis.

> Proposition #2: "The modern Jewish state is not a part of the messianic kingdom of Jesus Christ. Even though it may be affirmed that this particular civil government came into being under the sovereignty of the God of the Bible, it would be a denial of Jesus' affirmation that his kingdom is 'not of this world order' (John 18:36) to assert that this government is a part of his messianic kingdom."

To be honest, this writer knows of few premillennialists who would declare that the modern state of Israel is presently part of the messianic kingdom of Jesus Christ other than in a potential sense. Though they would certainly believe that such a blessed economy will emerge at the second coming of the Son of God. However, there are two related questions that must be faced here. First, is the land of Palestine today still a valid part of God's promise to the national seed of Abraham, Isaac, and Jacob, irrespective of present unbelief or whether a number of Jews, large or small, inhabits it? One fundamental reason that this covenant promise abides is Paul's declaration, significantly in the present tense, that "the promises" still belong to the Israelites (Rom 9:4). To suggest that this expression excludes the land would be quite unthinkable according to the apostle's use of accepted Hebrew parlance. Second, does God have any present covenantal regard for unbelieving, carnal, national, ethnic Israel? While a more complete positive answer is given in chapter 11 of this book, it is plain in Rom 11:28 that God continues to have a covenantal interest in unbelieving Israel. Robertson attempts to identify those "loved because of their forefathers" as elect Jews, not unbelieving Israel in a national sense.[55] The overwhelming opinion of

---

[54] Ibid., 193–96.
[55] Ibid., 189–90.

most commentators, however, is that, as Barrett concluded, "They [Israel] are the *race* [emphasis added] whom God elected to be his peculiar people, and their election rests in no way on their merits or achievements."[56] Thus, the positive answer to both of the questions raised leads to the conclusion that while there cannot be absolute certainty with regard to eschatological fulfillment in the present, the contemporary state of Israel, and especially its possession of Jerusalem, suggests a high degree of probability that eschatological fulfillment is in process before our very eyes.

Moreover, although Robertson concedes, as a Calvinist, that God's sovereignty was at work in the establishment of the state of Israel, this is obviously an inclusive understanding with regard to His general dominion over all creation; hence this would nevertheless exclude any divine, particular, sovereign, covenantal, national interest. Furthermore, he sees no distinctive divine involvement in the seeming secular process by which the European Zionist movement, along with the encouragement of Great Britain, resulted in the rebirth of the state of Israel since such involvement would violate the principle of John 18:36. Nevertheless, David Larsen's *Jews, Gentiles, and the Church* documents the historic development of Zionism that was substantially secular but was nevertheless often directed and permeated by Christian sympathy, investment, and biblical presuppositions. Consider that

> while doubtless there were complex motives of self-interest on the part of Great Britain, [Chaim] Weizmann stoutly maintained in his memoirs that the sincere Christian beliefs of Balfour, Lloyd-George, and Jan Christian Smuts were more responsible than anything else for the new opening for the Jews in Palestine.[57]

Concerning the broad principle of John 18:36, where Jesus declared, "My kingdom does not have its origin here," certainly no premillennialist would assert that the present-day nation of Israel is in fact a manifestation of the kingdom of God.[58] Having said this, it ought not to be implied then that, because of the present secularity and unbelief of Israel, therefore God

---

[56] C. K. Barrett, *Romans* (London: A & C Black, 1991), 225. Likewise, Cranfield, Hodge, Moo, Morris, Murray, Shedd, Schreiner.

[57] D. L. Larsen, *Jews, Gentiles and the Church* (Grand Rapids: Discovery House, 1995), 182; 131–221. Also see the catalog of providential circumstances mentioned in chapter 5 of this book.

[58] In John 18:36 where Jesus addresses Pontius Pilate, He is contrasting the holiness of His potential kingdom administration with the pervasive unholiness of the world order in which the Roman legate rules. There is no thought here of the non-material spirituality of Jesus' kingdom.

has no vested, particular, covenantal, loving interest in His people, as if a father had given up on his prodigal son. Quite the contrary, in the biblical parable surely the father lovingly followed the course of his son even when he was defiling himself in the far country. In this present age there is abundant evidence of God's dealing with godless mankind according to His prevenient grace whereby He woos and draws with cords of love the particular objects of His elective grace (John 6:44–45; 2 Thess 2:13; 1 Pet 1:1–2). They may appear as thoroughly secular and vehement despisers of Christ, nevertheless the divine pursuit of such renegades is unrelenting until such a time as sovereign grace claims them, as with Jacob (Gen 28:10–22; 32:24–32) and Paul (Acts 7:54–8:3; 9:1–9; Gal 1:15–16). Any Gentile similarly wooed by that same grace will appreciate this point. If so, is it not equally evident that God has also graciously pursued the nation of Israel through the centuries in its unbelief? Then how is it possible to so strenuously deny that God is now, in this twenty-first century, distinctively, covenantally dealing with the nation of Israel, especially since 1948? Indeed it is Romans 11 that so plainly describes this wooing through the centuries, even with the employed strategy of His temporary withdrawal.

> Proposition #3: "It cannot be established from Scripture that the birth of the modern state of Israel is a prophetic precursor to the mass conversion of Jewish people."

Doubtless in absolute terms this is correct even as it cannot be certainly proved that Robertson's denial of such an apocalyptic return and conversion of the Diaspora is correct. With the Word of God concerning eschatological events, at best we are dealing with cautious probability, so let each Christian be persuaded as he carefully studies Scripture. Theoretically, present-day Israel might be so assailed by the Arabs that it finds itself pushed into the Mediterranean Sea. This would in no way invalidate the premillennial hope, such as is portrayed in Ezekiel 36–37. But in such a situation, those of Robertson's convictions would readily confess God's work of judgment on Israel while denying His hand would ever bring consummate national blessing! Nevertheless, C. H. Spurgeon, J. C. Ryle, and Horatius Bonar did have such a premillennial hope concerning national Israel well before there was any aroused prospect in Europe of a possible Jewish state in Israel. In contrast, consider the rather imprudent prognostication of Philip Mauro who wrote that should Jerusalem "come into Jewish hands again" during the "times of the Gentiles," then "the prophecies would have been falsified and the entire New Testament discredited."[59] The pity is that he is not now able to provide an explanation of present circumstances, though the temper of his writings suggests that like some, he would simply deny any activity or national purpose of God whatsoever in the present state of Israel.

> *Proposition #4: "The land of the Bible served in a typological role as a model of the consummate realization of the purposes of God for his redeemed people that encompasses the whole of the cosmos. Because of the inherently limited scope of the land of the Bible, it is not to be regarded as having continuing significance in the realm of redemption other than its function as a teaching model."*

This matter is dealt with more fully in chapter 9 of this book. But consider C. H. Spurgeon's understanding of Ezek 37:1–10. By way of summary, the famous preacher is well aware that

> this vision has been used, from the time of Jerome onwards, as a description of the resurrection. . . . [However] there is no allusion made by Ezekiel to the resurrection, and such topic would have been quite apart from the design of the prophet's speech. I believe he was no more thinking of the resurrection of the dead than of the building of St. Peter's at Rome, or the emigration of the Pilgrim Fathers. That topic is altogether foreign to the subject in hand, and could not by any possibility have crept into the prophet's mind. He was talking about the people of Israel, and prophesying concerning them. . . . The meaning of our text, as opened up by the context, is most evidently, if words mean anything, first, that there shall be a political restoration of the Jews to their own land and to their own nationality; and then, secondly, there is in the text, and in the context, a most plain declaration, that there shall be a spiritual restoration, a conversion in fact, of the tribes of Israel.[60]

In contrast, consider Robertson's explanation of this same passage. His eschatological understanding of Ezekiel, quite apart from any immediate return of Israel after the Babylonian exile, is essentially a revamped interpretation that employs the resurrection motif while categorically excluding national Israel's resurrection to life through regeneration:

---

[59] P. Mauro, *The Gospel of the Kingdom, with an Examination of Modern Dispensationalism,* chap. 12, (http://www.gospeltruth.net/gospel_of_ the_kingdom/gotk_toc.htm); cited May 2007. In chap. 14, commenting on Zionism up to 1927, Mauro suggests that despite the Balfour Declaration, Zionism is a shabby movement in decline. But how times have changed, and will continue to change.

[60] C. H. Spurgeon, *The C. H. Spurgeon Collection, Metropolitan Tabernacle Pulpit,* X, no. 582, 1864 (Albany, Oregon: Ages Software, 1988), 533, 536.

This perspective [moving from shadow to reality] provides insight into the return to the land as described by Ezekiel and the other prophets. In the nature of things, these writers could only employ images with which they and their hearers were familiar. So they spoke of a return to the geographical land of Israel. Indeed there was a return to this land, though hardly on the scale prophesied by Ezekiel. But in the context of the realities of the new covenant, this land must be understood in terms of the newly created cosmos about which the apostle Paul speaks in Romans. The whole universe (which is "the land" from a new covenant perspective) groans in travail, waiting for the redemption that will come with the resurrection of the bodies of the redeemed (Rom. 8:22–23). The return to paradise in the framework of the new covenant does not involve merely a return to the shadowy forms of the old covenant. It means the rejuvenation of the entire earth. By this renewal of the entire creation, the old covenant's promise of land finds its new covenant realization.[61]

Romans 8:22–33 clearly presents a similar prophetic vision that anticipates the future glorious Messianic kingdom which will manifest Christ's reign from Jerusalem over Jew and Gentile. However, I would vigorously disagree with that mystical, indeed contorted incorporation of the land into the new cosmos in such a way that all territorial identity of Israel is lost. Thus we return to two basic problems here. First, there is a seeming unwillingness to accept that in the future blessed state there could possibly be a unity with diversity, that is, regenerate Jews and Gentiles in blissful subjection to the reign of Christ. Second, there is the basic fallacy that the land, as a mere shadow, is rooted in the old or temporal Mosaic covenant. Yet again we have been told that the land represents "a return to the shadowy forms of the old covenant." But I would strongly reassert that the land is rooted in the Abrahamic covenant (Gen 12:1,5–7; 13:14–15,17; 15:7–21) and as such is not limited by the temporal character of the Mosaic economy. God's fundamental dealing with Israel after redemption from Egypt continued to be based on the Abrahamic covenant that anticipated its inherent promise of the land (Exod 3:6–8,15–17; 6:1–9; 12:25; 13:5; 32:13–14; 33:1–3; Lev 20:24; 33:1–3; Num 13:27).

> Proposition #5: "Rather than understanding predictions about the 'return' of 'Israel' to the 'land' in terms of a geopolitical re-establishment of the state of Israel, these prophecies are more properly interpreted as finding consummate fulfillment at the 'restoration of all things' that will accompany the resurrection of believers at the return of Christ (Acts 3:21: Rom. 8:22–23)."

[61] Robertson, The Israel Of God, 26.

No premillennialist perceives the present "geopolitical re-establishment of the state of Israel" in a consummate sense. It is a precursor of that "restoration" (Acts 3:21) and "redemption" of the created order (Rom 8:22–23) in which saved national Israel will gloriously participate. However, this does not mean that we walk blindly through this world as if historic events have little significance. Surely not only the continued increasing material and military strength of national Israel, obtained in the face of seeming insuperable opposition, but particularly its possession of old Jerusalem after a hiatus of over 1,900 years, has troubled those of Reformed Augustinian convictions. There are published instances of their wrestling with these events since they tend to conflict with standard supercessionist explanations.

> *Proposition #7: "No worship practices that place Jewish believers in a category different from Gentile believers can be a legitimate worship-form among the redeemed people of God."*

Is this to suggest that the worship of the Gentile church at Antioch had an identical form when compared with that of the mother Jewish church at Jerusalem? If a church that is predominantly Jewish should desire to remember the Lord Jesus by means of a Seder, understood as being complementary to the Lord's Table, while a predominantly Gentile church ignores association of the Lord's Table with the Passover, who is to say that one order is more biblical than the other? If a church that is predominantly Jewish desires to initiate its children of Jewish parents and Jewish converts into Messianic Judaism by means of circumcision, where is the clear teaching in the NT that indicates that such a signification has been voided? How is it possible for the Council of Jerusalem's decision (Acts 15:1–35) to be construed as teaching the abolition of circumcision for the Jewish Christian? Paul later upheld the participation of Jewish Christians in distinctive Jewish practices (Acts 21:17–26).

> *Proposition #9: "The future manifestation of the messianic kingdom of Christ cannot include a distinctively Jewish aspect that would distinguish the peoples and practices of Jewish believers from their Gentile counterparts."*

This is a purely arbitrary statement that betrays a Gentile mindset. In effect Robertson is saying that the Gentile can worship in a purely Gentile manner, and the inference is that this will be the future messianic standard. But the Jew cannot incorporate distinctive Jewish aspects that are not appropriate for the Gentile. After all, this would be unfair for the Gentile. But how is it fair for the Jew to have to conform to Gentile worship?

An Open Letter to Evangelicals

Theological anti-Judaism, as distinguished from racial anti-Judaism, may be defined as the biblically derived conclusion that contemporary Judaism, especially its national and territorial representations, has no present or future covenantal legitimacy in the mind of God. Whatever present ethnic claims are made concerning Jewishness, such a perspective asserts the disenfranchisement of God's ancient people by means of the superseding new covenant of Heb 8:7–13. Many with Reformed convictions, upon hearing confessions of pro-Judaism, especially sympathy for the modern state of Israel and related eschatological matters, respond with disparaging epithets that at the same time are intended to commend a more enlightened, spiritual, and historic eschatology. At worst, such theological anti-Judaism extends to abusive and contemptuous regard for "carnal dispensationalism" and "worldly premillennialism." It is further protested that present day Judaism, in terms of its political alignment with Zionism, has unjustly oppressed and displaced the Palestinians who have been domiciled in the land "from time immemorial."[62] While theological anti-Judaism is based on biblical and religious convictions about the Jew, and racial anti-Judaism is based on antipathy toward social, cultural and ethnic characteristics inherent in the Jew, it cannot be denied that rabid interest in the former is capable of giving birth to the ethos of the latter. In this regard the legacy of God's servant, Martin Luther, is sufficient proof of this point.[63]

I readily allow that those committed to the preceding viewpoint demonstrate differing degrees of disapproval concerning national Israel, though the doctrinal underpinning of these expressions is essentially Augustinian. One more recent, definitive expression of the repudiation of distinctive covenantal Jewish identity in the sight of God has been published on the web site of Knox Theological Seminary. On the page headed "The Wittenberg Door," is featured *An Open Letter to Evangelicals and Other Interested Parties: The People of God, the Land of Israel, and the Impartiality of the Gospel.*[64]

---

[62] This expression is derived from the acclaimed, controversial study by J. Peters, *From Time Immemorial, The Origins of the Arab-Jewish Conflict Over Palestine* (Chicago: JKAP, 2002), 4.

[63] P. L. Rose, *German Question/Jewish Question: Revolutionary Antisemitism from Kant to Wagner* (Princeton, New Jersey: Princeton University Press, 1992).

[64] http://www.knoxseminary.org/Prospective/Faculty/WittenbergDoor/ (cited May 2007). Notable signatories to this "Open Letter" include Richard B. Gaffin, Michael S. Horton, Joseph

Here is a contemporary, anti-Judaic portrayal of the status, in fact non-status of Israel and the Jews today. Its denial of individual, national, and territorial Judaism in the sight of God calls for vigorous repudiation on account of explicit theological supercessionism. I conclude this chapter, therefore, with a critique of this "Open Letter" interspersed with quotations from the letter. One wonders if the symbolic panoply employed at this web site, concerning Martin Luther's historic forum of protest being the door of the Castle Church at Wittenberg in 1517, is also intended to represent alignment with the German reformer's eschatology, and especially the shameful anti-Judaism that so stained the conclusion of such an eventful and momentous life. No disassociation in this regard appears to be mentioned.

> *An Open Letter to Evangelicals and Other Interested Parties: The People of God, the Land of Israel, and the Impartiality of the Gospel*

> *Recently a number of leaders in the Protestant community of the United States have urged the endorsement of far-reaching and unilateral political commitments to the people and land of Israel in the Israeli-Palestinian conflict, citing Holy Scripture as the basis for those commitments. To strengthen their endorsement, several of these leaders have also insisted that they speak on behalf of the seventy million people who constitute the American evangelical community.*

Since the exact circumstances concerning the claim made by these Protestant leaders is not referenced, it is not possible or really necessary to make further comment. However it is asserted that indeed a large proportion of the American evangelical community would generally agree with the "endorsement," notwithstanding modern Israel's pervasive unbelief. By way of contrast, this "Open Letter" tends to oppose the people and land of Israel.

> *It is good and necessary for evangelical leaders to speak out on the great moral issues of our day in obedience to Christ's call for his disciples to be salt and light in the world (Matt. 5:13–16). It is quite another thing, however, when leaders call for commitments that are based upon a serious misreading of Holy Scripture. In such instances, it is good and necessary for other evangelical leaders to speak out as well. We do so here in the hope that we may contribute to the cause of*

A. Pipa, Jr., Robert L. Reymond, O. Palmer Robertson, R. C. Sproul, Cornelius P. Venema, and Bruce K. Waltke.

the Lord Christ, apart from whom there can never be true and lasting peace in the world (John 14:27).

Quite the contrary, I believe that the historic, Reformational eschatological repudiation of Israel is based on a Gentile, Augustinian, and Roman Catholic tradition more than clear exegesis, and as such wrongly filters Scripture through this doctrinal grid. In fact, it can hardly be said that the ethical fruit of this eschatology has contributed toward "true and lasting peace in the world." The record of history shamefully indicates quite the opposite result.

> *At the heart of the political commitments in question are two fatally flawed propositions. First, some are teaching that God's alleged favor toward Israel today is based upon ethnic descent rather than upon the grace of Christ alone, as proclaimed in the Gospel. Second, others are teaching that the Bible's promises concerning the land are fulfilled in a special political region or "Holy Land," perpetually set apart by God for one ethnic group alone. As a result of these false claims, large segments of the evangelical community, our fellow citizens, and our government are being misled with regard to the Bible's teachings regarding the people of God, the land of Israel, and the impartiality of the Gospel.*

While I heartily agree that God's saving favor is not based on ethnic descent any more than gender or learning, but rather grace through faith alone, I allege that as in the past, so in the future, God does have a distinctive, ongoing, covenantal regard for Israel after the flesh as beloved enemies (Rom 11:28). Reformational exegesis is particularly vulnerable with regard to the present relevance of this climactic verse (see chapter 11 of this book). If God can retain such grace for the nation of Israel, and Paul certainly did to the end of his ministry, then so ought the Gentile, engrafted wild olive branches.

However, the view espoused here in the "Open Letter" is far more representative of arrogant wild olive branches that are the subject of Paul's rebuke (Rom 11:17–20). Of course, as Ezekiel 36–37 plainly indicates, according to the sovereignty of God's covenant grace, national Israel after the flesh will become Israel after the Spirit. And indeed is not this the same essential experience of any Christian in terms of biblical conversion? Yes, as with the persuasion of Jonathan Edwards, Horatius Bonar, J. C. Ryle, and C. H. Spurgeon, I do believe that in grace God covenantally endowed the nation of Israel with the land in perpetuity so that ultimately it will be populated by those Hebrews who have authentically believed in Jesus as their Messiah. As with the aforementioned representatives, I do not believe that such a prospect in any way compromises the purity of the gospel. With both respect and loving regard for our fellow brothers and sisters in Christ, I believe that the Reformed eschatology of this "Open Letter" is misled with regard to the Bible's teaching, and that its ethical legacy in this matter concerning the Jews, according to Church history, is practical proof that this is so. Both Christians and unbelieving Jews will readily confirm this painfully sad truth.

> *In what follows, we make our convictions public. We do so acknowledging the genuine evangelical faith of many who will not agree with us. Knowing that we may incur their disfavor, we are nevertheless constrained by Scripture and by conscience to publish the following propositions for the cause of Christ and truth.*

It is good and commendable for conscience to be invoked here. Let every believer be guided by this principle, no matter what the cost. But conscience is very much enlivened by knowledge of the truth. So I urge that the history of the doctrine here espoused be studied in depth, especially its ethical outworking, since it is strenuously maintained that the record of Augustinian eschatology over the centuries with regard to Israel is shameful and unworthy of further loyalty. Even the Roman Catholic Church has more recently responded with some expressions of repentance. Nevertheless, historic tradition, however tainted, dies hard, although a return to the priority of fresh exegesis can emancipate. At the Reformation, this principle was certainly proved soteriologically, and to a lesser degree ecclesiologically, but not eschatologically.

> 1. *The Gospel offers eternal life in heaven to Jews and Gentiles alike as a free gift in Jesus Christ (Rom. 6:23). Eternal life in heaven is not earned or deserved, nor is it based upon ethnic descent or natural birth (Luke 3:8; Eph. 2:8–9).*

To this declaration I give happy yet qualified assent. Eternal life is solely according to God's free grace, that comes to earth from heaven for all who truly believe. Of course, there is eternal life for the inhabitants of heaven, though it will also come to this earth in a consummate eschatological sense, as even Hoekema, Strimple, Venema, and Waldron maintain (see chapter 8).

> *2. All human beings, Jews and Gentiles alike, are sinners (Rom. 3:22–23), and, as such, they are under God's judgment of death (Rom. 6:23). Because God's standard is perfect obedience and all are sinners, it is impossible for anyone to gain temporal peace or eternal life by his own efforts. Moreover, apart from Christ, there is no special divine favor upon any member of any ethnic group; nor, apart from Christ, is there any divine promise of an earthly land or a heavenly inheritance to anyone, whether Jew or Gentile (Rom. 3:9–10). To teach or imply otherwise is nothing less than to compromise the Gospel itself.*

Yes, to the Jews Jesus declared that "if you do not believe that I am He [the divine Son of God], you will die in your sins" (John 8:24). Yes, savingly "apart from Christ, there is no special divine favor on any member of any ethnic group." However, this in no way invalidates God's present regard for Israel after the flesh that will ultimately result in Israel after the Spirit (Rom 11:12,15,24–28). Paul maintained an evangelistic thrust "first to the Jew, and also to the Greek" (Rom 1:16), while also warning of "affliction and distress for every human being who does evil, first to the Jew, and also to the Greek" (Rom 2:9). Here is the incorporation of both priority for the Jew and at the same time impartiality for Jew and Gentile. Similarly with regard to the covenantally promised land, its consummate eschatological realization with regenerate Israel as its holy inhabitant, it will be grounded on the redemption that the holy Seed (Jesus Christ) of Abraham has accomplished. In this regard, this Messianic Savior will reign from Jerusalem over Israel in the land and the surrounding nations (Ezek 37:21–28; Zech 14:4,9–11). Again, in no way is this to suggest that this working of God's saving grace is compromised.

> *3. God, the Creator of all mankind, is merciful and takes no pleasure in punishing sinners (Ezek. 18:23,32). Yet God is also holy and just and must punish sin (Exod. 34:7). Therefore, to satisfy both his justice and his mercy, God has appointed one way of salvation for all, whether Jew or Gentile, in Jesus Christ alone (Acts 4:12; John 14:6).*

Without qualification, I join in upholding the glory of God's one gospel that saves both Jew and Gentile according to His elective grace through faith alone. However, just as the saved man and woman retain their gender identity following conversion, so the Jew and Gentile retain their ethnic identity. Absolute homogeneity is not a logical necessity, as distinctive giftedness in the church indicates. The oneness of God incorporates distinctive economic triunity. Even heaven is populated by the redeemed as well as holy angels having various ranks.

> 4. *Jesus Christ, who is fully God and fully man (John 1:1,14), came into the world to save sinners (1 Tim. 1:15). In his death upon the cross, Jesus was the Lamb of God taking away the sin of the world, of Jew and of Gentile alike. The death of Jesus forever fulfilled and eternally ended the sacrifices of the Jewish temple (Heb. 9:11–12; 10:11–12). All who would worship God, whether Jew or Gentile, must now come to him in spirit and truth through Jesus Christ alone. The worship of God is no longer identified with any specific earthly sanctuary. He receives worship only through Jesus Christ, the eternal and heavenly Temple (John 4:21,23; 2:19–21).*

The terms of the gospel are well stated here, and with them I am in full agreement. Further, this new covenant established through Jesus Christ's atoning death, in abrogating the Mosaic and Aaronic aspects of worship, specifically the sacrifices such as by the blood of bulls and goats, has primarily been made with Israel, into which stock the Gentiles are engrafted (Jer. 31:27–34; Rom 11:17). While "the worship of God is no longer identified with any specific earthly sanctuary" (see John 4:21–24) in the present, this in no way negates the eschatological prospect of Jesus Christ being personally worshipped from Jerusalem, even in association with the temple portrayed in Ezekiel 40–48. Since he is personally and gloriously present in that future kingdom, there is a sense in which such worship will have a local focus, while at the same time being universally spiritual. At that time, worship will not be confined to the heavenly realm; rather true spiritual worship will have come to earth.

> 5. *To as many as receive and rest upon Christ alone through faith alone, to Jews and Gentiles alike, God gives eternal life in his heavenly inheritance (Rom. 1:16; John 1:12–13).*

Again I give ready assent to this gospel declaration. Of course, both Jews and Gentiles retain their divinely appointed ethnic distinction even as they individually receive differing spiritual gifts, which diversity is incorporated within the unity of the one people of God. However, their "heavenly inheritance" is not some amorphous, ethereal existence, but rather the visitation of "the Holy City, [the] new Jerusalem coming down out of heaven [to earth] from God" (Rev 5:10; 21:2) in which Jews and Gentiles are destined to participate.

> 6. *The inheritance promises that God gave to Abraham were made effective through Christ, Abraham's True Seed (Gal. 3:16). These promises were not and cannot be made effective through sinful man's keeping of God's law (Rom. 4:13). Rather, the promise of an inheritance is made to those only who have faith in Jesus, the True Heir of Abraham. All spiritual benefits are derived from Jesus, and apart from him there is no participation in the promises (Gal. 3:7,26–29). Since Jesus Christ is the Mediator of the Abrahamic Covenant, all who bless him and his people will be blessed of God, and all who curse him and his people will be cursed of God (Gen. 12:3; Gal. 3:7–8). These promises do not apply to any particular ethnic group (Gal. 3:22; Matt. 21:43), but to the church of Jesus Christ, the true Israel (Rom. 2:28–29; Phil. 3:3). The people of God, whether the church of Israel in the wilderness in the Old Testament (Acts 7:38) or the Israel of God among the Gentile Galatians in the New Testament (Gal. 6:16), are one body who through Jesus will receive the promise of the heavenly city, the everlasting Zion (Heb. 13:14; Phil. 3:20; II Pet. 3:13; Rev. 21:9–14; Heb. 11:39–40). This heavenly inheritance has been the expectation of the people of God in all ages (Heb. 11:13–16; 12:22–24).*

Here we part company in a number of areas, but particularly with some ingenious exposition that seems more doctrinally than textually driven. To begin with consider: "Since Jesus Christ is the Mediator of the Abrahamic covenant, all who bless him and his people will be blessed of God, and all who curse him and his people will be cursed of God. These promises do not apply to any particular ethnic group, but to the church of Jesus Christ, the true Israel." While Jesus Christ is never declared to be the mediator of the Abrahamic covenant, let us grant the nuance of the assumption here. Nevertheless, the promise of Gen 12:3 is not made to Christ as the mediator but to Abraham, as this Scripture overwhelmingly affirms. Further, the seed of Abraham has application to Christ according to Gal 3:16, but this in no way invalidates the "seed" of Gen 12:1–3 being the nation of Israel anymore than does "seed" in Gen 13:15; 17:7. The exegetical reason is that God says to Abraham, your "descendants [seed]" shall be as the innumerable stars of heaven (Gen 15:5). These references are to the nation of Israel, not exclusively to Christ as an individual. Paul's employment of midrash (a distinctive Jewish, applicatory interpretation) incorporates Christ as the root of promised blessing without at all denying the obvious promise of national blessing, the plurality of "Abraham's seed, heirs according to the promise" (Gal 3:29).[65] Plainly the terms of the curse/blessing in Gen 12:2–3 principally refer to the national seed here, notwithstanding the attempted textual manipulation which betrays a difficulty that the obvious sense presents. To be sure, Christ is the ground of covenant blessing, but this does not nullify national blessing as is plainly indicated. Further evidence of this fallacious methodology is the desperate attempt here, according to standard Augustinian and Catholic practice, to conclude that "the church of Jesus Christ, [is] the true Israel," because Jesus said that "the kingdom of God will be taken away from you and given to a nation producing its fruit" (Matt 21:43). But here it is "the chief priests and the elders of the people" (Matt 21:23) who were addressed, though not with any indication that permanent disenfranchisement was intended in a national sense, as Matt 23:37–39 and Romans 11 make abundantly clear. Indeed, the twelve pillars of this new "nation producing its fruit" were all Jews, even as the new first church of Jerusalem was Jewish (see chapter 10 of this book).

> 7. *Jesus taught that his resurrection was the raising of the True Temple of Israel (John 2:19–21). He has replaced the priesthood, sacrifices, and sanctuary of Israel by fulfilling them in his own glorious priestly ministry and by offering, once and for all, his sacrifice for the world, that is, for both Jew and Gentile (Heb. 8:1–6; cf. 4:15–5:10; 6:13–10:18). Believers from all nations are now being built up through him into this Third Temple (Eph. 2:19–22; I Pet. 2:4–6), the church that Jesus promised to build (Matt. 16:18; Heb. 3:5–6).*

That the priesthood of Jesus has gloriously superseded the Aaronic priesthood incorporated within the Mosaic covenant is unquestionably true. However, this in no way has eliminated the essential character of distinctive Jewishness since, as Jer 31:27–34 indicates, the "new covenant," while abrogating the old covenant that was added following Israel's redemption out of Egypt, is made with "the house of Israel and the house of Judah," not the church. Further, Jesus as the superseding, incarnate spiritual "Temple" in no way negates the spiritual materiality of the eschatological temple from which Jesus Christ will reign (Isa 2:2–4; 56:6–7; Ezek 40–43; Mic 4:1–5; Zech 6:12–15), unless one understands this prospect in purely abstract, ethereal terms that a number of more recent amillennialists have

---

[65] D. H. Stern, *Jewish New Testament Commentary* (Clarksville, Maryland: Jewish New Testament Publications, 1999), 549. Difficult as this passage is, few commentators take such a narrow line here whereby unconditional blessing to Israel as a nation is eliminated from the original promise given to Abraham.

rejected. Thus Ezekiel was told concerning a future temple into which "the glory of the LORD entered, . . . 'Son of man, this [temple] is the place of My throne and the place for the soles of My feet, where I will dwell among the Israelites forever'" (Ezek 43:4,7). I believe this future temple, situated in Jerusalem, will accommodate the enthroned temple Jesus.[66]

> 8. *Simon Peter spoke of the Second Coming of the Lord Jesus in conjunction with the final judgment and the punishment of sinners (II Pet. 3:10–13). Instructively, this same Simon Peter, the Apostle to the Circumcision (Gal. 2:7), says nothing about the restoration of the kingdom to Israel in the land of Palestine (cf. Acts 1:6–7). Instead, as his readers contemplate the promise of Jesus' Second Coming, he fixes their hope upon the new heavens and the new earth, in which righteousness dwells (II Pet. 3:13).*

Undoubtedly it is right to presume that Peter was at the forefront of the question raised by the eleven disciples, "Lord, at this time are You restoring the kingdom to Israel?" (Acts 1:6). The restoration of Israel as declared by the prophets, which concept here surely incorporates the land, is a given that Jesus does not contradict; His concern is chiefly a matter of timing. As to Peter's understanding of 2 Pet 3:13, which is a quotation of Isa 65:17; 66:22, I believe the language here parallels "the restoration of all things, which God spoke about by the mouth of His holy prophets from the beginning" (Acts 3:21). When this kingdom of Messiah is consummated, then "all your people [Israel] will be righteous; they will possess the land forever" (Isa 60:21). Not for a moment would the mother church in Jerusalem have understood this promise in some esoteric sense.

> 9. *The entitlement of any one ethnic or religious group to territory in the Middle East called the "Holy Land" cannot be supported by Scripture. In fact, the land promises specific to Israel in the Old Testament were fulfilled under Joshua (Josh. 21:43–45). The New Testament speaks clearly and prophetically about the destruction of the second temple in A.D. 70 (Matt. 24:1–2; cf. Mark 13:1–2; Luke 21:20–24). No New Testament writer foresees a regathering of ethnic Israel in the land, as did the prophets of the Old Testament after the destruction of the first temple in 586 B.C. (Luke 21:24). Moreover, the*

---

[66] This raises the question of the interpretation of Ezekiel 40–48. While not denying difficulties here which *any* interpreter of this passage faces, detailed exegesis does not suit those who merely abstract general principles from the text.

land promises of the Old Covenant are consistently and deliberately expanded in the New Testament to show the universal dominion of Jesus (Exod. 20:12; Eph. 6:2–3; Gen. 12:1, cf. Rom. 4:13; Ps. 37:11; Matt. 5:5; Ps. 2:7–8), who reigns from heaven upon the throne of David, inviting all the nations through the Gospel of Grace to partake of his universal and everlasting dominion (Acts 2:29–32).

While presumably the signatories would believe in Israel's past entitlement to the holy land according to the terms of the Abrahamic covenant as indicated in the OT, we assume they are here referring to the modern day territorial possession of the State of Israel. However, I do not believe that the preceding promise in Isa 60:21, among numerous other instances, has been abrogated, any more than the preceding glorious pledges of Isa 60:15–20. Joshua 21:43–45 does not in any way speak of temporal possession. However, if, as seems to be claimed here, possession of the land relates to the time of Joshua, then why do we find so many of the prophets describing a future possession of the land in most concrete terms? Typical Gentile, exclusionary, either/or exegesis of Exod 20:12 and Eph 6:2–3 wrongly assumes that Paul's applicatory, more general reference to the Fifth Commandment nullifies the specific land reference (Exod 20:12; Deut 5:16). I have dealt elsewhere with the Hebrew Christian's free use of the OT, such as in Hebrews, that in no way invalidates the literal meaning of the text. The same point applies to the quotation of Ps 37:11, where the literal promise concerning the land still stands, yet in Matt 5:5 this truth is quoted in a more applicatory sense (see chapter 7 of this book).[67] It is incorrect to suggest from Gen 12:1 and Rom 4:13 that "the land promises of the old covenant are consistently and deliberately expanded in the New Testament to show the universal dominion of Jesus." That Abraham would be "the heir of the world" was not the expansion but the fulfillment of that which was originally promised, namely that "all the peoples on earth will be blessed through you" (Gen 12:3). Yet again, this unity with the Lord Jesus reigning over all does not exclude the diversity of Israel and the nations being under His dominion, as the original promise plainly distinguishes. In the same vein, concerning Ps 2:7–8, the fact that the Father declares to the Lord Jesus that to Him will be given "the nations for your inheritance, and the ends of the earth for your possession," in no way invalidates the diversity that this future holy ecumenicity will incorporate.

---

[67] Refer to David Stern's enlightening exegesis here from a Hebrew Christian perspective, *Jewish New Testament Commentary*, 23–24.

10. Bad Christian theology regarding the "Holy Land" contributed to the tragic cruelty of the Crusades in the Middle Ages. Lamentably, bad Christian theology is today attributing to secular Israel a divine mandate to conquer and hold Palestine, with the consequence that the Palestinian people are marginalized and regarded as virtual "Canaanites" (Deut. 20:16–18; cf. Lev. 27:28–29). This doctrine is both contrary to the teaching of the New Testament and a violation of the Gospel mandate (Matt. 28:19). In addition, this theology puts those Christians who are urging the violent seizure and occupation of Palestinian land in moral jeopardy of their own bloodguiltiness. Are we as Christians not called to pray for and work for peace, warning both parties to this conflict that those who live by the sword will die by the sword? (Matt. 26:52). Only the Gospel of Jesus Christ can bring both temporal reconciliation and the hope of an eternal and heavenly inheritance to the Israeli and the Palestinian. Only through Jesus Christ can anyone know peace on earth.

When one considers what the Crusades in the Middle Ages were about, it becomes quite astonishing that such an argument as this is offered. To begin with, it was the "bad Christian theology" of establishment Gentile Christianity that moved the armies of Western Europe to attempt a military recovery from Islam of the land of Israel, more familiarly regarded as the Christian holy land. We can be sure that there was no intent here to enable the dispersed Jews to return to their land; such a concept was unthinkable. Moreover, how disgraceful was the resultant persecution of the Jews by crusader bands traveling through Europe en route to the holy land so as to recapture Christian holy sites. "The leader of the First Crusade, Godfrey Bouillon, who had sworn to avenge the blood of Christ on Israel and 'leave no single member of the Jewish race alive', burnt the synagogue of Jerusalem to the ground, with all the Jews inside."[68] Here was the outworking of supercessionist theology that is rightly to be associated more with essential Augustinian, Medieval, and Reformed eschatology. There is simply no connection between the fundamental idea of the Crusades and the subsequent belief, especially resurrected during the seventeenth century, concerning the Jews' present and future covenantal claims to the promised land involving ultimate inhabitation by regenerated national Israel under Christ. This latter mentioned hope is the consummation of the "gospel mandate," not its violation.

[68] R. S. Wistrich, *Antisemitism: The Longest Hatred* (New York: Pantheon, 1991), 23–24.

Contrary to what the "Open Letter" suggests, in 1948 the State of Israel was reestablished through international assignment, not "conquest." However, particularly objectionable at this juncture is the obvious further bias that excoriates Israel's treatment of the pitiful, down-trodden, deprived Palestinians, the "violent seizure and occupation of Palestinian land," as if it were, in OT terms, heartlessly attempting to eliminate the Canaanites. The bias here is unabashed, though nonetheless offensive. Here is abhorrent theological anti-Judaism that is void of sympathy for the Jews, who presently occupy less than one percent of the middle-eastern Arab world, which at the same time is so obviously un-Pauline. Further in this regard, Joan Peters wrote, "There have been as many Jewish refugees who fled or were expelled from the Arab countries as there are Arab refugees from Israel, and that the Jews left of necessity and in flight from danger. . . . The Jews who fled Arab countries left assets behind in the Arab world greater than those the Arabs left in Israel."[69] This "Open Letter" plainly reveals the accusatory attitude, born of an Augustinian heritage similarly associated with the aforementioned anti-Judaic Crusades, that at the same time is presently represented in Reformed supercessionism. Yes, beyond question, "Only through Jesus Christ can anyone know peace on earth." But when an eschatology is centered, according to historic confession, in this same Christ and yet is productive of centuries of scandalous behavior and demeaning attitudes toward the Jews, even as is here reflected in the "Open Letter," then there needs to be further "Reformation" among many who so fervently proclaim their indebtedness to Reformed eschatology.

> *The promised Messianic kingdom of Jesus Christ has been inaugurated. Its advent marks the focal point of human history. This kingdom of the Messiah is continuing to realize its fullness as believing Jews and Gentiles are added to the community of the redeemed in every generation. The same kingdom will be manifested in its final and eternal form with the return of Christ the King in all his glory.*

I do not disagree with the essential thrust of what is here stated, though Scripture is much more specific concerning these matters. However, it is debatable if the inauguration of Jesus Christ's Messianic kingdom should take primacy over its consummation (1 Cor 15:23–28). Both natural and wild olive branches are being engrafted into the natural, Abrahamic olive tree so as to become partakers of the promise made with "the forefathers"

---

[69] Peters, *From Time Immemorial*, 25.

(see Rom 11:5,17–18,28), except that until the conclusion of the times of
the Gentiles, Jewish Christians constitute a remnant. But such participation does not eliminate present and future individuality. Then will come
for ethnic Israel "their full number," that is "life from the dead" for Israel,
when "all Israel [as a nation] will be saved" (Rom 11:12,15,26) at the personal return of the Lord Jesus Christ with great glory. This is basic to the
climactic optimism of Romans 11, and not so difficult to comprehend, as
most Hebrew Christians will testify, except for the attempt to filter this
truth through the presupposition of a Gentilic or an Augustinian grid.

> *Of all the nations, the Jewish people played the primary role in the*
> *coming of the Messianic kingdom. New Testament Scripture declares*
> *that to them were given the oracles of God (Rom. 3:2), the adoption,*
> *the glory, the covenants, the giving of the law, the service of God, and*
> *the promises (Rom. 9:3–4). Theirs are the fathers, Abraham, Isaac,*
> *and Jacob, and from them, according to the flesh, came Christ (Rom.*
> *9:5). Salvation is, indeed, of the Jews (John 4:22). While affirming*
> *the Scriptural teaching that there is no salvation outside of Christ,*
> *Christians should acknowledge with heartfelt sorrow and grief the*
> *frequent oppression of the Jews in history, sometimes tragically done*
> *in the name of the cross.*

This token acknowledgment of the significant role of the Jews up to the
time of the first coming of Jesus Christ will not suffice. The reason is that
while at this juncture there is a perfunctory giving with one hand, there is
overall a more vigorous taking away with the other, namely, the denial in
perpetuity of Jewish individuality, nationality, and territory. The suggestion
here of widespread oppression of the Jews in general that included some
modest participation by Christianity is in fact both evasion and distortion
of a most unpalatable truth. Since the ascendancy of Gentile dominion
within Christianity, this sway has resulted in a major anti-Judaic thrust,
born of replacement theology, which has not yet abated (see chapter 2).
As a result, much of Christianity has endeavored to justify this Gentilic
reign by means of supercessionism, even as is further indicated here by a
subtle misuse of Scripture: "Of all the nations, the Jewish people played
the primary role in the coming of the Messianic kingdom. New Testament
Scripture declares that to them were given the oracles of God (Rom. 3:2),
the adoption, the glory, the covenants, the giving of the law, the service of
God, and the promises (Rom 9:3–4)." Now in Rom 3:2, it is true that the
oracles of God were given (aorist) to the Jews. But Rom 9:3–4 does not

translate according to the same aoristic sense. Rather, this passage clearly declares that Paul regarded his brethren in the flesh as *presently Israelites:* "They are Israelites," *hoitines eisin Israēlitai,* and that *presently* to them, even in their unbelief, there belongs "the adoption, the glory, the covenants, the giving of the law, the temple service, and the promises." Tom Schreiner affirms this point: "The present tense verb (*eisin,* 'they are') indicates that the Jews still 'are' Israelites and that all the blessings named still belong to them."[70] In other words, Paul here confirms that in the mystery of God's dealings with national Israel in the flesh in unbelief He maintains a present covenant interest in them, even as beloved enemies (Rom 11:28). This being so, it is only right to understand this recognition in individual, national, and territorial terms.

> But what are we to make of the unbelief of Israel? Has their unbelief made the faithfulness of God without effect for them? (Rom. 3:1–4). No, God has not completely rejected the people of Israel (Rom. 11:1; cf. Rom. 11:2–10), and we join the apostle Paul in his earnest prayer for the salvation of his Jewish kinsmen according to the flesh (Rom. 9:1–3). There always has been and always will be a remnant that is saved (Rom. 11:5). While not all Israel will experience the blessing of participation in the Messianic kingdom (Rom. 9:6), yet Jews who do come to faith in Christ will share in his reign throughout the present age and into eternity. In addition, it is not as though the rejection of some in Israel for unbelief serves no purpose. On the contrary, because they were broken off in unbelief, the Gospel has gone to the Gentiles, who now, through faith, partake of the blessings to the fathers and join with believing Jews to constitute the true Israel of God, the church of Jesus Christ (Rom. 11:11–18).

The pejorative, utilitarian, anticlimactic tone here, "God has not completely rejected the people of Israel," betrays a reluctance to come to grips with Paul's exuberant, climactic expectation of Israel's national conversion in Romans 11, as is the obvious meaning with even a *prima facie* reading of this passage. How patronizingly gratifying it is to learn that, after all, the Jews have served a useful purpose! To sense the mood of the theological anti-Judaism in the whole of this "Open Letter," and then read that,

---

[70] T. R. Schreiner, *Romans* (Grand Rapids: Baker, 1998), 485. Similarly D. Moo, *The Epistle to the Romans* (Grand Rapids: Eerdmans, 1966), 560; E. Käsemann, *Commentary on Romans* (London: SCM Press, 1980), 258. Murray misses the point when he indicates that "they were 'Israelites'" (*The Epistle to the Romans* 2.4).

nevertheless, "we join the apostle Paul in his earnest prayer for the salvation of his Jewish kinsmen according to the flesh," is not to be impressed since this same prayerful concern was also expressed by Ambrose, Augustine, Chrysostom, and Luther. Tragically but not surprisingly in view of their deplorable attitudes, their petitions were not answered in a positive and comprehensive sense. However, "to join the apostle Paul" authentically in this matter is surely to imbibe his passionate interest in the Jews, which never flagged. But then what is meant here by the term "Jew," when it appears to have been evacuated of its obvious biblical meaning, so that only the shell of social convenience remains? Could any of the signatories of this "Open Letter" happily involve themselves in church planting in Israel today while at the same time, without compromise, making plain the gospel and presenting it in the framework of Jewish disqualification here presented? But there is further obfuscation in this regard when it is stated that, "Jews who do come to faith in Christ will share in his reign throughout the present age and into eternity." Again, what exactly is meant here by the term "Jews"? Is this really an honest declaration, for the teaching of the "Open Letter" is in fact that upon conversion the saved Jew loses his individual, national, and territorial Jewishness; in reality, according to Reformed Augustinianism, Judaism is finished. Some might attempt to avoid this problem by maintaining a temporary, quasi individuality for the Jewish Christian, though the aspects of nationality and territory would nevertheless be strenuously denied. This being the case, the language used here has the character of ambiguity and generality about it that fails to honestly reveal the real eschatological agenda.

> The present secular state of Israel, however, is not an authentic or prophetic realization of the Messianic kingdom of Jesus Christ. Furthermore, a day should not be anticipated in which Christ's kingdom will manifest Jewish distinctives, whether by its location in "the land," by its constituency, or by its ceremonial institutions and practices. Instead, this present age will come to a climactic conclusion with the arrival of the final, eternal phase of the kingdom of the Messiah. At that time, all eyes, even of those who pierced him, will see the King in his glory (Rev. 1:7). Every knee will bow, and every tongue will declare that Jesus Christ is Lord, to the glory of God the Father (Phil. 2:9–11). The kingdoms of this world will become the kingdom of our Lord and of his Christ, and he will reign forever and ever (Rev. 11:15).

Here is the harsh reality of theological anti-Judaism, the bottom line so to speak. The obvious and unavoidable conclusion then is that the present State of Israel is not of God; rather it is spiritually illegitimate if not fraudulent. Biblical Judaism, covenantally speaking, is passé. But nevertheless, "We love the Jews," is the hollow cry of the signatories of the "Open Letter." How strange it is for those of a Reformed persuasion who, while giving considerable place to the movements of God in human history, yet prefer to ignore the remarkable series of events involving significant Christian participation whereby the modern State of Israel came into being. How difficult it must be for these same people to brush aside the remarkable victories of the War of Independence of 1948, the Six Day War of 1967, and especially the reclamation of Old Jerusalem after 1,900 years of being "trampled by the Gentiles" (Luke 21:24). However, theological systems, while showing signs of becoming increasingly fractured because of historical enlightenment, nevertheless are not easily surrendered. Granted that Israel remains in unbelief, even so this in no way alters the fundamental issue of the ongoing legitimacy of the land in covenantal terms. Allowing for the worst of all scenarios, should Israel yet again be expelled from the land according to Arab and Gentile hegemony, even so this would in no way effect the abiding legitimacy of the land promise. However, one suspects that those who affirm modern Israel's present illegitimacy in the sight of God would, at such a tragic occasion, more assertively than ever declare this expulsion to be the will of God, with no prospective, covenantal return.

> *In light of the grand prophetic expectation of the New Testament, we urge our evangelical brothers and sisters to return to the proclamation of the free offer of Christ's grace in the Gospel to all the children of Abraham, to pray for peace between Israelis and Palestinians, and to promise all humanitarian sympathy and practical support for those on both sides who are suffering in this current vicious cycle of atrocity and displacement. We also invite those Christian educators and pastors who share our convictions on the people of God, the land of Israel, and the impartiality of the Gospel to join their names with ours as signatories to this open letter.*

> *Advent In the Year of our Lord 2002*
> *Soli Deo Gloria*

The inference here that we who are of a pro-Judaic persuasion are distracted from gospel proclamation has no more validity to it than the inference that those who are of a theologically anti-Judaic persuasion are more whole-heartedly committed to the proclamation of the gospel. Let us put aside such empty posturing. However, I do believe that faithful evangelism with regard to the Jews, as well as to the Palestinians, will inevitably have associated with it an ethical quality that commends the truth proclaimed. Further, I am convinced that the manner of our gospel preaching to Jews in particular will have a loving Pauline tone about it, even a special place as was his custom. In these two realms, I believe the evidence is conspicuous with regard to the lack in general that many Christians of Reformed convictions manifest. It may not sit well with those who staunchly identify themselves as Protestants, nevertheless it remains true at the present that, for all of its departure from the essential truth of the Bible, the Roman Catholic Church has more recently evidenced certain changes with regard to appreciation of the Jews and Judaism, however imperfectly and of debatable motivation, than those who glory in a Reformed heritage.

Chapter 4

ISRAEL AND CONTEMPORARY EXAMPLES OF CHRISTIAN ANTI-JUDAISM IN THE UK

Introduction

Ⓘn 1983 an Anglican clergyman and scholar named Colin Chapman published a book titled *Whose Promised Land?* in which he vigorously assailed biblical associations with the modern State of Israel. He also clearly asserted that pro-Judaic supporters today, in being pejoratively labeled as Christian Zionists, were unsympathetic to the injustice allegedly inflicted on the Palestinian cause by Israel. Though in constantly beating a drum in his cry for justice for the Palestinians, any similarly impassioned demand for justice with regard to centuries of inhumanity suffered by the Jews was merely referenced at a token level. The bias of the author was plain to read. For instance:

> I *do* have problems with the original vision of many Zionists to establish a Jewish homeland or a state in Palestine which would be exclusively or near-exclusively Jewish. . . . I feel bound to conclude that the promise of the land to Abraham and his descendants "as an everlasting possession" does *not* give the Jews a divine right to possess the land for all time. . . . I *don't* believe that the State of Israel is "of God" in the sense that it is the fulfillment (or even a preliminary stage in the fulfillment) of all that God promised and predicted in the Old Testament about the future of the land and its people. . . . I would go further and suggest that for Christians to interpret these events simply as the fulfillment of prophecy represents a kind of regression. . . . Could it be that God is challenging the whole Jewish people to think again about their destiny as a people? What is the whole enterprise of settling Jews in the land and setting up a Jewish state doing to the soul of Judaism? Did God really intend that they should be "a peculiar people" for ever and ever? Is there no alternative to the choice between traditional orthodox Judaism, assimilation and Zionism? Is there no other way by which the Jews can live securely among the nations without ceasing to be Jews?[1]

There is a chilling inference in the concluding three sentences here, in spite of the author's unconvincing protestation that he is not anti-Judaic. Moreover, the book remains essentially unchanged in its anti-Judaic style after four editions (the most recent in 2002). Incomprehensibly, the latest

---

[1] C. Chapman, *Whose Promised Land?* (Tring, Herts, England: Lion, 1983), 224, 226–28.

edition even incorporates in Appendix 3, without the slightest critical comment, "The Covenant of Hamas, the Islamic Resistance Movement," which includes the following:

> Hamas is for Muslims who favor Jihad. . . . Hamas aims for every inch of Palestine. . . . No part of it should be given up. . . . Hamas is opposed to initiatives, peaceful solutions and international conferences. Jihad is the only solution. . . . Enemy (i.e. Jews) responsible for the French Revolution, the Communist Revolution, etc. Allies of enemy: Freemasons, Rotary, Capitalist West, Communist East. Enemy caused the First and Second World Wars, etc. . . . Arab and Islamic countries should assist the anti-Zionist struggle.[2]

It seems unjust that Israel's *Proclamation of Independence* of May 14, 1948, was also not included:

> The Land of Israel was the birthplace of the Jewish people. Here their spiritual, religious and national identity was formed. Here they achieved independence and created a culture of national and universal significance. Here they wrote and gave the Bible to the world.
> Exiled from the Land of Israel the Jewish people remained faithful to it in all the countries of their dispersion, never ceasing to pray and hope for their return and the restoration of their national freedom.
> Impelled by this historic association, Jews strove throughout the centuries to go back to the land of their fathers and regain their statehood. In recent decades they returned in their masses. They reclaimed the wilderness, revived their language, built cities and villages, and established a vigorous and ever-growing community, with its own economic and cultural life. They sought peace, yet were prepared to defend themselves. They brought the blessings of progress to all inhabitants of the country and looked forward to sovereign independence.[3]

Chapman's tilt continues when he suggests that Israel may have fomented the formation of hard line terrorist organizations such as *Hamas* and *Islamic Jihad*, the result being that "distrust and despair have driven them to violence." Is there not here a degree of justification for the savagery of indiscriminate suicidal bombings that even employs children? The inference is that understanding of such terrorist groups is needed rather than a military response.[4]

In the whole of Chapman's most recent edition, particularly with regard to his sources, it is obvious that a doctrinal camaraderie has developed

---

[2] C. Chapman, *Whose Promised Land?* (Grand Rapids: Baker, 2002), 307. Qur'an/Hadith references are included.

[3] W. Laqueur and B. Rubin, *The Israel-Arab Reader* (New York: Penguin, 2001), 81.

[4] Chapman, *Whose Promised Land?* (2002), 272–76.

over the last twenty years among a number of Anglican scholars in England who reciprocate in their essential support of a supercessionist, if not theological, anti-Judaic agenda. Particularly prominent in Chapman's work are N. T. Wright (the most well-known, now Bishop of Durham and formerly Canon Theologian of Westminster Abbey), Stephen Sizer, Steve Motyer, Peter Walker, and Kenneth Cragg. Here is a coterie of Anglican scholars who have in common an amillennial, essentially Augustinian eschatology that plays out in a repudiation of the contemporary divine validity of National Israel. Stephen Sizer, Vicar of Christ Church, Virginia Water, Surrey, recently published his Ph.D. thesis, *Christian Zionism.* Similar in thrust to Chapman's book, it vigorously opposes any association with the modern State of Israel based on a premillennial, restorationist eschatology. Sizer's emphasis is more concerned, however, with a historical analysis of Christian Zionism, especially its alleged dispensational roots. He expresses particular indebtedness to Chapman, as well as Motyer, Walker, and American Presbyterian O. Palmer Robertson.

Motyer was editorially and sympathetically involved in the latest edition of *Whose Promised Land?* He is the author of *Israel in the Plan of God,* and in 2003 he presented a paper to the Evangelical Alliance titled "Israel in God's Plan" in which he broadly defined himself as "replacementist," arguing that it is Jesus who replaces Israel.[5] The writings of Peter Walker, lecturer at Wycliffe Hall, Oxford, have focused on Jerusalem and the land of Israel. Citing Wright, Chapman, and Motyer, he concludes that the land and related Zionist hopes have been absorbed into one people through Christ in fulfillment of God's universal purpose for the world.[6] Finally, the Islamophilic bias of Bishop Kenneth Cragg (former Assistant Bishop of Jerusalem and specialist in Christian-Muslim relations) is pointed out by Bat Ye'or (a pseudonym of Gisèle Littman, a British historian of non-Muslims in the Middle East and author of eight books), who relates how Cragg "criticized the European Kings and the popes for not having cooperated with the invading Muslim armies, a surrender which would have amounted to collaboration with their own demise."[7] I will now consider a number of emphases upon which these authors offer general agreement.

[5] S. Motyer, "Israel in God's Plan," *Evangelical Alliance Consultation,* June, 2003, http://www. eauk.org/theology/headline_issues/holyland/upload/S_Motyer_'Israel'_paper.pdf (cited 2007).

[6] P. Walker, "The land in the apostles' writings," and "The land and Jesus himself," in *The Land of Promise* (ed. P. Johnston and P. Walker; Downers Grove, Illinois: InterVarsity, 2000), 81–120.

[7] B. Ye'or, *Eurabia: The Euro-Arab Axis* (Madison, New Jersey: Fairleigh Dickinson University Press, 2005), 189.

All of them tend toward supercessionist, anti-Judaic antipathies with regard to modern Israel and also pro-Arab, Muslim, and Palestinian sympathies. The doctrinal kinship here certainly confirms the religious dimensions that are detailed in the warnings of Bat Ye'or in her *Eurabia: The Euro-Arab Axis*, and Melanie Phillips in her *Londonistan*.[8]

Law Precedes Grace

In varying degrees, these Christian authors would readily confess to doctrinal alignment with a broad Anglican, Protestant, and Reformed heritage. This would also mean belief in salvation by grace through faith alone in Jesus Christ, which is inevitably to result in the growth of manifest gracious and godly living. This being so, it is astonishing to behold these very same people regressing into a denial of this truth in so far as God's promised dealings with Israel in the OT are concerned. For instance, Sizer is critical of the fact that virtually all Christian Zionists insist that the Abrahamic covenant remains unconditional, whereas,

> subsequent references to the land in Scripture stress that humility and meekness rather than "chosenness" became a precondition for inheriting or remaining in the land, whereas arrogance or oppression were legitimate grounds for exile. For example, the psalmist explains, "But the meek will inherit the land and enjoy great peace" (Ps. 37:11). . . . The ethical requirements for continued occupancy are clearly outlined in the Law.[9]

We may conclude that to Sizer it is obedience to Torah that establishes participation in the Abrahamic covenant for the Jews, in particular the land promises, while this is exactly antithetical to the very heart of the Christian gospel, especially as it is confessed according to Reformed teaching. Many of Reformed convictions resort to this inconsistent belief, as is further detailed in chapter 9 of this book. What about "chosenness" according to sovereign grace? What about the priority of election and subsequent saving response of *sola fide* in relation to consequent good works (Eph. 2:8–10)? If Sizer claims these for himself, how can he deny the sovereignty of grace inherent in the election of Israel through Abraham? Do we have a different gospel standard represented in the OT in contrast with that of the NT, at least with regard to the salvation of Israel? Perish the thought, though it is simply amazing to note further how Sizer then leads us to consider the ethical demands of the prophet Ezekiel in 33:25–29. This concerns Israel being guilty of bloodshed

---

[8] M. Phillips, *Londonistan* (New York: Encounter Books, 2006).

[9] S. Sizer, *Christian Zionism* (Leicester, England: Inter-Varsity, 2004), 163.

and abominable things that threaten desolation and exclusion from the land. So quite apart from any mention of future grace, he comments,

> On the basis of sober warnings such as this, the question may legitimately be asked whether, due to its present expansionist policies, the State of Israel might not expect another exile rather than a restoration.[10]

Evidently Sizer's graceless intimation here, after the manner of the prophet Jonah's complaint (Jonah 4:1–4) as well as that of Habakkuk (Hab 1:2–4), seems to be that he prefers the judgment of modern Israel. Furthermore, his avoidance of the subsequent glorious truth of Ezekiel 34–37 appears dismissive of the ultimate triumph of God's saving power.[11] Yet it is this eventual consummate reign of sovereign grace that will bring about the national regeneration of Israel. So God declares,

> I will make them one nation in the land, on the mountains of Israel, and one king will rule over all of them. They will no longer be two nations and no longer will be divided into two kingdoms. They will not defile themselves any more with their idols, their detestable things, and all their transgressions. I will save them from all their apostasies by which they sinned, and I will cleanse them. Then they will be My people, and I will be their God (Ezek 37:22–23).

Here, and in many other instances, Sizer appears to long for the heavy hand of God to judge the nation of Israel, whereas God promises eventual national salvation—not on account of obedience but rather issuing in obedience. Sizer is eager for the law of God to thrash Israel,[12] in contradistinction to Habakkuk who nevertheless eventually cried out, "In wrath, remember mercy" (Hab 3:2). God declares that He will eventually restore His people according to sovereign grace. Sizer's problem here is exactly the same as that of Philip Mauro who was so soundly corrected by Samuel Wilkinson (see Appendix C).

Chapman calls Ezekiel 36–37 "a favorite hunting ground for students of prophecy." Twisting and turning to avoid the literal meaning at any cost lest his whole eschatological edifice should come tumbling down, he explains,

---

[10] Ibid., 163–64.

[11] Sizer only refers critically to the "futuristic" views of Christian Zionists concerning these chapters without any explanation whatsoever (Ibid., 40, 154–56). He probably follows Motyer and Robertson who merely abstract the concepts of regeneration and resurrection.

[12] Sizer further writes, "the present brutal, repressive racist policies of the State of Israel would suggest another exile on the horizon rather than a restoration." *Whose Promised Land: Israel and Biblical Prophecy*, http://www.christchurch-virginiawater.co.uk/articles/debate.html (cited May 2007).

the alternative is to try to interpret the language of the vision and translate it into a message which was relevant to the original hearers and is relevant to anyone who wants to listen today. . . . It is hard to think that a prophet would be given a message to his people in the eighth century BC which related to events that would not take place until the twentieth or twenty-first centuries.[13]

What assumptions lurk beneath what this scholar finds "hard to think"? Yet it was Daniel who declared that "I heard but did not understand," and he was then told that "the words [of prophetic revelation] are secret and sealed until the time of the end" (Dan 12:8–9). Daniel, along with his contemporary audience, was not expected to understand everything that had been immediately revealed. According to Chapman, what then was the meaning for Ezekiel's immediate audience that would reach through the centuries for us today? He quotes approvingly from John Goldingay, Professor of OT at Fuller Theological Seminary:

> When Ezekiel declared that such and such a return to the land or such and such a battle was to take place, he was not announcing events scheduled for two and a half millennia after his day. He was addressing and bringing God's word to people in his own day, warning them of calamities and promising them blessings that could come about in their day. He was not revealing a timetable or fixture list of events that had to unfold over thousands of years; he was bringing a specific message to a particular context. A fulfillment in 1948 of a prophecy given to Ezekiel to people who lived in the 580s BC is thus nonsense: it is not a fulfillment of promises and warnings that were part of God's relationship with those people. Prophets did sometimes speak about the End of all things, but there are relatively few of these prophecies.[14]

So a literal understanding of Ezekiel 36–37 is "nonsense"? If this is the fruit of Chapman and Sizer's eschatology and their exegesis of Ezekiel 36–37, then we can only conclude that its taste is most unpalatable and its ingestion most unhealthy. Our God does indeed prophesy of revelatory, cataclysmic, and climactic events that may be either imminent or generations away, even as the Son of God plainly indicated in Matt 26:13.

Covenantalism

Stephen Sizer explains that the purpose of his book,

> has been to make a case for a covenantalist approach to the Palestinian-Israeli conflict by focusing on and critiquing its antithesis, namely dis-

---

[13] Chapman, *Whose Promised Land?* (2002), 135, 288, 292.

[14] Ibid., 292–93; citing J. Goldingay, "The Jews, the Land, and the Kingdom", *ANVIL*, vol. 4, no. 1, 1987, 17.

pensational Christian Zionism. A covenantalist recognizes, for example, that the Bible consistently teaches that God has only ever had one people throughout history—those who share the faith of Abraham, whether Jews or Gentiles—and one means of atonement, the sacrifice of the Lord Jesus Christ in our place. Based on passages such as Romans 9–11, covenantalists recognize the Jewish people are loved by God, have fulfilled a unique role in history leading to the truth of Christianity and pray that one day all Jews will come to recognize Jesus as their Messiah. Covenantalism affirms that the church is Israel renewed and restored in Christ but now enlarged to embrace people of all nations. . . . Unlike Christian Zionism, covenantalism finds it unnecessary to justify or sacralize the State of Israel through tenuous biblical and theological arguments. It also distances itself from those who seek to impose a predetermined and apocalyptic agenda on the people of the Middle East.[15]

Actually, there is nothing distinctively "covenantal" in this definition when compared with differing eschatological opinions. Premillennial or Judeocentric eschatology is very much "covenantal." It would be more accurate to speak here of an Augustinian approach to the Palestinian-Israeli conflict. Perhaps the most galling comment here is the patronizing expression that "covenantalists recognize the Jewish people are loved by God, have fulfilled a unique role in history leading to the truth of Christianity and pray that one day all Jews will come to recognize Jesus as their Messiah." But Chrysostom, Ambrose, and Augustine would say the same thing while, like Sizer, denying the modern Jew of divine individuality, nationality, and territory. Most Jewish Christians who have read Sizer's writings will be put off by what appears to be a cover for an anti-Judaic agenda. What exactly does he mean here by "Jews"? At best there is the allowance of token, temporal individuality, apart from nationality and territory, that is, until the "Jews" have been absorbed into the one, homogenous people of God. What is meant by the ingratiating comment that "the Jewish people . . . have fulfilled a unique role in history leading to the truth of Christianity"? It sounds as though the Jews should say, "Thank you very much Mr. Sizer, for your recognition of a past national existence that has fulfilled its usefulness." His prayer is that Jews become saved through their Messiah to the end that they might then forfeit their national Jewishness. Sizer claims, "They simply have to understand that they have really become spiritually fulfilled Jews," as with any believer in Jesus. However, Mr. Sizer, who are you, a Gentile Christian, to tell a Jewish Christian he has been reconstituted, as if the church at Antioch in a similar manner lorded it over the

---

[15] Sizer, *Christian Zionism*, 261, 263.

church at Jerusalem? This is exactly what Paul warns about in Rom 11:18
when he exhorts the Gentile believers at Rome, "Do not brag that you are
better than those branches. But if you [Gentile believers] do brag— you
do not sustain the root, but the root sustains you." To suggest that "the
church is Israel renewed and restored in Christ but now enlarged to embrace people of all nations" is to fiddle with the language of the NT that in
reality nowhere declares that the church is Israel renewed. This fictional
extrapolation is in reality warmed over Augustinianism, and in light of
such an indecent eschatological legacy that Sizer and his associates so obviously embody (more fully described in chapter 2 of this book), this is
nothing to boast in.

Romans 11

The understanding of Rom 11:26, "and in this way all Israel will be
saved," has been fraught with controversy, especially over the three main
interpretations of the identity of "all Israel."[16] I suggest that there usually
runs here the current of a problem reaching much deeper than textual nu-
ances might suggest. The doctrine of salvation also has been associated
with controversy of historic proportions. But the evangelical Christian convinced that the redemption of a human soul is by means of the pure gospel of free grace personally embraced through faith alone in Christ (Rom
3:22–24) is not in the slightest shaken in his faith when controversy and
a plethora of interpretations swirl all around him. Ask Hebrew Christians
concerning their *prima facie* understanding of the Hebrew Christian Paul
in Rom 11:26, and their response will usually be common agreement that
the eschatological conversion of national Israel is envisaged. On the other
hand, ask a Gentile Christian the same question, especially one who has
assimilated the Augustinian/Catholic/Reformed doctrinal heritage of centuries in this regard, and he will probably reject that understanding. The
reason is that having assimilated the traditional supercessionist teaching
that transfers the blessings of Israel to the Christian Church, that body of
truth is unconsciously imposed on the text of Romans in such a way that
no national future for Israel is considered a possibility.

For instance, consider R. C. H. Lenski's approach to Romans 11. As a
classic conservative Lutheran scholar, he clearly wished to avoid any sug-

---

[16] "All Israel" refers to (1) the people of God that comprises Jew and Gentile, (2) the remnant of Rom 11:5 that gradually accumulates over the centuries and remains a remnant, or (3)
the nation of Israel that will be saved climactically, *en masse*, at the end of this age.

gestion that Paul had a future hope for national Israel. In his comment on Rom 11:10 he wrote:

> To this day "Jew" is an opprobrious epithet even in our best countries. Read their long history. The sum of that history is not the fact that the Jews innocently suffered these centuries of woe; it is that they have ever brought these woes upon themselves anew. Ever they keep acting as an irritant among the nations. . . . They crucified their own Christ; to this day their hatred of the crucified stamps them more than anything else as "Jews"; their segregation is of their own choosing. The more they retain the character of "Jews," the more does this appear; and during the long centuries this their character made them the irritant they have been. . . . "forever" (*diapantos*) does not sound like a future conversion of the Jews.[17]

The tone here is obviously anti-Judaic, reminiscent of Pieters and Boettner (see chapter 2) and definitely not Paul. It is not so surprising when Lenski interprets "all Israel" in v. 26 as the accumulating total of the elect remnant in conjunction with vv. 5,7. In this interpretation, which minimizes any national eschatological hope for the Jews, Lenski's anti-Judaic conviction finds solace.

An interpretation of Romans 11 focused through historic doctrinal tradition that is supercessionist inevitably leads to the search for an alternative understanding to the clear meaning of v. 26. The interpretation of "all Israel" that especially fits the bill here for those who are theologically anti-Judaic is that it refers to a cumulative Jewish Christian remnant. Both Chapman and Sizer in particular appear to follow a common cause, that is, an understanding which tends to repudiate an eschatological national future for Israel in Romans 11. Like Lenski's, their understanding of "all Israel" in Rom 11:26 by its very nature obviates the possibility of an eschatological hope for the nation of Israel. If one were to believe in this Jewish Christian remnant that accumulates over centuries of church history as the "all Israel" of Rom 11:26, then it would wholly exclude an eschatological hope for the salvation of national Israel. As a consequence, only a remnant would be saved and nothing more. That this is the predominant understanding with regard to the Anglican scholars and authors heretofore mentioned will now be indicated in more detail, particularly in terms of their interactive agreement.

---

[17] R. C. H. Lenski, *The Interpretation of St. Paul's Epistle to the Romans* (Peabody, Massachusetts: Hendrickson, 2001), 691.

As previously mentioned, Wright's exegesis appears to be particularly influential.[18] It is not uncommon for those of Chapman's persuasion to first declare, echoing Wright, that

> it is never appropriate for Christians to think that Christianity has "taken the place of Israel". This idea, which is sometimes described as "supercessionism" and sometimes as "Replacement Theology", finds no support in the New Testament.[19]

But at this juncture the aide of Wright is mustered whereby it is asserted:

> From the earliest evidence, Christians regarded themselves as a new family, directly descended from the family of Israel, but now transformed. . . . Those who now belonged to Jesus' people were not identical with ethnic Israel, since Israel's history had *reached its intended fulfillment*; they claimed to be the continuation of Israel in a new situation, able to draw freely on *Israel-images* to express their self-identity, able to read Israel's scriptures (through the lens of Messiah and spirit) and apply them to their own life. They were thrust out by that claim, and that reading, to fulfill Israel's vocation on behalf of the world.[20]

Chapman concludes with regard to a matter that seems to be of such pressing concern for him.

> There is no suggestion that they [Jewish and Gentile Christians] believed it was important for Jews to express their distinctive identity through having a Jewish state in the land.[21]

Here I can only conclude that to avoid the stigma associated with replacement and supercessionist theology, that is, of Israel being robbed of its inheritance by means of a Gentile takeover, there is a more deft employment of language. Instead of "replacement" and "supercession" we have substituted here the concept of "fulfillment" whereby an attempt is made to carry over more subtly Israel's covenant privileges to the homogenous "people of Jesus." Of course the end result is still the same, as Chapman is so intent on upholding, and that being Israel's national and territorial disqualification. So

---

[18] This is not meant to ignore the differing minority view that there will be an eschatological conversion of national Israel resulting in absorption into the church, and thus nullification of any ultimate national hope for Israel.

[19] Chapman, *Whose Promised Land?* (2002), 224; see N. T. Wright, *The Climax of the Covenant* (Edinburgh: T&T Clark, 1991), 253.

[20] Ibid., citing N. T. Wright, *The New Testament and the People of God* (London: SPCK, 1992), 457–58 (emphasis added).

[21] Chapman, *Whose Promised Land?* (2002), 224.

in a similar vein Wright elsewhere describes "transference" in Romans 11 whereby Paul

> has systematically *transferred* the privileges and attributes of "Israel" to the Messiah and his people. It is therefore greatly preferable to take "all Israel" in v. 26 as a typically Pauline polemical *redefinition*, as in Galatians 6:16.[22]

Paul's supposed "redefinition" of "Israel" in Gal 6:16 is today a minority interpretation (see chapter 10 of this book). The end result of Wright's interpretation of Romans 11 here, hence that of Chapman and Sizer, is that Jewish identity, nationality, and territory are all absorbed into the Christian church. Yet this is said not to be "replacement theology" or "supercessionism"? Without any doubt, what we have here is the outworking of classic Augustinianism in modern dress. So it is not surprising that as the centuries have witnessed resultant shameful anti-Judaism issuing from this doctrinal heritage, the revamping of this doctrine by Chapman and Sizer is likewise productive of a new strain of virulent anti-Judaism.

What then did Paul have in mind when in Rom 11:26 he asserts so enthusiastically that "all Israel will be saved"? While Wright admits that his alignment here is with a minority interpretation, he also finds a degree of refuge in Käsemann's belief that "the text [of Romans] has a central concern and a remarkable inner logic that may no longer be entirely comprehensible to us."[23] But those of a Judeo-centric persuasion find such a retreat to agnosticism quite unnecessary. So Wright believes that "it remains God's will that the present 'remnant' of believing Jews might be enlarged by the process of 'jealousy,'"[24] that is, by means of cumulative incorporation into the church as the people of God over the centuries of church history. In other words, as a remnant, a small number of Jews is progressively being saved alongside the mass of Gentiles also being saved; in this manner "all Israel will be saved." Wright makes no mention of the temporal sequence that v. 25 indicates whereby Israel's hardening is to be "until" [*achri*] the full number of the Gentiles has come in."[25] Also, his denial of a temporal significance for *houtōs* ('in this way") in v. 26 ignores the temporal reference in context here, as the temporal reference to *houtōs* in 11:4–5 well indicates, or the implications of the future rather than the present tense of

---

[22] Wright, *The Climax of the Covenant*, 25 (emphasis added).

[23] Ibid., 246–47.

[24] Ibid., 250.

[25] O. P. Robertson admits: "Initially it might seem that the word 'until' (*achris hou*) implies that the hardening of Israel will stop after the full number of the Gentiles has been realized." *The Israel of God* (Phillipsburg, New Jersey: P&R, 2000), 177.

"will be saved."[26] Of course with Wright there is no suggestion here that "all Israel" retains divinely recognized Jewish national and territorial identity since individual "Jews" have become absorbed into the one people of God in the new economy where former ethnic distinctions have no validity. But consider Matt Waymeyer's persuasive point that "they" in Rom 11:28 ("they are enemies . . . they are loved"), being unbelieving national Israel, is identical to the national "them" in v. 27 ("this will be My covenant with them when I take away their sins"), which is identical to "Jacob" and to national or "all Israel" in v. 26, and so is not a mere remnant.[27] The most unsatisfactory aspect of Wright's interpretation is that a "cumulative Jewish Christian remnant" is so obviously anticlimactic. It stands out toward the conclusion of Romans 11, especially vv. 25–36, that Paul anticipates such an enthralling climax concerning Israel's ultimate destiny. To suggest that "all Israel" is the aggregate of a relatively small number of converted Jews gleaned from the centuries of church history is to fly in the face of Paul's enthusiastic hope. Obviously, the apostle anticipates that more than a remnant will be saved. The remnant is certainly the guarantee of God's continued covenant faithfulness over the centuries, but Israel's conversion in terms of the "full number . . . acceptance . . . full number" (vv. 12,15,25–26) is what He ultimately longs for. It is easy to discern from Chapman and Sizer that at all costs they desire to eliminate any prospect for national Israel and thus suggest that Paul did not really mean what he appears to say. In this regard Romans 11 remains an enormous problem from which even N. T. Wright cannot satisfactorily deliver them.

Heaven Without Earth

While the question of spiritual materiality is dealt with in chapter 8 in greater detail, at this juncture it is appropriate to consider how both Chapman and Sizer raise the question of the carnality of Christian Zionism and its contrast with what they perceive to be the spirituality of the kingdom of Jesus Christ.

---

[26] See chapter 10 of this book as well as D. Moo's comprehensive study in which he concludes "that *houtōs*, while not having a temporal meaning, has a temporal reference: for the manner in which all Israel is saved involves a process that unfolds in definite stages," *The Epistle to the Romans* (Grand Rapids: Eerdmans, 1996), 720. In this regard, also consider that with *houtōs* commencing Rom 11:5, it is with temporal reference to the past of v. 4 and "the present time" of v. 5.

[27] M. Waymeyer, "The Dual Status of Israel in Romans 11:28," *The Master's Seminary Journal* (Spring 2005), 57–71.

Yes, there is cause for complaint here concerning those who portray eschatology in terms of sensationalist, materialistic pop-prophecy. Though it would be better, and probably more effectual, if such criticism were to come from those who evidence a genuine and heartfelt love for the Jewish people, who while remaining enemies of the gospel are at the same time beloved by God because of His fidelity to the Abrahamic covenant (Rom 11:28). But Chapman and Sizer retain an ardent repudiation of the present nation of Israel allegedly on account of its well-earned nullification by God. They claim that Christian justification for the renunciation of modern Israel's racist militancy is especially warranted because of unbelief, secularity, extreme military defense of its borders, and the unjust mistreatment and displacement of many Palestinians within its domain. So in place of an earthly eschatological hope for Jerusalem within the land of Israel, Chapman and Sizer propose a heavenly redefinition with material and spiritual dichotomies below and above. A particular cluster of references is then appealed to, especially Gal 4:25–26 and Heb 11:10,16; 12:22–23. At stake here is the vital matter of hermeneutics dealt with especially in chapter 7 of this book (see also chapters 8–11). We may only note at this point that for Sizer Jerusalem as the capital of Israel no longer has any historic, earthly role of divine, biblical significance.

> The New Testament . . . knows nothing of a preoccupation with a nationalistic and materialistic earthly Jerusalem, let alone Zionism as it exists today. . . . Jesus explained further, saying, "My kingdom is not of this world. If it were, my servants would fight to prevent my arrest by the Jews. But now my kingdom is from another place" (John 18:36). . . . Christians are told instead to inhabit Jerusalem by faith and look forward to the heavenly Jerusalem. . . . Paul takes a promise originally referring to the earthly Jerusalem [Gal 4:26] and applies it to the Jerusalem above, which is the home of all who believe in Jesus Christ.[28]

It is asserted that the Christian anticipates a nebulous, ethereal, non-material, Platonic higher level of existence in the economy of heaven above. But I believe that the Lord Jesus Christ did anticipate an earthly Jerusalem of spiritual materiality which would gloriously supplant the carnal materiality of Jerusalem that He wept over. He declared that the present Jerusalem was about to be left desolate in judgment. Yet the strong inference is that this humiliation would eventually yield to a glorious reversal of circumstances since Jesus continued, "For I tell you, you will never see Me again

---

[28] Sizer, *Christian Zionism*, 169.

until you say, 'Blessed is He who comes in the name of the Lord!'" (Matt 23:38–39). So in this regard Alford described

> that day, the subject of all prophecy, when your [Jerusalem's] repentant people shall turn with true and loyal Hosannas and blessings to greet "Him whom they have pierced:" (Deut. 4:30–31; Hos. 3:4–5; Zech. 12:10; 14:8–11). Stier well remarks, "He who reads not this in the prophets, reads not yet the prophets aright."[29]

When Paul wrote of "the Jerusalem above," he was not indicating that the Jerusalem below had been forever discarded for some abstract, amorphous Jerusalem, but rather that eschatological transformation of Zion whereby the holiness of heaven will have come down to regenerate the earthly Jerusalem. The result is, as John Milton described, a time when,

> Earth be chang'd to Heav'n, and Heav'n to Earth,
> One Kingdom, Joy and Union without end.[30]

Then will have come to pass "the Messianic Age [lit. "rebirth, regeneration," *palingenesia*], when the Son of Man sits on His glorious throne" (Matt 19:28; cp. Acts 3:21), which I believe to be that place, that new Jerusalem, from where Jesus Christ will reign with heavenly glory upon earth (Jer 3:17; Ezek 43:7; Zech 6:12–13).

Unity Without Diversity

One of the most fundamental errors of Chapman and Sizer concerns an oft-repeated logical fallacy, namely, that God's design that the redeemed of all ages become one in Christ Jesus excludes the possibility of any diversity happily existing within this unity. While the matter concerning the land of Israel is dealt with in more detail in chapter 9 of this book, both Chapman and Sizer suggest that it is the paradise of Eden that leads to the promised land flowing with milk and honey and ultimately the whole world as inherited by Abraham (Rom 4:13). It seems that this concept is derived from O. Palmer Robertson who references Christopher Wright, although N. T. Wright made the same point and expresses indebtedness to W. D. Davies.[31] Whatever the source of this concept, the argument runs that because redemption in Christ eventually encompasses the whole earth as the new promised land, so to speak, the OT boundaries of the land of Israel have

---

[29] H. Alford, *The Greek Testament*, I (London: Rivingtons, 1856), 216.
[30] John Milton, *Paradise Lost*, vii (New York: Hurd and Houghton, 1869), 203.
[31] Wright, *The Climax of the Covenant*, 174.

become inconsequential. In other words, a new, transcendent unity has eliminated the possibility of diversity incorporating Israel and the Gentile nations.

> He [Jesus] had not come to rehabilitate the symbol of the holy land, but to subsume it within a different fulfillment of the kingdom, which would embrace the whole creation. . . . Jesus spent his whole ministry redefining what the kingdom meant. He refused to give up the symbolic language of the kingdom, but filled it with such new content that . . . he powerfully subverted Jewish expectations.[32]

Sizer makes the same point, except that in caustically denouncing the literal hermeneutic of Christian Zionism which, it is alleged, "provides a theological endorsement for racial segregation, apartheid and war [within the contemporary State of Israel]," he invokes Robertson to describe a new covenant perspective.

> In the process of redemptive history, a dramatic movement has been made from type to reality, from shadow to substance. The land which once was the specific locale of God's redemptive working served well within the old covenant as a picture of Paradise lost and promised. Now, however, in the era of new-covenant fulfillment, the land has been expanded to encompass the cosmos. . . . In this age of fulfillment, therefore, a retrogression to the limited forms of the old covenant must be neither expected or promoted. Reality must not give way to shadow.[33]

In response, the fundamental error of identifying the promised land with the bilateral Mosaic covenant rather than the unilateral Abrahamic covenant is once again most prominent (dealt with in more detail in chapter 9 of this book). Adding to the confusion here is the ignoring of the fact that the new covenant was directly made with "the house of Israel and with the house of Judah" (Jer 31:31–34), and only indirectly with the church. Though of course, Romans 11 makes it clear that the Gentiles, as wild olive branches, are grafted into the Abrahamic natural olive tree so that they might become partakers of new covenant blessings. Furthermore, since Chapman, Wright, Sizer, and Robertson wrongly identify the land with the shadowy nature of the Mosaic covenant, they also ignore the fact that Jeremiah 31, where the new covenant supersedes the old, is further described in Jeremiah 32. Here it is "an everlasting covenant" (v. 40)

---

[32] N. T. Wright, *Jesus and the Victory of God* (London: SPCK, 1996), 446, 471; cited by Chapman, *Whose Promised Land?* (2002), 151..

[33] Sizer, *Christian Zionism*, 260; O. P. Robertson, "A new-covenant perspective on the land," 140.

including God's promise that He "will plant them [Israel] faithfully in this land with all My mind and heart" (v. 41) "because I will restore their fortunes" (v. 44). Plainly the land is part of the inheritance of the new covenant (see Ezek 36:24–28; 37:1–14).

To return to the original point of disagreement, let us happily assert the glorious truth that awaits all the people of God, namely, the universal, sole reign of His Son over this universe when, "the earth will be filled with the knowledge of the LORD's glory, as the waters cover the sea" (Hab 2:14; see Isa 11:9; Zech 14:9). Then how is it necessary that this heavenly economy on earth will be strictly and indistinguishably homogenous? Could angels then endure such a distinct existence? If there is economic and personal diversity within the triunity of the one true and living God, and His church manifests the diversity of giftedness within that one body, then how is it not to be expected, with the personal, distinguishable presence of Moses, Elijah, David, and Paul that there will also be an ethnic, national, and territorial diversity within the perfect ecumenicity of that kingdom? And how will it faintly be inconsistent with the gospel when the nation of redeemed Israel will distinctively reign with the redeemed Gentile nations while manifesting a diversity within the perfect unity of the kingdom of Christ?

Anti-Judaic Tone

What we have observed in the previous sections exhibits a tone of evident animosity and resentment toward the Jewish people, and especially the modern nation of Israel, whose very distinctive Jewish existence, they are told, has been forever forfeited. Steve Motyer has illustrated how a Christian understanding of the OT radically transcends that of orthodox Judaism: "It's more like a group of aliens meeting a Rolls Royce for the first time, when previously all they have seen is the Reader's Digest Guide to Car Maintenance."[34] Such pseudo-Marcionism belittles and does away with the whole framework of Judaism, not simply the old covenant. Of course, there is sufferance, an artificial, grudging tokenism of the worst kind that tolerates a Jewish Christian being called "Jewish," at least in a nominal social sense, even though his ultimate future will be the total loss of his Jewishness. Yet the Jewish Christian's divine nationality and territory are vehemently denied. Consequently, whereas racial anti-Judaism in the twentieth century culminated in a process of physical elimination, the extermination of Jews, theological anti-Judaism

---

[34] Motyer, "Israel in God's Plan."

in the twenty-first century culminates in identity elimination, the extermination of Jewishness in the name of Jesus the Jew.

With this in mind we again consider both Chapman and Sizer, principally because they have themselves staked out prominent positions in their intentional campaigning against "Christian Zionism" as they broadly designate it. First, in sympathizing with the cause of Palestinian Christians, Palestinian Arabs, and Muslim Arabs overall, Chapman takes issue with Jewish Christians and their supporters, and especially as enthusiastically represented in America. I have already catalogued explicit, distasteful expressions of his aversion to modern Israel. The sour aura is simply unmistakable, and I seriously question whether it finds the remotest reflection in the apostolic mood concerning the Jews, especially that of Paul (see chapter 11).

Perhaps even more vociferous in this regard is Sizer, who has also identified with the cause of Palestinian Christians, Palestinian Arabs, and Muslim Arabs. His tilt is thus heavily against biblical restorationism, while like Chapman he is happy to embrace the extremely critical, leftist/liberal, anti-Judaic views of Noam Chomsky, Norman Finkelstein, Grace Halsall, and others. Further, although he identifies with the evangelical wing of the Church of England, he happily associates as well with the Middle East Council of Churches (MECC) and its opposition to the modern State of Israel. The official web site of MECC explains that:

> The Middle East Council of Churches (M.E.C.C.) is a fellowship of churches relating itself to the main stream of the modern ecumenical movement, the same which gave birth to the World Council and other regional ecumenical councils throughout the world.[35]

Consequently, Sizer also invokes the declaration of MECC that Christian Zionism represents "a heretical interpretation of Scripture," a "deviant heresy,"[36] while further bolstering his tirade by claiming the agreement of John Stott that it is "biblically anathema."[37] Hence we are told that Christian Zionism

> provides a theological endorsement for racial segregation, apartheid and war [on the part of modern Israel]. This is diametrically opposed to the

[35] *The Middle East Council of Churches*, http://www.mec-churches.org/main_eng.htm (cited May 2007).

[36] Sizer, *Christian Zionism*, 22, 259.

[37] Ibid., 22, 261, citing D. Wagner twice. In this regard, I would much prefer the eschatology of Bishop J. C. Ryle who, in being in firm disagreement with Stott, yet expressed himself with far more grace.

inclusive theology of justice, peace and reconciliation which lie at the heart of the new covenant. . . . The present brutal, repressive and racist policies of the State of Israel would suggest exile on the horizon rather than a restoration. . . . Israel is a materialistic society, an apartheid state practicing repressive and dehumanizing measures against the Palestinians in flagrant disregard of the United Nations and UN declaration of human rights.[38]

The tone is revealing, and so is the language that resonates with the verbal mantras of liberation theology and baptized Marxism. However unbelieving Israel may presently be, surely there is something fundamentally wrong with an underlying eschatology that so demeans the Jewish people and their nation, in contrast to the oracles of God which are so thoroughly Jewish and uphold a Jewish Savior. In no way do we excuse aspects of Christian Zionism that may at times express prophetic carnality. Nor do we excuse the errors of national Israel after the flesh, for, enemies though they presently are in Christ, we do love them for the sake of the fathers, and thus the land that remains their inheritance. In this pro-Judaic scenario, there remains open and unashamed affection and respect for the Jews, after the manner that Paul encouraged in Rom 9:1–5. The reason for this is the fundamental underpinning of God's eschatological hope for ethnic, national, and territorial Israel as delineated in the Old and New Testaments. A supercessionist theology produces an anti-Judaic demeanor with regard to the Jews, and church history is the terrible, unavoidable proof that this is so. I grant that Chapman does attempt to deal with the matter of anti-Judaism, though to be frank it is quite inadequate in its selectivity and the shallowness of its assessment in nominal terms. Where he fails most is at the root of the matter, for while referencing the anti-Judaism of Chrysostom, Augustine, Aquinas, and Luther, he completely neglects to deal with the underlying doctrinal cause.[39] Had he done so, he would have been forced to see a reflection of the essence of his own supercessionist views.

Another aspect of tone to be considered, which again Chapman well represents, concerns his wrestling with the ancient conquest of the land of Canaan under Joshua. Here the tone is one of necessary accommodation, even with regard to the moral purposes of God. In this section one senses a relentless attempt to nullify modern Israel's "illicit" present possession of the land while attempting to confront ancient Israel's ques-

[38] Ibid., 260; N. Cornell and S. Sizer, "Whose Promised Land: Israel and Biblical Prophecy Debate," Guildford Diocesan Evangelical Fellowship, March, 1997, http://www.cc-vw.org/articles/debate.html (cited May 2007).

[39] Chapman, *Whose Promised Land?* (2002), 44–49.

tionable militant capture of the land. The biblical account is skeptically addressed as follows:

> Is it conceivable that a God of love could actually have ordered the Israelites to engage in what we today would call "ethnic cleansing"? . . . One way of resolving the problem is to see these stories simply as a Jewish interpretation of their history. Since they believed that they were "the chosen people" who enjoyed a special relationship with God, they wrote their history in such a way as to justify their ideas about their special status and their superiority over other people. The Old Testament should therefore be seen as a very ethnocentric interpretation of Israelite history.[40]

Chapman makes not the slightest attempt to repudiate this warped regard for the OT record in terms of its divinely inspired character. Describing these "stories" as "Jewish [i.e., very ethnocentric] interpretation" which "Israel believed" empties Scripture of its character as authoritative divine instruction. Instead, Chapman retreats to cultural, subjective accommodation. But sadly this assessment does not allow us to stop at a misuse of interpretive method. Rather, such method is wielded to accomplish the disqualification of the modern State of Israel. This appears to be Chapman's overriding concern, and Scripture is not allowed to get in the way. Thus he has written,

> No doubt we would all want to say that by the standards of today many of the actions of Joshua and the Children of Israel in the conquest of the land were evil and should never be held up as an example for people to follow today. . . . Anyone, therefore, who sees Christ as the fullest possible revelation of what God is like and of the kind of moral standards that God sets for human beings, will see many of the actions of Joshua as very wrong and abhorrent. But if, as the biblical account suggests, God was involved in the conquest of the land under Joshua, it was because he had to work within a particular cultural and religious context, revealing gradually as much new truth as people were able to grasp. Given the level of culture and religion at the time, God's revelation of a new way had to be gradual. He had to work *within* a culture that practiced ethnic cleansing as something that was acceptable, in order ultimately to change the culture from within by exposing this evil in its true light and showing the human race a better way.[41]

It is not difficult to sense a specific, controlling agenda at work, that is, the condemnation of the present Jewish occupation of Israel. To do this, somehow Joshua's campaigns of "ethnic cleansing" must be accommodated, as if God turns a blind cultural eye from this "shameful but vital stage, one

[40] Ibid., 120.
[41] Ibid., 121, 124–25.

that was not to be repeated, and need never be repeated."[42] The fallacy of
this reasoning is exposed when we are then told,

> So those who see Jesus as the climax of God's revelation to the human race
> can never imagine him acting in the way that Joshua did. It is inconceivable
> that Jesus would have taken up weapons to attack the Romans in the way
> that Joshua attacked the Canaanites.[43]

Jesus made it plain that His first coming was to save and not judge (John
12:47). Even then His wrath occasionally erupted (Matt 21:12–13; 23:1–
33). But this in no way alters the fact that at His Second Coming He will
indeed "judge the world in righteousness" (Acts 17:31), that is, with "flam-
ing fire dealing out retribution to those who do not know God" (2 Thess
1:7–8), at which time men and women will call for rocks to "fall on us and
hide us from the face of the One seated on the throne and from the wrath
of the Lamb" (Rev 6:16). For this reason, progress of revelation *does not*
involve divine advance from moral tolerance of immoral ethnic cleansing
to its moral condemnation, otherwise God's holy consistency is compromised. Rather, progress of revelation leads us from the moral rightness of
Joshua's campaigns according to divine mandate in an earthly sphere to the
moral rightness of Jesus Christ's campaign against sin in the human soul by
means of justification and judgment.

In conclusion, the anti-Judaic tone here, particularly in the writings of
Chapman and Sizer, betrays a deep-seated drive to nullify, at all costs, any
biblical validity claimed for the Jews and the modern State of Israel. Should
this theological end be accomplished, then the cause of the Palestinians
and Arabs could be pursued on a strictly secular, egalitarian basis due to
the elimination of supposed biblical claims. I strenuously maintain that
God, according to the good pleasure of His will, continues to regard Israel
after the flesh with favor according to elective grace that streams through
His distinctive covenantal regard for the Jews as beloved enemies (Rom
11:28). From a Christian perspective, election presupposes divine, particular, saving purpose directed toward sinful individuals (Rom 5:8). But
I maintain that God's elective regard for Israel rests on the same essential
gracious basis. One wonders how Chapman and Sizer cope with the priority that Paul continuously gave to the Jews throughout his Gentile ministry (Rom 1:16; 2:9–10), though no explanation is given. Was this divine
racism? Such a perspective is in no way intended to justify every military

---

[42] Ibid., 125.
[43] Ibid.

initiative of the State of Israel any more than the indiscriminate terrorism of the Arab/Palestinian *intifada*. Nevertheless, I do believe that the loving Pauline tone of distinctive regard for the Jews, even in unbelief, finds its antithesis in the anti-Judaic tone of Chapman and Sizer which so obviously conflicts with the apostle's indefatigable interest.

Furthermore, Chapman and Sizer plainly regard with disfavor the considerable role that Britain and America have played in the formation, maintenance, and prosperity of the State of Israel. Seeming to have more the spirit of Sanballat and Tobiah, they are obviously displeased that anyone should "seek the well-being of the Israelites [lit. 'sons of Israel']" (Neh 2:10). The biased tone here is unmistakable. Chapman and Sizer appear to wish that modern Israel had never been established because it was a wholly carnal endeavor to begin with without any biblical justification. It is not surprising to find intimations of their desire that this development should be reversed. There is constant niggling against the present support that America supplies. Yet should this nullification prevail, who can tell what horror might then result in terms of Arab attempts at the fulfillment of their stated goal, namely, the ethnic cleansing of Palestine. Does Sizer have this in mind when he suggests the possibility of "another exile on the horizon rather than a restoration."[44] Is this wishful thinking? The tone here certainly suggests preference for the severe condemnation of the law to fall on Israel, quite apart from any prospect of grace; on the other hand, grace should be showered on the Palestinians by means of substantial land reclamation.

Overall, it is difficult to avoid the conclusion that Chapman and Sizer have an intractable, theological aversion to modern Judaism and the State of Israel. Whether there is consideration of the land, Jerusalem, or even the OT, at best we have here a legacy of shadows that, while remaining memorable, is yet hardly of substantial importance. What counts is the absorption, indeed reformation, of these figures and patterns into the reality of Jesus Christ. There is a relentless effort to nullify Jewish identity, nationality, and territory, except where these terms are reinterpreted according to their NT and ecclesiological hermeneutic. However, notwithstanding a subtle appropriation of Jewish terminology, a token portrayal of interest in Jews as individuals, and the beguiling claim of being christocentric, I reemphasize the belief that this whole approach is nothing more than a revision of historic Augustinian eschatology. As such, I also believe it is

---

[44] Cornell, Sizer Debate, *Whose Promised Land: Israel and Biblical Prophecy*, http://www.christchurch-virginiawater.co.uk/articles/debate.html (cited May 2007).

not only biblically and theologically flawed but also ethically wanting as a consequence. In particular, the focus on being exclusively christocentric in fact necessitates a dual rather than a singular hermeneutic. That is, there is broad agreement that the NT should be interpreted by means of a literal, grammatical, historical, contextual hermeneutic whereby the person of Christ is expounded from the text. However, we are also told that this hermeneutic is not to be consistently applied to the OT as well. Rather, according to Augustinianism, a distinctive Christocentric method of interpretation is to be applied whereby the OT is understood strictly through a Christocentric and New Covenant lens. The result is, as Willem VanGemeren perceptively stated,

> the "new" Reformed hermeneutic is no longer "the Old is in the New revealed and the New is in the Old concealed," but rather "the Old is by the New restricted and the New is on the Old inflicted."[45]

Next we look at the issue of Zionism in greater detail, both historically and with regard to a Christian perspective. Then in chapters 6 and 7 we will concentrate on this vital matter of hermeneutics as it relates to the interpretation of the OT in the light of the NT, but especially with regard to Israel.

---

[45] W. A. VanGemeren, "Israel as the Hermeneutical Crux in the Interpretation of Prophecy," *WTJ*, 46 (1984), 268.

Chapter 5

ISRAEL AND CHRISTIAN ENCOUNTER WITH ZIONISM

The denigration of modern Judaism, especially its national and territorial Zionist aspirations, go hand in hand with sympathy for the cause of the Arab states, being predominantly Muslim, and particularly a national Palestinian agenda. One only has to read Colin Chapman, Stephen Sizer, Kenneth Cragg, Naim Ateek, and Donald Wagner.[1] It is not simply that their theology is Augustinian whereby the Christian Church is the new spiritual Israel, though it is decidedly that, but rather they plainly side with and regularly conference with both Christian and Muslim Palestinians while at the same time incessantly censuring modern Israel at every hand. All are guilty of a nominal, minimalist regard for Israel, based more on pragmatic, status quo social standards rather than abiding biblical principles. For instance, there will be acceptance of the need for Israel to have a national home somewhere, perhaps according to the 1948 borders established by the United Nations. But this is merely a concession to the existing state of affairs that usually abides more passionately with Arab and Muslim demands that ultimately have in mind the total elimination of national Israel from Palestine.

A classic example of the foregoing is the Fifth International Sabeel Conference held in Jerusalem, 2004, directed by Naim Ateek, the theme being "Challenging Christian Zionism: Theology, Politics, and the Palestine-Israel Conflict." The featured speaker was Stephen Sizer, and other presenters included Donald Wagner and Gary Burge. The Conference also met in Ramallah for a day and consulted there with terrorist Yasser Arafat under confinement. The whole aura here was incessantly anti-Judaic and pro-Palestinian, with the official Sabeel Conference Statement declaring:

> Christian Zionism is a modern theological and political movement that embraces the most extreme ideological positions of Zionism, thereby becoming

[1] Naim Ateek is referenced later in this chapter, as well as in appendix D. In this volume there is minimal reference to Donald D. Wagner, professor of religion and Middle Eastern studies at North Park University in Chicago, also director of the Center for Middle Eastern Studies. His supercessionist, anti-Judaic bent is plainly evident, especially in his *Anxious for Armageddon* (Scottdale, Pa.: Herald Press, 1995) and *Dying in the Land of Promise: Palestine and Palestinian Christianity from Pentecost to 2000* (London: Melisende, 2001). Not surprisingly, Stephen Sizer confesses his indebtedness to Wagner for inspiration in *Christian Zionism*, 14.

detrimental to a just peace within Palestine and Israel. The Christian
Zionist program provides a worldview where the Gospel is identified with
the ideology of empire, colonialism, and militarism. In its extreme form,
it places an emphasis on apocalyptic events leading to the end of history
rather than living Christ's love and justice today. We also repudiate the more
insidious form of Christian Zionism pervasive in the mainline churches that
remains silent in the face of the Israeli occupation of Palestine. Therefore,
we categorically reject Christian Zionist doctrines as a false teaching that
undermines the biblical message of love, mercy, and justice.[2]

Not unrelated to his attitude, by way of Arab association, is the comment
of David Shipler:

For the Arabs, the word "Zionism" has an ugly connotation that stirs up
deep revulsion and dread, with overtones as heavy as those that "commu-
nism" carries for many Americans. "'Zionist,' in Arabic is like 'Nazi,' one
Arab explained. "Since I was a child I have heard that the word Zionist is
the worst. I didn't understand the meaning of it, I just thought Zionist was
like criminal, thief, killer.[3]

Nevertheless, "Zion" is in the Bible a noble term, found there 161 times
(seven of those in the NT). For instance,

The LORD of hosts says this: I am extremely jealous for Zion; I am jealous
for her with great wrath" (Zech 8:2).
The Liberator will come from Zion; He will turn away godlessness from
Jacob" (Rom 11:26).

So what is this "Zionism" as a historic development that is especially derided in its Christian manifestation?

The Foundation of Zionism

When David became king over all Israel, "The king and his men
marched to Jerusalem against the Jebusites [Canaanites] who inhabited the
land. . . . Yet David did capture the stronghold of Zion, the city of David"
(2 Sam 5:6–7). More specifically, it was a citadel on the southeastern hill
within Jerusalem, being most suitable for fortified defense against enemies.
Here David's palace was also built. Supremely it was "the City of the LORD,
Zion of the Holy One of Israel" (Isa 60:14). Later the title Zion incorporated
the adjoining temple region (Ps 20:2), then Jerusalem overall (Isa 10:12).
This Zion then became acknowledged as the capital of the land of Israel

---

[2] Sabeel, Ecumenical Theology Center, Jerusalem, http://www.sabeel.org/documents/
5thConfStatementfinal.htm (accessed May 2007).

[3] D. K. Shipler, *Arab and Jew* (New York: Times Books, 1986), 70.

(Isa 66:8; Joel 2:18,21; Zech 2:10–12). Even after the War of Independence in 1948, for 19 years Arab Jordan did not allow Jews from Israel to have access to the Old City of Jerusalem. However, prior to the Six-Day War of 1967 when Israel eventually captured the Old City of Jerusalem, it had not been freely inhabited by the Jews since the Maccabean/Hasmonean revolt against the Seleucids. A hundred hears after the temple was cleansed and rededicated in 164 BC, Pompey of Rome captured Jerusalem (63 BC). The land of Israel continued to be heavily populated by Jews until the destruction of Jerusalem in AD 70 by Titus and again in 135 by Emperor Hadrian (although even after that a remnant continued living in the land, especially in the north). Following the resultant Jewish dispersion or Diaspora that the OT had prophesied (see Lev 26:32–33; Deut 4:27–28; 28:64–68; Ezek 22:15; 36:18–20; Zech 7:14; Luke 21:24), the perennial prayer of the Jews, whatever their scattered and downtrodden circumstances, has been the prayer at the conclusion of the Passover Seder, "Next year in Jerusalem." This heartfelt religious longing became embodied in the expression "Zionism," that is, the collective Jewish passion for free reestablishment in the land of Israel as a Jewish nation. Not surprisingly, when the Old City of Jerusalem was recaptured during the Six-Day War in 1967, Rabbi Goren blew his shofar or ram's horn trumpet at the wailing wall "in Zion" (see Jer 4:5; Joel 2:1,15) and proclaimed, "I, General Shlomo Goren, chief rabbi of the Israel Defense Forces, have come to this place never to leave it again."[4]

The Remnant of Israel

Being wholly evacuated from Jerusalem, Jews retreated westward to Jabneh and northward to Galilee and to many rural villages within Israel. The surprising result was an increase in and consolidation of Jewish literature, including the eventual compilation of the Mishnah and the completion of the Jerusalem Talmud. The synagogue also flourished. In spite of such intense devastation, even Jerusalem eventually saw the return of Jews to its fold, though with recurring episodes of humiliation. However, love for Zion never failed at home or abroad. In spite of great suffering, there were always returnees who built up the periodically diminishing remnant.

---

[4] M. B. Oren, *Six Days of War* (New York: Oxford, 2002), 246.

The Exile of Zionism

The Scattering of Jews Following AD 135

Although Emperor Hadrian renamed Jerusalem as Aelia Capitolina and the land of Israel as Syria Palestina, or Palestine in AD 135, I generally prefer the more historic "land of Israel," and related Hebrew titles. This is more than a matter of ancient semantics. Contrary to widespread misunderstanding, as Bernard Lewis has explained,

> From the end of the Jewish state in antiquity to the beginning of British rule, the area now designated by the name Palestine was not a country and had no frontiers, only administrative boundaries; it was a group of provincial subdivisions, by no means always the same, within a larger entity.
>
> With the British conquest in 1917–18 and the subsequent establishment of a mandated territory in the conquered areas, Palestine became the official name of a definite territory for the first time since the Middle Ages. To begin with, this designation was acceptable neither to Jews nor to Arabs. From the Jewish point of view . . . the very associations . . . were hateful. . . . For Arabs, . . . there was no such thing as a country called Palestine. The region which the British called Palestine was merely a separated part of a larger whole. For a long time organized and articulate Arab political opinion was virtually unanimous at this point.[5]

James Parkes made the same point even more comprehensively:

> During all this period of two thousand years, Palestine was not even a name on the political map of the world. It was a portion of a larger province, whether Roman, Byzantine, Arab or Turkish; and its people were never conscious of themselves as a national unit, nor did they ever attempt, as they had done in early and later Israelite days, to form an independent kingdom. During the long period of Islamic rule, with its kaleidoscopic changes of dynasty, no claimant to the throne of the caliphs, or even to a separate identity, ever emerged from the Palestinian population. It was the alternative prey of dynasties ruling from Damascus, Baghdad, Cairo or Istanbul. Only in the twentieth century has it resumed a separate identity, and that by the will of outsiders rather than of the majority of its own population; and the result has been conflict, uncertainty and one of the most delicate and difficult problems of modern international politics.[6]

[5] B. Lewis, "The Palestinians and the PLO," *Commentary*, January, 1975, 32–33. Stephen Sizer is either evasive or ignorant of the essential truth here and, without a shred of evidence to the contrary, castigates Dave Hunt who similarly, though more bluntly, states, "There never was a Palestinian people, nation, language, culture, or religion. The claim of descent from a Palestinian people who lived for thousands of years in a land called Palestine is a hoax." *Christian Zionism*, 244–45.

[6] J. Parkes, *A History of Palestine from 135 A.D. to Modern Times* (New York: Oxford, 1949),

Furthermore, granted that successive possession of the land of Israel was by Roman, Byzantium, Islam, Crusader, Mamluk, Ottoman, and British invasion, this in no way invalidated the covenanted bestowal of this territory on the seed of Abraham, Isaac, and Jacob. Nevertheless, the scattered people of Israel not only suffered this judgment from God as promised, but also endured such discipline throughout the four corners of the earth.

Jerusalem under Roman Dominion (AD 135–330)

The savage suppression of nationalism by Rome nevertheless brought a measure of stability, even Herodian glory. Then Jewish-born Christianity expanded in parallel with increasing Christian anti-Judaism and Gentile dominance; consequently, to begin with, it fled Jerusalem because of militant Jewish opposition (Acts 8:1). But its flourishing influence did much to gradually purge Palestine of imposed Roman paganism. The growing rift with Judaism became more established until a dominant Gentile church existed in Jerusalem. Notwithstanding the diminished Jewish population, two Roman emperors looked more favorably toward Judaism and Christianity during the Severan Dynasty of 193–235. Then Emperor Constantine's embrace of Christianity in 312 resulted in the construction of churches in Bethlehem, Jerusalem, the region of Hebron, and on the Mount of Olives. At the same time Jews continued to inhabit the land of Israel and periodically revolted for the cause of Zion against continuing iron-fisted imperialism. Nevertheless there was an easing by Rome of some former strictures, such as concerning formerly banned circumcision.[7]

Jerusalem under Byzantium Dominion (AD 330–640)

Outside the walls of Rome just prior to its conquest in 312, Constantine is reputed to have seen in the sky a vision of a cross bearing the inscription, "In this [cross], conquer!" He founded Constantinople in 330 as the "New Rome," and it became the capital of the Byzantine Empire and therefore controlling center of Christianity. The Eastern Roman Empire administered Palestine until the Arab conquest. While Christian prosperity enhanced Jerusalem, there were no Jewish residents there until the Roman Empress Eudocia (394–460) granted permission. Then throughout the Roman Empire the patriarchal house of Hillel was accepted as the

13. Indebtedness to this work concerning much that follows is readily acknowledged.

[7] J. Parkes, *Whose Land? A History of the Peoples of Palestine* (London: Penguin, 1970), 42; J. G. Gager, *The Origins of Anti-Semitism* (New York: Oxford, 1983), 55–66.

supreme authority for the Jewish community. Jerome of Bethlehem wrote of a few Christians and a predominance of Jews, yet by the seventh century the Jewish population of Palestine had dwindled to under 250,000. This decline paralleled an increasing intolerance of Jews and Samaritans by Christianity, as evidenced by the legal prohibition against building synagogues. The Persian invasion of Palestine (611–614) involving the massacre of Christians, perhaps aided by Jews in the north who hoped for greater autonomy, was short-lived. Desolation and ruin became widespread throughout the land. Under Heraclius Rome recaptured Palestine in 629, and the Jews themselves experienced a bloody massacre. Yet at this very same time, Muhammad conquered Mecca, and in 640 he also captured Caesarea and ended Byzantine rule.[8]

Jerusalem under Islamic Dominion (AD 640–1099)

Following the conquest of Persia, Syria, and Egypt, the Islamist Arabian pall eventually covered all the Middle East. In Palestine the Christian majority and Jewish minority endured subjection as *dhimis,* that is, Christians and Jews who though not Muslims were considered people of an inferior, superseded revelation and thereby were granted fewer rights under Islamic law than Muslims, though more than other less submissive non-Muslims. They paid heavy taxes, retained their churches and synagogues, but were not allowed to erect new buildings. Their social presence was required to appear subdued, and of course proselytizing was forbidden. In 691 the Dome of the Rock was built on the temple area in Jerusalem, becoming the third most holy shrine in Islam. Compared with earlier Eastern Orthodox and Roman oppression, the Jews, though small in numbers, indicated preference for their Arab overlords.

> Nevertheless, we have evidence that Jews lived in all parts of the country and on both sides of the Jordan, and that they dwelt in both the towns and villages, practicing both agriculture and various handicrafts. During the seventh and eighth centuries Tiberias continued to be their center; but some Jews began to return to Jerusalem shortly after the Moslem conquest in spite of the fact that in the original negotiations for the surrender of the city, the [Eastern Orthodox] Christians had wished to insist that no Jews should be admitted to it. At first Jews lived in the southern quarter near the Wailing Wall. . . . At some period they purchased the slopes of the Mount of Olives facing the Temple, and there used to be a considerable pilgrimage to this spot at the chief festivals, especially at the Feast of Tabernacles.[9]

[8] Parkes, *Whose Land?* 42–61.
[9] Ibid., 72–73.

Surely at those times, before the vista of Zion and the temple mount, there was a great lament: "There we sat down and wept, when we remembered Zion. . . . If I forget you, Jerusalem, may my right hand forget its skill. May my tongue stick to the roof of my mouth if I do not remember you, if I do not exalt Jerusalem as my greatest joy" (Ps 137:1,5–6). Nevertheless, vigorous spiritual life was productive of the completion of the Jerusalem Talmud as well as the Hebrew Masoretic text of the OT that remains the standard for today.

Muslim Arab rule was then from Damascus, but sectarian conflict, such as between the Shiites and Sunnis, resulted in civil war and instability within Palestine.

> It was now but a remote and unimportant province; and though strong rulers might suppress insurrection, yet tribal disorders and Bedouin raids might at any time make life insecure for Muslims as well as Jews and Christians.[10]

Now earlier toleration for Muslim rule began to wane. Synagogues and Christian churches were periodically destroyed, though an annual mercantile fair still survived in Jerusalem from Byzantine times. At the end of the tenth century, the Fatmid dynasty became the new conqueror of Palestine as well as Syria, tracing its descent from the daughter of Muhammad. A period of toleration was followed by further destruction of synagogues and churches, even the Church of the Holy Sepulchre, which especially aroused animosity in Europe and thus triggered the first Crusade. Yet again peace followed, then unrest and the challenge of Turkish invaders. Even Jewish sectarianism became more vigorous with the Babylonian Talmud now supplanting the Jerusalem Talmud. Even so the whole population was beginning to speak Arabic, and certainly a majority residing in Palestine was now Muslim.

Jerusalem under Crusader Dominion (AD 1099–1187)

The call to crusade for the cause of the holy land was instigated by the papacy in response to the Byzantine emperor facing the threat of advancing Seljuk Turks. Christians also desired more open access to Palestine. The first Crusade captured Jerusalem in 1099, during which most of the Muslims and Jews in Jerusalem were slaughtered. As a result a medieval structure was imposed including military orders of knights, impressive castles, and prosperous tourism. But neither the Muslims nor the Jews, the

[10] Ibid., 75.

representation of the latter having already been weakened, were allowed to reside in Jerusalem. Both entities thrived in the surrounding regions, but

> when a brilliant soldier of Kurdish origin, Salah ed-Din (Saladin), came to rule over both Syria and Egypt, the end of the European interlude was inevitable. . . . For the Jews a return or migration to Europe offered no attraction. They stayed, to share and suffer from the disorder which followed the disappearance of the crusader's feudalism.[11]

The anti-Semitic King Richard I came on a third Crusade to rescue the situation. Although he was within sight of Jerusalem, his weakened position led to a truce with Saladin. He then retreated homeward to England.

Jerusalem under Mamluk Dominion (AD 1187–1453)

A mamluk was a slave soldier, often a Turk, who converted to Islam and served the Sunni Ayyubid dynasty of Saladin. They eventually sacked Jerusalem, massacring most of the Christians and looting the Church of the Holy Sepulchre. There followed a line of mamluk sultans that captured the crusader sea ports and the knights' castles. An attempted Cypriot crusade further ravaged the coast of Syria and Palestine. In revenge the mamluks closed the Church of the Holy Sepulchre for five years. European trade sanctions were ventured but failed. Hence the land presents a sad picture of decline. Jerusalem became unwalled, though both the Dome of the Rock and the El Aksa Mosque were adorned and preserved. But Christian churches, along with synagogues, fell into decay or were confiscated. Muslim opposition became more fanatical, leading to imprisonment and torture. Franciscan settlement in Palestine, involving suffering and heroism, led to some gains including land on Mount Zion and the room where the Last Supper of Jesus was reputed to have been held. Their accumulating wealth gained some security through bribery. The Jews endeavored to buy the site of David's tomb, which led to loss for the Franciscans. The Eastern churches also suffered, though heavy taxation impoverished most Christians, as well as the Jews. The wealthy among the Dispersion became more devoted to support of their bethren in Zion. Some 300 Jewish immigrants settled in Acre on the coast in 1211. Then the aged scholar Nachmanides, commonly known as Ramban, fled Spain and settled in Jerusalem where he revived synagogue life. Many more Jews came from Spain following the persecution of 1391. Another scholar even respected by the Muslims, Obadiah ben Abraham of Bertinoro, arrived in 1488, estab-

---

[11] Ibid., 99.

lished a significant rabbinical college in Jerusalem, and testified to tolerable Arab treatment of the Jews. Nevertheless, northern and western areas suffered impoverishment; particularly galling was the Muslim imposition of their shrines upon Jewish OT sites.

> This penetration of Islam into what had previously been Jewish or Christian sites had this justification—or at least explanation: that it is during the Mamluk period that it first becomes possible to speak of The Land as a primarily Muslim country. During the first century and a half of the Arab period the Christian and Jewish communities certainly constituted the majority of the population. . . . But during the Mamluk centuries both Jewish and Christian communities suffered tremendous losses through conditions which made life intolerable. . . . There is nothing improbable in the estimate that the two and a half centuries of their [Mamluk] power cost the country two thirds of its population.[12]

Jerusalem under Turkish Ottoman Dominion (1453–1918)

In 1453 Constantinople fell to the siege of King Mehmed, ruler of the Ottoman sultans, who made this prize the capital of his huge Turkish empire that soon included all the Middle East yet extended to Greece, Persia, and North Africa. The Mamluk Empire was now in full decay. Jerusalem, Gaza, Nablus, Sidon, and Beirut now came under the authority of Ottoman Damascus. In need of a southern fortress, Sultan Suleiman the Magnificent (1520–1566) rebuilt the walls of Jerusalem, even as they surround the Old City today. A resultant feudal system that imposed harsh taxation and even more harsh penalties, experienced initial glory, yet the inherent seeds of corruption and tribal conflict led to progressive decline in a self-fulfilling spiral. Within Palestine a falling population led to nomadic abuse and in turn greater wasteland, especially when compared with former agricultural prosperity. One debauched and cruel sultan ordered the massacre of all non-Muslim subjects, though intervention by Muslim authorities prevailed. During the seventeenth century several rulers governed more by terror over the regions of Galilee, though in being challenged, the ensuing conflict brought more misery to the land. During the eighteenth century this tribal conflict continued, which necessitated the extraction of ever larger sums from peasants to finance such conflicts. In one instance, Ramleh, Gaza, and Jaffa revolted against this increased tax burden.

---

[12] Ibid., 113–114.

In 1770 the Mamluk ruler of Egypt took steps to invade Syria. With some intrigue, he was eventually successful in capturing Damascus. Yet on returning to Egypt he was expelled; returning yet again, he was seized and killed by a rival. Such was the ceaseless tension of those times in the midst of a most unhappy empire, full of extortion, lacking in security. The ruler of Sidon, "the butcher," was renowned for his avarice and cruelty. Nevertheless, the Turkish reign provided more opportunities for the Jewish than for the Christian population. Some "Marronos" Christians expelled from Spain, that is, converts of coercion and convenience, were encouraged to immigrate, though others from Europe also came. Then,

> the Jewish community under the Turks passed from a very rapid and bril-
> liant expansion, during which the land became for a brief while again
> the center of the whole Jewish world, to almost as rapid and catastrophic
> decline.[13]

The cause was not only due to distinction between the Sephardic and Ashkenazic Jewish communities in Palestine, but also the persecution and suffering they endured because of the indifference of Turkish rulers to incessant local conflict. This led to greater poverty and desolation than was experienced under the Mamluks. Even travellers' accounts testified to the wilderness existence that had now come about.

Certainly eighteenth century Europe had not the slightest interest in securing, let alone enhancing, the monolithic Turkish empire. Further, the expansion of Russia and then Great Britain presented a new challenge to the Middle East. Yet a further rising contestant on the horizon concerned the expansionist ambitions of Napoleon Bonaparte, and especially his conquest of Egypt and Syria. But he was defeated by Nelson at the Battle of the Nile. Entering coastal Palestine, Napoleon reached as far as Acre and then was forced to retreat, having never approached Jerusalem. Further retreat to Europe ended in his defeat at Waterloo. Thus the land sank back into obscurity, including rivalry within the weakening Turkish dominion. A new and independent-minded sultan in Egypt, Mehmet Ali, favored the French, drove out the British, and instituted a totalitarian regime. Then, along with his son, Ibrahim, in ambitiously moving northward, he captured Gaza, Jaffa, Jerusalem, Acre, and Damascus. After Ali threatened to take Constantinople, Russia came to the rescue and forced Ali's eventual retreat back to Egypt. Nevertheless Egyptian rule had opened Palestine to western visitors, including British and American missionary societies, re-

---

[13] Ibid., 128–29.

sulting in biblical research. Ibrahim also received consuls in Jerusalem, first from Great Britain, then France, Prussia, Sardinia, and America. Then a rabbi was recognized for Russian and Austrian Jews. An English bishop was sent out jointly by England and Prussia, as well as a patriarch from Rome, by means of which the interests of Jews and Christians were better suited, even if they did continue to be at unrest with each other. In 1852 the sultan decreed that competing claims to holy places be established as the *status quo*, and at least in this area some peace prevailed.

In 1870 reformer Midhat Pasha established a more representative form of government for the empire, a Turkish parliament, but only for some months until the reign of the evil tyrant Abdul Hamid commenced. His redistribution of Syria, hence the land, led to the independent territory of Jerusalem. Through his becoming friends with the German Kaiser, Jerusalem sprouted several notable German and Lutheran edifices. But Hamid's oppression led to his overthrow by the idealistic, reforming "Young Turks," offering centralized government, even for the non-Muslim and non-Turkish population, as well as equal participation in Turkish political life. Yet the Arabs wanted no such change. Thus with the outbreak of the World War I in 1914 Turkey aligned itself with Germany, this being a decision of momentous importance. Indeed British Prime Minister Herbert Asquith prophetically declared that "the Turkish empire has committed suicide."[14] Jewish Zionist leaders in Europe were well aware of the potential this turn of events presented, and Palestine was soon in turmoil as many fled to Egypt. However, the bulk of the agricultural settlers stayed on the land. Hence the population in 1917, when the Balfour Declaration was issued, was between 85,000 and 100,000 Jews living in Palestine, out of a total population of 600.000.[15]

In Arab sections of the empire, there was by no means a sense of loyalty toward the disintegrating Turkish empire or toward Germany that hoped for participation in a *jihad*, a holy war against Britain. For this reason the Germans failed to win over the Arabs to their cause, whereas the British did so by giving assurances of their prospective independence in Syria, Arabia, and Mesopotamia (except for western Syria).[16] In 1916 the British crossed the Suez Canal against strong Turkish resistance and reached al-Arish. The

---

[14] P. Johnson, *A History of the Jews* (New York: Harper & Row Publishers, 1987), 423.

[15] Ibid., 241–250, 430.

[16] H. M. Sachar, *A History of Israel* (New York: Alfred Knopf, 1991), 92–93. Also Parkes, *Whose Land?* 253–54.

revolt of desert Arabs who found British assistance through T. E. Lawrence, was confronted with a scorched earth,

> a ruthless policy of oppression [by the Turks], which resulted in the deliberate destruction of houses, roads, fruit trees and crops, and the execution or imprisonment of considerable numbers of the population. . . . Nearly all the improvements of the previous fifty years were swept away. When the British entered Judea and Jerusalem they found a land on the brink of starvation, and for the first year of administration the feeding of the population, countrymen as well as townsmen, proved their most urgent task.[17]

Held back at Gaza, General Edmund Allenby took charge of the British Expeditionary Force which led to the rout of the Turks at Beersheba. Taking Jaffa, Allenby finally captured Jerusalem and on December 11, 1917, he marched bareheaded into the historic capital to address a gathering of Muslim, Christian, and Jewish notables on the steps of the Tower of David.

Jerusalem under British Dominion (1918)

By 1918 the end of Ottoman rule in Palestine at the same time raised the question of settlement for the recent Middle Eastern conquests of Britain and France. However, in anticipation of the capture of Jerusalem and the odd prospect of Berlin also making a pro-Zionist declaration, the Balfour Declaration had been composed a month before Allenby's formal entry into the Holy City, by means of which "the British Government gave the [European] Zionist enterprise formal recognition."[18] As the Foreign Secretary, Arthur James Balfour, of evangelical stock,

> had been nurtured on the Old Testament, and his extensive study of Jewish history had filled him with inner remorse about Christendom's treatment of the Jews. "They have been exiled, scattered and oppressed," he told [journalist] Harold Nicholson in 1917. "If we can find them an asylum, a safe home, in their native land, then the full flowering of their genius will burst forth and propagate."[19]

Guided by a draft statement that Balfour solicited from the Zionists, a final compromise declaration was approved:

> His Majesty's government views with favor the establishment in Palestine of a national home for the Jewish people, and will use their best endeavors

---

[17] Parkes, *Whose Land?* 190, 249.

[18] B. Lewis, *The Middle East* (New York: Simon & Schuster, 1995), 348.

[19] Sachar, *A History of Israel*, 106.

to facilitate the achievement of this object, it being clearly understood that nothing shall be done which may prejudice the civil and religious rights of existing non-Jewish communities in Palestine, or the rights and political status enjoyed by Jews in any other country.[20]

But James Parkes made some very telling comments concerning this historic document that clarify common misunderstanding:

> The Balfour Declaration for the first time established a unit called Palestine on the political map. But there were two essential elements in political realism which it could not create. In the first place the Jews, who had through all the centuries clung to their right to settle in the Holy Land, had been so reduced in numbers and importance that they were not a recognized and accepted presence to the rest of the population as were the Christians in Lebanon. In the second place, though the word 'Arab' was rapidly coming to be accepted as covering the indigenous inhabitants who spoke Arabic, independently of their religious or ethnic affiliation, there was no such thing historically as a 'Palestinian Arab,' and there was no feeling of unity among 'the Arabs' of this newly defined area. Hence the unfortunate phrase used to describe the majority of the population in the Declaration—'the non-Jewish communities'.
>
> The Balfour Declaration did not 'give Palestine to the Jews'. It recognized that here existed already a historic Jewish right, not *to* but *in* the country; and it promised to assist the Jewish people in its development in such a way that the other rights in the country were not endangered. It equally did not 'give away what belonged not to it but to the Arab people'; for it had already refused to recognize, also on historical grounds, that the Arab claim to be exclusive owners of the country was justified.[21]

So to Britain had fallen a responsibility of momentous proportions. To begin with, it seemed to grasp its calling with sharp insight born of its Christian heritage. Sad to say, the noble fulfillment of this vocation seemed to gradually wither. But notwithstanding a degree of apostasy, divine Providence would not be diverted from His vision.

The Birth of Zionism

The preceding historic turn of events also needs to be appreciated in terms of the founding Zionist movement in Europe that opportunely coalesced with the providential leadership in Britain of Lloyd George, Balfour, Allenby, Jan Smuts, and others.

---

[20] W. Laqueur and B. Rubin, *The Israel-Arab Reader* (New York: Penguin, 2001), 16.
[21] Parkes, *Whose Land?* 256–57.

The Shame of European Anti-Semitism

The heritage of Augustinian anti-Judaism has been detailed in chapter 2. Its arousal of Zionism during the late nineteenth century is beyond dispute. As already mentioned, Jewish hope of return to the land had remained undying. The dawning of modern Europe saw a fresh awakening of the Jew for *aliyah* (the right of return to the land) in response to new forms of hatred clothed in supposed enlightenment and social revolution. By way of material encouragement there was the philanthropy from England of Sir Moses Montefiore and Edmund de Rothschild in France. There was also Moses Hess in Germany who sought for the establishment of Jewish colonies in Palestine. Then Leon Pinsker in Russia first headed an illegal organization there named Lovers of Zion which encouraged immigration. Most significant was the vision of Lithuanian Eliezer Ben Yehuda who immigrated to Palestine in 1881 with the passionate vision to establish the Hebrew language there in the midst a polyglot population.

The Agency of Theodore Herzl

Theodore Herzl (1860–1904) is commonly acknowledged to be the visionary founder of modern political Zionism that led to the establishment of a Jewish state in Palestine. A secular Jew educated in the high culture of Vienna, Austria, having received a doctorate in law in 1884, Herzl's confrontation with European anti-Semitism led to the eventual conclusion that the only solution was the establishment of a distinct nation for this distinctive people. His journalistic coverage of the Dreyfus trial in Paris with its blatant revelation of anti-Semitism especially prompted him in this direction.

At first Herzl would consider any location, though he eventually concluded that only relocation in the land of Israel was a satisfactory solution. His pamphlet, *The Jewish State*, published in German in 1896, was catalytic in leading to the first Zionist Congress in Basle, Switzerland, in 1897. As a result, the World Zionist Organization was established with Herzl as its first elected president. Having died in 1904 with his dream unfulfilled, in 1949 his remains were transferred to a mountain in western Jerusalem which became Mount Herzl, and is today a major military cemetery.

Much of Herzl's remaining time was spent in courting world leaders, both Jewish and non-Jewish, with the goal of enlisting financial and political support for his dream of a Jewish state. Walter Laqueur wrote,

> He wanted to appeal to the Pope: help us against anti-Semitism and I in turn will lead a great movement amongst the Jews for voluntary and hon-

orable conversion to Christianity. . . . It was pointed out to Herzl that, all other considerations apart, the Pope would never receive him.[22]

But in 1904 he became acquainted with a Papal Count, B. Lippay, who assured Herzl that should he visit Rome, he could arrange an audience with Pope Pius X. In a short while, such a meeting was arranged, and the following account of this meeting is taken from *The Diaries of Theodor Herzl* by Marvin Lowenthal. The relevance of the conversation that took place between this secular Jew and a professed world Christian leader will become obvious.

In an early entry of Herzl's diary there is an interesting confession in which, at the age of 35, he reflects upon his earlier encounter with Christianity:

> At first the Jewish question [of European anti-Semitism] vexed me bitterly. There was perhaps a time when I would have gladly slipped over into some corner of the Christian fold. But, in any case, this was only a faint vagary born of adolescent weakness. For I can say to myself with the honesty demanded by this diary—which would be utterly worthless if I played the hypocrite with myself—that I never thought seriously of becoming baptized or changing my name.[23]

In the light of this, it would not seem unreasonable to speculate what might have been the effect of Christianity upon Herzl had he grown up in a Gentile Christian society that had seriously taken into account the apostle Paul's admonition: "Do not brag that you are better than those [Jewish] branches [under discipline]. But if you do brag—you do not sustain the root, but the root sustains you. . . . Do not be arrogant, but be afraid" (Rom 11:18,20). But further, even as Herzl is now close to his judicial encounter with the Lord, how better it would have been that a more merciful, Christlike witness had been conveyed by the supposed vicar of Jesus Christ. How profoundly sad it is that a harsh and most un-Christlike witness was communicated. So Herzl records in his diary:

Rome. January 26, [1904].

> Yesterday I was with the Pope [Pius X]. . . . I arrived ten minutes ahead of time, and without having to wait I was conducted through a number of small reception rooms to the Pope.
>
> He received me standing and held out his hand, which I did not kiss. Lippay had told me I had to do it, but I didn't. I believe this spoiled my chances with him, for everyone who visits him kneels and at least kisses his

[22] W. Laqueur, *A History of Zionism* (New York: Schocken, 2003.), 88–89.

[23] M. Lowenthal, *The Diaries of Theodor Herzl* (New York: Grosset & Dunlap, 1962), 4–5.

hand. This hand kiss had worried me a great deal and I was glad when it was out of the way.

He seated himself in an armchair, a throne for minor affairs, and invited me to sit by his side. He smiled in kindly anticipation. I began:

Herzl: I thank Your Holiness for the favor of granting me this audience. [I begged him to excuse my miserable Italian, but he said:]

Pope: No, Signor Commander, you speak very well.

Herzl: [He is an honest, rough-hewn village priest, to whom Christianity has remained a living thing even in the Vatican. I briefly laid my request before him. But annoyed perhaps by my refusal to kiss his hand, he answered in a stern categorical manner.]

Pope: We are unable to favor this movement [of Zionism]. We cannot prevent the Jews from going to Jerusalem—but we could never sanction it. The ground of Jerusalem, if it were not always sacred, has been sanctified by the life of Jesus Christ. As the head of the Church I cannot answer you otherwise. The Jews have not recognized our Lord, therefore we cannot recognize the Jewish people.

Herzl: [The conflict between Rome and Jerusalem, represented by the one and the other of us, was once again under way. At the outset I tried to be conciliatory. I said my little piece. . . . It didn't greatly impress him. Jerusalem was not to be placed in Jewish hands.] And its present status, Holy Father?

Pope: I know, it is disagreeable to see the Turks in possession of our Holy Places. We simply have to put up with it. But to sanction the Jewish wish to occupy these sites, that we cannot do.

Herzl: [I said that we based our movement solely on the sufferings of the Jews, and wished to put aside all religious issues].

Pope: Yes, but we, but I as the head of the Catholic Church, cannot do this. One of two things will likely happen. Either the Jews will retain their ancient faith and continue to await the Messiah whom we believe has already appeared—in which case they are denying the divinity of Jesus and we cannot assist them. Or else they will go there with no religion whatever, and then we can have nothing at all to do with them.

The Jewish faith was the foundation of our own, but it has been superseded by the teachings of Christ, and we cannot admit that it still enjoys any validity.[24] The Jews who should have been the first to acknowledge Jesus Christ have not done so to this day.

Herzl: [It was on the tip of my tongue to remark, "It happens in every family: no one believes in his own relative." But, instead, I said:] Terror and persecution were not precisely the best means for converting the Jews. [His reply had an element of grandeur in its simplicity:]

[24] Here unrelenting supercessionist theology is plainly upheld as the norm of the Roman Catholic Church. Further, this confession, along with the whole tone of the Pope in his meeting with Herzl, indicates the perpetuation of a doctrinal emphasis that has resulted in centuries of degrading behavior toward the Jews.

Pope: Our Lord came without power. He came in peace. He persecuted no one. He was abandoned even by his apostles. It was only later that he attained stature. It took three centuries for the Church to evolve. The Jews therefore had plenty of time in which to accept his divinity without duress or pressure. But they chose not to do so, and they have not done it yet.[25]

Herzl: But, Holy Father, the Jews are in a terrible plight. I do not know if Your Holiness is aware of the full extent of their tragedy. We need a land for these harried people.

Pope: Must it be Jerusalem?

Herzl: We are not asking for Jerusalem, but for Palestine—for only the secular land.

Pope: We cannot be in favor of it.

Herzl: Does Your Holiness know the situation of the Jews?

Pope: Yes, from my days in Mantua, where there are Jews. I have always been in friendly relations with Jews. Only the other evening two Jews were here to see me. There are other bonds than those of religion: social intercourse, for example, and philanthropy. Such bonds we do not refuse to maintain with the Jews. Indeed we also pray for them, that their spirit see the light. This very day the Church is celebrating the feast of an unbeliever who became converted in a miraculous manner—on the road to Damascus. And so if you come to Palestine and settle your people there, we will be ready with churches and priests to baptize all of you.[26]

Herzl: [At this point Count Lippay had himself announced. The Pope bade him be admitted. The Count kneeled, kissed his hand, and joined in the conversation by telling of our "miraculous" meeting in the Bauer beer-hall at Venice. The miracle was that he had originally intended to stay overnight in Padua, and instead, it turned out that he was given to hear me express the wish to kiss the Holy Father's foot.

At this the Pope made no movement, for I hadn't even kissed his hand. Lippay proceeded to tell how I had expiated on the noble qualities of Jesus Christ. The Pope listened, and now and then took a pinch of snuff and sneezed into a big red cotton handkerchief. It is these peasant touches which I like about him best and which most of all compel my respect.

[25] This response has the "grandeur" of total avoidance of what Herzl had intimated, namely, that the abusive reputation of Roman Catholicism toward the Jews was unlikely to foster conversion. Further, if "it took three centuries for the Church to evolve," it was that very same period of time that it took for the Church to consolidate and launch its thrust of anti-Semitism through the following centuries.

[26] This would not have impressed Herzl, especially since he would have been well aware of the notorious kidnapping of a six-year-old Jewish boy from his home in Bologna, Italy, by the Roman Catholic authorities in 1858. The reason was that since a Gentile nurse had secretly "baptized" Edgardo Mortara as a baby, the Church determined that he had to be brought up under a Roman Catholic environment. The prior Pope Pius IX was deeply complicit in this whole sordid affair that attained to world-wide notoriety. Refer to D. I. Kertzer, *The Kidnapping of Edgardo Mortara* (New York: Alfred Knopf, 1997).

Lippay, it would appear, wanted to account for his introducing me, and perhaps ward off a word of reproach. But the Pope said:]

Pope: On the contrary, I am glad you brought me the Signor Commendatore.

Herzl: [As to the real business, he repeated what he had told me, until he dismissed us:]

Pope: Not possible!

Herzl: [Lippay stayed on his knees for an unconscionable time and never seemed to tire of kissing his hand. It was apparent that this was what the Pope liked. But on taking leave, I contented myself with shaking his hand warmly and bowing deeply. The audience lasted about twenty-five minutes.

While spending the last hour in the Raphael gallery, I saw a picture of an Emperor kneeling before a seated Pope and receiving the crown from his hands. That's how Rome wants it.][27]

When Chaim Weizmann visited Rome in 1922, his several concerned enquiries—up to the level of Cardinal Gaspari, with regard to Vatican opposition to the Zionist movement—remained unrelieved.[28]

The British Encouragement of Zionism

During the nineteenth century, Great Britain witnessed not only widespread evangelistic and missionary outreach through the agency of Anglican and nonconformist Christianity, but also an intensity of biblical ministry that focused on outreach to the Jews with parallel eschatological concern. Consider the formation of the Church Missionary Society (1799, Anglican), the London Society for Promoting Christianity amongst the Jews (1809, Anglican), the Free Church of Scotland Jewish Mission, (1840, Presbyterian), and the British Society for the Propagation of the Gospel amongst the Jews (1842, non-denominational).

Providence in British Millennial Fervor

During this same period, historic, pro-Judaic premillennialism and post-millennialism were equally concerned with the future consummation of the age in relation to the glorious personal, bodily return of Jesus Christ. In the main, both perspectives anticipated a climactic mass conversion of Jews along with their restoration as a nation to the land of Israel. Then there erupted a premillennial subset called dispensationalism, under the

---

[27] Lowenthal, *The Diaries of Theodor Herzl*, 427–30.

[28] C. Weizmann, *Trial and Error* (London: East and West Library, 1950), 284–86.

leadership of John Nelson Darby and Benjamin Wills Newton, which proposed a more specific formulation of future events with regard to the return of Jesus Christ and the relationship between Israel and the Church. In all this there was a Judeo-centric focus that laid a significant foundation for integration of prophetic Bible truth with political events, but especially the secular European Zionist movement. In this regard, and allied with the aforementioned missionary outreach, there was a considerable number of prominent evangelical pastors and leaders who in a variety of ways, and broadly speaking, expressed millennial expectations with regard to the destiny of the Jews and the restoration of national Israel. They included Charles Simeon, Lord Palmerston, the Earl of Shaftsbury, Bishop Edward Bickersteth, British chaplain William Hechler of Vienna, Bishop J. C. Ryle, barrister Lewis Way, Horatius Bonar, and C. H. Spurgeon, and many others. As the British Foreign Secretary, Lord Palmerston had written to the British Ambassador in Constantinople as early as 1840 so that he might encourage the Sultan to allow the migration of Jews to Palestine.

Providence in British Political Fervor and Beyond

The vastness of the British Empire and its pervasive Christian heritage during the nineteenth century meant that a leavening effect was to be expected at both social and political levels. A biblical mindset was common in all aspects of English life. So a number of the leaders of the British government, including the military, most naturally approached the question of Palestine from a biblical perspective. For instance, the entry of victorious General Allenby into Jerusalem was regarded as an event of deep significance. But replacement and supercessionist theology now tends to disparage this and subsequent events that have resulted in an appointed Jewish homeland. Colin Chapman associates Zionism and its Christian devotees with implicit violence, racial discrimination, American hegemony, and misguided biblical fundamentalism.[29] In a similar vein, Stephen Sizer brings the accusations of colonialism, apartheid, Islamic demonization, and dubious, selective biblical exegesis. Moreover,

> the overall consequences of such uncritical support for the State of Israel, especially among American evangelicals who identify with Christian Zionism in larger numbers than in Britain, are inherently and pathologically destructive. [30]

[29] C. Chapman, *Whose Promised Land?* (Grand Rapids: Baker, 2002), 242–48, 262–66.
[30] S. Sizer, *Christian Zionism* (Leicester, England: Inter-Varsity, 2004), 202–53.

Gary Burge charges modern Israel with discrimination as an exclusivist state, the stealing of land and water, the destruction of homes and villages, human rights abuses, imprisonment and torture, street violence and religious compromise.[31]

Not surprisingly, Chapman, Sizer, and Burge (see chapters 3 and 4) in varying degrees attempt to dull the admirable shine of the leadership roles of Lloyd George, Arthur Balfour, and General Allenby, as well as Herzl and Weizmann, especially by means of the attribution of naiveté, secularism, cynicism, and intrigue rather than participation in authentic providential, covenantal oversight. But many events of that time and onward have indicated surprising circumstances that strongly suggest divine providence, in the midst of great conflict, that is difficult to discount.

The prompting of Herzl to seek a national home for the Jews due to the persecutory character of Europe, while being essentially secular, yet involved both remarkable circumstances and Christian encouragement. By way of providence, consider the following sequence of events recorded by Martin Gilbert:

> The Sixth [Zionist] Congress was held in Basle [August, 1903]. The idea of Uganda instead of Palestine, even as a temporary place of refuge, led to stormy arguments. . . . Herzl worked busily behind the scenes to win over [Max] Nordau and to secure a majority. He succeeded: 295 for the Uganda scheme, 175 against, and 99 abstentions. The Zionist movement was certainly split. . . . Then in July, at the early age of forty-four, Herzl died. He had been worn out by his frenetic, fevered, disputed labors and endless travels. . . . The Uganda scheme was finished; Herzl's death effectively killed it, and even the British government had lost its enthusiasm.[32]

In the same vein, and possibly due to the savage conflict between the British and the Jews toward the end of the World War II, there then came the death of President Roosevelt on April 12, 1945.

> In his last weeks he had turned anti-Zionist, following a meeting with King Ibn Saud after the Yalta Conference. The pro-Zionist presidential assistant, David Niles, later asserted: "There are serious doubts in my mind that Israel would have come into being if Roosevelt had lived."[33]

I have already referenced the fateful alignment of Turkey with Germany and the Axis powers at the commencement of World War I and the con-

---

[31] G. Burge, *Whose Land? Whose Promises?* (Cleveland, Ohio: The Pilgrim Press, 2003), 135–64.

[32] M. Gilbert. *Israel* (New York: William Morrow, 1998), 22.

[33] Johnson, *History of the Jews*, 525.

sequence of Britain conquering Ottoman Palestine. This was through the notable instrumentality of General Allenby. But what of providential espionage data he received from the NILI organization (whose initials in Hebrew means "The Eternal One of Israel Will Not Lie") under the bravery of Aaron and Sarah Aaronsohn?

"It was very largely the daring work of the young [Aaronsohn] spies . . . ," wrote Captain Raymond Savage, Allenby's deputy military secretary, "which enabled the brilliant Field-Marshall to accomplish his undertaking so effectively."[34]

At the same time in England, consider the Christian encouragement that came from the close acquaintance of Chaim Weizmann, a pivotal successor of Herzl, with

the nation's political leaders, including Lloyd George, Winston Churchill, and Lord Robert Cecil. His relationship with these men was further strengthened by a vital service he performed for the British Admiralty. In March of 1916, Weizmann was summoned to London to help solve the shortage of acetone, an ingredient in the naval explosive cordite. After two years of laboratory research, he accomplished the task by devising a special fermentation process.[35]

The timing of the issuance of the Balfour Declaration was in itself quite remarkable:

Even twelve months later it would not have been possible. As it was, Weizmann pulled the Zionists through a brief window of opportunity, fated never to open again.[36]

Then consider that shortly after this remarkable event,

In London, Lloyd George and Balfour thought they had taken advantage of the most odious war in human history at least to produce some benefit: to give the Jews a home. When Weizmann lunched with the Prime Minister on Armistice Day he found him reading the Psalms, in tears.[37]

But further, not all the Zionist leaders were wholly secular. At the critical Paris Peace Conference of 1919, with the Jewish delegation headed by Weizmann, another of the four representatives, Menachem Ussishkin

---

[34] Sachar, *A History of Israel*, 105.
[35] Ibid., 98.
[36] Johnson, *History of the Jews*, 430.
[37] Ibid., 431.

passionately spoke in Hebrew of the "God of Israel," on behalf of over one million Jews in Russia, as follows:

> Nowhere have we found rest for our weary spirit nor for our aching feet. Persecution, expulsion, cruel riots, unbroken distress—such have been our lot during all these generations in all the countries of the world, and in these very days—when the wielders of the world's destiny have proclaimed the liberation of the nations, the equality of the nations, and the self-determination of every separate nation—Russian Jewry, which I represent here, is undergoing fresh torrents of murder and rioting the like of which were never known even in the Middle Ages.
>
> For us there is no way out save to receive, under your authority and subject to your supervision, one secure place in the world where we shall be able to renew our own lives and revive the national and cultural tradition which has come down to us from ancient times, and where can that secure spot be save in out historic country? Throughout all these generations we have not ceased to yearn for it, but have prayed the God of Israel for our return thither. Not for a moment have we forsaken our God, our tongue and our culture.
>
> We let ourselves be slain for these possessions of ours rather than betray them. And on this very day I address you in our Hebrew tongue, the tongue of our kings and prophets which we have never forgotten. This tongue is bound up with all our national aspirations. At the beginning of the national revival in the Land of Israel, when we had barely begun our upbuilding work there, even before the war, we devoted our efforts to the revival of our language and our culture.[38]

Then there was Sir Arthur Wauchope, British High Commissioner (1931–1938), who was a Bible-reading Scott. In spite of later differences that arose due to the more anti-Mandate policies emanating from London, under his governance Weizmann attributed to him the greatest overall advance in Palestine.[39]

But further still, what shall we say of the remarkable preservation of Israel during five major wars, all of which threatened either national extermination or total expulsion from the land of Israel by means of the surrounding Arab nations? Consider just two of these victories. The War of Independence involved assaults and invasion from surrounding Lebanon, Syria, Iraq, Egypt, and the Transjordan Arab Legion, which formally commenced on May 15, 1948. This was the day after David Ben-Gurion, who was to become the first Israeli Prime Minister, declared the establishment of a Jewish State in Palestine. Early the next morning, on May 15, he broad-

---

[38] Gilbert, *Israel*, 41–42.
[39] Sachar, *A History of Israel*, 189; Chaim Weizmann, *Trial and Error*, 335.

cast to the US. As he spoke, the sound of Egyptian aircraft bombing Tel Aviv could clearly be heard. Furthermore, from the very beginning of this savage conflict, the leadership of the withdrawing British armed forces expressed itself in unequivocally hostile terms about the struggle of the Jewish population. Yet in spite of being disadvantaged in terms of personnel and equipment, victory was obtained by means of innovation and flexibility. Even so, it appeared that the fate of Israel hung precariously in the balance. It was saved by the great and historic leadership of Ben-Gurion leading a nation endowed with a desire to live and be prepared to make every sacrifice to achieve this end.[40]

The Six Day War was prompted by Egypt's closure to Israeli shipping of the Straits of Tiran leading to the Gulf of Aqaba on May 22, 1967, along with the aggressive posture of the armies of Egypt, Jordan, Syria, and Iraq. After a stunning pre-emptive attack by the Israeli Air Force on the Egyptian Air Force, and later in the day the Jordanian Air force, 416 Arab aircraft had been destroyed, 393 of which were destroyed on the ground; only 26 Israeli aircraft had been lost in action. The result was Israel's complete superiority in the air and thus its freedom to support advancing Israeli ground formations. Here was further innovation and daring that surprised the world, let alone the Middle East.[41] During the same conflict, Major-General Israel Tal's division pushed through the Sinai wilderness. Egyptians mistook Israeli tanks for their own and allowed Israeli paratroopers to slog through the dunes unmolested.

> "Apparently someone in heaven was watching over us," remarked the commander, Rafael (Raful) Eytan, after the war, "Every unintended action they took and every unintended action we took always turned out to our advantage." But Israeli advances were more than a product of luck. Egyptian intelligence had concluded that enemy movements in the sector were merely diversions for the main axis of attack, opposite Rafah and Khan Yunis.[42]

The British Discouragement of Zionism

There was great euphoria resulting from the Balfour declaration. In 1918 Lord Robert Cecil, a subsequent architect of the League of Nations, declared, "Our wish is that Arabian countries shall be for the Arabs, Armenia for the

---

[40] C. Herzog, *The Arab-Israeli Wars* (New York: Vintage Books, 1984) 17–108; J. Westwood, *The History of the Middle East Wars* (North Dighton, Mass.: World Publication, 2002), 8–27.

[41] Herzog, *The Arab-Israeli Wars*, 145–53.

[42] Oren, *Six Days of War*, 179.

Armenians, and Judea for the Jews." Winston Churchill spoke of "a Jewish State by the banks of the Jordan . . . which might comprise three or four million Jews." Field Marshal Jan Smuts (1870–1950), South African statesman, anticipated the rise of "a great Jewish State." Balfour added that,

> the notion that Jewish immigration would have to be artificially restricted in order to ensure that the Jews should be a permanent minority never entered into the heads of anyone engaged in framing the policy. That would have been regarded as unjust and as a fraud on the people to whom we were appealing.[43]

Nevertheless, the window of opportunity did begin to close. The British Mandate of Palestine concerned territory in the Middle East, including the modern regions of Israel, Jordan, the West Bank, and the Gaza Strip. These had formerly belonged to the Ottoman Empire, which the League of Nations entrusted to the United Kingdom for administration in the aftermath of World War I. Arab nationalist leaders expressed growing misgivings about a scheme permitting Jews to share even limited consultative authority with Arabs, so they boycotted elections. After three failed attempts at arranging some form of Arab and Jewish administrative cooperation, the High Commissioner for Palestine, Herbert Samuel, continued from 1923 onward as the first of successive high commissioners who administered with almost total authority, that is, until the end of Britain's tenure in 1948. In 1921 through negotiation with Winston Churchill, that part of Palestine named Transjordan, east of the Jordan, was separated and handed over to the charge of Emir Abdullah from Arabia, who was thus dissuaded from interfering in Syria. In 1950 Transjordan annexed the West Bank, declaring itself now as Jordan, and this with the recognition of the United Kingdom. At this time, Abdullah significantly conferred Jordanian citizenship on the population of the West Bank, including the inhabitants of Arab Jerusalem.[44]

The Expansion of the Jewish National Home (1920–1935)

The ensuing period of 28 years leading to nationhood saw great economic advance under British direction, including the reclamation of malarial swamps and wilderness, and reforestation. In particular the 1920s witnessed the beginning of Jewish industry in Palestine with an attitude of near unparalleled vigor. Along with this many Palestinian Arabs also enjoyed unprecedented affluence, although there continued much village poverty. One of the pioneers of this labor intensive, often regimented pro-

[43] Sachar, *A History of Israel*, 110.
[44] Ibid., 126–28, 434.

gram was the charismatic Joseph Trumpeldor, a Russian dentist. The commitment he sought was from

> people to serve at any cost at whatever task Palestine requires. . . . The metal, whatever is needed to forge anything, whatever the national machine will require. Is there a wheel lacking? I am that wheel. Nails, screws, a block? Take me. Must the land be dug? I will dig it. If there is shooting to be done, are soldiers needed? I will enlist. Policemen, doctors, lawyers, teachers, water-carriers? If you please, I am ready to do it all. I am not a person. I am the pure embodiment of service, prepared for everything. I have no ties. I know only one command: Build.[45]

By 1930, 57 percent of Jewish land holdings had been either swamp or land never before cultivated. Such industriousness and resultant accomplishment even up to the present, to which the Mamluk and Ottoman empires over the preceding eight hundred years never remotely attained, is something that Christian anti-Judaism is loath to acknowledge. Today, modern Israel has, by far, the highest per capita gross domestic product in all the countries of the Middle East, even among those that are fabulously oil rich.

So in the 1930s a new wave of immigration brought additional Jewish citizens and a resurgence of hope to the land. In 1932 immigration rose to 12,500; then 37,000 in 1933; 45,000 in 1934; and 66,000 in 1935. Between 1932 and 1935 the population of the Jewish settlement in Palestine doubled from 185,000 to 375,000. Indeed the reputation of the kibbutz movement, as well as capitalist villages, throughout Europe provided a kind of built-in, ongoing dynamism and encouragement for further migration. By the end of the first decade, the Jewish share of contributions to the public revenues totaled approximately 45 percent, and it was the Arabs who benefited most impressively from government expenditures. This expansionism, but preeminently the international interest in encouraging increased migration, resulting in the more rapid enlargement of the Jewish population, inevitably led to growing conflict, indeed sporadic warfare between Jews and Arabs.[46] In Britain as well, a cloud of diminished support had come to hover over the Zionist cause. Within the Labor Government of Ramsay McDonald (1929–1935), Colonial Secretary Sidney Webb, later Lord Passfield, one of the early founders of the Socialist Fabian Society, bluntly told Weizmann that he opposed mass Jewish immigration to Palestine. Not surprisingly, the subsequent Passfield White Paper of 1930 attempted revision of the

[45] Ibid., 147–48.
[46] Ibid., 138–94.

Mandate, at which Winston Churchill anathematized the document in a heated House of Commons debate.[47]

The Shame of British Appeasement (1935–1948)

Britain was also faced with a dilemma concerning successful Jewish national growth and dominance that aggravated the Arab population in the direction of rising militancy. In 1935 upon the introduction of the Nuremberg racial laws, Hitler received telegrams of congratulations and praise from all corners of the Arab world. Hardly a German Arabic-language newspaper or magazine appeared in the Middle East without a sharp thrust against the Jews. In 1936 a major Arab revolt arose in Jerusalem, Galilee, and Samaria; there was a further revolt on 1937. These uprisings gave birth to the formation of the Haganah defense agency that received professional training for three years from British Captain Orde Wingate, a devout Christian, which in turn eventually gave rise to the Israeli Defense Forces. At the same time there also resulted economic Arab threatenings that would present a real problem for British industry, especially in the realm of petroleum necessary for an imminent Second World War. Further, there was British concern that burgeoning Germany might attract Arab loyalty which, nevertheless, did result through the flight of the Mufti of Jerusalem, Haj Amin el-Husseini, to Iraq, and Hitler's protection in Germany in 1941. He had already provoked several Arab uprisings in Palestine during 1922–1936. So the unchanging and ever more shrill demand of the Arabs was for the termination of the League of Nations mandate so that independence might be awarded to Palestine in the form of an Arab-dominated state. To the great consternation of British Jewry, and especially Weizmann, the White Paper of Unitarian Neville Chamberlain's government issued on May 17, 1939, indicated appeasement was in the air. This mood was already evident in terms of Britain's willingness to yield to Germany's appetite for Czechoslovakia and Poland, when Chamberlain returned from Munich with the paper thin assurance of "peace for our time" in September 1938.[48] Clearly there was revisionism afoot when it was now to be required, by means of a notorious British White Paper, that Jewish immigration be restricted to 10,000 for each of the next five years, plus an overall 25,000 refugees. After this no further Jewish immigration would be permitted without Arab agreement. Further, the sale of land to Jews was to be prohibited immediately. This

---

[47] Ibid., 171–77.
[48] M. Gilbert and R. Gott, *The Appeasers* (Boston: Houghton Mifflin, 1963).

declaration of British policy was a foreclosure on any subsequent growth for the Jewish National Home. Here was the Chamberlain government's stringent, newly forged, anti-Zionist mandate.[49]

During the World War II, humanity reached its lowest ebb when orchestrated genocide focused on the annihilation of European Jewry. The inauguration of the Holocaust inevitably led to the flight of Jews who attempted various means of reaching Palestine, but especially by ship. The shame of Britain must surely be its closure of Palestine to these desperate hordes resulting in thousands perishing, notwithstanding the thrust generated by massacres in Eastern Europe. After some hesitancy in Britain, at the encouragement of Churchill, in 1944 a Jewish brigade was formed which served in Italy and subsequently supplied Haganah. The end result was the service of 30,000 Jews during the war who often bore the shield of David, except when it had to be removed upon entering the land lest the Arabs might be offended! The number of Arabs also serving the Allied cause was about 12,000, though not all from Palestine. Actually Palestine prospered at this time.

During the three years immediately after the war, waning confidence in British support saw a rise in Jewish terrorism through Haganah under Ben-Gurion's direction, and the more radical Irgun, fathered by Vladimir Jabotinsky, mentor of Menachem Begin. Both defense agencies consorted in the blowing up of the King David Hotel in Jerusalem, though Ben-Gurion attempted to withdraw. Weizmann objected, but to no avail so that 91 were killed, including 28 British, on July 22, 1946. This was the result of 2,718 Jews being arrested in a dawn raid on Haganah, just three weeks before. As a result, the British Government attempted a tripartite division of the land that was rejected by both Jews and Arabs. Consequently, on February 14, 1947, Foreign Secretary Ernest Bevin announced that he was handing over the Palestinian problem to the United Nations. Nevertheless bitter conflict between the British and the Jews continued to the end of the relationship. The Jews were prepared to establish their own state, but the Arabs refused to make any such move since they had war plans afoot.[50] So the only solution was partition of Palestine according to United Nations investigation and administration. This was agreed to by the General Assembly of the United Nations, with Britain abstaining, on November 29, 1947. Also Haifa was to be opened as a free port for Jewish immigration on February 1, 1948. By March 1948, the whole country was in disorder. Yet by a seeming

[49] Parkes, *Whose Land?* 282–301; Sachar, *A History of Israel*, 147–226.
[50] Johnson, *History of the Jews*, 522–24.

miracle of providence, and in spite of virulent Arab hatred, on May 14, 1948, in Jerusalem, the State of Israel was inaugurated with Ben-Gurion as its first Prime Minister and Minister of Defense. Even then, that same day, Egyptian aircraft bombed Tel Aviv![51]

The Recovery of the State of Israel

The Fledgling State of Israel (1948–1973)

The War of Independence in 1948 immediately tested Jewish ingenuity, flexibility, and tenacity, especially in view of outmoded equipment:

> So in the first hectic weeks after the Declaration of the State, I worked almost continuously round the clock at Sde Dov, fitting those little planes with Venturi Tubes and basic night-flying instruments, so that they could be used as bombers, with crude hand-made bombs chucked over the side. The role of these little planes, the Austers, Pipers, Fairchilds, in the first crucial weeks before the Czechoslovakian airlift brought Messerschmitts, . . . tends to be overlooked. But they were vital in checking the better equipped enemy's rapid advances, flying in mail and urgently needed medical supplies to isolated areas. One of those little Austers stood mounted on a plinth outside Sde Dov, in recognition of the role they played. Sadly it was later removed. A great pity, as it put the inequality of resources into perspective [as with Egyptian Spitfires] and served as a reminder of the grave danger the new little State was in, in May 1948.[52]

After two uneasy truces and an armistice agreement involving territory gains, in 1949 Israel's control of the Negev was now unquestioned while the State was more substantially established, having been forged in the heat of bloody war. Now a reserve army was also created,[53] and at the same time membership of Israel in the United Nations was approved.[54]

The Suez and Sinai conflict of 1956, lasting but a week, was called by one British war strategist as "a work of art." Precipitated by the incursion of murderous Arab fedayeen, closer ties between Egypt and Syria, and ultimately Egyptian President Nasser's seizure of the Suez Canal, after just six days Israel had overrun Sinai. Standard equipment for Egyptian officers was an Arabic edition of Hitler's *Mein Kampf*. After fierce fighting, the capture of Sharm el-Sheikh led to the reopening of the Straits of Tiran. Captured

---

[51] Gilbert, *Israel*, 170–90.

[52] Ibid., 189–190, quoting John Barrard, an overseas volunteer.

[53] Herzog, *Arab-Israeli Wars*, 105–8.

[54] Sachar, *A History of Israel*, 315–53.

territory was eventually returned subject to United Nations supervision. Continuing economic growth was always under the shadow of surrounding Arab neighbors. Adolf Eichmann was captured, tried in 1961, and executed. The heightening of an Israeli-Syrian border conflict and Nasser's Pan-Arabism were forebodings of Israel being confronted with enlarged threatenings.

The Six Day War of 1967 was "a work of exquisite execution" in which timing was everything. A coalition of Arab rumblings became louder than ever, especially in view of deceptive confidence based on reception of large amounts of equipment and weaponry from the Soviet Union. Apart from my summary description of the spectacular opening thrust, it is well to remember the great risk that was involved, for only twelve fighter planes had been left in Israeli air space. All the rest set out on the mission to destroy Egyptian air power at its source. From another perspective, this was but preliminary, even when added to the capture of the Golan Heights and Sharm el-Sheikh by which access was regained to the Gulf of Aqaba. The ultimate, incomparable, yet bloody conquest was that of the Old City of Jerusalem on June 7, 1967.[55] Concerning this event, Reformed theologian R. C. Sproul ambivalently makes an interesting comment with regard to Rom 11:26, "And in this way all Israel will be saved":

> I don't know whether this restoration is going to be sudden or gradual, or even if it is going to follow the return of the Jews to their own land. There is still quite a bit of debate about that. I remember sitting on my porch in Boston in 1967, and watching on television the Jewish soldiers coming into Jerusalem, dropping their weapons and rushing to the Wailing Wall, and weeping and weeping. Immediately I telephoned one of my dear friends, a professor of Old Testament theology, who does not believe that modern day Israel has any significance whatsoever. I asked him, "What do you think now? From 70 AD until 1967, almost 1900 years, Jerusalem has been under the domination and control of Gentiles, and now the Jews have recaptured the city of Jerusalem. Jesus said that Jerusalem will be trodden under foot by the Gentiles, until the fullness of the Gentiles be fulfilled. What's the significance of that?" He replied, "I am going to have to rethink this situation." It was indeed startling.
>
> Well, 1967 was many years ago, and we have not seen the restoration of the Jewish nation, although we have seen the greatest concentration on eschatology that the church has ever known. . . . Perhaps it will be another thousand years before the Jews have complete control of Jerusalem. Maybe present arrangements are just a temporary interlude. It is possible that the Arabs will drive the Jews out of Jerusalem and the Jewish people will be put

---

[55] Gilbert, *Israel*, 384–395; Herzog, *Arab-Israeli Wars*, 143–223.

in exile again, and this present attempt to recover the Promised Land will be abortive—who knows? I don't know what the significance of it all is. But I will tell you this: we should be watching very carefully.[56]

The War of Confrontation and Attrition of 1967–1970 was a "work of endurance" since it followed shortly after the spectacularly brief Six Day War and aimed at testing the staying power of the Israeli spirit. It involved three borders, those of Jordan, Lebanon, and Egypt. The north Jordan valley area involved the thwarting of a Palestine Liberation Organization and Syrian aided takeover of the Kingdom of Jordan at the instigation of terrorist leader Yasser Arafat. Never was a man less qualified for peace recognition than he. The PLO's defeat and retreat to Lebanon led to this country's decimation and later occupation by Syrian forces, and therefore increased northern threatenings to Israel. The third and major front involved periodic conflict along the Suez Canal. Having expelled the Russian military from Egypt, while yet securing further military supplies, Nasser maintained strict observance of the Suez Canal cease-fire, while exchanging spasmodic incursions with Israel. Then there was the Egyptian sinking of the Israeli flagship, the destroyer *Eilat* patrolling a distance from Port Said. In response Israel severely attacked major Egyptian petroleum installations. However, while rigorously training his army, Nasser craftily attempted lulling Israel into a false sense of safety, that is, until the surprise Yom Kippur War erupted and caught the Israeli military unawares.

The Yom Kippur War of 1973 was a "work of recovery," though nevertheless a very costly one at that. There had been indications of enemy build-up early in October of 1973 that were not well heeded. Then at 2:00 p.m. on Saturday, October 6, Yom Kippur, the Day of Atonement, the holiest day of the year, when the nation was at relative ease and religiously focused, Egypt and Syria simultaneously unleashed a surprise attack on the south and north of the land. The onslaught began with 250 warplanes that attacked unsuspecting Israeli fortifications in the Sinai. Some 2,000 guns delivered an artillery barrage involving 10,000 shells that fell on Israeli positions during the first minute. In addition, 2,000 tanks were deployed. Egypt expected 10,000 dead Israelis at the end of the day, though in reality it turned out to be only 208. Syria advanced with 1,400 tanks and recaptured the Golan heights along with the Israeli base on Mount Hermon. Yet by October 8 they yielded again to the Israelis when all lost territory was regained. On October 16, after intense conflict on the east bank of the

---

[56] R. C. Sproul, *The Gospel of God: Romans* (Fearn, Scotland: Christian Focus, 1999), 191–92n.

Suez and in the Sinai involving fierce tank battles, Israeli troops eventually crossed the Suez Canal, humiliated the Egyptian third army of 20,000 and surrounded it by October 21. In spite of Russia's heavy investment in the region with weaponry, with Israel's mastery of the air and both sides of the Canal, a weakened Egypt agreed to a cease-fire on October 24, brokered between Nixon and Kissinger of the US and Brezhnev of the USSR. So Israel recovered from a critical assault, though the cost was the loss of 2,522 lives, and a sobering investigation followed.

Chaim Herzog significantly described this bruising conflict of 1973 as ushering in "a new era of military conflict."[57] This was certainly true, especially on account of improved Egyptian planning. But at the same time, another new era was introduced in terms of President Sadat's subsequent visit to Jerusalem in 1977 at Prime Minister Begin's request. At that time he also appeared before the Israeli parliament and then signed the Camp David Accords in 1978. His assassination by Islamic Jihadists in 1981 upheld the ongoing mood of much of the Arab world which indicated that it was not enthused about rapprochement with the Jews. Putting aside the successive military humiliations of Israel's neighbors since 1948, the two conflicts of 1967–1973 in particular ushered in a radically new tactic that would call for the engagement of Europe with the Arab cause, and that with considerable enticement. Martin Gilbert made a perceptive assessment concerning this very same period:

> Beyond Egypt the oil-producing Arab states had found a new strength. An oil embargo on those States that supported Israel was followed by the rise of the Organization of Petroleum Exporting Countries (OPEC), dominated by Saudi Arabia, which used its ability to raise oil prices at will, and to raise them to unprecedented heights, to cast the Western economies into chaos. This spawned what came to be known as "petro-dollar diplomacy', which led to pressure being put on Israel by those States which felt threatened (and were threatened) by a rise in oil prices *if they did not act against Israel in the diplomatic arena.*[58]

The European Arab and Augustinian Resurgence

Following a succession of post-independence wars that in the main were initiated by the surrounding Arab countries and not simply the Palestinian Arabs, the State of Israel found itself more firmly established, both economically and militarily, than ever. This series of conflicts also resulted

---

[57] Herzog, *Arab-Israeli Wars*, 323.
[58] Gilbert, *Israel*, 460–61. Emphasis added.

in the expansion of Israel's territorial boundaries, though often followed by negotiated cut-backs. In general it appears that the more the Arab nations raged against Israel, the more they lost out to their increasingly industrious and prosperous neighbor. Especially following the 1967 debacle as well as the loss of the Yom Kippur war in 1973, the Arab nations, in licking their wounds, appeared to have conceived a new battle plan of a radically different nature. And the nature of this change of strategy has evidently had a profound effect on Europe in general and (as I shall note) the United Kingdom in particular with regard to Israel and Zionism. So we now consider post-World War II Europe from 1973 onwards and its relation to modern Israel and its Arab neighbors, both politically and theologically.

The Witness of Bat Ye'or

Fundamental to an understanding of the aforementioned new Arab strategy is a ground-breaking book by historian Bat Ye'or which Sir Martin Gilbert highly commended for repeated reading.

> This is a provocative and disturbing book. With all the drama of a master writer, Bat Ye'or presents a wide range of historical and contemporary documents and facts to tell the story of how the European Union is being subverted by Islamic hostility to the very ethics and values of Europe itself. . . . It is also a warning to Europe not to allow the anti-American and anti-Israel pressures of Islam to subvert Europe's true values.[59]

By way of summary, Ye'or reveals the transformation of Europe into "Eurabia" as she defines it, a region of dhimmitude or non-Muslim subjection to Islam, having become a cultural and political appendage of the Arab/Muslim world. Eurabia is fundamentally anti-Christian, anti-Western, anti-American, and anti-Semitic. The institution that has been responsible for this transformation, and that continues to propagate its ideological message, is the Euro-Arab Dialogue (EAD), developed by European and Arab politicians and intellectuals over the past 30 years. Since 1967–1973 and the associated succession of military defeats at the hands of Israel, a new strategy was brought into effect by the Arab world that involved an integration of economic, political, cultural, and religious elements. In particular it involved the transfer of culture from the Arab world to Europe, but not necessarily, as we shall see, from Europe to the Arab world, especially with regard to religion. For example, in 1974 at the Sixth Arab

---

[59] B. Ye'or, *Eurabia: The Euro-Arab Axis* (Madison, New Jersey: Fairleigh Dickinson University Press, 2005). Outside back cover commendation by Sir Martin Gilbert, an acclaimed historian, whose magnum opus is the official and definitive biography of Sir Winston Churchill.

Summit Conference in Algiers, which was addressed to Western Europe, Nijmeddin Dajani, the Jordanian minister of industry and justice addressed the central issue.

> As much as the Arab side attaches utmost importance to the economic development of their countries and the improvement of the standard of living of the Arab peoples, the Arabs were not ready to let the Dialogue proceed at the expense of the national interests, foremost of which was the Palestinian problem.[60]

Then in 1975 Dr. Ibrahim A. Obaid, Saudi Arabia's director of the Ministry of Petroleum and Mineral Resources,

> aptly expressed the spirit of the Dialogue at a 1975 meeting of Euro-Arab Cooperation experts in Amsterdam. "Together as equals, the Europeans and the Arabs can through a 'strategy of interdependence' forge ahead to remove the thorn in their sides—the Israeli problem—and attend to the Herculean task ahead of them." In his statement, "Political Preconditions for Cooperation with Western Europe," Obaid stressed that for the sake of peace, the European Community should stop all military and economic assistance to Israel and work toward "an Israeli withdrawal from occupied Arab territories foremost of which is Jerusalem." He affirmed that it was in the interest of Western Europe to attempt to assume a more active role in the Middle East and this would be facilitated, if the PLO were recognized by the European Community as the official representative of the Palestinians. "The Arab-Israeli conflict and the oil problem are not only related but inseparable. Had it not been for the said conflict the oil weapon would not have been unleashed," he declared.[61]

It is the religious aspect of Ye'or's work, however, that especially draws our attention. She makes it very clear that the Islamization of Europe in the economic, political, and cultural realms brings with it the Arab-Muslim desire for the Islamization of Christianity. At the same time this has associated with it an inevitable anti-Judaism and philo-Islamic worldview concerning which an increasing number of Christians have indicated considerable sympathy. Ye'or's evidence here is voluminous, though I especially focus on individuals she references who have already been mentioned in chapter 4. More specifically, the problem concerns the merging of Christianity with Palestinianism in such a way that the Arab world gradually conquers by stealth.

[60] Ibid., 71–72.

[61] Ibid., 71. This Arab/European collusion, especially with regard to Arafat's PLO, is further attested to in D. Selbourne, *The Losing Battle with Islam* (New York: Prometheus, 2005), 314, 321.

A full-blown "Palestinian replacement theology" was created and spread throughout Europe, encouraged by EAD pro-PLO indoctrination. The new Arab Jesus unites in his Palestinianism both Muslims and Christians against Israel. . . . "Palestinianism," the new Eurabian cult, thus conferred a theological value upon Palestinian sufferings. Palestinian victimology—the Jewish victimization of innocent Palestinians—was drummed into the European political conscience through the church institutions, the media, and Eurabian networks. Arab Palestine came to symbolize the crucifixion of Jesus by Jewish evilness. Such was the thesis preached by Kenneth Cragg, the assistant Anglican bishop in Jerusalem from 1970 to 1973.[62]

Concerning politicians who suggested that Europe needed Islamic spiritual values for its own moral regeneration, that past wars resulted from Europe's resistance to Islam in the past, the same Bishop Cragg supported such views and also

criticized the European kings and the popes for not having cooperated with the invading Muslim armies, a surrender which would have amounted to collaboration in their own demise.[63]

It should be recalled that both Chapman and Sizer, also referenced in chapter 4, happily call on Cragg in support of their own Islamophile, pro-Palestinian, anti-Judaic bias.[64]

Ye'or also mentions some scholars who have revived ancient Christian supercessionist writings that held that Jews had lost all rights to their land because of the crucifixion. From the early 1970s onward, a trend developed whereby

Eastern Christian communities were blackmailed and threatened. Any criticism of the pejorative characteristics attributed to Jews by the church fathers—especially those of Augustine and St. Chrysostom—was considered blasphemous by Muslims, since they are echoed in the Qur'an.[65]

Biblical history that had legitimized Israel became ever more contemptible and discredited, unless purified of its Jewish interpretation by Palestinian Liberation Theology. Its conceiver, canon Naim Ateek, is revered in European Protestant Churches. Theologians aligned on Ateek's interpretation called for a new Christian reading of the Bible, in line with the Qur'an, that would expel Israel from its biblical identity as well as its patrimony. These Christians believe that they would thereby obey God's will by helping to destroy Israel by whatever means.[66]

[62] Ibid., 176.
[63] Ibid., 189.
[64] Chapman, *Whose Promised Land?* 224–226; Sizer, *Christian Zionism*, 14, 259–60.
[65] Ye'or, *Eurabia*, 186.
[66] Ibid., 177.

Here then is yet another anti-Judaic, anti-Zionist scholar whom Chapman, Sizer, and Burge devoutly respect.[67] Here also is a variation of replacement theology that is not so far removed from the Muslim variety whereby Christianity is both preceded by and superseded by Islam. According to Ismail Raji al-Faruqi who taught at the Universities of Chicago and Syracuse and was a professor in the Department of Religion at Temple University,

> Islam precedes Judaism and Christianity and was present at humanity's birth. Islam recognizes the Hebrew and Christian "prophets," but only as Muslim prophets. . . . For this reason, the Christian belief that Jesus, the apostles, Jesus' disciples and Christianity itself are related to Judaism is—according to al-Faruqi—a monumental error. Jesus rebelled against Judaism precisely to restore Islam, his religion. Christianity is an outgrowth of Islam; the Hebrew prophets, Jesus, his mother, his disciples, and apostles were all Muslims who preached Islam. Hence, because Christians belong to the Muslim creed, they cannot settle their relations with the Jews apart from the Muslims.
>
> However strange it may seem, these assertions have been constantly affirmed and proclaimed by the *dhimmi* Arab Churches and supported in Europe and America by the anti-Zionist trend in the Church and in academia. . . . Above all, al-Faruqi warns that Christian voices allied to Zionism must be silenced.[68]

Is it any wonder then that the proponents of the broad Arab agenda delight in the supercessionist contributions of the likes of Chapman, Sizer, Burge and Cragg to their cause.

The Witness of Melanie Phillips.

Yet further proof of Ye'or's thesis is her referencing of the London journalist Melanie Phillips, especially her analysis of the dire state of Jewish-Christian relationships in the United Kingdom due to the burgeoning yet polarizing influence there of resurgent Islam. As an example, writing under the heading of "The Moral Bankruptcy of the Church of England," Phillips is quoted as indicating that

> Muslim records and texts testify to the usefulness of the Churches' collaboration in the anti-Israel policy. Now, terrified by Islam, the Churches seek their security by advocating openly an anti-Israel policy.[69]

[67] G. Burge, *Whose Land? Whose Promise?* (Cleveland, Ohio: The Pilgrim Press, 2003), 104–5, 193, 214–15; Chapman, *Whose Promised Land?* 196, 210, 215–16, 234–35. Both of these authors highly esteem and quote N. Ateek's *Justice and only Justice: A Palestinian Theology of Liberation* (Maryknoll, N.Y.: Orbis Books, 1989).

[68] Ye'or, *Eurabia*, 221–22.

[69] Ibid., 267, 346n. 5.

Even more to the point is the fact that this "anti-Israel policy" is driven by replacement or supercessionist theology (also see appendix D). In Phillips' recent volume, *Londonistan*, she makes the same essential point with far greater emphasis: the Islamization of Europe, and especially London by way of example, has associated with it the intentional Islamization of Christianity, particularly through the encouragement of anti-Israel supercessionism.

One chapter in particular brings this point home. "On Their Knees before Terror" deals with the cringing attitude of British clergy toward the European thrust of Islam, as with regard to the perpetrators of the terrorist London bombings of July 7, 2005:

> The first instinct of many British clerics was to emphasize and agonize not with the victims of the atrocity but with the community of faith in whose names it had been committed—and to deny that religion had anything to do with it at all.[70]

Concerning the origins of this capitulation, Phillips confirmed the argumentation of Ne'or:

> The real motor behind the [Anglican] Church's engine of Israeli delegitimization is theology—or, to be more precise, the resurgence of a particular theology that had long been consigned to ignominy. This is "replacement theology," sometimes known as "supercessionism," a doctrine going back to the early Church Fathers and stating that all God's promises to the Jews— including the land of Israel—were forfeit because the Jews had denied the divinity of Christ.
>
> This doctrine lay behind centuries of Christian anti-Jewish hatred until the Holocaust drove it underground. The Vatican officially buried it, affirming the integrity of the Jewish people and recognizing the State of Israel. This was because the Catholic Church faced up to the excruciating role it had played over centuries in dehumanizing and demonizing the Jewish people, a process which had paved the way for the Holocaust. But the Anglican Church failed to conduct a similar process, leaving unaddressed and unresolved the key issue of how in doctrinal terms it should regard the Jews. The ancient calumny that the Jews were the murderers of God and had denied His love thus still had resonance for Anglicans. So when Arab Christians reinterpreted Scripture in order to delegitimize the Jews' claim to

---

[70] M. Phillips, *Londonistan* (New York: Encounter Books, 2006), 138–39. It is interesting that although this author had previously published in the United Kingdom, like D. Selbourne, *The Losing Battle with Islam* (New York: Prometheus, 2005), difficulty concerning British acceptance for both necessitated publication in the United States. Refer to "Terrified publishers won't print truth about Islam, says author [Selbourne]," *London Daily Telegraph*, 12/13/2005.

the land of Israel, this kick-started replacement theology, which roared back into the imaginations, sermons and thinking of the Anglican Church.[71]

By way of further example, there is an appropriate dissection of Naim Ateek along with his Sabeel Center in Jerusalem, "a source of systematic demonization of the Jewish State."[72] His book *Justice and Only Justice* inverts history, defames the Jews, and sanitizes Arab violence. Real anti-Semitism, says Ateek, is found within the Jewish community in its treatment of the Palestinians. Zionism was a retrogression into the Jews' primitive past. While asserting belief in Israel's existence, it is "not based on divine revelation but on a resolution of the United Nations."[73]

Next is an analysis of Colin Chapman, whose book *Whose Promised Land?* Phillips charges is a poisonous travesty that uses theology to delegitimize Israel. Chapman's history grossly downplays the extent of Arab violence against Jews in the decades of Jewish immigration to Palestine before the State of Israel was created. It is absurd for him to claim that no US president could win without Jewish votes. Since American Jews are overwhelmingly Democrats, the victory of Republican presidents must remain, on this theory, a complete mystery.[74]

She also includes a critical review of Stephen Sizer. His supercessionism is similar to that of Ateek and Chapman, though he vociferously asserts that Israel is fundamentally an apartheid state because it is based on race; indeed it is even worse than South Africa was. The reason the Israelites were expelled from the land was their breaking of the conditional Mosaic covenant with God. Being more interested in money and power, they treated the poor and aliens with contempt. Today's Jews, it appeared, were no better![75]

Christian Sympathy with Zionism

The Christian Zionist feels himself torn in two directions, even as did Paul when he described the unbelieving nation of Israel in his day as God's beloved enemy (Rom 11:28). On the one hand the modern State of Israel, with its predominantly unbelieving Jewish constituency, is an "enemy" of God because it continues to declare, "We don't want this man [Jesus Christ]

---

[71] Ibid., 152. We would modify some elements of this statement. But the essential thrust is true.

[72] Ibid.

[73] Ibid., 152–53.

[74] Ibid., 154–55.

[75] Ibid., 156.

to rule over us!" (Luke 19:14). But we are told that, at the same time, this identical modern State of Israel, along with the diaspora, is "loved because of their forefathers." This tension is further reflected in Paul's expressed frustration with the fierce opposition of the Jews that he personally experienced (1 Thess 2:14–16), and yet his tireless loving devotion poured out toward them, come what may (Rom 9:1–5).

Another aspect of this tension regards the Christian Zionist's sympathy for the modern State of Israel—this thriving, secular, dynamic nation in the midst of opposing, raging nations. While identifying with this ongoing travail rooted in spiritual blindness, commiseration is also born of anticipation of the glory—through sovereign, saving, covenantal grace—that shall eventually overtake this same nation, as the prophets have repeatedly promised. So there will be a future consummate renovation and manifestation of the Jewish people by means of heaven coming down to earth. Of course the supercessionist plainly offers no such sympathetic affection, only merciless condemnation and ultimate extinction; he does not envisage any eschatological hope for the nation of Israel, especially in view of his pliable use of the OT.

To be sure, there is no place here for dual covenant theology since the evangelistic mandate continues both to encourage faith in Christ and to warn the Jewish people, even as from the lips of Jesus when He declared, "if you do not believe that I am He [the Son of God come from the Father] you will die in your sins" (John 8:24).

The Contemporary State of Israel

I have plainly indicated that, notwithstanding Israel's ongoing rebellion and ungodliness even to date, God retains a deep covenantal interest in His people of the flesh in the same manner that He indicated this loyal love toward Israel as an adulterous people by means of the prophet Hosea (Hos 2:14–23; 14:1–9; cp. Mal 3:6). For this reason we love the modern State of Israel, we weep over it, we desire to proclaim to it "the glory of our great God and Savior, Jesus Christ" (Tit 2:13), and yet we also anticipate that time when the Lord Jesus will be welcomed by the joyous exclamation of Israel, "Blessed is He who comes in the name of the Lord" (Matt 23:39).

The present status of Israel, its providential existence, its current earthly achievements, its immersion in conflict and consequent ceaseless groanings, have to be carefully and sensitively assessed. In considering current events in the Middle East and viewing them through the lens of the Word of

God, my perspective is one of cautious probability. But there are two matters I believe to be firm and non-negotiable. First, the present, unbelieving, Jewish people and their national manifestation are the object of God's ongoing, distinct, covenantal interest. Second, it is the inviolate promise of God that the land originally promised to Abraham is a perpetual inheritance of the Jewish people, whether they remain in it or are expelled from it yet again. This is a most fundamental issue that controls any discussion concerning the claims of the Palestinian Arabs and a just settlement of the present problems in that region.

The Israeli/Palestinian Dispute

The initial and continuing opposition to the nation of Israel subsequent to its founding in 1948 was principally engineered by the surrounding Arab nations, not the Palestinian Arabs. Yet this animosity was also the result of centuries of hatred having already been poured out on the Jews. The major Middle Eastern wars against Israel of 1948–1949, 1956, 1967, and 1973 were all primarily instigated by the nations of Egypt, Jordan, Iraq, Syria, Saudi Arabia, and Lebanon, and not the Palestinian Arabs. It is the Arab world of the Middle East, holding 99.8 percent of that sector which, with such virulent hatred, would wholly exclude Israel from the minuscule territory that it occupies, which is presently under .2 percent of that region.[76]

During the Sinai Campaign of 1956, Jonathen Etkes, an Israeli Mustang P-51 pilot, crash landed and was captured by the Egyptians. After interrogation and torture, he was released and returned to the wreck of his aircraft after 1967. He commented,

> They [his captors] were so full of hate. . . . The heart of the problem is the lack of acceptance of Jews here by Arabs," he declared. "This is the heart of the problem, not the Palestinians.[77]

Bat Ye'or came to a similar conclusion when she described a major element of EU policy toward Israel. It concerns the

> Arab demand to which the EU has submitted: the internationalization of what was essentially a regional conflict. The Israeli/Palestinian dispute could have been settled decades ago by an adjustment of frontiers and the integration of Arab and Jewish refugees by each side in an exchange of populations—in the same way that many other conflicts were resolved

[76] B. Netanyahu, *A Durable Peace* (New York: Warner Books, 2000), 45.

[77] Shipler, *Arab and Jew*, 27.

> throughout the twentieth century [e.g., India and Pakistan]. But the Arab-Israeli conflict has been kept alive by the imposition of unacceptable conditions on Israel and European support for the most radical Arab leaders [such as Yasser Arafat].[78]

Plainly, it was not until after the 1967 and 1973 wars that there was a call for a separate Palestinian nation adjacent to Israel. The reason is that from 1948 to 1967 the hope of the Arab nations was the defeat and total expulsion of Israel from the land. But when this hope faded, the alternative strategy was a separate Palestinian territory that was contemplated as a launching pad for further gains, yet never sufficient in itself. This being the case, the proposal of a separate Palestinian state incorporating the West Bank and the Gaza Strip is a hopeless prospect.

It is interesting to recall the early character of Transjordan, which was originally allocated in its larger configuration for habitation by the Palestinian Arabs. In 1950 Transjordan annexed the West Bank and then declared itself to be Jordan, and it did this with the recognition of the United Kingdom. It is significant that, at this time, King Abdullah conferred Jordanian citizenship on the population of the West Bank, including the inhabitants of Arab Old Jerusalem. But in 1967 Jordan was drawn into the Six Day War and as a result lost the West Bank and Old Jerusalem to Israel. Consequently, in 1988 Jordan renounced all claims to the West Bank. So it should be remembered that West Bank Palestinians were formerly Jordanians. This could have presented a window of opportunity except for the fact that Yasser Arafat and the PLO muddied the waters in 1970 when his Black September uprising against King Hussein in Jordan was ruthlessly put down. Arafat fled to southern Lebanon which he soon took over. After the War of Independence armistice of 1949, the Gaza Strip remained under Egyptian control until the 1967 Six Day War. Yet neither Jordan nor Egypt have subsequently showed any interest in absorption of their Arab Palestinian relatives; rather, they have fostered only aggravation with the Jewish people. Under the circumstances, Israel must remain strong and vigilant until such time as Arab leadership should turn from its fiercely anti-Judaic ways.

Christian Zionist Involvement in the Cause of Israel

Christian Zionists are often challenged concerning any degree of political and material support they might offer to the cause of the nation of

---

[78] Ye'or, *Eurabia*, 113.

Israel. This criticism frequently suggests that such practical aid leads to a neglect of evangelism. Indeed, Augustinian-like, there is also the intimation that the Jews should be kept in a state of constant humiliation; prosperity and independence would only reinforce their unbelieving ways! How this attitude of the Gentiles would make the Jews jealous, as is Paul's hope in Rom 11:14, defies understanding, especially when the apostle rather encourages merciful interest (Rom 11:18–20), even as is the divine intent (Rom 11:31–32). When brought down to a more personal level, such an objection borders on Pharisaism that would make even the Good Samaritan blush. Yet we are told that practical support for the political and material improvement of the downtrodden Palestinians, often in socialist and neo-Marxist terms, is to be considered ethically noble.

As Christians our desire for the conversion of a dearly loved relative calls for patience and sensitivity to earthly needs that ought to be boundless. Yet would we shy away from offering such care when this dear one is in deep need since it might distract us from the priority of witnessing to them about the gospel? Yes, the gospel is for the spiritually poor and captive and blind and oppressed (Luke 4:18), and certainly modern Israel qualifies in this regard. But for Christians to suggest that political and material support should be restricted is quite outrageous and is thoroughly condemned in Jas 2:15–17. This is not to suggest that all Israeli policy should be blindly supported, as some would suggest. But in spite of the tireless efforts of supercessionists to evacuate Gen 12:3 of its plain teaching (cp. Gen 27:29; Zech 2:8), I adamantly maintain that the Jew in the flesh is to be treated with a special kindness in view of the Pauline priority of going "first to the Jew" (Rom 1:16). Furthermore, experience undoubtedly proves that this approach is far more likely to gain a respectful hearing.

The Consummate State of Israel

Ultimately Christian Zionism represents a most glorious hope that even Israel after the flesh does not faintly grasp today. Nor can supercessionism, with its hermeneutics of divestment, finally subtract from the eschatological luster that is to come. The reason is that Zion will be the dwelling place of the Lord Jesus Christ, through which entrance gates only the objects of saving grace will enter and behold His glory and praise His name (Pss 9:11,14; 102:12–13,16,21; Isa 46:12–13). At that time Israel will weep over its tragic past (Zech 12:10–14), yet the children of Zion will also rejoice in their King (Ps 149:2). This city is to be the joy of the whole earth, the city of the great King (Ps 48:1–2). There will be a reversal of former dispersal and desolation. The wilderness will become like Eden, the desert will become like the garden of the Lord, discomfort will yield to gladness and singing. The scattered will return to Zion with joy, while sorrow and sighing will vanish (Isa 51:3,11). Then the inhabitants will be told by the Lord, "You are My people" (Isa 51:3,11,16). So evangelists will proclaim to the future heirs of Zion, "Your God reigns!" Isa 52:7–8). Then the Lord will roar from Zion in declaration of His being a refuge for His people, while they will be reassured of their security under His dominion (Joel 3:16–17,21). Zion will become a place of worship, instruction, and outreach to the nations (Mic 4:2–3). For this reason, "Jerusalem will be called the Faithful City, the mountain of the LORD of Hosts, and the Holy Mountain" (Zech 8:3).

> Let Zion's time of favor come;
>   Oh, bring the tribes of Israel home;
> And let our wandering eyes behold
>   Gentiles and Jews in Jesus' fold.
>
> *William Shrubsole, 1759–1829*

Chapter 6

ISRAEL AND CHRISTIAN ANTI-JUDAIC HERMENEUTICS IN HISTORY

I n chapter 3, and especially chapter 4, we considered allegations by a number of scholars that the disqualification of national Israel, according to the broken terms of the old covenant, led to transference, via imagery, of its promised blessings to the NT people of God. As a result, a new, distinctive, even apostolic principle of interpretation arose. In simple terms it was the necessity of focusing on the OT text through the clarifying lens of Jesus Christ's NT revelation. The argument runs that because NT writers appear to have freely interpreted many passages in the OT revelation christologically and ecclesiologically, then we must employ this same hermeneutical method in interpreting the OT as a whole, and its eschatology as well. In other words, by a process of reinterpretive imposition, the revelation of Jesus Christ has nullified a normative literal understanding of the OT. However, before we take a closer look at this interpretive methodology, which is really an upgraded Origenistic and Augustinian hermeneutic, some further historical background concerning its origin will prove helpful.

Reformed Connection with Roman Catholicism

Numerous Reformed writers have been inclined to boast in their amillennial eschatology's long-standing heritage going back to Augustine. They rightly claim that their essential prophetic perspective overwhelmingly dominated the church following the fourth century. The illustrious, indeed God-blessed Reformation perpetuated this inherited eschatology, even though the gospel and the doctrine of the church were subject to considerable, indeed radical change and apostolic recovery at that time. For example, contemporary conservative Reformed writer Kim Riddlebarger makes this point most emphatically when he describes amillennialism as "the historic Protestant understanding of the millennial age."[1] One is led to believe that to be Reformed in the fullest sense of that term is to be amillennial and that Augustinian eschatology, channeled through Luther, ought to be regarded as the traditional scheme of prophetic revelation. Implicit is Riddlebarger's belief that the vagaries of premillennialism, repudiated as carnal *chiliasm*, along with its dispensational subset, should yield to the more historic stream.

---

[1] K. Riddlebarger, *A Case for Amillennialism* (Grand Rapids: Baker, 2003), 11.

The Protestant orthodox also used the more polemical term *chiliasmus crassissimus*, "the grossest millennialism," regarding those who stressed the earthly and Jewish elements of the millennial age, much like contemporary dispensationalists. Most Protestants regard chiliasm as incompatible with Reformation orthodoxy. This may come as a surprise to many American evangelicals, who assume that Bible-believing Christians throughout the centuries have held to premillennialism.[2]

For the believer of Reformed convictions, there is a strong allegiance to historical roots and continuity, especially insofar as connection with the historic Reformation is concerned, distinctively emanating from Wittenberg, Geneva, and Westminster. So Riddlebarger further claims,

> First given systematic expression by Augustine in his famous *City of God*, amillennialism developed a distinctive Reformed emphasis. . . . Because amillennialism has its roots deep in historic Christianity, when it comes to comparing amillennialism with dispensationalism, clearly the burden of proof lies with dispensationalists to prove their case. Evangelicals often assume the opposite. It should also be noted that all major thinkers in Christian history have held something akin to the amillennial position (e.g. Augustine, Aquinas, Luther, and Calvin). This does not mean that amillennialism is true simply because it has historical support within Catholic Christianity and historic Protestantism. Nevertheless this is an impressive point, which is often not considered.[3]

Such claims call for a response that clearly exposes the shameful legacy of historic amillennialism, which is really the eschatology of Roman Catholicism. According to Chapman, Burge, Robertson, and Sizer, the Christian Church has, through inheritance, become the new Israel of God. Such language is nothing new according to Roman Catholicism. Consider the following:

1. In fact, from the beginning of his ministry, the Lord Jesus instituted the Twelve as "the seeds of the new Israel and the beginning of the sacred hierarchy."[4]
2. As Israel according to the flesh which wandered in the desert was already called the Church of God (2 Esd. 13:1; see Num. 20:4; Deut. 23:1ff.), so too, the new Israel, which advances in this present era in search of a future and permanent city (cf. Heb. 13:14), is called also the Church of Christ (cf. Matt. 16:18).[5]

---

[2] Ibid., 20.

[3] Ibid., 32.

[4] *Catechism of the Catholic Church* (New York: Doubleday, 1994), Para. 877.

[5] *Second Vatican Council*, L. Gentium, "The People of God" (New York: Viking Press, 1964), Chapter II.

3. Modern Israel is not the true heir of the biblical Israel, but a secular state. . . . Therefore, the Holy Land and its sacred sites belong to Christianity, the true Israel.[6]

4. His [Jesus Christ's] intention in employing the term [*qahal*], hitherto used of the Hebrew people viewed as a church, to denote the society He Himself was establishing cannot be mistaken [Matt. 16:18]. It implied the claim that this society now constituted the true people of God, that the Old Covenant was passing away, and that He, the promised Messias, was inaugurating a New Covenant with a New Israel.

Hebrew prophecy relates in almost equal proportions to the person and to the work of the Messias. This work was conceived as consisting of the establishment of a kingdom, in which he was to reign over a regenerated Israel. The prophetic writings describe for us with precision many of the characteristics which were to distinguish that kingdom. Christ during His ministry affirmed not only that the prophecies relating to the Messias were fulfilled in His own person, but also that the expected Messianic kingdom was none other than His Church.

In the Apostolic teaching the term *Church*, from the very first, takes the place of the expression *Kingdom of God* (Acts 5:11). Where others than the Jews were concerned, the greater suitability of the former name is evident; for *Kingdom of God* had special reference to Jewish beliefs. But the change of title only emphasizes the social unity of the members. They are the new congregation of Israel—the theocratic polity: they are the people *(laos)* of God (Acts 15:14; Rom. 9:25; 2 Cor. 6:16; 1 Peter 2:9; Heb. 8:10; Rev. 18:4; 21:33).[7]

But since the time of Augustine, the amillennial doctrine of the supercession of national Israel by the Christian church has resulted in the vilification of the Jewish people over the centuries, which has not excluded participation by Reformed individuals and congregations, notwithstanding some notable exceptions. It is interesting to consider that more recently, while within the Roman Catholic Church there has been some sorrowful confession of this tragic heritage, those of conservative Reformed convictions have appeared to be reluctant to confront the ethical shame of their eschatological roots. Of course, the Roman Catholic Church, despite *Nostra Aetate* of Vatican II, in which anti-Semitism was denounced,[8] nevertheless

---

[6] *L'Osservatore Romano*, May, 1948. Cited in D. Selbourne, *The Losing Battle With Islam* (New York: Prometheus, 2005), 424.

[7] "The Church," *The Catholic Encyclopaedia*, http://www.newadvent.org/cathen/03744a. htm,1908 (accessed May 2007).

[8] "True, the Jewish authorities and those who followed their lead pressed for the death of Christ (John 19:6): still, what happened in His passion cannot be charged against all the Jews, without distinction, then alive, nor against the Jews of today. Although the Church is the new people of God, the Jews should not be presented as rejected or accursed by God, as if this followed from the Holy Scriptures. . . . The Church, mindful of the patrimony she shares with

continues to maintain that it is the new Israel. The root of the Church of Rome's problem here has not been excised.

Other Christian denominations have also recently repudiated anti-Judaism in a confessional sense. As examples, Michael Vlach refers to the Central Board of the Swiss Protestant Church Federation, the Mennonite European Regional Conference, the Synod of the Evangelical Church of the Rhineland, the Texas Conference of Churches, the General Assembly of the Presbyterian Church (U.S.A.), though associated with disinvestment concerning Israel, that have issued a variety of high-sounding statements repudiating replacement theology in one form or another. Yet none of these specifically declare agreement with Israel's divine covenantal rights in terms of ethnicity, nationality, and territory.[9]

Those of a Reformed persuasion are faced with the embarrassment of alignment with a sordid eschatological lineage (see chapter 2) and the alternative of alignment with divine, uncompromising recognition of National Israel in the present, after the manner of Rom 11:28. This would also involve the recognition of divine acknowledgment of Jewish ethnicity, nationality, and territory as being intrinsic to the modern Hebrew people of God, notwithstanding their unbelief. The dilemma then concerns an eschatological vision that inescapably draws close to a broad premillennial perspective with regard to Israel, especially concerning the interpretation of passages such as Ezekiel 36–37, Zechariah 14, and Romans 11. By contrast, there is the disgraceful eschatology that has dominated Augustinian, Roman Catholic, and Reformed church history for centuries.

Israel and Judeo-centric Premillennialism up to the Reformation

The classic eschatological distinction for centuries was between the supercessionism of Augustine, as reflected in his *City of God*, and chiliasm that was often maligned for its alleged carnality and Judeo-centricity. As will be demonstrated, chiliasm and subsequent premillennialism have continued to uphold a closer identity with the perpetuation of the Jewish people as a nation with a distinct eschatological hope. This being so, and in light of

the Jews and moved not by political reasons but by the Gospel's spiritual love, decries hatred, persecutions, displays of anti-Semitism, directed against Jews at any time and by anyone." *Documents of Vatican II Council*, http://www.vatican.va/archive/hist_councils/ii_vatican_council/documents/vat -ii_decl_19651028_nostra-aetate_en.html, 1965 (cited May 2007).

[9] M. J. Vlach, *The Church as a Replacement of Israel: An Analysis of Supercessionism* (Ph.D. diss., Southeastern Baptist Theological Seminary, 2004), 72–75.

the theological anti-Judaism that flowed forth with dominant influence out of Augustine's eschatology, it is easier to understand how premillennialism suffered Cinderella-like belittlement as a consequence. Over the centuries that led up to the Reformation, the commanding influence of classic amillennialism was not a matter of choice according to the free biblical enquiry of Christians in general. During this period, the normative eschatology was upheld by the ecclesiastical powers, according to the lineage of Augustine and Aquinas, and it admirably suited the perpetuation and consolidation of the Church triumphant on earth as the new Israel that was rigidly intolerant of any suggestion of a revived and regenerated old Israel. Thus, at the dawning of the Reformation,

> in the sixteenth century, the rejection of the doctrine of a future terrestrial millennium was so common in Puritanism, and in Protestantism more generally, that it represented a mainstream position at the time. Luther and Melanchthon, Zwingli and Bullinger, and Calvin and Beza repudiated the millenarian doctrine, as did the Elizabethan Anglicans John Bale and John Foxe and their Puritan contemporaries Thomas Cartright and William Perkins. These and other "amillennialists," as they are often called, either assigned the millennium to a past historical epoch that antedated the supposed corruption of the apostolic church by Roman Catholicism, or saw the millennium as the whole period of the Christian dispensation between the incarnation and the second coming, or regarded the millennium as a purely spiritual condition existing only in heaven or perhaps in the souls of living believers. But in the early to mid-seventeenth century, this amillennialist consensus unraveled as the idea of a future millennium on earth gained popularity, particularly in Reformed circles.[10]

Only with the advent of printing and the freedom to publish that coalesced during the early seventeenth century did a more independent pastorate result and the people at all stratas find themselves exposed to a revival of more millennial interpretations of Scripture, especially as eventually designated as premillennialism and postmillennialism.

Israel and Judeo-centric Premillennialism Beyond the Reformation

In broad terms, the eschatology of the late sixteenth century perpetuated Augustinianism, the result being that chiliasm continued to be associated with certain extremist segments of Anabaptism. But the seventeenth century

---

[10] R. W Cogley, "The Fall of the Ottoman Empire and the Restoration of Israel in the 'Judeo-centric' Strand of Puritan Millenarianism," *CH*, 72:2 (2003): 306–7.

introduced an openness to millennial speculation that has continued to the present, though the reason for this eruption and consequent flurry of discussion is a matter that has already been indicated briefly in chapter 2 with regard to Puritanism. At the conclusion of Crawford Gribbens' published doctoral thesis, he draws attention to the observations of Christopher Hill which prove to be most enlightening.

> If, as [Christopher] Hill claims, English Calvinism was crumbling in the 1590s, then after the 1640s both strict church discipline and Calvinist theology finally "lost their grip": "Calvinism broke down when the Revolution established freedom of discussion." . . . The revolution's literary implications were also enormous. . . . As Thomas Manton noted in 1655, "The press is an excellent means to scatter knowledge, were it not so often abused. All complain there is enough written, and think that now there should be a stop. Indeed, it were well if in this scribbling age there were some restraint. Useless pamphlets are grown almost as great a mischief as the erroneous and profane." Hill has noted that, "The collapse of censorship saw a fantastic outpouring of books, pamphlets and newspapers. Before 1640, newspapers were illegal; by 1645 there were 722. Twenty-two books were published in 1640; over 2,000 in 1642. As both sides in the Civil War appealed for support from the ordinary people, the issues at stake had to be discussed. But it went farther than that . . . No old shibboleths were left unchallenged in this unprecedented freedom." Perhaps Owen had been right in hoping "we might have less writing, and more praying."[11]

The result was a resurgence of millennialism that continued to be opposed by much of the Anglican, European Reformed and Lutheran establishments. Nevertheless,

> on the Continent, the key figures in the transition to millenarianism were two German Reformed theologians, Johann Piscator and Johann Heinrich Alsted; and in England, they were Thomas Brightman and Joseph Mede, an Anglican whose influence on the emergence of Puritan millenarianism was profound.[12]

---

[11] C. Gribben, *The Puritan Millennium* (Dublin, Ireland: Four Courts Press, 2000), 194–95.

[12] Cogley, "'Judeo-centric' Strand of Puritan Millenarianism," 307. Basic millennial distinctions during the late sixteenth and seventeenth centuries were not so clearly defined. Nevertheless, millennialism in general spawned the arousal of a more affectionate, philo-Judaic attitude. Along with Mede (having been influenced by Alsted), considered the father of English premillennialism, were other English premillennialists such as John Archer, Jeremiah Burroughs, Thomas Goodwin and William Twisse. See R. G. Clouse, "The Influence of John Henry Alsted on English Millenarian Thought in the Seventeenth Century" (Ph.D. diss., Graduate College of the State University of Iowa, 1963); C. Gribben, *The Puritan Millennium* (Dublin, Ireland: Four Courts Press, 2000); Iain Murray, *The Puritan Hope* (London: Banner of Truth, 1971); P. Toon, *Puritans, the Millennium and the Future of Israel: Puritan Eschatology, 1600 to 1660* (Cambridge: James Clarke, 1970).

As eschatological study of Scripture and resultant speculation fomented fresh discovery, two distinctive schools of millennialism emerged and came to the fore. There was premillennialism, which anticipated the future return of Jesus Christ just prior to the commencement of his earthly thousand-year reign, and postmillennialism, which anticipated the future earthly millennium at the end of which Jesus Christ would personally return to earth. However, "the three major eschatological traditions which the Christian church has developed—a-, pre- and postmillennialism—each found expression within the puritan movement."[13]

Wilhelmus à Brakel

A further example of a more pro-Judaic, European eschatology that appeared in the seventeenth century was that expressed by Wilhelmus à Brakel (1635–1711), an esteemed Dutch Reformed theologian who ministered in Rotterdam, Holland, having eschatological views that contrasted with the more standard Augustinian variety. Willem VanGemeren explains that, in objecting to Calvin, Brakel held that,

> the Church could not be identified with the New Israel. When Paul wrote about "all Israel" (Rom. 11:25) he was referring to the nation, and not the totality of the church and national Israel. This rejection of Calvin was also found in Brakel's contemporaries. Brakel expected *all* twelve tribes to repent and express faith in Jesus as the Messiah. He also held that the Jews would be privileged to return to their land. The promise of the land is not just a type of the eternal rest or of heaven, rather it is part and parcel with the covenant of grace which God made to and affirmed with Israel. Brakel kept Israel and church together.[14]

Brakel's whole tone is also particularly Pauline since it breathes a tenderness that at the same time did not see the necessity of denying Jewish distinctiveness. So he wrote,

> Will the Jewish nation be gathered together again from all the regions of the world and from all the nations of the earth among which they have been dispersed? Will they come to and dwell in Canaan and all the lands promised to Abraham, and will Jerusalem be rebuilt?
> We believe that these events will transpire. We deny, however, that the temple will be rebuilt, and that therein the previous mode of worship will be observed, which prior to Christ's coming was of a typifying nature and

[13] Gribben, *The Puritan Millennium*, 16.

[14] W. VanGemeren, "Israel as the Hermeneutical Crux in the Interpretation of Prophecy," *WTJ*, 45 (1983): 142–43.

would then be of a reflective nature. We also deny that Israel will then have dominion over the entire world—and other such things which the Jews imagine and some Christians dream about. Rather, they will be an independent republic, governed by a very wise, good-natured, and superb government. Furthermore, Canaan will be extraordinarily fruitful, the inhabitants will be eminently godly, and they will constitute a segment of the glorious state of the church during the thousand years prophesied in Revelation 20.[15]

It is notable that, like Jonathan Edwards, for Brakel the unity of the redeemed people of God will yet comprise a diversity, incorporating territory, in which Israel is a distinctive part of the whole. What is also significant concerning Brakel's belief in the regenerate future of national Israel is his evident loving attitude, without compromise concerning Israel's unbelief, that is manifest in his consideration of how Christians should respond to unbelieving Jews. Surely his kindly temperament was the result of his Judeo-centric eschatology. Consider his "various reasons . . . for focusing upon the conversion of the Jewish Nation":

(1) Attentively observe the immutability of the covenant God made with Abraham and his seed. Consider that God, in spite of all their sins and stiff-neckedness under it, does not break His promise nor will He permit any of the good words spoken to them to fall to the earth.

(2) Do not despise the Jewish nation. "Boast not against the branches" (Rom. 11:18), the natural branches of that olive tree into which you, as branches of a wild olive tree, have been grafted contrary to nature. "Be not high-minded, but fear" (Rom. 11:20). 1) They have received more than enough contempt from the unconverted. 2) They are in one and the same covenant with Abraham, their father. 3) "They are beloved for the father's sakes" (Rom. 11:28). Therefore, let there be the love of benevolence toward them. They are the children of the covenant (Acts 3:25). 4) They will once be converted and be a glorious and holy people above all the nations on the face of the earth. Therefore, esteem, honor, and love them.

(3) Have pity upon their state, which is so wretched according to the flesh, being despised and detested among the nations—this is a righteous judgment of God upon them for their rejection of Christ. They hate the Lord Jesus, the true Messiah, with an evil hatred, and are living without the true religion—yes, have a religion which does not even resemble a religion. Nevertheless, they find a wonderful delight in it; thus they live in a state in

---

[15] W. à Brakel, *The Christian's Reasonable Service*, IV (Ligonier PA: Soil Deo Gloria, 1992), 530–31. From a premillennial perspective, one does not have to agree with Brakel's postmillennialism and the common optimism of that "new world" period within church history to nevertheless admire his loyalty to the Scriptures concerning a godly, distinctive, and territorial future for national Israel.

which they cannot be saved, but have nothing to look forward to but eternal damnation.

(4) Pray for their conversion. How they have prayed for the conversion of the Gentiles! How they rejoiced in the prophecies that one day the Gentiles would be converted! Therefore, you ought to do likewise for their conversion, for you can pray this in faith, since they will certainly be converted.

(5) By way of a holy life show that you are walking in the footsteps of their father Abraham. The life of so many so-called Christians offends them and keeps them from exercising faith in Christ. They do not know, except it be to a very limited extent, that among Christians there are presently many who fear and love *Jehovah*, the God of Israel. Therefore, manifest the image of Christ by way of a holy walk, so that they may be convicted by it and yet be aroused to jealousy. Occasionally make use of opportunities to speak in a friendly manner with them, making your affection known to them, as well as your anticipation of their restoration in Canaan. Speak to them about the Lord Jesus by the name of Messiah. Speak of the dreadfulness of sin and of eternal damnation to follow upon sin, and show this from the Scriptures of the Old Testament if you are able to do so. Show them that man cannot be justified before God by works, and that all their deeds cannot justify them. Show them from the Old Testament that the Messiah would make satisfaction for sin by His death, reconcile God with man, and convert souls, proving this from Isaiah 53; 61, and Daniel 9. The fact is that in doing so you have done your duty, and it will be a delight to your soul that you have done so. Be very careful not to quarrel, however, thereby giving them an opportunity to slander and grieve you by their diatribe.[16]

Luther's Eschatological Legacy

The inheritance from the Augustinian tradition that modern Europe received, notwithstanding the opposition of Melanchthon and others to Luther's excesses, resulted in the continuance of an eschatology that upheld the essentially anti-Judaic thesis, namely, the transference of blessings, formerly promised to Israel, to the Christian Church for its fulfillment. As a consequence, the Jews continued to be an offence to western civilization, especially within Europe, a claimant forever disinherited of their Jewishness. The Catholic, Protestant, and Reformed churches gave encouragement to this anti-Judaic course. The end result, however, was a Germany that, having shaken the world with its call back to biblical Christianity, yet became the shame of the world whereby it caused the name of God to be blasphemed among the Jews. Thus Robert Wistrich concludes:

[16] Ibid., 534–35.

The German Reformation, under Luther's guidance, therefore led in a very unfavourable direction for the Jews, when compared with parallel developments in English, Dutch or Swiss Protestantism. The seed of hatred sown by Luther would reach its horrible climax in the Third Reich, when German Protestants showed themselves to be particularly receptive to Nazi anti-Semitism.[17]

Evidence of continuity concerning this eschatological lineage is not difficult to find. Consider a contemporary expression of Luther's Augustinian anti-Judaism by The Lutheran Church-Missouri Synod, titled "The eschatology presented in The Lutheran Confessions is clearly amillennialist."[18] The whole content of this document adds unqualified support to this statement. Then in an "Excursus Regarding the Jews," anti-Semitism is nevertheless repudiated while at the same time we are told quite defensively that, "Martin Luther, in his last sermon, said concerning the attitude of Christians toward the Jewish people, 'We want to treat them with Christian love and to pray for them, so that they might become converted and would receive the Lord.'"[19] However, what is unsaid here is just as significant, for Williamson also explains that "Luther's last sermon, preached a few days before his death, importunately appealed that all Jews be driven from Germany."[20] Then *The End Times" Report* concludes:

> Believing Jews, together with Gentiles, constitute the New Israel. In Christ "there is neither Jew nor Greek" (Gal. 3:28). In speaking of the place of Jews within saving history, the Scriptures do not ascribe a political fulfillment to Old Testament texts which deal with the future of "Israel." The modern Israeli state is not the fulfillment of Old Testament prophecy. The view of an earthly millennium with the temple rebuilt cannot be substantiated. Quite simply the Scriptures are silent regarding modern political events in the Middle East and any Jewish right to the land there. Judgments concerning such matters are therefore not theological questions.[21]

As we have already seen, the exegesis of Lutheran commentator R. C. H. Lenski follows the same course. In a similar, though more vociferous vein, the eschatology of Herman Otten, editor of the Lutheran *Christian News*, has been vehemently anti-Judaic in doctrine, and especially so with regard

---

[17] R. S. Wistrich, *Antisemitism, The Longest Hatred* (New York: Pantheon, 1991), 42.

[18] *The "End Times": A Study on Eschatology and Millennialism*. A Report of the Commission on Theology and Church Relations of The Lutheran Church—Missouri Synod (St. Louis: The Commission, 1989), 7.

[19] Ibid., 38.

[20] C. M. Williamson, *Has God Rejected His People?* (Nashville: Abingdon, 1982), 102.

[21] *The "End Times" Report*, 39.

to the modern State of Israel. Francis Pieper's *Christian Dogmatics* (1953), a standard Missouri Synod work, is also thoroughgoing in its amillennialism. Here theological anti-Judaism plainly rears its head. Pieper opposed the modern State of Israel because its establishment would

> divert the attention of the Jews from the Gospel which in their dispersion they now hear and are to believe to a future age. This pernicious effect is intensified if this dream of a future "time of the Jews" is made attractive to them by promises of Jewish nationalism, a return to, and possession of, the land of their forefathers, and a rebuilding of the Temple in Jerusalem, with re-establishment of its elaborate worship. One of the many deplorable consequences of the World War is the promise of the Allies to give Palestine to the Jews as their national home. Instead of repenting of their sins and believing in the Messiah who has come, the Orthodox Jews dream of a return to Palestine and the rebuilding of the Temple with its worship (Zionism), and the Reform Jews envision a spiritual domination of the world by Jewish intellectual superiority and erudition, to be achieved by means of a Jewish university on the Mount of Olives.[22]

What further proof is needed of the shameful eschatological spirit of Augustine living on in Augustinian Lutheranism? Whereas the Bishop of Hippo rejected the concept of extreme persecution of the Jews (that is, elimination), he favored their being kept in subjection and impoverishment.[23] So Pieper would similarly have them remain as vagabonds for their own spiritual good! The whole spirit of this doctrinal expression is repugnant in the light of Rom 11:18–20.

Departure from Luther

By the time of the late seventeenth century, the creedal formulation of Lutheranism had deteriorated into cool dogmatic orthodoxy resulting in a nation in spiritual decline, out of which arose the pietistic movement. It was prompted by Philipp Jacob Spener of Frankfurt and Berlin, who was concerned about the spiritually bleak and parched state of Lutheranism.[24]

While Spener considered himself a dwarf when compared with Luther's stature, yet he maintained that standing on the shoulders of this giant he was enabled to see further ahead. He was pained when Lutherans spoke evil of Luther's Reformation but was insistent that spiritual reform should

---

[22] F. Pieper, *Christian Dogmatics* (St. Louis, Missouri: Concordia, 1953), 3:533–34.

[23] J. Carroll, *Constantine's Sword* (Boston: Houghton Mifflin, 2001), 385.

[24] See A. H. Newman, *A Manual of Church History* (Philadelphia: American Baptist Publication Society, 1931), 2:525.

continue toward personal sanctification and piety.[25] Joined by A. H. Franke, a new movement grew that resulted in the founding of the University of Halle and a large growing body of spiritually zealous pastors. Through Spener's godson, Count Nicolaus Ludwig von Zinzendorf, the Herrnhut community developed, which greatly influenced John Wesley.

The pietistic movement developed with a more millenarian emphasis with greater tolerance toward the Jews. This contrasted with the *Augsburg Confession*, Article XVII, which condemned those "who now scatter Jewish opinions, that, before the resurrection of the dead, the godly shall occupy the kingdom of the world, the wicked being every where suppressed."[26] Spener evidenced a mild postmillennialism[27] that helped stem the tide of anti-Semitism in his day.

> It has been suggested that Spener, in Frankfurt, treated the Jewish people not only as potential Christians, but also as neighbors assigned by God. . . . His forthright and frequent denunciation of the teasing and mobbing of Jewish people on the streets by Christian children caused that malicious practice to occur with less frequency. . . . Spener replied affirmatively to the question, "Can Christian midwives attend Jewish women?" . . . Spener in numerous later opinions advised against expulsion of Jews or abolition of their synagogues. . . . Spener was a promoter of Christian missions to Jews. He himself baptized a number of Jewish converts to Christianity at Frankfurt. He conceded, however, how difficult it was to help these people, now bereft of family and position, to recapture financial security. He, therefore, concluded that reborn Christians could best help in this difficult task by living out their faith in love-filled lives that would make the Gospel attractive to Jews.[28]

As we have already seen with Brakel, here is further proof that Judeo-centric doctrine, in giving right biblical acknowledgment of the Jews even in unbelief, while having evangelism in mind, is best suited for the production of a loving attitude toward the Jews. A scholarly lineage of Lutheran premillennialists developed that included Bengel, Zahn, Delitzsch, Godet, Auberlen, and Rothe, along with van Osterzee who was Dutch Reformed. Thus "American Lutherans were aware of these European theologians. Some Lutherans emigrating to America brought these millennialistic views

---

[25] K. J. Stein, *Philipp Jakob Spener, Pietist Patriarch* (Chicago: Covenant Press, 1986), 264–65.

[26] P. Schaff, *The Creeds of Christendom* (Grand Rapids: Baker, 1969), 3:18.

[27] J. M. Brenner, *American Lutheran Views on Eschatology and How They Related to the American Protestants*, http://www.wlsessays.net/authors/B/ BrennerEschatology/BrennerEschatology.rtf, 6 (accessed May 2007).

[28] Stein, *Philipp Jacob Spener*, 246–47.

with them."[29] In the United States, three particular Lutherans encouraged Judeo-centric premillennialism: Samuel Simon Schmucker, Joseph Seiss, and George N. H. Peters.

Reformed Development

On a much larger scale the Reformed movement maintained its allegiance to Augustinian eschatology, which especially found authoritative expression in the writings of Francis Turretin (1623–1687) who studied at Calvin's Academy in Geneva and later taught there for 30 years. His monumental *Institutes of Elenctic Theology* became the epitome of Reformed doctrine. Not surprisingly, his quotations of Augustine are copious, even far exceeding references to Calvin. Consequently Turretin's eschatology is almost predictable. With regard to the prophetic expectations of Israel's restoration beyond the return from Babylon,

> the expressions are not to be pressed literally because they are symbolical, not proper; typical, not literal; to be explained spiritually and not carnally. Israel is to be restored, not according to the flesh and letter, but according to the promise and spirit (Rom. 9); the holy city, not Jerusalem, but the church.[30]

Certainly there will be a remarkable conversion of the Jews before the end of the world,

> not that all will be converted, but that many will . . . (although we cannot be certain either in what way or when precisely it will take place). . . . But whatever that calling of them shall be, a restitution of the Jewish polity in the land of Canaan is not to be dreamed of. . . . Besides, this polity was to last only until Christ. . . . Finally, if God had wished to restore that polity, he would not have suffered it to be abolished for so long a time (for over sixteen centuries).[31]

Of course such a mass incorporation into the Church is to the exclusion of any perpetuation of Jewish identity. In classic Augustinian fashion, there is token recognition of Jewish individuality for a time, though any form of a Jewish restoration was considered to be a gross form of chiliasm.[32] Turretin's *Institutes* became the central textbook for Systematic Theology in American Ivy League Colleges during the later half of the

---

[29] Brenner, *American Lutheran Views on Eschatology*, 6.
[30] F. Turretin, *Institutes of Elenctic Theology* (Phillipsburg, N.J.: P&R, 1992–1994), 2:163.
[31] Ibid., 3:587–88.
[32] Ibid., 3:574–75.

eighteenth century. It is not surprising that the early theologians of Princeton Theological Seminary highly esteemed this most influential legacy, and of course its eschatology.

> Charles Hodge agreed with Dr. [Archibald] Alexander that Turretin's *Institutio Theologiae Elencthicae* was "incomparably the best book as a whole on systematic theology" and continued its use as the principal text.[33]

In 1845 Hodge replaced student recitation of Turretin with his own theological lectures,[34] but when his *Systematic Theology,* was first published in three volumes in 1872, its replacement of Turretin brought no change in essential emphasis, as the copious references to his Reformed mentor indicate.

Fairbairn, Bavinck, and Vos

In the eschatological milieu of the western world toward the close of the eighteenth century, a defensive response against resurgent premillennialism came to the fore which resulted in a "new hermeneutic" that actually proved to be nothing more than revamped Augustinianism. As VanGemeren explained,

> By the end of the nineteenth century amillennialism as an eschatological position had arisen out of the new hermeneutic for which [Patrick] Fairbairn [1805–1874] was a leading spokesman. The writings of Herman Bavinck (1895–1964) [of the Free University of Amsterdam] and Geerhardus Vos (1862–1949) [of Princeton Seminary] are representative of the change. Both theologians interact with chiliasm in affirming that their eschatological position is normative. Both Bavinck and Vos are amillennial in their views and engage in argumentation against premillennialism. . . . Instead of taking the OT language for what it is, Bavinck argues that there lies an eternal truth "in the earthly, sensual forms of the prophecies." . . . He strongly objects to millennialism as a hermeneutic in which the earthly forms of the OT are understood literally.[35]

We now consider these three Reformed scholars in terms of their eschatology with regard to Israel and the all too obvious historic connection with fundamental Augustinianism.

Patrick Fairbairn

Patrick Fairbairn was born in Hallyburton, Scotland, in 1805. After graduating from the University of Edinburgh in 1826, he tutored at the Orkney

---

[33] D. B. Calhoun, *Princeton Seminary*, I (Edinburgh: Banner of Truth, 1994), 262.

[34] Ibid., 2:32.

[35] W. VanGemeren, "Israel as the Hermeneutical Crux in the Interpretation of Prophecy (II)," *WTJ*, 46 (1984): 261.

Islands and advanced in his study of Hebrew and German. Following his first pastorate in Glasgow, evangelical convictions led to his alignment with the Free Church of Scotland; he took a leading part in organizing the Free Church Presbytery of Haddington. In 1853 he was appointed by the General Assembly to the Chair of Theology in Aberdeen. When the Free Church College was founded in Glasgow in 1856 Fairbairn became Principal and Professor of Church History and Exegesis there and presided over the institution till his death in 1874.

Fairbairn (1838–39) versus Fairbairn (1864).

In 1838–39 Fairbairn delivered twelve lectures on "Future Prospects of the Jews—Restoration to Their Own Land—Universal Conversion to the Faith of Christ." Here the young Presbyterian minister of Glasgow presented arguments for a millennial eschatology anticipating a distinct national future and conversion of the Jewish people. In 1864 the older Fairbairn, as Principal of the Presbyterian Free Church College in Glasgow, authored *Fairbairn on Prophecy* in which was included, from an amillennial perspective, "The Prophetical Future of the Jewish People." Fairbairn's *The Typology of Scripture* (1852), *Hermeneutical Manual* (1858), and *Commentary on Ezekiel* (1863) are similarly amillennial. In 1950 Albertus Pieters[36] edited a book including both articles under the title, *The Prophetic Prospects of the Jews, or Fairbairn vs. Fairbairn.* The later writing of Fairbairn proposes three views—the Jewish, semi-Jewish, and spiritualistic—the last mentioned being his more recently embraced amillennial perspective, namely, "that the proper meaning of the prophecies, in so far as they bear on the future of Israel, is to be made good simply by the conversion of the people [Jews] to the Christian faith, and their participation in the privileges and hopes of the church of Christ."[37]

The older Fairbairn's regard for Israel and the Jews was simply a recapitulation of essential Augustinianism, though filtered through a prism of German scholarship. Passing by this author's unwillingness to face the Jewish realities of Matt 19:28, Luke 21:24, and Acts 1:6–7,[38] we will consider his wrestling with the vital question:

---

[36] See this author's theological anti-Semitism in Chapter 3.

[37] Albertus Pieters, ed., *The Prophetic Prospects of the Jews, or Fairbairn vs. Fairbairn* (Grand Rapids: Eerdmans, 1930), 91. Of course this incorporation of Israel into the Church of Christ means that all Jewish identity, whether individual, national, or territorial, has become null and void.

[38] Fairbairn frequently disparaged "literalism." With the same tone of depreciation he wrote "Prophetical Literalism Essentially Jewish," *Prophecy*, Second Edition (New York: Nelson &

May not the natural Israel in some other respect have the prospect of a separate and peculiar standing in the church? . . . Even when the kingdoms of this world have become the kingdom of our God and of His Christ, shall the Jewish nation stand out and apart from the rest? . . . Were it to do so, *it would not be a continuation or a renewal of the past, but the introduction of an entirely new principle into the Church of God.*[39]

David E. Holwerda, professor of NT at Calvin Theological Seminary, commenced a study of Romans 9–11 with the question, "Is there a future for Jewish Israel?" He at least confessed that "there is nothing in the Gospels and Acts that either biblically or logically entails an absolute or definitive rejection of Jewish Israel."[40] But Fairbairn was quite unyielding at this juncture, explaining that Israel was

the nation that held the truth, and, as such, stood apart from the idolatrous nations of heathendom. But when that distinction virtually ceased to exist by the mass of the people abandoning the truth, and espousing the corruptions of heathenism, the Lord held the ground of separation to be abolished, and addressed and treated them as heathen (Isa. 1:1–10; Amos 9:7–8; Ezek. 16–23).[41]

Yet ensuing revelation from all three of the prophets Fairbairn referenced gives encouragement concerning the vital truth of Paul that "where sin increased, grace abounded all the more" (Rom 5:20; see Isa 2:1–4; Amos 9:11–15; Ezek 28:25–26; chaps. 34, 36–37). Such triumph of sovereign grace is acknowledged by Fairbairn and others with regard to the new covenant dispensation, yet denied for Israel.

Why then cannot the future people of God incorporate a diversity of Jews and Gentiles, as Edwards, Bonar, Ryle, and Spurgeon affirmed? Fairbairn explained:

If converted Israelites were still to stand apart from and above them [the remainder of the kingdom], it would not be the same thing that existed under the law, but something essentially different—something foreign even to Judaism; how much more, then, to Christianity?[42]

Phillips, 1874), 505–7. Is a true and more figurative biblical hermeneutic in the realm of eschatology non-Jewish?

[39] Ibid., 131, 133–34.

[40] D. E. Holwerda, *Jesus & Israel, One Covenant or Two?* (Grand Rapids: Eerdmans, 1995), 150.

[41] Pieters, *Prophetic Prospects of the Jews*, 132.

[42] Ibid., 134.

Yet the essence of Judaism is rooted in the Abrahamic covenant, not the temporal Mosaic legal covenant. A future distinctive Hebraic/Judaic distinction would not be essentially different. Granted that there would be new features in this perfected Messianic Judaism, but it is simply not correct to suggest that there could not be variety among the people of God. After all, we might ask if angelic beings will also be participants in the future, new glorious order.

Concerning Fairbairn's regard of the land of promise, we encounter a similar problem. He declared

> that the typical character which attached to the people and the religion of the old covenant, attached also to the inheritance—the land of Canaan; and that the transition to gospel times is represented as effecting the same relative change in respect to this as to the others. . . . The land was, in a manner, the common basis of the people and the worship—the platform on which both stood, and in connection with which the whole of their religious observances, and their national history, might be said to move. To except this, therefore, from the typical territory, and withdraw it from the temporary things which were to pass to something higher and better in Christ, were to suppose an incongruity in the circumstances of ancient Israel, which we cannot conceive to have existed, and could only have led to inextricable confusion. . . . The former relation of the Israelites to the land of Canaan affords no ground for re-occupation by them after their conversion to the faith of Christ, no more than for expecting that the handwriting of ordinances shall then be restored. [43]

For all the twisting and turning here, the fact remains that God's promise of the land was made unilaterally to Abraham, Isaac, and Jacob (Gen 12:1; 15:1–21; 26:2–4; 28:13), and Fairbairn seems uncomfortably aware of this. The reality is that the multilateral Mosaic covenant was a temporary administration imposed on Israel (Ps 147:19–20), which could not nullify that which had been promised to Abraham (Gal 3:17); it "was added because of transgressions" (Gal 3:19; see Rom 5:20), and thus could not invalidate the promise of the land. Yes, I agree that Abraham would become "heir of the world" (Rom 4:13), that the seed of Abraham, being Christ and His seed (Gal 3:16,29), would inherit the world. But I reject Fairbairn's suggestion that this necessarily brings about the nullification of Israel's future possession of the land, as if it were part of "the handwriting of ordinances" (Eph 2:15; Col 2:14) that were specifically Mosaic. So again here is the rigid unwillingness of amillennial doctrine to incorporate diversity within unity. But the prophets repeatedly incorporated the diversity of the

---

[43] Ibid., 140, 142.

land, the prominence of Jerusalem, and the surrounding nations within the unity of the whole redeemed, inhabited earth (Isa 60:1–4; 62:1–12; Mic 4:1–5; Hag 2:1–7; Zech 14:16–21).

Ezekiel 34, 36–38.

Fairbairn's overall approach considering the future of national Israel in these classic references is portrayed in his answer to this question:

> *Could* the promise of Messiah, and of the affairs connected with his work and kingdom, have been unfolded to the Church [of ancient Israel] beforehand, and with any degree of detail, excepting under the form and shadow of Old Testament relations? We unhesitatingly answer, No; not unless the Spirit had violently controlled the minds of the prophets, and superseded the free exercise of their faculties. . . . [This] prophecy . . . bears the natural impress of the time to which it belonged. But if any, determined to hear of nothing but the letter, will still hold by the watchword of literality,—will maintain that as it is a literal Israel that is the subject of promise, a literal Canaan, a literal dispersion, and a literal return from it, such too must be all that is to come,—then, we say, let them carry it out, and the shepherd by whom the good is to be accomplished must be the literal David, for David alone is expressly named in the promise; and so the Messiah altogether vanishes from the word of which he is the very heart and center. And there must be no advance in the Divine dispensations, nothing but the formal reproduction of the past. Such is a slavish adherence to the letter; it ends in shutting up the new wine of Messiah's kingdom in the old bottles of a transitory and provisional economy. . . . Thus, as the David of the promise is Christ, so the covenant-people are no longer the Jews distinctively, but the faithful in Christ; and the territory of blessing no longer Canaan, but the region of which Christ is king and lord.[44]

So these passages, and thus the human author, although directed by the Holy Spirit, were culturally landlocked, constrained by "the time to which [they] . . . belonged." To be sure, the tone of the exilic period is to be expected in Ezekiel's style of communication (Ezek 1:1–3). But to suggest that God could only present the future of His kingdom strictly within these exilic parameters is to rashly constrain Him contrary to Daniel who was not so restricted, for he "heard but could not understand," and was further told, "Go your way, Daniel, for these words are concealed and sealed up until the end time" (Dan 12:8–9). Here Fairbairn begs the question since the necessity of "violent control of the minds of the prophets" in predicting the future is quite unproven, and indeed an unnecessary restriction of the

---

[44] P. Fairbairn, *Ezekiel* (Edinburgh: T&T Clark, 1863), 385, 388, 421.

Divine Will. After all, the vital terms concerning the meaning of "Judah" and "Israel" and "land" and "Jerusalem" and Zion" and "nations" are certainly not restricted by a particular culture. I would suggest that Fairbairn's attempt to generalize with regard to the promised rapprochement concerning "Judah" and "Israel" (Ezek 37:15–23)—so that it merely represents the result of the resurrection of God's people whereby "the direct result of this was to unite them to God"[45]—borders on the fanciful. I would maintain that "Judah" means "Judah" and "Israel" means "Israel," so that God "will make them one nation in the land, on the mountains of Israel; and one king will be king for all of them" (Ezek 37:22).

Concerning David following his future resurrection, we would first enquire of the amillennialist as to what his distinctive role will be in the future kingdom of God. As with Moses and Elijah, surely he will have great prominence, in which case it is quite likely that he will indeed be a regent/prince over Israel under the King of kings, Jesus Christ, the "righteous Branch of David" (Jer. 23:5). To suggest that such an understanding results in "Messiah altogether vanishing from the word" is simply absurd. Thus, "My servant David will be a prince among them" (Ezek 34:24), that is, "My flock" (v. 22). However, this prince is not identical with Christ since he offers a sin offering for himself (45:22) and has distinctive sons (46:16–17).

Fairbairn's conclusion is that at the consummation of the church, peculiar and historic Jewishness will have been done away with, superseded, absorbed into the one people of God, and particularly with regard to any distinction concerning the territory of Israel. Augustinianism, Catholic eschatology, and Fairbairn are in essential agreement at this point. So the good news for the Jew today is that his distinctive Jewishness is divinely passé, a biblical anachronism. Those Christians who believe this will nevertheless declare their desire for the Jews to be saved. But they dare not explain to these same Jews their whole agenda, which includes salvation from Jewishness. But this approach flies in the face of Paul's whole attitude toward the Jews (Rom 11:28), especially in his evangelistic endeavors, in that he freely confessed that he remained one of them (Acts 21:39; 22:3; Rom 9:3; 11:1). And surely he spoke truly.

Ezekiel 40–48

Fairbairn explains four categories of interpretation and then argues for his "Christian-spiritual" interpretation. He claimed that

---

[45] Ibid., 416.

the whole representation was not intended to find either in Jewish or Christian times an express and formal realization, but was a grand, complicated symbol of the good God had in reserve for his church, especially under the coming dispensation of the gospel. From the Fathers downwards this has been the prevailing view in the Christian church.[46]

I would thoroughly agree with this historic representation, except that "from the Fathers downwards" only describes the eschatology of Augustine and the Roman Catholic Church, namely, supercessionism. When Ezekiel was instructed concerning his final vision, "Report everything you see to the house of Israel" (Ezek 40:4),[47] he was confirming the earlier promise: "When My sanctuary is among them forever, the nations will know that I, the LORD, sanctify Israel" (Ezek 37:28). Thus "Israel" and "the nations" are to become distinct, yet complementary, worshipping entities.

I admit to Fairbairn's consistent application of his method of interpreting prophetic Scripture. But here in Ezekiel 40–48 he blithely rides over the astonishing particulars in terms of future fulfillment. This is not to suggest that such a grand and glorious vision is easily comprehended, though it does test our willingness to accept the transcendent glory of God's future, holy, spiritual materiality. However, it is the "spiritual interpretation" here that is so evidently unspiritual in that it implies an unnecessary verbosity that ends up in justifying any number of vague interpretations, provided one makes an attempt to deal with the particulars. Horatius Bonar explained the problem well:

> Every word of prophecy is big with meaning. Hence it must be most carefully and exactly interpreted. To attach a general meaning to a whole chapter, as is frequently done, shows not only grievous irreverence for the Divine Word, but much misconception of the real nature of that language in which it is written. Yet such is often the practice of many expositors of prophecy. They will take up a chapter of Isaiah, and tell you that it refers to the future glory of the Christian Church; and that is the one idea which they gather from a whole chapter, or sometimes from a series of chapters. Their system does not admit of interpreting verse by verse and clause by clause, and affixing an exact and definite sense to each. Bring them to this test, and their system gives way. It looks fair and plausible enough, so long as they can persuade you that the whole chapter is one scene, out of which it is merely designed that one grand idea should be extracted; but bring it to

---

[46] Ibid., 443–44.

[47] In the commentary by the Puritan, W. Greenhill (1591–1671), *An Exposition of Ezekiel* (Edinburgh: Banner of Truth, 1994), Ezekiel 40:4 is considered as referencing the Christian church in the extreme. Any distinctive regard for national Israel is wholly absorbed into a Gentile worldview.

the best of minute and precise interpretation, and its nakedness is at once discovered. Many prophecies become in this way a mere waste of words. What might be expressed in one sentence, is beaten out over a whole chapter; nay, sometimes over a whole book.[48]

These expositors think that there is nothing in prophecy, except that Jew and Gentile are all to be gathered in, and made one in Christ. Prophet after prophet is raised up, vision after vision is given, and yet nothing is declared but this one idea! Every chapter almost of Isaiah foretells something about the future glory of the world; and every chapter presents it to us in some new aspect, opening up new scenes, and pointing out new objects; but, according to the scheme of some, every chapter sets forth the same idea, reiterates the same objects, and depicts the same scenes. Is not this handling the Word of God deceitfully?[49]

The Response of Horatius Bonar.

Bonar was a Scottish contemporary of Fairbairn who responded with perceptive vigor and critical enlightenment. Bonar's *Prophetical Landmarks*, and *The Quarterly Journal of Prophecy* which he edited from 1849 to 1873, contain detailed refutations of Fairbairn's hermeneutic and resultant eschatology. I give a summary of two significant areas of criticism.

1. All prophecy is, to some degree, conditional.

Classic Reformed theology has commonly distinguished between prophecy that is predestined or certain, and prophecy that is contingent or conditional, usually in harmony with the distinction between God's decretive will and His preceptive will. Fairbairn addressed this matter in his *Prophecy, viewed in respect to its Distinctive Nature, its Special Function, and Proper Interpretation* (1856), and included a qualifying appendix in the Second Edition (1865). This was doubtless due to the controversial nature of his opinion, that is, his alleged departure from the accepted Calvinist stance to that which was more Arminian. In this regard, Bonar responded in *The Quarterly Journal of Prophecy* (1858) with marked disagreement concerning this particular item in *Fairbairn on Prophecy*, to which Fairbairn replied with some displeasure in the preface to his *Hermeneutical Manual* (1858).

---

[48] Bonar footnotes the following reference. "The latter chapters of Ezekiel, describing the erection of a certain temple, are involved in so much obscurity, that it seems difficult to arrive at any determinate conclusion respecting the import of this mysterious prophecy. *It is certain that the attempt to spiritualize it produces little besides perplexity and confusion; nor have we any example in Scripture of an allegory so perfectly dark and enigmatic, as it must be confessed to be, on that supposition.*"—Robert Hall, *Works*, IV (New York: Harper, 1844), 405.

[49] H. Bonar, *Prophetical Landmarks* (London: James Nisbet, 1876), 234–35.

The heart of Bonar's concern, as a Calvinist, was Fairbairn's belief "that there is in all prophecy an element of contingency,"[50] which reflects a more Arminian perspective. Thus Fairbairn believed that the Second Coming was certainly decreed in a general sense, although circumstances could change in terms of the time of its eventual occurrence. For example, Bonar referred to the following declaration of Fairbairn:

> The prophecies, for example, relating to the second coming of the Lord, . . . may be regarded . . . as protracted beyond what the natural import of the language might have seemed to indicate, on account of the forbearance of God waiting for the conversion of men. . . . Yet when [this Advent is] spoken of, as it often is, of being "near," of "drawing nigh," or being "at hand," while now so many centuries have elapsed without its taking place, we can scarcely help admitting (however we may choose to express it) that some after-respect has been had to moral considerations as influencing the time of the predicted event; in other words, that there has been the operation of a conditional element to the effect of delaying longer than the original predictions might have led us to expect the actual occurrence of the event predicted.[51]

Bonar responded,

> We are at a loss to conceive how it [this quotation] can be reconciled with any theory of predestination whatever. To say that God did not from all eternity decree the time when the Savior should come the second time, is to admit at once the Arminian notion of conditional decrees. . . . Nothing can well be more dishonoring to the Divine Being than to suppose, as Dr. Fairbairn's words imply, that there was enough in the earlier predictions to warrant an expectation of the advent at a period which has passed by without it; and that "the course of things in the world" has led to the postponement of the Church's hope.[52]

To criticism such as this Fairbairn responded with seeming irritation,

> To divide, as he [Bonar] and his authorities do, between prophecy, considered as equivalent to Divine decrees, and prophecy, as involving matter of commination or promise—the former absolute, the latter conditional—does not satisfy my "exegetical conscience," and I am afraid never can.[53]

A further illustration of Fairbairn's understanding of conditionality concerns the institution of the Davidic covenant in 2 Sam 7:1–17. He stated,

---

[50] H. Bonar, "Professor Fairbairn and Conditional Prophecy," *The Quarterly Journal of Prophecy* (October, 1858): 313.

[51] Fairbairn, *Prophecy*, 63–64.

[52] H. Bonar, "Fairbairn on Prophecy," *The Quarterly Journal of Prophecy* (September, 1857): 275.

[53] P. Fairbairn, *Hermeneutical Manual* (Edinburgh: T&T Clark, 1858), vii.

David himself knew perfectly well, that there was an implied condition, and that the prophecy must be read in connection with the whole plan and purposes of God in the administration of the affairs of His church.[54]

We wonder what conditionality, in any sense, could be understood in the Noahic covenant of Gen 8:20–9:17. Could an unprecedented surge in human moral decline bring about an unexpected divine interference in which the seasons fail and a similar universal flood reoccurs? But what interests us most is where this distinctive hermeneutic leads, and we now discover that it very much concerns the destiny of Israel. Fairbairn further explained,

> If the *threatened judgments* of the prophetic word, then also its *promised blessings*, are to be regarded, not as primarily and absolutely predictions of coming events, but rather as exhibitions of the Lord's goodness, prospective indications of his desire and purpose to bless the persons or communities addressed, yet capable of being checked, or even altogether cancelled, in the event of a perverse and rebellious disposition being manifested by men. . . . The Apostle Paul re-announces the principle with special emphasis on this particular branch of its application, when he says, at the close of his reasoning on the case of the Jewish people, "Behold, therefore, the goodness and the severity of God: on them which fell severity, but toward thee goodness, if thou continue in his goodness; otherwise, thou shalt also be cut off" (Rom 11:22),—that is, the prophetic intimations of future blessing are to be understood as valid only so long as the spiritual relation contemplated in them abides. When that ceases, a new and different state of things has entered which the promise did not contemplate, and to which it cannot in justice be applied.[55]

In the face of such a disturbing course of reasoning, I would simply ask whether this same conditionality applies to the application of the new covenant gospel to believing sinners? If it does, then surely the sovereignty of grace has been done away with and in its place has been substituted a subtle form of Galatianism.

2. The unhelpful influence of German scholarship.

It is refreshing to discover a conservative scholar such as Bonar who is not wholly enamored with, even hypnotized by, German scholarship so that both its strengths and weaknesses are clearly distinguished. Bonar provided the following estimate.

---

[54] Fairbairn, *Prophecy*, 64–65.

[55] Ibid., 75. The third class conditional clause of Romans 11:22, A. T. Robertson, *Word Pictures in the New Testament* (Nashville: Broadman, 1931), 4:397, is defined as being a "More Probable Future Condition," H. E. Dana and J. R. Mantey, *Manual Grammar of the Greek New Testament* (Toronto, Canada: Macmillan, 1969), 290.

The German style of thought is now widely leavening both Britain and America; and the issue of this is matter for suspicion and fear, in so far as pure Bible exposition is concerned. It is a style entirely self-revolving, in which, as one of their poets has described it, the soul is,

> "Chasing *its own dream* for ever,
> On through many a distant star;"

turning in upon its own actings, instead of out upon God's; making man's interior self the great region of research, not God's manifested self; dealing with spiritual truths as with abstractions or ideas, not as connected with Divine personality and life.

In spite of all the admiration in which it is fashionable to hold German critics, and with the full admission that their researches have not been unrewarded, their system of criticism, as a whole, cannot but be regarded as a failure, if not something worse. Its results have been inconsiderable for good, but vast for evil. Dwelling in the region of their own thoughts, they have lost the power to grasp, and the taste to appreciate the thoughts of God. They may be interpreters of words, but they are not expounders of thought, in so far as Scripture is concerned. In the former they excel, in the latter they fail. They have not brought forth the fullness, the richness, the vastness of Scripture language; they have rather diluted and emptied it. They have taken their own thoughts as their standard in measuring, their law in interpreting the thoughts of God. Hence, in prophecy, where the language is doubly pregnant with the thoughts and purposes of God, they have totally broken down. Few of their works on prophecy are possessed of much value beyond that of verbal criticism. And it is sad to see their American imitators rapidly coming up to them, if not outstripping them, in the race of irreverence and error.[56]

Fairbairn had obviously spent much time studying German theologians and exegetes. In reviewing *Ezekiel, An Exposition*, Bonar commented, "We must profess our great dislike to the many *abstract* and *German* forms of expression employed throughout Mr. Fairbairn's volume."[57] He further included in *The Quarterly Journal of Prophecy* the following correspondence, presumably with some agreement:

You [Bonar]have carefully abstained from saying many things regarding Dr. Fairbairn's works in general which you might have said, and which are freely ventilated in private among German scholars, viz., that Dr. F. has taken most of his good things, as well as some of his bad things, from German critics. A great part of his *Commentary on Ezekiel* is from

---

[56] Bonar, *Prophetical Landmarks*, 191–93.
[57] H. Bonar, "Ezekiel," *The Quarterly Journal of Prophecy* (July, 1851): 218n.

Hävernick, as every German scholar knows. His other works are said to be in like manner large debtors to foreign sources. . . . [Signed] A Calvinist.[58]

While much of German scholarship has been Augustinian and amillennial in its leaning, especially with regard to Lutheran writings even to this day, it remains to be seen if a direct connection can be made between this and the eschatology of Fairbairn's later writings.

Herman Bavinck

Born in the town of Hoogeveen in the Netherlands in 1854, Herman Bavinck first went to theological school at Kampen, but then moved on to Leiden where he graduated in 1880 after completing a dissertation on Ulrich Zwingli. In 1882 he taught theology at the Theological School of the Christian Reformed Churches, also at Kampen. In 1902 when Abraham Kuyper left the Free University for a time to become Prime Minister of the Netherlands, Bavinck joined the faculty as Professor of Systematic Theology at the Free University of Amsterdam where he served until his death in 1921.

In his massive *Reformed Dogmatics*, in true Augustinian fashion, Bavinck approaches the whole of the OT as follows:

> The spiritualization of the Old Testament, rightly understood, is not an invention of Christian theology but has its beginning in the New Testament itself. The Old Testament in spiritualized form, that is, the Old Testament stripped of its temporal and sensuous form, is the New Testament. . . . All Old Testament concepts shed their external, national-Israelitish meanings and become manifest in their spiritual and eternal sense.[59]

Bavinck declared further, with a decidedly anti-Judaic tone,

> Chiliasm [millennialism] includes the expectation that shortly before the return of Christ a national conversion will occur in Israel, that the Jews will then return to Palestine and from there, under Christ, rule over the nations. . . . Those of the Jews who reject Christ are not really true Jews (Rom. 2:28–29). They are not the "circumcision" but the "mutilation" (Phil. 3:2). They are the irregulars, idle talkers, deceivers, who must be silenced (Tit. 1:10–11). They have killed the Lord Jesus and their own prophets as well. They persecute believers, do not please God, and oppose everyone. . . . Real Jews, the true children of Abraham, are those who believe in Christ (Rom. 9:8; Gal. 3:29, etc.). The community of believers has in all respects replaced carnal, national Israel. The Old Testament is fulfilled in the New.[60]

[58] *The Quarterly Journal of Prophecy*, ed. H. Bonar, Correspondence (October, 1858), 410.
[59] H. Bavinck, *The Last Things* (Grand Rapids: Baker, 2000), 96–97.
[60] Ibid., 99, 102.

The salvation of "all Israel" in Rom 11:26, unlike Calvin's inclusion of converted Jews and Gentiles,

> remains a remnant chosen by grace (Rom. 11:5). . . . There is no room left
> in Paul's sketch [in Romans 11] for a national conversion of Israel as the
> chiliasts expect. . . . Even if Paul expected a national conversion of Israel at
> the end, he does not say a word about the return of the Jews to Palestine,
> about a rebuilding of the city and a temple, about a visible rule of Christ: in
> his picture of the future there simply is no room for all this.[61]

Thus Bavinck, as a thoroughgoing supercessionist, revealed his vigorous opposition to restorationist premillennialism, his militant demeanor here being characteristic of the Reformed environment in which he worshipped and was educated. Concerning these strong eschatological convictions, VanGemeren offered the following critique:

> Bavinck's treatment of his subject exemplifies the amillennial approach
> toward the prophetic word. On the one hand, he summarizes the teach-
> ing of the OT prophets with respect to the future of Israel, which includes
> the conversion of Israel, the Messiah's coming, the benefits to be enjoyed
> by the people of the Messiah including the return from the land of captiv-
> ity, a restoration of temple and worship, and the Gentiles sharing in the
> blessings of the kingdom. Instead of taking the OT language for what it is,
> Bavinck argues that there lies an eternal truth "in the earthy, sensual, forms
> of the prophecies." He strongly objects to millennialism as a hermeneutic in
> which the earthly forms of the OT are understood literally.[62]

So Bavinck relentlessly imposed the NT over the OT, resulting in the assembly of Christian believers completely supplanting ethnic Israel. For this reason VanGemeren frankly concluded,

> He sacrifices the OT prophetic hope to a harmonious understanding of the
> NT, in which the NT passages which hold out a hope for Israel and different
> exegetical options are either harmonized or not fully considered. The au-
> thority of the OT as well as of the NT seems to be sacrificed out of concern
> for unity, harmony, and systematization.[63]

What then is the response of Bavinck to the European development of Zionism with which he must have become familiar during his lifespan (1854–1921)?

> The question of the Near East is approaching solution, for Turkey owes its
> existence to the mutual jealousies of the great powers. Once Turkey is de-

---

[61] Ibid., 107.

[62] VanGemeren, "Israel as the Hermeneutical Crux in the Interpretation of Prophecy (II)," 261.

[63] Ibid., 263.

stroyed there is every chance that Palestine will be assigned to the Jews to whom by rights it belongs. Furthermore, in the hearts of many Jews, as is evident from the Zionism that has emerged in recent years, there is a longing to return to Palestine and to form an independent state there. . . . However we may view these political combinations, the New Testament furnishes not the slightest support for such an expectation.[64]

Those who hold this classic and influential representation of Reformed, Augustinian eschatology, channeled through Calvin and Turretin, would do well to consider exactly what evangelistic outreach to the Jews they might advocate? The position does not appear to reflect the pro-Judaic passion and methodology of Paul.

Geerhardus Vos

Since the close of the nineteenth century, probably the most influential and esteemed Reformed scholar in the realm of eschatology, not unrelated to his pioneering studies in biblical theology, would be Geerhardus Vos. Many of the Reformed writers we consider will be found to have placed considerable reliance on Vos—especially Hoekema, Riddlebarger, Robertson, Venema, and Waldron. Born at Friesland, the Netherlands, in 1862, he was raised in a Christian Reformed Church manse in Michigan. Later he studied at the Theological School of that denomination in Grand Rapids, then Princeton Seminary, Berlin and Strasburg. He was personally exposed to Abraham Kuyper and Herman Bavinck in the Netherlands. Returning to a faculty position in Grand Rapids, he eventually settled back at Princeton Seminary as professor of biblical theology in 1893 until his retirement in 1932. Vos's theological environment was decidedly intolerant of premillennialism—for example, Bavinck,[65] the Christian Reformed Church,[66] and

---

[64] Bavinck, *The Last Things*, 100.

[65] Ibid.

[66] The Christian Reformed Church, in being traditionally amillennial, has critically responded to the emergence of any premillennialism within its ranks. Consider the instances of both Rev. H. Bultema and Prof. D. H. Kromminga being under synodical investigation. J. Kromminga, *The Christian Reformed Church* (Grand Rapids: Baker, 1949), 72–75; H. R. Boer, "The Premillennial Eschatology of Diedrich Honrich Kromminga," in *Perspectives on the Christian Reformed Church* (ed. P. De Klerk and R. R. De Ridder; Grand Rapids: Baker, 1983), 153–69. Boer's fair-minded conclusion is significant: "The virtue of Kromminga's contribution is that he has alerted us to eschatological possibilities in a manner and on a scale that the Reformed tradition up to now has not taken into account. Most especially an appreciation of Kromminga's eschatological vision should raise the question by what legitimate rationale can public discussion of it be ecclesiastically prohibited," 169.

to a lesser extent, Princeton Theological Seminary.[67] Since the Christian Reformed Church was rooted in the Reformed Church of the Netherlands, along with confessional allegiance to the Belgic Confession, the Heidelberg Catechism, and the Canons of the Synod of Dort, there was the conviction that this creedal heritage was incompatible with chiliast beliefs. That Vos himself was vehemently opposed to premillennialism is plainly indicated in his *Pauline Eschatology*, specifically the chapter "The Question of Chiliasm in Paul," which includes the following:

> Chiliasm has to its credit the astounding readiness it evinces of taking the O.T. Scriptures in a realistic manner, with simple faith, not asking whether the fulfillment of these things is logically conceivable, offering as its sole basis the conviction that to God all things are possible. This attitude is, of course, not attained except through a reckless abuse of the fundamental principles of O.T. exegesis, a perversion invading inevitably the precincts of N.T. exegesis likewise, heedless of the fact that already the O.T. itself points to the spiritualizing of most of the things in question. Apart from accidental features, and broadly speaking, Chiliasm is a daring literalizing and concretizing of the substance of ancient revelation. Due credit should be given for the naïve type of faith such a mentality involves. It is a great pity that from this very point of view premillennialism has not been psychologically studied, so as to ascertain whence in its long, tortuous course through the ages it has acquired such characteristics. Although pre-millennialism is by no means a local phenomenon, there are evidently certain milieus in which it has found a more fertile soil than elsewhere. In certain countries it comes to meet an eccentric interest in the superficial, visible, curiosity-attracting events in eschatological perspective. The evil is not so much an evil in itself: it is a malformation or over-rank outgrowth drawing to itself a surplusage of religious interest, at the expense of what is more essential and vital in the eschatological sphere. The resulting evil lies largely in the deficit thus caused in the appraisal of other eschatological processes far overshadowing in importance this one feature, at least to the normally-constituted Christian mind.[68]

It is difficult for me to recall a more graceless, indeed intellectually arrogant denunciation of an opposing Christian perspective than this. While Richard Gaffin commended the gentle, retiring, pious manner of Vos,[69] such virtue is quite absent here. Furthermore, within this whole chapter by Vos, although numerous European sources are employed in support of his

---

[67] Calhoun refers to a "tolerant dissatisfaction" at Princeton Seminary concerning premillennialism, *Princeton Seminary*, II, 183.

[68] G. Vos, *Pauline Eschatology* (Princeton, NJ: Published by the author, 1930), 227.

[69] G. Vos, *Redemptive History and Biblical Interpretation* (ed. R. B. Gaffin Jr.; Phillipsburg, NJ: P&R, 2001), xiii.

critical analysis, there does not appear to be so much as one reference to a premillennialist of standing. Hence, it is not so surprising, as VanGemeren has pointed out, that Vos was fearful of any considerations of a future, eschatological conversion of the Jews. Nevertheless, commitment to the exposition of Romans 11 led Vos to yield to what he felt the apostle Paul incontrovertibly taught, namely, a future conversion of Israel *en masse*. So VanGemeren explained,

> In his *Dogmatiek* Vos answers the question why it is so difficult to enter into detail on the future conversion of Israel by saying: "Because it has been connected on the one hand with the restoration of the Jews to the Holy Land and on the other hand with the millennial kingdom. . . . The fear existed to encourage chiliasm" (p. 26). Vos affirms, nevertheless, the exegetical ground for the hope in Israel's conversion. He thinks "that the conversion of Israel is clearly predicted" (p. 27) and bases this conclusion on "all the prophets of the Old Testament who speak of the apostasy and the return of the Jews, particularly Zechariah 12 and Romans 11" (p. 26). . . . He expects the conversion to be a true spiritual revival, when the Jews have sufficiently been provoked to jealousy . . . by the Gentiles who have found salvation in Jesus Christ. When the fullness of Jewish and Gentile Christians has been achieved, the *parousia* will follow. Vos admits that the chronological connection is implied in the text, but not explicitly stated (p. 88). Though Vos vehemently opposes a premillennial reading of the NT. The exegesis of the text itself forces him to expect a future conversion of the Jews.[70]

However, like John Murray who confessed to a similar "mass conversion,"[71] Vos was careful not to express belief in any related, present, covenantal, national Jewish identity—or present, covenantal, land inheritance rights for Israel in unbelief—according to Rom 11:28–29. He was well aware that, had he done so, he would have been crossing over the divide, so to speak, into millennial territory.[72] Nevertheless, in not following this path, his understanding of what constitutes "Jews" by his designation with regard to their mass conversion, in their having individuality but no national or territorial inheritance, is a common weakness of this approach. It is as if Paul, in claiming to be an "Israelite" (Rom 11:1), nevertheless repudiated national and territorial identity according to divine recognition.

---

[70] VanGemeren, "Israel as the Hermeneutical Crux in the Interpretation of Prophecy (II)," 263–64.

[71] J. Murray, *Romans* (Grand Rapids: Eerdmans, 1965), 2:98.

[72] To use OT Scripture for justification of such land and nation legitimacy would involve passages that, using the same hermeneutic, would lead to acknowledgment of a millennial economy in which a distinction is maintained between Jew and Gentile within the one people of God (see Ezek 36–37; Zech. 8, etc.).

Such a bifurcated perspective is quite untenable from a biblical and Hebrew understanding of Jewishness. In this regard, concerning the reticence of Vos at this point to clarify exactly what he meant by the term "Jew" in terms of a future mass conversion, consider his article, "Eschatology of the New Testament," which lists two events that will precede the *parousia*. They are first, the conversion of Israel, and second, the coming of the Antichrist. The former event is succinctly explained in approximately 115 words; the latter event is comprehensively explained in approximately 2900 words.[73]

Further indication of the reluctance of Vos to give explanation beyond his declaration that "in the future there will be a comprehensive conversion of Israel (Rom 11:5,25–32)"[74] is found in an article, "The Second Coming of Our Lord and the Millennium." It is his contention that OT Jewishness is ultimately superseded by the NT kingdom of God. This being so, then distinctive, eschatological, covenantal significance for the nation of Israel and the land has been done away with, whatever conversion of the Jews toward the end of this present age might entail. Vos declared: "The theory [of premillennialism] has its preformation in a certain scheme of Jewish eschatology dating back as far as the New Testament period or even earlier."[75] One is inclined to enquire how, at that period, any other than a "Jewish eschatology" would be understood in the early church. Vos continued:

> In Judaism there existed two types of eschatological outlook. There was the ancient national hope which revolved around the destiny of Israel. Alongside of this existed a higher form which had in view the destiny of the creation as a whole. The former has its scene on earth, the latter in a new world, radically different from the present one. Now, in certain of the apocalyptic writings a compromise is effected between these two schemes after this manner, that the carrying out of the one is to follow that of the other, the national earthly hope receiving its fulfillment in a provisional messianic kingdom of limited duration (400 or 1,000 years), to be superseded at the end by the eternal state. It was felt that the eschatology of this world and that of the world to come would not mix, therefore the two were held together on the purely mechanical principle of chronological succession. This Jewish compromise was distinctly due to a lack of spirituality in the circles where it appears. . . .
>
> As stated, the Old Testament avails itself of earthly and eternal forms to convey heavenly and spiritual things. Sincere attachment to the Old Testament Scriptures and a profound conviction of their absolute veracity

---

[73] G. Vos, "Eschatology of the New Testament," *ISBE*, ed. J. Orr (Grand Rapids: Eerdmans, 1939), 2:983–86.

[74] Ibid., 983.

[75] G. Vos, *Redemptive History and Biblical Interpretation*, 416.

could and can still underlie a desire to see them in their whole extent literally fulfilled, and since the eternal world offers no scope for this, to create a sphere for such fulfillment in the millennial kingdom. Instead of casting upon such a state of mind the stigma of unspiritualness and narrow-mindedness, we should rather admire the faith-robustness which it unquestionably reveals. None the less, we believe such faith to be a misguided faith.[76]

So since a millennium would unsatisfactorily result in a mere upgraded universe, "the consummation of this world and the bringing in of the world to come, this and nothing else can at this point effect the necessary change."[77] Thus, by means of a quasi-Platonic/Gnostic hermeneutic, "the world to come" is radically different from "this present world," especially its transcendence of any earthly Jewish heritage. But I would suggest that the Bible does indeed describe an upgraded, thoroughly refurbished rather than a supplanted universe, that is, a victoriously recovered rather than a new world supplanting that which was defeated by Satan; this is the point of the "restoration/rebirth *[apokatastasis]* of all things about which God spoke by the mouth of His holy prophets" (Acts 3:21), in which purified Judaism will retain a distinctive role as the prophets make very clear. The same point is true with regard to the nature of the future bodily glorification of the believer. He will receive a changed body, not that which is wholly new (1 Cor 15:51). As this "corruptible [body] must be clothed with incorruptibility" (15:53), so this perishing world will be renewed, yet retain essential connection with its original form. Certainly purified Judaism will be a distinctive part of that retained essence. But for Vos, this "world to come" has left behind any Jewish essence. Concerning this present world, he described how Paul "outlines for us in Romans a program of the uninterrupted progress of the kingdom of God and points as its goal the Christianization of all the nations and the salvation of all Israel."[78] However, beyond this present age is "the world to come" that leaves behind any thought of Israel in relation to its distinctive nationality and territory. Why is this so? Vos responded,

> Indiscriminate insistence upon the literal import of prophecy were [sic] not merely a weak, but an impossible basis to build chiliasm upon. In point of fact, even the most radical chiliasts discriminate between what they expect and do not expect to see materialized in the millennium. On the ground of the Old Testament alone there is no warrant for such distinction. The prophets proclaim as emphatically the restoration of the temple, the priesthood, and the sacrificial system as they predict the return of the people to

---

[76] Ibid., 416–17.
[77] Ibid., 419.
[78] Ibid., 420.

Palestine and the rebuilding of Jerusalem. Besides, the serious difficulty arises that the Old Testament ascribes to the fulfillment of these things eternal validity and duration.[79]

The heart of the complaint here is not that of "the return of the people to Palestine and the rebuilding of Jerusalem," which events are not rooted in the old Mosaic covenant, as clear as these events are prophesied about in the OT. Rather, in mentioning "the restoration of the temple, the priesthood, and the sacrificial system," the inference chiefly concerns Ezekiel 40–48 and supposed conflict here with the abolishment of the Mosaic sacrificial order according to Hebrews. How Vos interpreted this passage is not indicated, though perhaps we can assume he took a path here similar to Patrick Fairbairn. Be that as it may, spurning a premillennial perspective hardly enlightens us with a positive interpretation of a passage that presents considerable mystery whatever one's understanding may be. I would simply quote some judicious comments of A. B. Davidson at this juncture concerning Ezekiel 40–48.

> We should go very far astray if on the one hand fastening our attention on the natural elements of the picture . . . [these] were [regarded as] mere figures or symbols, meaning nothing but a higher spiritual condition after the restoration [from Babylon], and that the restoration described by Ezekiel is no more than one which might be called natural, and which took place under Zerubbabel and later. Ezekiel of course expects a restoration in the true sense, but it is a restoration which is complete, embracing all the scattered members of Israel, and final, being the entrance of Israel upon its eternal felicity and perfection, and the enjoyment of the full presence of Jehovah in the midst of it. . . .
> Consequently we should go equally far astray on the other hand if fastening our attention only on the supernatural parts of Ezekiel's picture, . . . that all this to the prophet's mind was nothing but a lofty symbolism representing a spiritual perfection to be eventually reached in the Church of God of the Christian age. To put such a meaning on the Temple and its measurement and all the details enumerated by the prophet is to contradict all reason. The Temple is real, for it is the place of Jehovah's presence upon the earth; the ministers and the ministrations are equally real, for His servants serve him in his Temple. The service of Jehovah by sacrifice and offering is considered to continue when Israel is perfect and the kingdom the Lord's even by the greatest prophets (Isa. 19:19,21; 60:7; 66:20; Jer. 33:18).
> There can be no question of the literalness and reality of the things in the prophetic program, whether they are things natural or supernatural, the only question is, What is the main conception expressed by them?[80]

---

[79] Ibid., 418.

[80] A. B. Davidson, *The Book of the Prophet Ezekiel* (Cambridge: Cambridge University Press, 1906), 288–89.

Chapter 7

ISRAEL AND CHRISTIAN ANTI-JUDAIC HERMENEUTICS TODAY

Our concern is now the hermeneutical principle that imposes the NT revelation of Jesus Christ on the OT in such a way that the new covenant (upper layer) has become the controlling hermeneutic whereby the old covenant (lower layer) is christologically reinterpreted. Colin Chapman, Steve Motyer, Stephen Sizer, Peter Walker, and N. T. Wright, representing UK Anglicanism, and Anthony Hoekema, William Hendriksen, Hans K. LaRondelle, and O. Palmer Robertson, representing US scholarship, provide further basic scholarly agreement. With variation in tone, they all draw on the same essential Augustinian root to examine the OT through the controlling lens of the NT. They would all agree with the fundamental hermeneutical approach of Turretin, Fairbairn, Bavinck, and Vos, representing four hundred years of Reformed eschatology. But all of these scholars without exception—and this in no way being a coincidence—emphatically assert the covenantal nullification of ethnic, national, and territorial Israel.

"But does not this galaxy of Reformed scholars represent a weighty, scholastic fraternity?" Yes, without a doubt we have here a concert of notable, esteemed, and influential theologians. But I maintain that the eschatological lineage here is not vindicated by resultant, attractive, ethical fruit that parallels Paul's biblical esteem for the Jews. The reason is that the study of centuries of church history has led to the unraveling of closely woven strands of shameful anti-Judaism by Lutheran, Anglican, Dutch Reformed, Nonconformist, or Presbyterian scholars, exceptions notwithstanding. But perhaps, it is protested, "Do not these various strands nevertheless present sound hermeneutical reasons for their biblical exegesis?" To answer this I would respond with two further questions. Is it admitted that the root of this sound exegesis takes us back to the esteemed Augustine? Richard Muller suggests that this is so when he writes,

> Reformed theology appears not as a monolithic structure—not, in short, as "Calvinism"—but as a form of Augustinian theology and piety capable of considerable variation in its form and presentation.[1]

---

[1] R. A. Muller, *Christ and the Decree* (Durham, N.C.: Labyrinth, 1986), 176.

If this is the case, then is Augustine's seminal exegesis of Ps 59:11 ("Do not kill them [the Jews]; otherwise, my people will forget. By Your power, make them homeless wanderers") whereby he established centuries of shameful treatment of the Jewish people, representative of his contemporary biblical successors? I maintain that Augustine was grievously wrong in his exegesis at this point, and in so doing he bequeathed a hermeneutical legacy that has proved to result in dire consequences for the people of Israel. Furthermore, I suggest that the traditional Reformed exegesis at this point is likewise in error since it is grounded on the same Augustinian root and has resulted in similar Augustinian fruit. The various Reformed strands have similarly humiliated the Jews through tokenism and the denial of ethnicity, nationality, and territory according to divine mandate. So we must consider the fallacy of the essential Reformed hermeneutic insofar as it is concerned with the eschatology of Israel. But before doing so, there is one significant author in this regard who merits special consideration.

The Hermeneutic of George Eldon Ladd

George Ladd is often upheld today as the quintessential historic premillennialist, though I seriously question his representative status in this regard. I would maintain that earlier premillennialists, being more Judeo-centric, better qualify as being characteristic of historic premillennialism. They would include Joseph A. Seiss, David Baron, Adolph Safir, B. W. Newton, H. Grattan Guinness, J. C. Ryle, C. H. Spurgeon, George Peters, Nathaniel West, and Horatius Bonar. As such, they were far more historic in the accepted sense of that term when their lineage is traced back at least to the millennial awakening originating in Protestant England and Europe. Concerning Israel, without exception, these latter mentioned authors all upheld the expectation of a distinctive, glorious, prominent, national prospect for Israel in the land under the personal reign of Jesus Christ, and this expectation came with the explicit support of numerous OT and NT passages. Their Judeo-centricity qualified them as far more authentically historic in their premillennialism. On the other hand, Ladd has maintained that Revelation 20 explicitly and exegetically provides the *sole*, albeit conclusive proof from the Bible for the premillennial school of eschatology. When pressed concerning the degree to which the OT gave further support to premillennialism, he responded that it provided none whatsoever! His reason here was that he perceived OT passages that have been commonly understood in millennial terms as finding their fulfillment, not with regard to national Israel's future glory, but rather the Christian church. This new covenant community comprised of Jews and Gentiles has inherited God's OT promised blessings as the newly constituted people of God. Consequently he identified at this point with a more Augustinian and Reformed appropriation, by the Christian church, of promises formerly made to abandoned OT Israel, so that the new body of God's people had become the new spiritual Israel. Thus,

> Old Testament prophecies must be interpreted in the light of the New Testament to find their deeper meaning. . . . I do not see how it is possible to avoid the conclusion that the New Testament applies Old Testament prophecies to the New Testament church and in so doing identifies the church as spiritual Israel.[2]

For example, Ladd cites Rom 9:24–26 where Paul employs Hos 2:23; 1:10 to describe God's call to the Gentiles. Yet the context of Hosea 1–2 deals with the nation of Israel and the promised land. It is here that Ladd's Gentile logic, rather than a Hebrew perspective represented by Paul, concludes that Hosea's prophecy finds a broader, more inclusive fulfillment which nullifies a more narrow, national, eschatological interpretation of the prophet. Thus, "the prophecies of Hosea are fulfilled in the Christian church. . . . It is clearly what the NT does to the OT prophecies."[3] Therefore, other national promises in the OT may similarly be understood as being fulfilled in the church. So Ladd elsewhere concluded that "it is highly probable that when Paul speaks of the 'Israel of God' (Gal. 6:16) he is referring to the church as the 'true spiritual Israel.'"[4]

Concerning the reference to the quotations in Romans 9 from Hosea, an explanation is in order, and it will somewhat justify the prior reference to Ladd's "Gentile logic." As a converted Jewish rabbi, Paul confessedly remained a Jew (Rom 11:1; Acts 21:39; 22:3) who, in quoting the OT in a manner that a Gentile is not accustomed to, made use of Hosea in an applicatory or analogical manner which nevertheless does *not* nullify the obvious, original literal interpretation. David Stern, a Hebrew Christian scholar, commented,

---

[2] G. E. Ladd, "Historic Premillennialism," *The Meaning of the Millennium* (ed. R. G. Clouse; Downers Grove, Ill.: InterVarsity Press, 1977), 23. Similarly, Ladd concludes, concerning these OT passages, as employed in the NT, that "the church is in fact the true Israel of God." *A Theology of the New Testament* (Grand Rapids, Mich.: Eerdmans, 1993), 433.

[3] Ibid., 23–24.

[4] Ladd, *A Theology of the New Testament*, 584. But see chapter 10, where it is indicated how far more improbable Ladd's opinion here proves to be.

Sha'ul [Paul] uses these texts from Hoshea midrashically. Hosea was not referring to Gentiles but to Israel itself; he meant that one day Israel, in rebellion when he wrote, would be called God's people. Sha'ul's meaning, which does not conflict with what Hoshea wrote but is not a necessary inference from it, is that 'God's people' now includes some Gentiles. How this has come about and for what purpose are examined at [Rom] 9:30–10:4 and 11:17–32, as well as in the book of Ephesians.[5]

In a similar way Sanday and Headlam commented,

St. Paul applies the principle which underlies these words [of Hosea], that God can take into His covenant those who were previously cut off from it, to the calling of the Gentiles. A similar interpretation of the verse was held by the Rabbis.[6]

If this basic hermeneutical principle is true, it opens up a world of understanding concerning how the Hebrew authors of the NT could legitimately quote from the OT in a more applicatory, illustrative sense without invalidating the original literal meaning, as Ladd's rigid exclusionary approach demands, and as is frequently the case with Reformed amillennialists.[7]

Nevertheless, according to his exclusionary hermeneutical method, Ladd is led necessarily to introduce the term "reinterpretation," which has doubtful legitimacy.[8] Obviously, he appreciated that careful exegesis of eschatological texts within the OT, employing his interpretive methodology, presents difficulties. As a result, he found himself willingly boxed into a corner of generalization and suggestion according to his imposition of the NT on the OT. Proof of this is found in his dealing with such classic eschatological passages as Ezek 36–37 and Zech 8; 14, especially as they relate to

---

[5] D. Stern, *Jewish New Testament Commentary* (Clarksville, MD: Jewish New Testament Publications, 1992), 392. Also refer to this author's commentary on the quotation of Hosea 11:1 in Matthew 2:15, where he lists the four basic modes of Scripture interpretation used by the rabbis. These are explained in more detail later in this chapter under the heading, "A Christocentric Hermeneutic for the Hebrew Scriptures."

[6] W. Sanday and A. C. Headlam, *A Critical and Exegetical Commentary on Romans* (Edinburgh: T&T Clark, 1977), 264. Similar analogical interpretations are upheld by S. Lewis Johnson, "Evidence from Romans 9–11," *The Coming Millennial Kingdom* (ed. D. K. Campbell and J. L Townsend; Grand Rapids: Kregel, 1997), 203–11, and J. Murray, *Romans* (Grand Rapids: Eerdmans, 1965), 2.38.

[7] Consider the same form of amillennial argumentation, employing Romans 9:24–26; see Hos. 2:23; 1:10, in O. T. Allis, *Prophecy and the Church* (Philadelphia: Presbyterian and Reformed, 1945), 156; W. J. Grier, *The Momentous Event* (London: Banner of Truth Trust, 1970), 44; W. Hendriksen, *Israel and the Bible* (Grand Rapids: Baker, 1968), 57; H. K. LaRondelle, *The Israel of God in Prophecy* (Berrien Springs, Mich.: Andrews University Press, 1983), 130–31; C. P. Venema, *The Promise of the Future* (Edinburgh: Banner of Truth Trust, 2000), 271–72.

[8] G. E. Ladd, *The Last Things* (Grand Rapids: Eerdmans, 1978), 9–18.

Israel's national and territorial destiny. Regarding these references in Ladd's *A Theology of the New Testament*, instead of specifically referencing "Israel," "nations," "land," and "Zion/Jerusalem," he repeatedly and accommodatingly substitutes "his/God's people." Thus he will not particularize in a precise exegetical manner since his hermeneutic is more arbitrary and inclusive with regard to the OT. So we should not be surprised at the diminutive place that the Jews hold in Ladd's eschatology. He did acknowledge Jewish individuality; even nationality seems to find some brief, indistinct, uncertain mention; but consideration of the land and its validity for national Israel is virtually nonexistent. I believe, however, that the specificity and historic reality of the Prophets is of much greater importance than mere NT window dressing. I further believe that the NT authors, according to a Hebrew mindset, when rightly comprehended, would be startled to discover that they are chargeable with the principle of "reinterpretation" that tends to denigrate the plain, original meaning of the Prophets. A final perceptive objection to Ladd's hermeneutic of NT imposition on the OT is that of Walter C. Kaiser Jr.:

> It is widely held that the most obvious corollary to the Christocentric hermeneutic is the *theologia crucis* that the New Testament must always be our guide to interpreting the Old Testament. But why would a rule be imposed on the revelation of God that demands that the Old Testament passages may not become the basis for giving primary direction on any doctrines or truths that have relevancy for New Testament times? This is only to argue in the end for a canon within a canon. . . . We misjudge the revelation of God if we have a theory of interpretation which says the most recent revelation of God is to be preferred or substituted for that which came earlier.[9]

The Instructive Example of Hebrews

Of all the books of the NT, Hebrews has the most concentrated collection of quotations from the OT. In P. Ellingworth's commentary on Hebrews, which draws heavily on his doctoral research (1977), he assesses 35 explicit quotations, including 14 from the Psalms and 13 from the Pentateuch.[10] This leads us immediately to refer to the cautionary comment of John Owen on Hebrews: "There is not any thing in this Epistle that is attended with more difficulty than the *citation of the testimonies out of the*

---

[9] W. C. Kaiser Jr., "The Land of Israel and the Future Return (Zechariah 10:6–12)," *Israel, the Land and the People: An Evangelical Affirmation of God's Promises* (ed. H. Wayne House; Grand Rapids: Kregel, 1998), 219. 222.

[10] P. Ellingworth, *Commentary on Hebrews* (Grand Rapids: Eerdmans, 1993), 37, 39.

Old Testament that are made use of in it."[11] The reason is that the author of Hebrews was comfortable with the flexible use of the OT in a number of ways. Therefore, it is both cavalier and misleading to suggest that a controlling NT hermeneutic kicks in, so to speak, with the result that the original meaning of the OT quotations is now invalidated. With this in mind, it must be noted that Hebrews was written by a Hebrew Christian to Hebrew Christians. So we need to approach the interpretation of this epistle, not so much with a Gentile frame of reference as with the frank conclusion of Simon Kistemaker in mind:

> In contrast to the NT authors the present day writer is bound in his writing and thinking by profane [secular] motifs, by grammatico-historical principles, which characterize him as a child of his time. Hence our motifs and principles may never be foisted upon the writers and literature of the first century of our era.[12]

Then he concludes the section dealing with hermeneutical principles as follows:

> It is quite understandable that this type of [*Midrashim*] sermon delivery was transferred from the Synagogue to the Early Church. Many of the characteristics in the Jewish manner of expounding a portion of Scripture in respect to method, were directly passed on to the sermons preached by the apostles and evangelists. There are still a few of these early Christian *Midrashim* extant. The Second Epistle of Clement, usually considered a homily, is in fact an early midrash. It may be said conclusively that the recipients of the Epistle to the Hebrews were addressed in accordance with the literary methods prevalent in that day.[13]

Horatius Bonar, although writing over a century earlier, nevertheless appreciated this same approach concerning the presupposition of a Hebrew hermeneutic when he wrote,

> Much is to be learned in the way of typical exposition from the Epistle to the Hebrews, not merely in reference to the passages cited, or the events referred to, but respecting a multitude of others to which there is no allusion at all. The apostle proceeds upon certain principles of interpretation recognized among his countrymen. *He did not write as one who had discovered a new theory of interpretation which he called on them to receive* [emphasis added]; but he proceeds upon principles owned by and familiar

---

[11] J. Owen, *An Exposition of Hebrews*, I (Evansville, IN: Sovereign Grace Publishers, 1960), 106.

[12] S. Kistemaker, *The Psalm Citations in the Epistle to the Hebrews* (Amsterdam: W. G. van Soest, 1961), 89n.

[13] Ibid., 93.

to them. He takes his stand upon their own application of the prophecies regarding Messiah, and reasons with them upon principles which both he and they acknowledged. To ascertain these is of much importance. They are the principles adopted by the nation to whom the prophecies were addressed, and, therefore, acquainted with the circumstances in which they were spoken; a nation to whom the language and dialect of prophecy were as their native tongue, and of whose history every event had been an accomplished prophecy; a nation who had not only prophets to predict, but also to guide them to the right meaning of "what manner of things the Spirit of Christ, which was in them, did signify" [1 Pet 1:11]; a nation that in their last days had the Messiah himself to expound to them in all the Scriptures the things concerning Himself [Luke 24:17], to correct their principles wherein they were false, and to confirm them wherein they were true.[14]

In this regard due credit should also be given to John Calvin who, in considering the manner in which some of the OT quotations are employed in Hebrews, came to a conclusion similar to that of Stern, Kistemaker, and Bonar. In commenting on Heb 2:7 where Ps 8:5–6 is quoted, he declared,

This Psalm which he [Paul?] quotes must be examined, for it seems to be unfitly applied to Christ. . . . He [David] does not, then, speak of any particular person, but of all mankind. To this I answer, that all of this affords no reason why the words should not be applied to the person of Christ. . . . It was not the Apostle's design to give an exact explanation of the words. For there is nothing improperly done, when verbal allusions are made to embellish a subject in hand, as Paul does in Romans 10:6, from Moses. . . . He only bids us to consider the abasement of Christ, which appeared for a short time, and then the glory with which he is perpetually crowned; and this he does more by alluding to expressions than by explaining what David understood.[15]

I conclude that the hermeneutic of reinterpretation and transference is illegitimate, which takes the adapted quotation of the OT in the NT to be justification for nullifying the literal interpretation of that same OT passage. The reason is that it not only ignores a fundamental, Hebrew, hermeneutical frame of reference, but it also brings about a serious distortion of meaning, especially where the eschatological message of the Prophets is concerned. Representatives of this hermeneutic of reinterpretation and transference are now considered.

---

[14] H. Bonar, *Prophetical Landmarks* (London: James Nisbet, 1876), 211–12.

[15] J. Calvin, *Commentary on the Epistle to the Hebrews* (Grand Rapids: Eerdmans, 1949), 56, 58–59.

A Christocentric Hermeneutic
against the Hebrew Scriptures

An anti-Judaic eschatology is most often grounded on a NT re-inter-pretation of the OT. By this means the "Christianizing" of the OT results in it being evacuated of its distinctive Jewish roots and substance. Some definitive examples of this teaching are as follows, along with subsequent comment. What stands out here is that, apart from some variations in emphasis, the essentially Augustinian transference hermeneutic unfailingly results in the national and territorial nullification of Israel.

N. T. Wright stated,

> He [Jesus] had not come to rehabilitate the symbol of the holy land, but to subsume it within a different fulfillment of the kingdom, which would embrace the whole creation. . . . Jesus spent his whole ministry *redefining* what the kingdom meant. He refused to give up the symbolic language of the kingdom, but filled it with such new content that, as we have seen, he powerfully subverted Jewish expectations.[16]
>
> Through the Messiah and the preaching which heralds him, Israel is transformed from being an ethnic people into a worldwide family.[17]
>
> Those who now belonged to Jesus' people were not identical with ethnic Israel, since Israel's history had reached its intended fulfillment; they claimed to be the continuation of Israel in a new situation, able to draw on Israel-images to express their self-identity, able to read Israel's Scriptures (through the lens of Messiah and spirit) and apply them to their own life. They were thrust out by that claim, and that reading, to fulfill Israel's vocation on behalf of the world.[18]

So historic Israel and the holy land, while having come to a substantial conclusion, yet are "universalized" through "symbolic language" and "images" (as in "The song is ended, but the melody lingers on"). Here is an attempt to linguistically adorn what in reality is the offensive face of supercessionism. The result is that today the Jews, their nation, and their territory are "subsumed" within the kingdom of God, that is, they are absorbed into glorious homogeneity. The OT promises concerning a distinctive restoration were a literary accommodation, a mere shadowy representation that should not be taken too seriously.

---

[16] N. T. Wright, *Jesus and the Victory of God* (London: SPCK: 1996), 446, 471.

[17] N. T. Wright, *The Climax of the Covenant* (Edinburgh: T&T Clark, 1991), 240.

[18] N. T. Wright, *The New Testament and the People of God* (London: SPCK, 1992), 457–58.

Colin Chapman wrote,

> It was not that Jesus was simply "spiritualizing" Old Testament prophe-
> cies, and thereby leaving open the possibility that they might one day be
> interpreted literally. Rather, according to him, the gathering of believers
> into the kingdom of God was the true fulfillment of these prophecies.
> Some Christian writers have pointed out that the prophets predicted the
> return of the exiles from all countries—from north, south, east and west.
> Moreover, they say, some of the prophets (notably Zechariah) specifi-
> cally predicted that exiles of the northern kingdom of Israel would return
> to the land as well as exiles from the southern kingdom of Judah [Ezek
> 37:15–23; Zech 8:13]. They go on to ask: has anything happened in history
> which fits this description—*except* the recent return of Jews to the land?
> The question at first sight seems unanswerable; it sounds a convincing
> 'knock-down' argument. But if the Christian is to interpret Old Testament
> prophecy in the light of the teaching of Jesus, the question simply does
> not arise. Why? Because in the perspective of Jesus, the ingathering of
> the exiles—from north, south, east and west—takes place when people of
> all races are gathered into the kingdom of God. This is the true, the real,
> the intended fulfillment of prophecy. . . . Christians today do not have the
> liberty to interpret the Old Testament in any way that appeals to them.
> Everything in the Old Testament has to be read through the eyes of the
> apostles. It is they who, so to speak, give us the right spectacles for a genu-
> inely Christian reading of the Old Testament. Therefore if Christians today
> find that certain details in books like Ezekiel appear to fit certain situations
> in the Middle East today, they should resist the temptation to draw direct
> connections with these contemporary events. The reason is that since the
> apostle John has given *his* interpretation of Ezekiel's visions, this should be
> seen as *the normative Christian interpretation* of these visions, and not only
> *one possible interpretation.*[19]

The subjective arbitrariness of the supposed "interpretation" of Zechariah
here is simply breathtaking. Though in all this one senses a suppressed un-
ease. The plain teaching of the exilic and postexilic prophets is obliquely
confessed as obvious, then put down. After all, if Ezekiel and Zechariah are
allowed to stand according to their plain and obvious sense, then a whole
eschatological edifice comes tumbling down. As a result, there would
be an eschatological future for national Israel. But this would never do!
Consequently, Chapman must turn to the Jewish apostles, such as John,
who have renounced that carnal Jewish focus of the past and ascended to
more spiritual heights whereby Ezekiel and Zechariah are reinterpreted in
more universal, Christocentric terms. Be warned that this is the one and
only interpretation; yield to it as the new norm lest one become beguiled

---

[19] C. Chapman, *Whose Promised Land?* (Grand Rapids: Baker, 2002), 150, 172.

by the deceitful, obvious clarity of literal interpretation. But then we turn to Acts 5:31 where these same Jewish apostles declare concerning Jesus Christ, "God exalted this man to His right hand as ruler and Savior, to grant repentance to Israel, and forgiveness of sins." This does not sound like supercessionism any more than was the case when Paul declared to the leading Jews in Rome that his captivity was "for the hope of Israel" (Acts 28:20). These Jewish apostles do not mislead us with ambiguous terminology whereby reinterpretation of "Israel" in fact means the homogenous people of God. No, I must assert that these Jewish apostles held to a future hope for national and territorial Israel whereby the nation would eventually be saved by its Messiah and retain its identity among the saved nations (Isa 66:8,12; Acts 3:21–22; Rom 11:26–28).

Stephen Sizer wrote,

> As Palmer Robertson also observes, by the end of the Apostolic era, the focus of God's redemptive work in the world has shifted from Jerusalem to places like Antioch, Ephesus and Rome. There is, therefore, no evidence that the apostles believed that the Jewish people still had a divine right to the land, or that the Jewish possession of the land would be important, let alone that Jerusalem would remain a central aspect of God's purposes for the world. On the contrary, in the Christological logic of Paul, Jerusalem as much as the land, has now been superseded. They have been made irrelevant to God's redemptive purposes. . . . Their selective and dualistic hermeneutic leads Christian Zionists to ignore how Jesus and the apostles reinterpreted the Old Testament. . . . Under the old covenant, revelation from God came often in shadow, image, form and prophecy. In the new covenant that progressive revelation finds its consummation in reality, substance and fulfillment in Jesus Christ and his church.[20]

To suggest that the Jewish apostles, especially at the time of the Council at Jerusalem and apparently under the headship of James, did not believe that "the Jewish people still had a divine right to the land, or that the Jewish possession of the land would be important," is sheer nonsense. In the plainest terms, we are told here that not only have Jerusalem and the land of Israel become irrelevant to God, but also that now they have become superseded. Here is unclouded, arrogant anti-Judaism that Paul so adamantly opposed in Romans 11. Perhaps we should be grateful here for the honest confession of supercessionism which others of a similar persuasion have attempted to ingeniously dance around. To attempt to claim support from Paul's "Christological logic" is to fly in the face not only of the apostle's passionate, persistent, pro-Judaic stance, but also of his repeated

---

[20] S. Sizer, *Christian Zionism* (Leicester, England: Inter-Varsity Press, 2004), 170, 204.

claim that he retained full status as a Jew or Israelite (Rom 11:1; Acts 21:39; 22:3). For Paul to be told that his Jewishness, so integrated with Jerusalem and the land as a "Benjamite," was "irrelevant" would have invited the strongest disavowal (Rom 3:1–2; 9:1–5; 11:18–21). Yet the original promise of the land was *not* part of the old covenant; rather it was integral to the promise God originally gave to Abraham, 430 years before Moses, that eventually found the beginning of fulfillment through Joshua. The land is not identical with the shadows established through the Mosaic covenant (see chapter 9).

Steve Motyer has stated,

> Throughout the New Testament, we see the first Christians wrestling with the relationship between the "new" thing that God has now done in Christ, and the "old" thing which he had done in Israel, and re-interpreting the latter in the light of the former. If we are to be New Testament Christians, we must do the same. . . . Distinctive Jewish Christianity finally died out. . . . The first Christians set themselves the wonderful, exciting task of completely re-thinking their understanding of the Scriptures, in the light of Jesus Christ. . . . The New Testament 're-reading' of the Old Testament promises sees their climax in Jesus, and makes him the 'end' of the story. The interpretation of Old Testament prophecy and other 'Israel' texts must be approached from the perspective of this basic New Testament teaching, and must follow the guidelines of New Testament interpretation. . . . The New Testament writers are 'normative' for us, in showing us how to interpret Old Testament prophecy.[21]

To suggest that "the first Christians set themselves the wonderful, exciting task of completely re-thinking their understanding of the Scriptures, in the light of Jesus Christ," especially by a "'re-reading' of the Old Testament promises," is simply a reflection of Gentile blindness and bias. For theological convenience Motyer sets aside the Jewish apostles' continuing Jewish, albeit clarified, regard for the OT. They would be offended at the suggestion here that they had instigated a radically new hermeneutic. There was no such novel formulation. To declare that "distinctive Jewish Christianity finally died out" is to avoid mentioning the doctrinal conflict whereby it was "put to death" by proud Gentile ascendancy through Justin Martyr and Melito of Sardis on through to Augustine. If the NT writers' re-interpretation of the OT had established a new, Christological, normative hermeneutic, then what of those frequent occasions in which they interpreted the

---

[21] S. Motyer, "Israel in God's Plan," *Evangelical Alliance Consultation*, June, 2003, http://www.eauk.org/theology/headline_issues/holyland/upload/S_Motyer_'Israel'_paper.pdf (accessed 2007).

OT quite literally? Has this literal hermeneutic now become sub-normal? Consider Bonar's comment:

> In so far as prophecy has been already fulfilled, that fulfillment has been a literal one. Take the predictions regarding the Messiah. His being born of the house of David; of a virgin; at Bethlehem; being carried down to and brought up out of Egypt; His healing diseases; His entering Jerusalem on an ass; His being betrayed by one of His disciples; His being left by all His familiar friends; His being smitten, buffeted, spit upon; His side being pierced; His bones unbroken; His raiment divided by lot; His receiving vinegar; His being crucified between two thieves; His being buried by a rich man; His lying three days in the tomb; His rising on the third day; His ascending up on high, and sitting at the right hand of God; these and many others, have all been fulfilled to the very letter; far more literally than we could have ever conceived. And are not these fulfillments strong arguments in favor of the literality of all that yet remains behind? Nay, do they not furnish us with a distinct, unambiguous, and inspired canon of interpretation?[22]

O. Palmer Robertson said,

> Any transfer from the old covenant to the new covenant involves a movement from shadow to reality. The old covenant appealed to the human longing for a sure and settled land; yet it could not compare with the realities of new covenant fulfillment. This perspective is confirmed by a number of references in the new covenant documents. Abraham is declared to be heir, not of "the land," but of "the world" (Rom. 4:13). By this comprehensive language the imagery of the land as a picture of restored paradise has finally come of age. No longer merely a portion of this earth, but now the whole of the cosmos partakes of the consummation of God's redemptive work in our fallen world.
>
> This perspective provides insight into the return to the land described by Ezekiel and the other prophets. In the nature of things, these writers could only employ images with which they and their hearers were familiar. So they spoke of a return to the geographical land of Israel. Indeed there was a return to this land, though hardly on a scale prophesied by Ezekiel. But in the context of the realities of the new covenant, this land must be understood in terms of the newly recreated cosmos about which the apostle Paul speaks in Romans. The whole universe (which is "the land" from a new covenant perspective) groans in travail, waiting for the redemption that will come with the resurrection of the bodies of the redeemed (Rom. 8:22–23). The return to paradise in the framework of the new covenant does not involve merely a return to the shadowy forms of the old covenant. It means

---

[22] Bonar, *Prophetical Landmarks*, 246–47.

the rejuvenation of the entire earth. By this renewal of the entire creation, the old covenant's promise of land finds its new covenant realization.[23]

To read Robertson's *The Israel of God* is to quickly discover his intoxication with the representation of virtually the whole OT as "shadowy, temporal forms."[24] This is especially true with regard to the land's alleged temporal significance in view of Abraham's subsequent inheritance of the world in Rom 4:13. For some reason, it is vital for Robertson that this universal prospect should absorb, rather than include, the particularity of Israel, and thus eliminate national identity. The same emphasis on absorption, or supercession, is made by Wright, Chapman, and Sizer. Whereas it seems perfectly clear that since "in you [Abraham] all the families of the earth [the Gentile nations] will be blessed" (Gen 12:3), this broad prospect does not at all eliminate the distinctive inclusion of national Israel dwelling in the promised land under Christ surrounded by these same saved Gentile nations who are also under Christ. So Barrett rightly related Paul's exposition of Rom 4:13—which "summarize[s] the content of the promise [to Abraham]"—to Gen 22:17–18.[25] Thus the world includes the land of Israel "at the center of the world" (Ezek 38:12). Yet for Robertson, even the explicit restorationist language of Ezekiel is merely a necessary geographic accommodation to the times of the prophet that calls for a more universal perspective. But Bonar's response to this was that such a hermeneutic of accommodation, evidently unoriginal, was not at all necessary:

> So far, then, from conceding the opinion that the prophets used language of the peculiarly Jewish, or, as we might call it, Mosaic cast, because they had no other by which to convey their representations of the future glory of the Church, we maintain just the opposite. . . . The reason for which they [the prophets] used their peculiar style was, because it was the fullest, richest, and most exact that could be adopted; nay, because it was especially constructed by God to express that vast variety of ideas which prophecy unfolds, with a correctness, and, at the same time, with a power, of which common language did not admit.[26]

I agree with Robertson that there will certainly be an eschatological "newly created cosmos" according to Rom 8:22–23. Yet I am once again at a loss to understand how this universal of a redeemed creation cannot include

---

[23] O. P. Robertson, *The Israel of God* (Phillipsburg: P&R, 2000), 25–26.

[24] Ibid., 82.

[25] C. K. Barrett, *The Epistle to the Romans* (New York: Harper & Row, 1957), 94. Similarly D. Moo, *Romans* (Grand Rapids: Eerdmans, 1996), 273–74.

[26] Bonar, *Prophetical Landmarks*, 238.

the particular of a redeemed national Israel, that is, except that the author cannot break free from the shackles of a rigid, unbiblical, eschatological homogeneity.

A Misguided Christocentric Hermeneutic

In the foregoing it should be noted that the anti-Judaic or supercessionist hermeneutic of Wright, Chapman, Sizer, Motyer, and Robertson is declared to be founded on a supremely Christocentric reinterpretation of the OT, even as Ladd propounded. In this view, a Judeo-centric eschatology is not sufficiently Christocentric since it is impeded by a more literal understanding of OT Judaism whereby its shadows are allowed to obscure the reality of Christ. In response it simply needs to be pointed out that the risen, glorified Christ never declared that His Jewishness would ever be abandoned, though a supercessionist hermeneutic would tend to require this. On the Emmaus road the two Jewish disciples were enthralled when "beginning with Moses and all the prophets, He [Jesus] explained to them the things concerning Himself in all the Scriptures" (Luke 24:27). Here was no imposition of Himself on Scripture, no reinterpretation of Scripture, but rather Jesus' fulfillment of Scripture at every hand which the disciples embraced, not as radically new, but rather as wonderfully fulfilling in terms of the promises of the OT.

We need to consider with closer scrutiny the extent to which Jesus Christ ought to be dominant in the interpretation of biblical eschatology as an overriding hermeneutical principle. Some would emphatically suggest that the more we "see only Jesus," even in the OT, the more we are keeping to the heart of the Bible. So this Christocentricity in interpreting the OT, even as accentuated by Reformed hermeneutics, has to be right. But I must carefully assert, in upholding a Trinitarian perspective with regard to the headship of the Father, that it is possible for such an understanding of Christocentricity to be misguided.[27] This is not an insignificant point since it is common today, especially within Reformed Christianity as Thomas Smail pointed out in *The Forgotten Father*, for an incorrect prominence to be given to Jesus Christ (as though impossible to challenge) that results in biblical distortion.[28] For this reason, I believe Chapman, Sizer, Motyer,

---

[27] While the Christocentricity of the Gospel of John might be considered beyond dispute, in fact the ministry of Jesus throughout this record is "patercentric" and repeatedly subsidiary to the will, calling, and exaltation of His Father (4:34; 5:19; 8:29).

[28] T. A. Smail, *The Forgotten Father* (Grand Rapids: Eerdmans, 1981). Initially captivated by the charismatic movement, this Anglican author became troubled by a seeming primary em

Robertson, and others take a legitimate Christological interpretive principle and give it a disproportionate primacy and driving emphasis. Bernard Ramm provided a more balanced approach when he recommended four principles for the interpretation of the prophetic segments of Scripture. The third was, "The interpreter should take the literal meaning of a prophetic passage as his limiting or controlling guide," and the fourth, "The centrality of Jesus Christ must be kept in mind in all prophetic interpretation."[29]

Steve Motyer provides an example of this radical christocentricity. His perspective represents a variation of the more common type of supercessionism in which Jesus Christ replaces national Israel rather than the church. But the end result is identical, that is, the nullification of Jewish nationality and territory:

> The view for which I am arguing in this paper does not see *the church* as the "replacement" for Israel, but sees Jesus in this role. . . . In the opening chapters of his Gospel, Matthew deliberately tells the story of Jesus' birth, baptism, temptations and entry into ministry in such a way that *Jesus' history replays the Exodus history of Israel*. This is a dramatic re-telling of Israel's story, which would have been immediately obvious to Jewish readers, but can easily be overlooked by us. Jesus, too, goes down to Egypt by divine guidance, just like Jacob and his family. Then he comes out of Egypt in fulfillment of Hosea 11:1, "Out of Egypt have I called my son' (Matt. 2:15). Matthew knows full well that he is applying to *Jesus* a verse originally about *the Exodus!* He is giving a clue to help us interpret the significance of Jesus. Armed with this clue, we then see how Jesus passes through water, just like Israel on her way out of Egypt, and, just as for Israel, this is a defining moment in Jesus' relationship with God (Matt. 3). Then he is tested in the wilderness, just like Israel after the Exodus (Matt 4:1–11), and he quotes to the Devil three verses all drawn from the story of that wilderness testing of Israel, with flying colors. Finally, just as Israel came to a mountain where she heard God's ten "words", constitutive of her life with him, so now Jesus climbs a mountain and utters the nine 'words' constitutive of life in the kingdom of God—statements not of duty, but of blessedness (Matt. 5:1–12). We could hardly ask for a clearer presentation of the conviction that Jesus steps into he role of Israel, in God's plan.[30]

phasis on pneumatology that gave little place to God the Father. He further mentions that this lack of biblical proportion "was indeed characteristic of the kind of Reformed Christocentric emphasis in which I had been grounded. Indeed when one widens the scope and looks at vital modern Christian movements of any kind, one has to admit that emphasis upon and devotion to the Father has not been a main characteristic of many of them," 18–19.

[29] B. Ramm, *Protestant Biblical Interpretation* (Grand Rapids: Baker, 1956), 234, 248.

[30] Motyer, "Israel in God's Plan," *Evangelical Alliance Consultation*, June, 2003 [cited 28 June 2007]. Online: http://www.eauk.org/theology/key_papers/holy-land/upload/S_Motyer_'Israel'_paper.pdf.. Emphasis original.

It is the hermeneutic that especially concerns us here. To begin with, apart from this conjectural extrapolation, there is not one explicit statement in the NT which supports the suggestion that Jesus Christ is the new covenant replacement for old covenant Israel. Strictly for the sake of argument, however, let us grant the rationale here that Matthew subtly portrays Jesus as the OT revelation of Israel. In allowing this subjective representation, where in all this is there the *necessity* for Jesus to replace Israel, and not simply be identified with them? A wonderful case can be made for the representation of Jesus by Joseph in Genesis, in spite of the fact that there is not one explicit verse of justification for this analogy to be found in the NT. Of course, this being the case, at best we are left with a good and helpful illustration. So Motyer's proposal is likewise at best a good and helpful illustration. However, to build a doctrinal case on this for the replacement of national Israel by Jesus is both extreme and unsound!

Robert Strimple, another Reformed theologian making a defense of the amillennial disenfranchisement of national Israel, likewise declared,

> The true Israel is Christ. . . . Yes, Israel was called to be God's Servant, a light to enlighten the nations and to glorify God's name. But since Israel was unfaithful to her calling and failed to fulfill the purposes of her divine election, the Lord brought forth his Elect One, his Servant, his true Israel.[31]

This particular claim of supercession is made without the slightest warrant from the NT. Yes, there is a sense in which the suffering Servant of Isaiah does take the name of "Jacob" and "Israel" (Isa 44:1), though I believe it is entirely arbitrary and unwarranted to suggest that it is a matter of replacement. I would suggest that by such terminology in Isaiah the Messiah intimately identifies with Israel because of a specific saving purpose that is in mind: "I [the Lord] will keep you [my servant], and I make you a covenant for the people [Israel] and a light to the nations" (Isa 42:6; see 44:21–23). But that "Israel" is consistently defined in the NT as the nation rooted in Abraham and never as the Gentiles wholly excludes the idea that Christ, or for that matter the church, have superseded Israel's national identity. As William Campbell explained,

> Although we do acknowledge Jesus as the true Israelite, the ideal servant of God, we must not totally identify him with Israel. We cannot claim that Christ is Israel. . . . Nor is it legitimate to claim that Christ displaces or becomes Israel. In such a theology, the humanity of Christ is obliterated with

---

[31] R. Strimple, "Amillennialism," *Three Views on the Millennium and Beyond* (ed. D. L. Bock; Grand Rapids: Zondervan, 1999), 87–88.

Israel, and the outcome is that we are left with a theological docetism that manifests itself as individualism.[32]

Certainly I accept the truth that Jesus Christ, as the seed of Abraham, both represents and embodies the nation of Israel in a vivid sense; His intimate identification in this respect must not be downplayed. I would further agree that there does appear to be a helpful analogy between the exodus of Israel and the life of our Lord Jesus Christ.[33] But I object to the out of bounds portrayal here of Jesus Christ replacing national Israel to the point of elimination through transference.

A Christocentric Hermeneutic for the Hebrew Scriptures

In contrast with the foregoing, I maintain that there is a right Christocentric method of interpretation that is relevant to all of Scripture. In the light of modern supercessionism, this hermeneutic especially addresses both the OT and the NT according to the unifying principle of Judeo-centricity. In other words, as the Scriptures of the whole Bible are mainly of Hebrew origin, and the Savior was Hebrew along with the founding church, then we should never cease to keep this Hebrew perspective before us. The Hebrew character of OT Scripture ought not to be regarded, in its literal form, as passé, and therefore the object of reinterpretation by the NT Gentile Christian. Tet-Lim N. Yee concluded,

> It is my hope that the lasting impression of this study will be that the substantial contribution of Christianity is Jewish. Our assessment of Ephesians within the "new perspective" which helps us to gain a clearer view of the first-century Jews and Judaism has shown abundantly clearly that the theme of Jewish attitudes toward the Gentiles and ethnic reconciliation cannot be fully appreciated unless we give the enduring Jewish character of Christianity which is represented in Ephesians its due weight.[34]

[32] W. S. Campbell, "Church as Israel, People of God," *Dictionary of the Later New Testament and Its Developments* (ed. R. P. Martin and P. H. Davids; Downers Grove, Ill.: InterVarsity, 1997), 217. Similarly, C. Blaising, "A Premillennial Response to Robert B. Strimple," *Three Views on the Millennium and Beyond* (ed. D. L. Bock; Grand Rapids: Zondervan, 1999), 145–47.

[33] P. D. Feinberg, "Hermeneutics of Discontinuity," *Continuity and Discontinuity* (ed. J. S. Feinberg; Westchester, Ill.: Crossway Books, 1988), 121–22.

[34] T. N. Yee, *Jews, Gentiles and Ethnic Reconciliation: Paul's Jewish Identity and Ephesians* (Cambridge: Cambridge University Press, 2005), 228. Although this revision of a doctoral thesis at Durham University, especially focusing on Ephesians 2, draws upon the "new perspective" emphasis of E. P. Sanders, J. D. G. Dunn, and N. T. Wright, disagreement with some of the conclusions of this movement does not detract from appreciation of the fundamental approach that

This does not simply involve being acquainted with extra-biblical Jewish sources but with that Jewish hermeneutic with which the apostles almost unconsciously breathed. This is especially to be the case when Gentiles desire to understand the Word of God. When the OT is quoted in the NT by a Hebrew author, we anticipate his use of an established Hebrew hermeneutic, not necessarily so familiar to the Gentile mind, though certainly not some supposed new, superseding, and radical hermeneutic. This is the point that Horatius Bonar made so well (see n. 14): "The apostle [as the author of Hebrews] proceeds upon certain principles of interpretation recognized among his countrymen. *He did not write as one who had discovered a new theory of interpretation which he called on them to receive* [emphasis added]." It follows that when the NT Jewish author quoted the OT, sometimes with a methodology that is not following the exact literal meaning, it is presumptuous to conclude that this usage nullifies the possibility of the original passage retaining literal validity. A more Hebrew based hermeneutic is preferred that remains based on a literal understanding of the text. I echo David Stern's comment that "the New Testament is a Jewish book, written by Jews in a Jewish context,"[35] as well as his explanation of the four basic modes of Scripture interpretation used by the rabbis. These are:

(1)*P'shat* ("simple")—the plain, literal sense of the text, more or less what modern scholars mean by "grammatical-historical exegesis," which looks to the grammar of the language and the historical setting as background for deciding what a passage means. Modern scholars often consider grammatical-historical exegesis the only valid way to deal with a text; pastors who use other approaches in their sermons usually feel defensive about it before academics. But the rabbis had three other modes of interpreting Scripture, and their validity should not be excluded in advance but related to the validity of their implied presuppositions.

(2)*Remez* ("hint")—wherein a word, phrase or other element in the text hints at a truth conveyed by the *p'shat*. The implied presupposition is that God can hint at things of which the Bible writers themselves were unaware.

(3)*Drash* or *midrash* ("search")—an allegorical or homiletical application of a text. This is a species of eisegesis—reading one's own thoughts into the text—as opposed to exegesis which is extracting from the text what it actually says. The implied presupposition is that the words of Scripture can legitimately become grist for the mill of human intellect, which God can guide to truths not directly related to the text at all.

calls for heightened regard for the essential Jewish nature of biblical Christianity. See chapter 10 for further references to Dr. Yee's study in relation to Ephesians 2.

[35] D. Stern, *Jewish New Testament Commentary* (Clarksville, MD: Jewish New Testament Publications, 1992), 13.

(4)*Sod* ("secret")—a mystical or hidden meaning arrived at by operating on the numerical values of the Hebrew letters, noting unusual spellings, transposing letters, and the like. . . . The implied presupposition is that God invests meaning in the minutest details of Scripture, even the individual letters.

These four methods of working a text are remembered by the Hebrew word "PaRDeS," an acronym formed from the initials; it means "orchard" or "garden."[36]

Michael Vlach points to the same four categories, as referenced by Richard N. Longenecker, that would have been common knowledge to the authors of the NT.[37] Keeping these Judeo-centric hermeneutic principles in mind, we now turn to three examples frequently referenced concerning the manner in which OT passages are quoted in the NT. In these instances, it is wrong to allege that a new covenant hermeneutic, previously unknown, is introduced that nullifies the original, literal OT meaning (see my previous discussion of Hos 2:23; also see Rom 9:24–26).

(1) **Hosea 11:1 and Matthew 2:15.** At face value, the strict meaning of Hos 11:1 seems at variance with its use Matt 11:1. Hosea was plainly speaking of "Israel" when he declared, "out of Egypt I called My son." But Matthew, having advised that the child Jesus had found refuge in Egypt from Herod, then anticipated His eventual return from Egypt as the fulfillment of Hosea's explanation, "out of Egypt I called My Son." Has Matthew then introduced a new Christocentric hermeneutic that nullifies the former reference to Israel? Is Christ now identified as Israel? To begin with, it is important that the subsequent context of Hos 11:1 be considered. Whereas v. 1 introduces God's original redemptive love for Israel, vv. 2–7 tell of His relentless, compassionate pursuit, mingled with judgment, for a constantly rebellious, betrothed people. Yet vv. 9–11 reveal the eventual triumph of God's sovereign grace: "I will not turn back to destroy Ephraim. . . . They will follow the LORD; . . . Then I will settle them in their homes. This is the LORD's declaration." Clearly, the ultimate restoration of Israel is envisaged here, but if Matthew has introduced a new hermeneutic, this can be reinterpreted as simply the inclusive triumph of God's love for His people, quite apart from any more exclusive national considerations that have now been superseded. Not only is this unnecessary, but it also does not satisfy our reading of vv. 2–11. On the one hand, the literal interpretation of Hosea

[36] Ibid., 11–12.

[37] M. J. Vlach, "The Church as a Replacement of Israel: An Analysis of Supercessionism" (Ph.D. diss., Southeastern Baptist Theological Seminary, 2004), 176n. R. N. Longenecker, *Biblical Exegesis in the Apostolic Period* (Grand Rapids: Eerdmans, 1999), xxxiii, 14–35.

stands, and especially as this so obviously agrees with Ezekiel 36–37 concerning the future salvation of national Israel. On the other hand, as we have already considered, Matthew identified Jesus as the personification of Israel, though certainly not as a replacement, even as Isaiah identified the suffering Servant of the Lord as both Messiah and the personification of Israel. David Stern sees here "a [Hebrew] *remez*, a hint of a very deep truth. . . . the Messiah is equated with, is one with, the nation of Israel."[38] Therefore, Matthew did not reinterpret Hosea; he simply understood Hosea as fulfilled, for the restoration of national Israel will be inseparably related to that time when "the people of Israel will return and seek the LORD their God and David their king [Messiah]. They will come with awe to the LORD and His goodness in the last days" (Hos 3:5).

(2) **Amos 9:11–12 and Acts 15:16–18.** According to Amos 9:11–15, the future restoration of Israel is declared in terms of *reconstruction* for the house of David, inclusive of national deliverance for the Gentiles (vv. 11–12), *recovery* from destitution (v. 13), *return* from captivity (v. 14), and *relocation* in the promised land (v. 15). The quotation of vv. 11–12 by James in Acts 15:16–18 is deemed by those of a supercessionist persuasion to be proof that the Christian church has inherited the promises originally made to Israel through Amos. As amillennialist Kim Riddlebarger stated,

> James saw the prophecy as fulfilled in Christ's resurrection, exaltation, and in the reconstitution of his disciples as the new Israel. The presence of both Jew and Gentile in the church was proof that the prophecy of Amos had been fulfilled. David's fallen tent had been rebuilt by Christ.[39]

It is important to notice here that Riddlebarger, along with others who take a similar supercessionist stance, seems eager to disqualify the Jewish eschatological implications of the whole of Amos 9:11–15. For him, the hermeneutic of James—this quintessential Jewish Christian leader of the Jewish church at Jerusalem and the author of the Epistle of James—is supposed to have completely nullified the nation of Israel, the future restoration, and the land as he would have understood it, with one fell blow. This I believe to be highly unlikely, in spite of Motyer's extreme language that "in Acts 15:13–21 James dramatically re-reads Amos' prophecy of the restoration of Israel (Amos 9:11–12) . . . [concerning] what God has done in saving Gentiles. It's a new action, demanding a new reading of Scripture."[40] But

---

[38] Stern, *Jewish New Testament Commentary*, 12.

[39] K. Riddlebarger, *A Case for Amillennialism* (Grand Rapids: Baker, 2003), 39.

[40] S. Motyer, "Israel in God's Plan," *Evangelical Alliance Consultation*, June, 2003, http://www.eauk.org/theology/headline_issues/holyland/upload/S_Motyer_'Israel'_paper.pdf (accessed 2007).

James referenced Amos simply to indicate his agreement with Peter's experience that the Gentiles have been included in God's gospel program. In no way does this "reinterpret" Amos 9:13–15 where Israel's restoration to the land is specified. Even Robertson admitted that all of Amos 9:11–15 cannot be exclusively equated with the blessings of the present church age:

> The present fulfillment of Amos' prophecy may be seen as only the "first stage" of God's consummation activity. The restoration of the Davidic throne takes on the lowly form of a "booth" or tent. Yet the first installment of the Spirit as possessed by Gentiles today guarantees the future restoration of all things. Endowed in the end with bodies transformed by the resurrection power of the same Holy Spirit, believers in Christ ultimately shall participate in the restoration of all things at the re-creation of heaven and earth.[41]

The obvious weakness remaining here is that Robertson still refuses to allow the inclusion of any eschatological future for the nation of Israel in the land. This is in spite of Amos 9:14–15 explicitly declaring, "I will restore the fortunes of My people Israel. . . . I will plant them on their land, and they will never again be uprooted from the land I have given them." As Kenneth Barker states,

> What happened in Acts 15 constitutes a stage in the progressive fulfillment of the entire prophecy in Amos 9 (cf. Acts 15:12–15). It is an instance of direct fulfillment, but not the final and complete fulfillment, as the following verses in Amos (9:13–15) plainly indicate.[42]

Similarly, from a Hebrew Christian perspective, Stern comments, "The complete fulfillment of Amos' prophecy will take place when the undivided realm of David's time is restored. Meanwhile, this is a beginning."[43] In other words, the either-or hermeneutic of Reformed eschatology in which saved national Israel cannot coexist with the Gentile nations in the consummate kingdom of Christ does not mesh with the prophetic revelation here. The supposed necessity of Judaic exclusion, dressed in the language of supercession or transference, must yield to the both-and eschatology of one people of God in which Israel and the Gentile nations distinctively

---

[41] O. Palmer Robertson, "Hermeneutics of Continuity," *Continuity and Discontinuity* (ed. J. S. Feinberg; Westchester, Ill.: Crossway Books, 1988), 108.

[42] K. L. Barker, "The Scope and Center of Old and New Testament Theology and Hope," *Dispensationalism, Israel and the Church* (ed. C. A. Blaising and D. L. Bock; Grand Rapids: Zondervan, 1992) 327. Also refer to H. Heater, Jr., "Evidence from Joel and Amos," *The Coming Millennial Kingdom* (ed. D. K. Campbell and J. L. Townsend; Grand Rapids: Kregel, 1997), 147–57.

[43] Stern, *Jewish New Testament Commentary*, 277.

exist under Christ. When this fundamental issue is accepted, a change of temperament results whereby a shameful anti-Judaic attitude is supplanted by Pauline, pro-Judaic passion.

(3) **Zech 12:10–14; John 19:37; Rev 1:7.** According to Zech 12:1–9, the final eschatological attack on Jerusalem results in the Lord's intervention. So David Baron described prophetically,

> Israel's great national deliverance and the destruction of the armies of the confederated anti-Christian world-powers which shall be gathered in the final siege of Jerusalem. That will, indeed, be a great and wonderful day in their history. . . . But yet there is something greater, more solemn and more blessed, than mere outward deliverance and triumph over their enemies that Israel is to experience on "that day," and that is God's final conquest over them.[44]

Then the house of David will be redeemed by means of "the Spirit of grace and supplication" (v. 10). Here is the crowning act by which the Lord saves Israel. It is *this* Spirit which causes Israel to *look, mourn,* and *weep* (Ezek 36:26–27; 37:1–4,9–10,14; 39:25–29) concerning its crucified Messiah. By way of application, God saves the Jews in the same way as He saves the Gentiles, through Holy Spirit regeneration that gives the repentant sinner eyes to see Jesus as Savior. So there will be the piercing of the Lord's first-born (vv. 10b–14). Whereas it was Roman soldiers who pierced Jesus Christ, it was at the instigation of the Jews (Acts 2:22–23).

But what of John 19:37? Is this the sole and complete fulfillment of Zech 12:10? In view of the rest of vv. 10–14, undoubtedly not. Furthermore, consider the additional reference of Rev 1:7. As *all* of Israel paid off its shepherd (Zech 11:12), so *all* Israel pierced the Lord and will continue to do so in a corporate sense to the end of this age. In effect, John 19:37 refers to a fulfillment in part, that is, the specific incident of Messiah's piercing, but certainly not the whole of the national mourning yet to come. It is similar to the previous study of Amos 9:11–12, which was seen by James to be fulfilled in part in Acts 15:16–18. After Israel's national eschatological regeneration (Rom 11:12,15,26) there will be national, bitter, and prolonged weeping (Zech 12:10c–14). Undoubtedly such intensive and extensive mourning has not yet come to pass, though in recollection of the centuries of rejection, such thoroughgoing, consummate grief is not to be considered unexpected or inappropriate. Israel has grief "as one mourns for an only son," even "over a firstborn," and thus the deity of Christ as

---

[44] D. Baron, *Zechariah* (London: Hebrew Christian Testimony to Israel, 1951), 436.

the only begotten of the Father is suggested. Feinberg added, "When the one who is greater than Joseph makes himself known to his brethren, they will be heartbroken with grief and contrition"[45] (Gen 45:14–15). There will not only be special mourning in Jerusalem (v. 11), but also total mourning throughout the land (vv. 12–14). Nevertheless, if Israel should so weep, then should any saved Gentile weep the less on account of his guilty participation in the piercing of the Lord Jesus Christ (Acts 4:27)?

The partial soteriological fulfillment of Zech 12:10 according to John 19:37 in no way diminishes anticipation of the eschatological repentance of national Israel. It may be that Rev 1:7 should be translated, "And all the tribes of the land will mourn over Him"[46] (see Matt 24:30); but if not, and "tribes of the earth" is substituted, the overall eschatological expectation of Israel's national repentance and salvation according to Zech 12:10 is in no way diminished.

In conclusion, we return to the fundamental character of the Reformed eschatological hermeneutic, here severally represented, which so vehemently disallows a diversity within the unity of Jesus Christ's consummate kingdom. I believe that for reasons more philosophic than logical, more historic than biblical, more systematic than exegetical, there is a tenacious refusal to allow a both-and situation for Israel and the Gentile nations. Indeed there has come about a Gentile fear for the perpetuation of Judaic influence on Christianity, as if the church at Antioch should supersede the church at Jerusalem—though Acts 15 indicates how invalid such a proposal is. The ethical results in this regard have not been inconsequential. It is as if history dominates, that is, Augustinianism reigns and holds exegesis in captivity. But history also indicates that in the realm of eschatology, Augustine was terribly wrong and, so are those who follow in his eschatological steps regarding the disenfranchisement of national Israel. In this particular realm of divine truth, much of Reformed exegesis has been driven more by a historic hermeneutic rather than the principle of *semper reformandum*, "always reforming." After all, Luther, Calvin, Turretin, Fairbairn, Bavinck, and Vos could not possibly be wrong! Or could they? They are all part of the same eschatological lineage that peers through essentially Augustinian lenses. If this patristic root, with its unsavory eschatology, does not result in the ripening of its fruit through the sweetening of

---

[45] C. L. Feinberg, "Zechariah," *Wycliffe Bible Commentary* (ed. C. F. Pfeiffer and E. F. Harrison; Chicago: Moody Press, 1962), 909.

[46] So J. A. Seiss, *The Apocalypse*, I (New York, Charles C. Cook, 1865); Stern, *Jewish New Testament Commentary*, 790.

sovereign grace, its continuance and bitter influence, after the manner of centuries of church history, will only result in branches that bring forth tart produce during this twenty-first century.

Chapter 8

ISRAEL AND THE HARMONY OF SPIRITUAL MATERIALITY

All eschatological opinions are open to perversion, even with regard to the three major schools of interpretation. They each have attracted devotees who have strayed from the mainstream of the historic norm. Amillennialism has drifted in a gnostic and platonic direction through identification with a more spiritually amorphous, extraterrestrial, ethereal, egalitarian future kingdom that defies human comprehension. Postmillennialism has inclined toward a legislated political kingdom, somewhat Mosaic in character, that more recently has drifted toward extreme preterism. Premillennialism, in proclaiming a future earthly reign of Jesus Christ upon a renewed earth, has been associated with carnal Zionism that lacks authentic spirituality. It is this allegation against premillennialism that we are here concerned about, for it certainly does have a degree of validity with regard to *some* deviant proponents. Certainly there are those who have given undue prominence to Israel's prospective glorious dominion in predominantly political and sensationalist terms. But this remains quite invalid in the light of a classic, historic, premillennial understanding with regard to Israel's biblical future prospects.

It was Augustine who, in considering a seventh-day millennial Sabbath of a thousand years, commented that "this opinion would not be objectionable, if it were believed that the joys of the saints in that Sabbath shall be spiritual, and consequent on the presence of God; for I myself, too, once held this opinion."[1] But in further expounding Revelation 20, he opposed millennialism and characterized an extreme materialistic example of it as

> the leisure of immoderate carnal banquets, furnished with an amount of meat and drink such as not only to shock the feeling of the temperate, but even to surpass the measure of credulity itself, [so that] such assertions can be believed only by the carnal. They who do believe them are called by the spiritual Chiliasts, which we may literally reproduce by the name Millenarians.[2]

We can only designate this as an extreme representation which an authoritarian church perpetuated for centuries. A more biblical portrayal of

---

[1] Aurelius Augustine, *The City of God*, XX (Edinburgh: T&T Clark, 1872), 7.
[2] Ibid.

classic millennialism, even incorporating a form of Christian Zionism, is now presented according to the essential distinguishing characteristic of "spiritual materiality."

The Fall of Spirituality and Materiality

According to Gen 1:31, "God saw all that He had made, and it was very good [tôb]." This included the "light," "dry land," the "gathering of the water," the "earth," the "vegetation . . . plants . . . seeds . . . trees," "the two great lights," "the large sea creatures and every living creature . . . every winged bird," "the wildlife of the earth . . . the livestock . . . and creatures that crawl on the ground" (Gen 1:3–25). This whole creation was "very good" in its substance in conjunction with a hovering and inherent spirituality. Perhaps we could say that God's original creation comprised "spiritual materiality," and thus was wholly unpolluted, undefiled. There was nothing "carnal" or second-rate about this holy materiality. If "the Spirit of God was moving over the surface of the waters" (Gen 1:2) at the commencement of creation, how much more did this same Spirit inhabit the whole of that same creation at its completion, and especially the garden of Eden. Further, the fact that Adam and Eve in their innocence had intimate fellowship with God (Gen 3:8–9) indicates that there was blessed spiritual kinship and union. From God's perspective, His creation was good, spiritually and materially, especially in the sense of being admirable both ethically and aesthetically. Ps 104 well reflects the overall glory of God's creation, *not* its material, earthly inferiority that pales before spiritual, heavenly superiority.

> My soul, praise the LORD!
> LORD my God, You are very great;
> You are clothed with majesty and splendor.
> He wraps Himself in light as if it were a robe,
> spreading out the sky like a canopy,
> laying the beams of His palace on the waters above,
> making the clouds His chariot,
> walking on the wings of the wind,
> and making the winds His messengers,
> flames of fire for His servants.
> He established the earth on its foundations;
> it will never be shaken.
> You covered it with the deep as if it were a garment;
> the waters stood above the mountains. . . .
> How countless are Your works O LORD!

> In wisdom You have made them all;
> the earth is full of Your creatures. . . .
> When You send Your breath, they are created,
> and You renew the face of the earth.
> May the glory of the LORD endure forever;
> may the LORD rejoice in His works. (vv. 1–6,24,30–31)

When God rested, immediately following the creation, He reflected and mused upon the excellence, even perfection, of His labor, surely in greater terms of veneration than any psalmist could express.

Adam and Eve's fall in sin, however, contracted the curse of God on the whole created order over which they had been commissioned to have righteous dominion. The holy materiality of the creation became an unholy materiality. The consequences of this universal sinful pollution, being judgment on Adam and his posterity, also included judgment on the world in its broadest sense, not just humanity. In particular, decay and degradation in the human species also resulted in decay and degradation within the whole material order. Such is the world we inhabit today. It is difficult for redeemed man, let alone unredeemed man, to conceive of a world in which materiality and spirituality perfectly coalesce. Nevertheless, the promise that the child of God eagerly looks forward to is that future time when "the creation itself will also be set free from the bondage of corruption into the glorious freedom of God's children" (Rom 8:21), which includes "the redemption of our bodies" (Rom 8:23).

The Spirituality of Materiality in the Old Testament

Not only is the OT revelation a transcript of the truth of God communicated through a Hebrew prism, but also it reveals visceral earthiness and admiration of the imminent creation that is in confluence with transcendent spirituality reaching to God's glorious throne in heaven. As George Eldon Ladd explained:

> Hebrew thought saw an essential unity between man and nature. The prophets do not think of the earth as merely the indifferent theater on which man carries out his normal task but as the expression of the divine glory. The Old Testament nowhere holds forth the hope of a bodiless, nonmaterial, purely "spiritual" redemption as did Greek thought. The earth is the divinely ordained scene of human existence. Furthermore, the earth has been involved in the evils which sin has incurred. There is an interrelation of nature with the moral life of man; therefore the earth must also share in God's final redemption. . . . The fact that man is a physical creature is not the measure of his sinfulness and therefore a state from which he must be

delivered. Rather, the acceptance of his creaturehood and the confession of complete and utter dependence upon the Creator God are essential to man's true existence. . . . Salvation for man does not mean deliverance from creaturehood, for it is not an evil thing but an essential and permanent element of man's true being. Salvation does not mean escape from bodily, creaturely existence. On the contrary, ultimate redemption will mean the redemption of the whole man. For this reason, the resurrection of the body is an integral part of the biblical hope.[3]

Similarly, from a Hebrew Christian perspective, Baruch Maoz commented:

It is true that redemption from sin is not to be conceived of in terms that are primarily material. On this point the New Testament is as clear as the Old, though much more emphatic. But salvation is not to be thought of as exclusively spiritual and moral, as if Israel's living in the land had no spiritual and moral implications! The gospel message is replete with appreciation for the material realm. The New Testament makes it quite clear that the material is the arena in which ultimate salvation is to take place (Rom. 8:18–25), thus reconfirming Old Testament expectation. Even our bodies are to be redeemed.[4]

Thus we should reject imposing the shadowy character of the Mosaic covenant on the ethos of the OT as a whole. This is in no way meant to depreciate the significance of progressive revelation where type and promise in the OT proceed toward antitype and fulfillment in the NT. But Palmer Robertson's *The Israel Of God*, in repeatedly using the term "shadow" or "type" in a very comprehensive sense with regard to the OT, goes way beyond the obvious temporal, typological limitations of the Mosaic covenant. He did this by attempting to incorporate similar limitations within the Abrahamic covenant since it is here that the promise of the land is rooted.[5] He commented, "In speaking of Israel's land under the old covenant, it is necessary to think in categories of shadow, type, and prophecy, in contrast to reality, substance, and fulfillment under the new covenant."[6] This I believe to be a fundamental error. As I have repeatedly maintained, the land is rooted in the abiding Abrahamic covenant, not the transient old covenant.

---

[3] G. E. Ladd, *The Presence Of The Future* (Grand Rapids: Eerdmans, 1974). 59–60; also pp. 63–64.

[4] B. Maoz, "People, land and Torah: a Jewish Christian perspective," in *The Land of Promise* (ed. P. Johnston and P. Walker; Downers Grove, Ill.: InterVarsity, 2000), 196.

[5] O. P. Robertson, *The Israel of God* (Philipsburg, New Jersey: P&R, 2000). In the first chapter, "The Israel of God: Its Land," he refers at least 20 times to the land as "shadow" or "type," principally in parallel with Mosaic entities.

[6] Ibid., 4.

Furthermore, the materiality of this land should not be divorced from any prospective spirituality. Being aware of this, Robertson responded,

> Just as the tabernacle was never intended to be a settled item in the plan of redemption, but was to point to Christ's tabernacling among his people (cf. John 1:14), and just as the sacrificial system could never atone for sins but could only foreshadow the offering of the Son of God (Heb. 9:23–26), so in a similar manner Abraham received the promise of the land but never experienced the blessing of its full possession. In this way the patriarch learned to look forward to "the city with foundations, whose architect and builder is God" (Heb. 11:10).[7]

Robertson could not prove his point here apart from the further use of inappropriate identification of the land with the Mosaic covenant, along with an attempt at depreciation of the original Abrahamic covenant. He also turned to an incorrect, Gentile, antithetical understanding of Heb 9:23–26; 11:10, that is, the false dichotomy of a superior, other-worldly heaven above versus an inferior earth below. It appears to escape Robertson that here in Hebrews we have a learned Hebrew Christian author instructing Hebrew Christians concerning Hebrew Scripture using a Hebrew hermeneutic. When Abraham first entered and surveyed the promised land, it was manifestly unholy as a result of extreme Canaanite defilement. He was looking for the consummation of the promise originally given when heaven would come down and transform the unholy land into the land that was to become truly holy (Zech 2:12). At that glorious time, the land will have become regenerated and spiritually material, but it will still be the land of Israel (see chapter 9).

The Spirituality of Materiality in the New Testament

At the transfiguration of Jesus, it seems that for a fleeting period, the veil of perfect humanity is penetrated to reveal essential glory so that "His face shone like the sun. Even His clothes became as white as the light" (Matt 17:2). The account of Luke adds concerning Moses and Elijah, "They appeared in glory *[doxa]*" (Luke 9:31). Evidently Moses was identifiable as Moses while Elijah was identifiable as Elijah. Here was the embodiment of spiritual materiality on planet earth. So it is with the resurrection appearances of the Lord Jesus; He was transformed into tangible, spiritual materiality (Luke 24:13–16,30–31; John 20:15–16). In Galilee, "He Himself stood among them. He said to them, 'Peace to you.' But they were startled

[7] Ibid., 13.

and terrified and thought they were seeing a ghost" (Luke 24:36–37). Then He invited them, "Touch Me and see, because a ghost does not have flesh and bones as you can see I have" (24:39). Subsequently He ate fish, after which "He left them and was carried up into heaven" (Luke 24:51). Again, here is the formerly crucified, but now resurrected, Son of God plainly evidencing spiritual materiality. Paul similarly instructs us in 1 Cor 15:35–57 that the seed of the buried dead human body is to be raised with a distinctively new body. Concerning the more exact nature of this resurrection body Paul stated,

> So it is with the resurrection of the dead: Sown in corruption, raised in incorruption; sown in dishonor, raised in glory; sown in weakness, raised in power; sown a natural body, raised a spiritual body. . . . And just as we have borne the image of the man made of dust, we will also bear the image of the heavenly man [as a both/and result]. Brothers, I tell you this: [sinful] flesh and blood cannot inherit the kingdom of God, and corruption cannot inherit incorruption [except resurrection change be accomplished when]. . . . this corruptible must be clothed with incorruptibility, and this mortal must be clothed with immortality (1 Cor 15:42–44,49–50,53).

The Judeo-centric, premillennial hope anticipates that time when the spiritual materiality of the redeemed, who have been regenerated and resurrected, will have become gloriously manifest. They will comprise Israel and the Gentile nations; they will enjoy the consummation of their salvation on an earth of spiritual materiality where the glorious, spiritually tangible and spiritually material Jesus Christ will reign from the spiritually material Jerusalem. For those who continue to charge that premillennialism is carnal at its roots, Horatius Bonar has a persuasive response that is worth pondering. He maintained that a literal fulfillment of Scripture is often just as spiritual as any other, and he offered three compelling proofs that this is so. First he referred to the incarnation of Christ:

> Take the prophecies regarding the incarnation of Christ. Before that event took place, there might be a controversy as to whether they were to be literally fulfilled or not. A Jew might have argued with much apparent force against a literal meaning, What! Is God to take upon Himself the form of a man? Is Jehovah to become an infant of days, nay, to be born of a creature, to be a man of sorrows and acquainted with grief, to die and be buried, as men die and are buried? Impossible! the very idea is carnal beyond endurance. These prophecies cannot be interpreted in their literal sense; they must have some figurative, some spiritual meaning. So might a Jew have argued before Messiah came. . . . [However the] fact, the glorious but stupendous fact, made known in the fullness of time, proved not only that the

literal was the true sense of these prophecies regarding Messiah's first coming, but also established this truth, that the literal interpretation and fulfillment may be the more truly spiritual of the two.[8]

Second he referred to the resurrection of Christ:

> Take, as another illustration of the point in hand, the doctrine of the resurrection. That doctrine appeared to some, in the first ages, such a carnal doctrine, that they denied the literal accomplishment of those Scriptures which speak of it. Of these were Hymenæus and Philetis, mentioned in the Second Epistle to Timothy. They maintained that a literal resurrection was such a carnal thing, that those passages which refer to it must mean something spiritual,—the resurrection of the soul from sin. They "erred concerning the truth, saying that the resurrection was past already" [2 Tim 2:18]. Here, also, the literal was the more spiritual of the two interpretations.[9]

Third he referred to the biblical truth concerning spiritual unity that exists between Jewish and Gentile believers:

> It is said, "All are one in Christ Jesus [Gal 3:28], therefore there can be no national distinction of the Jews, no national restoration, no national pre-eminence." . . . Some have surely a strange notion of what is meant by being "one in Christ," when they make their spiritual oneness depend upon the uniformity of external circumstances. What a low idea of Christian oneness! They charge us with carnal views because we insist upon the future distinctiveness of the Jewish nation; but it appears that the charge of carnality belongs to them, not to us! We believe in the literal accomplishment of the prophecies regarding the Jews, in which there appear to be many promises of temporal blessings as well as spiritual; but we lay no further stress upon these than the Word of God lays; we admit spiritual blessings to be the highest and noblest. Our opponents, however, lay such stress upon external circumstances, as to insist, that if these exist the oneness in Christ is gone. We had always understood Scripture as telling us, not that there were no national distinctions, but that, in spite of these, there was a oneness which bound together all believers; a oneness so spiritual, so divine, so unearthly, so unapproachable, as not to be in the very least affected by temporal distinctions of time, or place, or rank.[10]

We might take this argumentation further by referring to the apostle John's insistence, not only that "the Word became flesh and took up residence among us" (John 1:14), but also that, "every spirit who confesses that Jesus Christ has come in the flesh is from God. But every spirit that does not confess Jesus [has come in the flesh] is not from God" (1 John

---

[8] H. Bonar, *Prophetical Landmarks* (London: James Nisbet, 1876), 231–32.
[9] Ibid., 232–33.
[10] Ibid., 240–41.

4:2–3). Indeed, added to this impeccable carnality of the Son of God was the vital sensual attestation that John esteemed to be of fundamental significance concerning "what we have heard, what we have seen with our eyes, what we have observed, and have touched with our hands, concerning the Word of life" (1 John 1:1). Surely this alludes to Christ's post-resurrection appearances that manifest a glorious and spiritual materiality promised as the form of His personal Second Coming (Acts 1:9–11). In Jesus Christ has come about the union of eternal deity and holy materiality, while at the same time He has received from His Father "the Spirit without measure" (John 3:34).[11]

The original creation before the fall, especially within the boundaries of the garden of Eden, was not of such a lowly and inferior status that it will be superseded by a heavenly existence. On the other hand, this is not to say that God's vindication by means of the future millennial reign of Jesus Christ on earth will be the employment of an economy identical with that of Eden.

The Influence of Platonism, Aristotelianism, and Stoicism on the Early Church

The early Christian fathers were Gentile Greeks and Romans. Having embraced Christian truth, they nevertheless were influenced by the dominant world view of their time, namely, Greek philosophy, particularly Platonism, Aristotelianism, and Stoicism, often in blended forms. Gager indicates that "the appropriation of Middle- and Neo-Platonic philosophy by such theologians as Justin, Clement of Alexandria, Origen, Ambrose, and Augustine eventually came to play an important role in the formulation of Christian doctrine."[12] Platonism also had ongoing relevance for Christian mysticism as represented by Dionysius the Areopagite and Bernard of Clairvaux. John Scotus in the medieval church, then in the Renaissance, John Colet, Thomas More, and Richard Hooker, imbibed this ongoing stream of Platonic thought. The prevailing philosophic understanding of Hellenistic deity was that of a transcendent, spiritual, unchanging being in contrast with the changing character of this material world. Thus Greek thought was predominantly negative about this earthly existence. It considered material life in this world to be temporal, transient, the creation of an inferior deity. The philosophical

---

[11] Concerning this interpretation of John 3:34, see the commentaries of C. K. Barrett, D. A. Carson, and L. Morris.

[12] J. G. Gager, *The Origins of Anti-Semitism* (New York: Oxford University Press, 1983), 160.

approach to this world was usually ascetic in which the philosopher sought to rise above the things of the world. The Greek or Hellenist despised the material world because it was tangible substance and thereby was changing, deteriorating as an inferior creation. Man's body was the mere clothing of the soul, which was regarded as the real essential person. Future hope consisted in release from the imprisonment of the earthly body. Of course, it is not difficult to recognize some agreement in certain areas here with biblical Christianity, especially in the realm of divine transcendence. But the thought that God would participate in human flesh, and indeed resurrect the body, was abhorrent to Greek thought (Acts 17:32; 1 John 1:1–3; 4:1–3; 2 John 1:7). We can easily see how other-worldly Hellenistic thought was in conflict with a more earthly Hebrew world view, except that some mode of reconciliation could be employed. Alfred Edersheim explained how rapprochement could be obtained, even among Jews influenced by Hellenism during the time of Jesus Christ:

> To those who sought to weld Grecian thought with Hebrew revelation, two objects would naturally present themselves. They must try to connect their Greek philosophers with the Bible, and they must find beneath the letter of Scripture a deeper meaning, which would accord with philosophic truth. So far as the truth of Scripture was concerned, they had a method ready at hand. The Stoic philosophers had busied themselves in finding a deeper *allegorical* meaning, especially in the writings of Homer. By applying it to mythical stories, or to the popular beliefs, and by tracing the supposed symbolical meaning of names, numbers, &c., it became easy to prove almost anything, or to extract from these philosophical truths ethical principles, and even the later results of natural science. Such a process was peculiarly pleasing to the imagination, and the results alike astounding and satisfactory, since as they could not be proved, so neither could they be disproved. This allegorical method was the welcome key by which the Hellenists might unlock the hidden treasury of Scripture.[13]

It should not surprise us then that the early Christian fathers, particularly Augustine, should be similarly influenced by Greek thought in such a way as to subtly include elements of Hellenism within their hermeneutical frame of reference concerning Scripture, especially with regard to eschatology.[14] In other words, the Augustinian concept of the *City of God* was

---

[13] A. Edersheim, *The Life and Times of Jesus the Messiah*, II (Grand Rapids: Eerdmans, 1969), 33–34.

[14] O. Heick, *A History of Christian Thought*, I (Philadelphia: Fortress, 1965), 133. He quotes Anders Nygren, *Agape and Eros*: "all his life he [Augustine] remained a Neo-Platonic Christian or, if you will, a Christian Platonist" (London: SPCK, 1953), 458.

based on an either/or, that is, an inferior/superior eschatological regard for earth and heaven rather then the Hebrew both/and eschatological hope concerning earth and heaven, materiality and spirituality. Herein lies a fundamental point of difference that I regard to be at the heart of much amillennial allegiance to anti-Semitic eschatology, often quite unconsciously. To embrace the Augustinian dichotomy between materiality and spirituality and impose it on the OT canon is to fly in the face of the Hebrew hope of spiritual materiality. However, of supreme importance is the consequence of this philosophical/theological amalgam that has lead to the depreciation of national and ethnic Israel. Augustine's *City of God* found its earthly expression in the Roman Catholic Church that, as the new Israel of God, would not suffer any legitimacy from a rival, the old Israel of God. B. B. Warfield wrote,

> It was particularly in the doctrine of the Church, which he [Augustine] thus took up and transfigured, that he became in a true sense the founder of Roman Catholicism, and thus called into being a new type of Christianity, in which, "the idea of the Church became the central power in the religious feeling" and "in ecclesiastical activity," "in a fashion which has remained unknown to the East." . . . To Augustine the Church was fundamentally the *congregatio sanctorum*, the Body of Christ, and it is this Church which he has in mind when he calls it the *civitas Dei*, or the Kingdom of God on earth.[15]

Considering the subsequent centuries of denigration of the Jewish people that have transpired through the widespread influence of Augustinian eschatology and ecclesiology, it is difficult to comprehend how a Christian today should boast in such an eschatology. Consider Jewish historian Robert S. Wistrich's opinion in this regard:

> The Augustinian theology reinforced the notion of the Jews as a wandering, homeless, rejected and accursed people who were incurably carnal, blind to spiritual meaning, perfidious, faithless, and apostate. Their crime, being one of cosmic proportions, merited permanent exile and subordination to Christianity. Israel, the older son, must be made to 'serve' the Church, the younger son, which is the true heir and rightful owner of the Divine promises enunciated in the Old Testament.[16]

When Reformed scholars write with admiration concerning their eschatological linkage with Augustine,[17] they might reconsider exactly what the

---

[15] B. B. Warfield, *Calvin and Augustine* (Philadelphia, PA: Presbyterian and Reformed, 1974), 313. He quoted Hermann Reuter, *Augustinische Studien*, vii (Gotha: F. A. Perthes, 1887), 499.

[16] R. S. Wistrich, *Antisemitism, The Longest Hatred* (New York: Pantheon Books, 1991), 19.

[17] W. J. Grier writes glowingly of Augustine as "one of the greatest men of the Christian Church of all time" since it has been said that he "laid the ghost of premillennialism so effec-

fruit of this legacy has produced, and how their derived understanding of national and ethnic Israel would help or retard their witness to unbelieving Jews.

The Redemption of Spirituality and Materiality

In rejecting the Platonic/Augustinian eschatological dichotomy between inferior, earthly materiality and superior, heavenly spirituality, the preferred alternative of both earthly materiality and heavenly spirituality in holy union should be carefully understood. Craig Blaising describes this essential distinction in the millennial debate in a manner that is well worth consideration at this juncture. He speaks of "Two Models of Eternal Life," the "Spiritual Vision Model," which is the presupposition or "preunderstanding" of amillennialism, and the "New Creation Model," which is the presupposition of premillennialism. The Spiritual Vision Model understands the "final state of the resurrected" as being in heaven. Advocates of this view base it not only on "biblical themes,"

> but also on cultural ideas common to the classical philosophical tradition. That tradition has contributed to the spiritual vision model in three basic convictions: (1) a basic contrast between spirit and matter; (2) an identification of spirit with mind or intellect; and (3) a belief that eternal perfection entails the absence of change. Central to all three of these is the classical tradition's notion of an ontological hierarchy in which spirit is located at the top of a descending order of being. Elemental matter occupies the lowest place. In the spiritual vision model of eternity, heaven is the highest level of ontological reality. It is the realm of spirit as opposed to base matter. This is the destiny of the saved, who will exist in that non earthly, spiritual place as spiritual beings engaged eternally in spiritual activity. . . . Following the classical tradition's identification of spirit with mind or intellect, the spiritual model views eternal life primarily as cognitive, meditative, or contemplative. With this point of emphasis, the place or realm of eternal life is really a secondary or even inconsequential matter. In its essential reality, eternal life is a state of knowing [God].[18]

tively that for centuries the subject was practically ignored." *The Momentous Event* (London: Banner of Truth, 1970), 27. C. P. Venema writes of "the great church father, Augustine" with regard to his instrumental role in establishing the predominant place of amillennialism over succeeding centuries and on through the Reformation. *The Promise of the Future* (Edinburgh: Banner of Truth, 2000), 236–37.

[18] C. A. Blaising, "Premillennialism," *Three Views on the Millennium and Beyond* (ed. D. L. Bock and S. N. Gundry; Grand Rapids: Zondervan, 1999), 161–62. He acknowledges that some amillennialists have attempted to retain materiality involving the present planet earth in their understanding of the future new heavens and new earth. But this must surely be seen as a precipitous situation in that it opens the door for a more earthly understanding of OT passages

On the other hand, the "New Creation Model"

> draws on biblical texts that speak of a future everlasting kingdom, of a new earth and the renewal of life on it, of bodily resurrection (especially of the nature of Christ's resurrection body), of social and even political concourse among the redeemed. The new creation model expects that the ontological order and scope of eternal life is essentially continuous with that of present earthly life except for the absence of sin and death. Eternal life for redeemed human beings will be an embodied life on earth (whether the present earth or a wholly new earth), set within a cosmic structure such as we have presently. It is not a timeless, static existence but rather an unending sequence of life and lived experiences. It does not reject physicality or materiality, but affirms them as essential both to a holistic anthropology and to the biblical idea of a redeemed creation.[19]

In other words concerning this more biblical perspective, materiality is not ultimately to be transcended, but rather transformed. Such a transformation is to be the rebirth that ushers in "the Messianic Age [*palingenesia*, "regeneration"], when the Son of Man sits on His glorious throne . . . judging the 12 tribes of Israel" (Matt 19:28). Then there will be "a new heaven and a new earth" (Isa 65:17; 66:22), that is, a spiritually renewed earth and cosmic order. Through the triumph of sovereign grace, both human and nonhuman aspects of creation, animate and inanimate, will be greatly blessed beyond the state of things prior to the transgression of Adam and Eve.

The Tension between Spirituality, Materiality and Augustinianism

Robert Strimple has furnished a critique of Blaising's view that introduces a more recent development within amillennial eschatology. Strimple disclaims a proven connection between amillennialism and the "Spiritual Vision Model," citing Charles E. Hill's *Regnum Caelorum: Patterns of Future Hope in Early Christianity*, which considers the streams of millennialism and amillennialism that flowed during the early church up to the mid-third century.[20] Hill concluded,

---

that, according to a *prima facie* reading, proclaim a glorious, holy, earthly existence. In such a case the door would then open even wider to Messiah inhabiting and reigning over a geographic Jerusalem, Israel, and the nations.

[19] Ibid., 162–63.

[20] R. B. Strimple, "An Amillennial Response," in *Three Views on the Millennium and Beyond* (ed. D. Bock and S. N. Gundry; Grand Rapids: Zondervan, 1999), 257–58.

Nor should it be thought permissible to portray all opposition to early chiliasm as "Greek," "allegorizing," or "spiritualizing." Doubtless chiliastic hopes must have seemed a chimera [a fantastic or gross result of imagination] to any who were favorably disposed to Platonism, but the eschatological scheme that looked for a return of Christ to be followed, without an interregnum, by a last judgment and an eternal state was no less "realistic," no less "historical," and no more "allegorical," "mystical," or "Greek" than was chiliasm. Nor was the amillennial tendency necessarily or ultimately "antimaterialistic"; it only looked for the next stage of material realization to be final, perfect, and eternal (Rom. 8:19–23), rather than intermediate, gradational, and temporal.[21]

Aside from this conclusion that spans a period of approximately 150 years, and thus hardly encompasses "the history of the church," as Blaising puts it, we must ask how Augustine, immediately following the period of Hill's consideration, arrived at his amillennialism. After all, his doctrine was, as previously pointed out, influenced by the dominant world view of that time. As Gager indicated, those especially impacted by this teaching were Justin, Clement of Alexandria, Origen, Ambrose, and Augustine.[22] Hill himself admitted, "We know that Augustine, in continuity with the non-chiliastic tradition, still reserved a large place in his exegesis for the 'Church triumphant' in heaven."[23] Not surprisingly, since Augustine was a Neoplatonist prior to his conversion, Warfield concluded, "It was as a Neoplatonist thinker that Augustine became a Christian; and he carried his Neoplatonic conceptions over into Christianity with him."[24] Not that this legacy remained; quite the contrary, Warfield suggested that it diminished. Augustine was not expounding "the Neoplatonist philosophy in Christian terms," but was "developing the philosophy of Christianity in terms of the best philosophic thought of the day."[25] With this in mind, as well as the subsequent Aristotelian legacy of Thomas Aquinas and centuries of Roman Catholic mysticism, it is not surprising that this era, up to the present, has indeed been dominated by what Blaising called the "Spiritual Vision Model."

Nevertheless, in the light of the preceding, it is interesting to consider that more recently a number of Reformed amillennialists have upheld a version

[21] C. E. Hill, *Regnum Caelorum, Patterns of Millennial Thought in Early Christianity* (Grand Rapids: Eerdmans, 2001), 251.

[22] J. G. Gager, *The Origins of Anti-Semitism* (New York: Oxford University Press, 1983), 160.

[23] Hill, *Regnum Caelorum*, 267.

[24] Warfield, *Calvin and Augustine*, 369.

[25] Ibid., 374.

of Blaising's "New Creation Model." From a premillennial perspective, I believe this is a step in the right direction. In considering the representations of Anthony Hoekema, Robert Strimple, Cornelius Venema, and Samuel Waldron, we find interpretations of the "new heavens and a new earth" which do appear to affirm a hope in future spiritual materiality. Hoekema raised the question "whether the new earth will be totally other than this present earth or a renewal of the present earth. . . . Lutheran theologians have often favored the former of these two options. . . . We must, however, reject the concept of total annihilation in favor of the concept of renewal."[26] Although I agree with Hoekema's rejection of the Lutheran perspective, I suggest that a far more broad legacy has prevailed within Christendom that, as I have already indicated, involved centuries of a mystical heavenly hope rather than anything earthly, especially Jewish, according to spiritual materiality. Even so, Hoekema appears to quote approvingly Edward Thurneysen who wrote,

> The world into which we shall enter in the Parousia of Jesus Christ is therefore not another world; it is this world, this heaven, this earth; both however, passed away and renewed. It is these forests, these fields, these cities' streets, these people, that will be the scene of redemption. At present they are battlefields, full of the strife and sorrow of the not yet accomplished consummation; then they will be fields of victory, fields of harvest, where out of seed that was sown with tears the everlasting sheaves will be reaped and brought home.[27]

Concerning Rev 21:24,26, Hoekema declared,

> One could say that, according to these words, the inhabitants of the new earth will include people who attained great prominence and exercised great power on the present earth—kings, princes, leaders, and the like. One could also say that whatever people have done on this earth which glorified God will be remembered in the life to come (cf. Rev. 14:13). But more must be said. Is it too much to say that, according to these verses, the unique contributions of each nation to the life of the present earth will enrich the life of the new earth? Shall we then perhaps inherit the best products of culture and art which this earth has produced?

Then he concluded,

> Whereas ecologists often picture the future of this earth in gloomy terms, it is encouraging to know that some day God will prepare a glorious new

[26] A. A. Hoekema, *The Bible and The Future* (Grand Rapids: Eerdmans, 1979), 280. Hoekema acknowledged his debt to P. Fairbairn's *Typology of Scripture* for the development of his teaching on "The New Earth" (p. 279). See chapter 6 for a consideration of Fairbairn in this regard.

[27] Ibid., 281. E. Thurneysen, as a pastor theologian, was a close colleague of Karl Barth in Germany.

earth on which the ecological problems which now plague us will no longer exist. . . . As citizens of God's kingdom, we may not just write off the present earth as a total loss, or rejoice in its deterioration. . . . As we live on this earth, we are preparing for life on God's new earth.[28]

All this is quite astonishing. Without blushing, language is used that is very similar to how premillenarians have spoken for generations. Even more startling is the mention of distinctive national contributions, which of necessity would surely have to include the cultural benefactions of Israel! But then, according to amillennialism, such a distinction is passé. So it is also fascinating to note that more recently, several amillennial authors have expressed their agreement with Hoekema's eschatological "New Earth." Three examples are Robert Strimple,[29] Cornelius P. Venema,[30] and Samuel E. Waldron.[31] Waldron confesses his dependence on Hoekema and declares,

> The heavenly country is not a country in heaven, but a country *from heaven*. The heavenly kingdom is the *kingdom from heaven* and not the kingdom in heaven. . . . Though heaven is the happy abode of the disembodied righteous during the present age, in the age to come heaven comes to earth. . . . This doctrine enables us to answer the best argument of both pre- and postmillennialists. What is this argument? It is the countless Old Testament and New Testament prophecies that clearly prophecy a future, earthly kingdom. In the past, those opposing millenarianism often failed to satisfactorily interpret such passages. They attempted to apply them to the church in the present age or to heaven. Such interpretations did not make sense to many good people. They shouldn't have! They were wrong. Only the doctrine of the new earth [Isa. 65–66] provides a proper interpretation of such passages.[32]

In reply, I very much appreciate the hermeneutical advance here from former classic amillennialism to that which is more genuinely literal. But Waldron struggles with the interpretation of Isaiah 65–66 and the possibility of death,[33] as did E. J. Young,[34] relegating an alleged premillennial

---

[28] Ibid., 286–87.

[29] Strimple, "Amillennialism," 256–76. He cites Bavinck and Vos in support and also draws on Hoekema's "even more earth-oriented vision."

[30] C. P. Venema, *The Promise of the Future* (Edinburgh: Banner of Truth, 2000), 454–88. Also citing Bavinck and Hoekema, he makes a significant though unexplained comment: "Ironically, the future millennium of dispensational expectations is in some ways a less literal fulfillment of the biblical promise of the new heavens and earth than that of Amillennialism" (469n).

[31] S. E. Waldron, *The End Times Made Simple* (Amityville, NY: Calvary, 2003), 225–41.

[32] Ibid., 240–41.

[33] Ibid., 235–38.

[34] E. J. Young, *The Book of Isaiah* (Grand Rapids: Eerdmans, 1972), 3:515. He commented on Isa 55:20, "The conditions of Paradise are to be restored, but the new age will surpass Paradise,"

economy to the eternal state, which will nevertheless constitute a millennial environment upon a renovated earth. Now I readily confess that Isaiah 65–66 is not an easy passage to interpret, whatever eschatology one follows. Yet our main objection to Waldron remains. In terms of Judeo-centric premillennialism, there is inconsistency in attributing millennial conditions to the eternal state because

> the emphasis on the earth and land is too pervasive and too deeply rooted
> in the biblical doctrine of creation itself to be explained away on this basis.
> To dismiss all the emphasis on the earth in favor of a more "spiritual" view
> of the eternal state raises serious questions.[35]

This being all too true, in again considering Isaiah 65–66 in this regard, it is astonishing that the distinction that will exist between "My people/ My chosen ones" (65:15,19,22) and the "nations" (66:12,18), as well as the identification of "Jerusalem/Zion/My holy mountain" (65:18–19,25; 66:8,10,13,20), is rejected because of supercessional presuppositions concerning Israel. Are these terms, while distinctively representing the community and geography of "heaven on earth," to be identified as the actual Jerusalem where Messiah will personally reign from Zion over "Israel, My servant" (49:3) as "the Holy One of Israel" (60:14)? Surely the pervasive Judeo-centric language of Isa 41:8–10; 43:1–7; 44:21; 45:17; 46:3–4,13; 49:5–7; 55:5; 60:9,14; 63:7–8 provides an eloquent and positive answer. In the glory of the earthly kingdom yet to come, Israel will have distinctive prominence. But supercessionist amillennialism plainly conflicts with such an expectation, while its eschatological outworking concerning Israel has proved to be historically shameful.

The Redemption of Israel's Fallen Spiritual Materiality

Surely the preeminent passage of Scripture that describes the regeneration, resurrection, and restoration of national Israel is Ezek 36:22–37:28. Spurgeon's sermon on Ezek 37:1–10 is well worth studying. He proposed that dispersed national Israel will experience national conversion as well as glorious residency in the land under Christ.[36] His plain exposition is in stark contrast with O. Palmer Robertson's attempt to spiritualize this passage in terms of a NT resurrection motif.[37] I would strongly maintain that Spurgeon

---

[35] Waldron, *End Times Made Simple*, 227.

[36] C. H. Spurgeon, *The C. H. Spurgeon Collection, Metropolitan Tabernacle Pulpit*, X, 1864 (Albany, Oregon: Ages Software, 1998), 582.

[37] Robertson, *The Israel of God*, 21–25.

is essentially and obviously correct, while it is difficult to avoid the conclusion that Robertson's explanation is born of avoidance, at all costs, of what is, according to Spurgeon, patently obvious. Two related matters should be considered at this point. First, the nation of Israel will enjoy the redemption of its fallen spiritual materiality. The language is full of the inert material becoming gloriously alive unto God. The national and personal form remains, but the bones come to life and are clothed with redeemed flesh that responds with submissive adoration. Second, Ezek 37:28 declares, "When My sanctuary is among them forever, the nations [Gentiles] will know that I, the LORD, sanctify Israel." There is no absorption here of the Jews into the Gentile community or of the Gentiles into the Jewish community. Rather, the Jews will inhabit the land, and the Gentiles will surround them, both distinct entities manifesting diversity within the unity of the seed of Abraham.

Carnal Zionism

In chapter 5, the predominant secularity of Zionism was described, as were many remarkable providential circumstances. David Larsen has written about the impressive rise of European Zionism:

> While doubtless there were complex motives of self-interest on the part of Great Britain, [Chaim] Weitzmann stoutly maintained in his memoirs that the sincere Christian beliefs of Balfour, Lloyd-George, and Jan Christian Smuts were more responsible than anything else for the new opening for the Jews in Palestine.[38]

Certainly the present leadership of Israel in general as well as the population and diaspora reflect no love for Jesus of Nazareth as its longed-for Messiah. Faced with such animosity, the apostle Paul never ceased to witness in synagogues wherever he traveled. Interestingly, whereas in 1967, when Israel regained ancient Jerusalem in the Six Day War, there were hardly any Messianic Jewish congregations in the world, by 1998 there were 350 gatherings.[39] And whereas in the 1950s in Israel there were at least 20 Christian churches, congregations, and groups, in the 1990s there were over 130.[40] However, as is pointed out in chapter 11 with reference

---

[38] D. Larsen, *Jews, Gentiles, and the Church: A New Perspective on History and Prophecy* (Grand Rapids: Discovery House, 1955), 182.

[39] G. Thomas, "The Return of the Jewish Church," *Christianity Today* (September 7, 1998).

[40] K. Kjær-Hansen and B. F. Skjøtt, *Facts and Myths About the Messianic Congregations in Israel* (Jerusalem: United Christian Council in Israel in cooperation with the Caspari Center for Biblical and Jewish Studies, 1999), 67–69.

to Rom 11:28, God still has a covenantal regard for His beloved enemies in the flesh, that is, a preponderance of severed natural olive branches (Rom 11:17,20–21).

In essence, carnal Zionism places a primary emphasis on circumcision of the flesh, related religious form, external legal conformity, and secular nationalism. In the realm of eschatology, it excludes the primacy of necessary spiritual renovation, both personal and national. By way of example, consider the common references to "Pray for the peace of Jerusalem" (Ps. 122:6). Stanley Ellison directed us to more seriously reflect on King David's plea:

> To pray this prayer intelligently in the will of God, it is important to discern more specifically what "peace" the Psalmist had in mind. Was he speaking of military triumph for the nation? Are we to pray for modern Israel's political dominance over the Arabs? Should we encourage her annexation of the West Bank and Gaza Strip? How about praying that the Muslim Dome of the Rock be replaced by a new Jewish temple? Or should we simply pray for Israel's international prominence and peaceful relations with her neighbors in the Middle East?[41]

Here is also exposed the very heart of carnal Christian Zionism. It is chiefly concerned with a prophetic agenda, the nation of Israel, as if it were merely a playing piece on a chess board. But there is no Pauline passion for the very soul of Israel after the manner of the Lord Jesus Christ weeping over Jerusalem (Matt 23:37–38).

Spiritual Zionism

By way of contrast, spiritual Zionism places a primary emphasis on circumcision of the heart, related godly virtue and Spirit-constrained worship, yet continuing to acknowledge the significance of circumcision, and national, territorial identity. But again with reference to Ps 122:6 (see also vv. 7–9), David's primary desire was to draw close to God within His house, in fellowship with authentic believing brethren. This then is the very source of the peace, with rejoicing, he so longed for. But he also acknowledges that ultimately this peace is a sovereign, gracious bestowment of God and not an achievement of man.

Ellison further explained,

> The context of this Psalm appears to have a very different emphasis. David's concern was for the house of the Lord, that is, the tabernacle in Jerusalem. As Hebrew pilgrims ascended the rugged hills to the city, they especially an-

---

[41] S. A. Ellison, *Who Owns The Land?* (Portland, OR: Multnomah, 1991), 184.

ticipated a time of fellowship with their covenant Lord, bringing with them various offerings. They came "To give thanks to the name of the Lord," as the psalmist expresses it. Warfare would restrict or deny this privilege, but that was not his main concern. The peace of which he speaks is not primarily outer, but inner peace—not political, but spiritual. "May peace be within you," is his emphasis. His concern throughout the Psalm is "the house of the Lord" and the spiritual peace that comes through a right relationship with God. For this "peace of Jerusalem" all creation groans, and all God's people are exhorted to fervently pray. It is the grand climax of the biblical drama of Israel, through whom God will bring the full blessing of Abraham to all the world.[42]

Of supreme importance is that, in the sovereignty of God's grace, Zion will undergo resurrection unto glorious, spiritual materiality. Because "the LORD of hosts says: I am extremely jealous for Jerusalem and Zion" (Zech 1:14), He "will once more comfort Zion and again choose Jerusalem" (Zech 1:17). As a result, "I [the LORD] will return to Zion and live in Jerusalem. Then Jerusalem will be called the Faithful City, the mountain of the LORD of hosts, and the Holy Mountain" (Zech 8:3). Commenting on this last reference and what follows, David Baron admirably described the essential character of spiritual Zionism:

> Jehovah, in the person of the Messiah, *"will dwell in the midst of Jerusalem,"* which shall become the center of His governmental dealings with the world, and the place whence light and truth shall go forth unto all the nations. "And Jerusalem shall be called *'Ir ha-emeth, the City of Truth"*; first, because it shall be the seat of the *El-emeth*, "The God of Truth"; and, secondly, because "the remnant of Israel," which shall then dwell in it, "shall not any longer do iniquity, nor speak lies" (Zeph. 3:13), but be known throughout the earth for their truth and fidelity toward God and man. *"And the mountain of Jehovah of hosts,"* i.e., Mount Zion, shall be called *"The Holy Mountain,"* because there the Holy one of Israel shall once more take up His abode, and by His presence in their midst sanctify His people, so that they, too, shall be holy; and, *Qodesh la-Yehovah*—"Holiness (or 'holy') unto Jehovah," shall be written, not only on their hearts and foreheads, but on all their possessions, down to the very "bells of their horses," and the "pots" which they shall use to prepare their food (14:20–21; Isa. 1:26; 60:14; 62:12).
>
> Now follows a beautiful picture of restored and flourishing Jerusalem. No longer shall the holy city, and the land of which it is the metropolis, be depopulated by war and other grievous calamities, and lie desolate. "The LORD of hosts says this: 'Old men and women will again sit along the streets of Jerusalem, each with a staff in his hand because of advanced age.

---

[42] Ibid., 185–86

The streets of the city will be filled with boys and girls playing in them."
Zech. 8:4–5).[43]

Here spiritual materiality shall have attained to that glorious consummation over which Jesus the Messiah shall reign, with the harmonious, distinctive incorporation of both Israel and the Gentile nations.

---

[43] D. Baron, *Zechariah* (London: Hebrew Christian Testimony to Israel, 1951), 233–34.

Chapter 9

ISRAEL AND THE INHERITANCE OF THE LAND THROUGH ABRAHAM

At the heart of the controversy surrounding the nation of Israel to-day and the Jews in particular, the matter which most frequently awakens fervent dispute concerns the ownership and inhabitation of the land of Palestine. The land of Israel—a specific geographic region, a material territory, a piece of historic real estate—generates world-shaking concern. In parallel with this, underlying biblical considerations raise the question of disputed legitimacy for the Jewish people who have constituted the State of Israel since 1948, and thus regained the land, *ha'aretz*. While Jews, as individuals, are barely tolerated in their dispersal throughout the world, it is the current dispute over the land, especially in relation to the hostile claims of the surrounding Arab nations and Arab Palestinians, that continually threatens to bring about calamity of international proportions. It seems that Jewish individualism is endured, while at the same time Jewish nationalism is more strenuously opposed, even within the United Nations. So the land has especially become a trigger, a catalyst that ignites world-wide animosity to Zionism. For Zionism is rooted in the biblical concept of the land, which epitomizes an indivisible union between territory and people. Baruch Maoz, a Jewish Christian and Reformed Baptist pastor in Israel, explained this distinctive phenomenon:

> [Linguistically] "Israel" denotes both people and land. . . . The land is no passive observer, a mere sphere in which Israel as a people operate. It is spoken of as altogether at one with the people—so much so that it becomes liable for the people's actions (Lev. 26:14; Deut. 6:12). It is also a privilege granted to the land (Lev. 25:4–5). Israel's sin brings punishment to the land (Lev. 26:33; Deut. 24:4,28–29), for God will be "angry with the land" be-cause of the people's sin. Conversely, when the people are true to God, he will bless them and the land (Deut. 30:9). Israel's destiny is that of the land (Ps. 122:1–2,6; 147:2).[1]

I repeat that while individual Jews are socially tolerated at best in Western society, their national identification with the land of Israel seems to awaken much greater controversy. This appears to be the case in the theological realm as well, particularly when replacement theology or supercessionism

---

[1] B. Maoz, "People, Land and Torah: a Jewish Christian Perspective," *The Land of Promise* (ed. P. Johnston and P. Walker; Downers Grove, Ill.: InterVarsity, 2000), 191–92.

is considered. Jewish individuality is suffered, in a token sense, while the nation and territory of Israel are repudiated by means of such misguided epithets as "carnal Zionism," "Dispensationalism," "a temporal earthly shadow," and so on.

Those who have no millennial sympathies that closely identify ethnic Israel with the land are usually quick to present a common objection, namely, that the NT revelation of the Word of God places no emphasis on the land of Israel in contrast with the OT where references are so numerous. These comments frequently arise in the consideration of Romans 9–11. With regard to Rom 11:25–26 Herman Bavinck commented,

> Even if Paul expected a national conversion of Israel at the end, he does not say a word about Palestine to the Jews, about a rebuilding of the city and a temple, about a visible rule of Christ: in his picture of the future there simply is no room for all this.[2]

Similarly, C. E. B. Cranfield wrote concerning Rom 11:26b–27,

> There is here no trace of encouragement for any hopes entertained by Paul's Jewish contemporaries for the re-establishment of a national state in independence and political power, nor—incidentally—anything which could feasibly be interpreted as a scriptural endorsement of the modern nation-state of Israel.[3]

Martyn Lloyd-Jones was even more shrill in tone when, in preaching on vv. 25–32 during 1964 and 1965, he declared,

> Where do you find any reference whatsoever to the land of Palestine or of Israel in this section? Where is there any mention of the restoration of the Jews to the land? Where is any mention of Jerusalem as such and the reigning there of the Lord for a thousand years?[4]

---

[2] H. Bavinck, *The Last Things* (Grand Rapids: Baker, 1996), 107.

[3] C. E. B. Cranfield, *The Epistle To The Romans* (Edinburgh: T&T Clark, 1979), 2.579.

[4] D. M. Lloyd-Jones, *Romans, Exposition of Chapter 11* (Edinburgh: Banner of Truth Trust, 1998), 231–35. Preaching during 1964–5, prior to the 1967 Six Day War, he was repetitive in this vein, even denying any relationship in this passage to the Second Coming. But one wonders if there was an adjustment in perspective by 1980, shortly before his passing in 1981. He said when interviewed by Carl Henry for *Christianity Today*, "To me 1967, the year that the Jews occupied all of Jerusalem, was very crucial. Luke 21:43 is one of the most significant prophetic verses: 'Jerusalem,' it reads, 'shall be trodden down of the Gentiles until the time of the Gentiles be fulfilled.' It seems to me that that took place in 1967—something crucially important that had not occurred in 2,000 years. Luke 21:43 is one fixed point. But I am equally impressed by Romans 11 which speaks of a great spiritual return among the Jews before the end time. While this seems to be developing, even something even more spectacular may be indicated. We sometimes tend to foreshorten events, yet I have a feeling that we are in the period of the end. . . . I think we are witnessing the breakdown of politics. I think even the world is seeing that.

Finally, Bruce Waltke gave similar strong criticism that relegated the premillennial/dispensational understanding of the land to a cheap representation of that which is transcendently enriching in its spiritual fulfillment.[5]

What is astonishing here is that such comments are made of Paul, the converted rabbi, who, especially in Romans 9–11, was so eager to maintain his passionate loyalty and love for ethnic Israel. In other words, he wrote as a Hebrew Christian, and it is a conspicuous weakness of some that they seem to avoid contemporary conservative scholarship that is rooted in a Hebrew Christian perspective similar to Paul's. Apart from such categorical Gentile criticism, where is there any breadth of Hebrew Christian scholarship that would add support with equal force to what these authors maintain? On the contrary, a preponderance of Hebrew Christian opinion does indeed repudiate such a Gentile understanding with equal vehemence.[6] Admittedly, amidst the dominance of contemporary Gentile Christianity this voice is not as influential. Nevertheless, ought not this neglected focus cause the Gentile student of the NT to more carefully consider Romans 9–11 in the light of the fact that is was written by a converted, highly qualified Jewish rabbi? Frankly, Paul might respond with exasperation at that exegesis that, while strangely tolerating limited individualism concerning the contemporary situation of the Jews, most vigorously opposes any territorial nationalism that might still be rooted in the Abrahamic covenant. Arguing from the absence of the term "land" in Romans 9–11 is a dubious argument from silence. One might just as well argue against the validity of repentance from the absence of the term in the Gospel of John, or against the importance of love from the term's absence in the Acts of the Apostles. To suggest that though boldly confessing, "I too am an Israelite, a descendant of Abraham, of the tribe of Benjamin" (Rom 11:1), the apostle still disavows any attachment to the land is ludicrous. Such an argument evidences the Gentile tendency towards detachment and aloofness from the "natural branches" (Rom 11:17–24) that has been the blight of the Christian church for centuries.

Civilization is collapsing" (C. Henry, "Martyn Lloyd-Jones: From Buckingham to Westminster," *Christianity Today* [February 8, 1980], 33–34).

[5] B. K. Waltke, "A Response," *Dispensationalism, Israel And The Church* (ed. C. A Blaising and D. L. Bock; Grand Rapids: Zondervan, 1992), 357–9.

[6] See the writings of Michael Brown, Arnold Fruchtenbaum, Dan Gruber, Baruch Maoz, Mark Nanos, David Stern, as well as the ministry of the Caspari Center, Jerusalem.

The Land in the Old Testament

As Stephen pointed out, the land promise originated when "the God of glory appeared to our father Abraham when he was in Mesopotamia, before he settled in Haran, and said to him: 'Get out of your country [pagan Ur of the Chaldeans] and away from your relatives, and come to the land that I will show you'" (Acts 7:2–3). In Haran, following the death of his father Terah, the call is repeated to Abraham: "The LORD said to Abram: 'Go out from your land, your relatives, and your father's house to the land [hā'āreṣ] that I will show you" (Gen 12:1). When Abram arrived at Shechem, God confirmed the promise: "The LORD appeared to Abram and said, 'I will give this land to your offspring'" (Gen 12:7). Hence, this specific territory is rooted in persistent promise (Gen 13:14–17) that is then covenantally, unilaterally signified or cut (Gen 15:7–21). The promise was in no way abrogated when, 430 years later, the temporary, intervening, foreshadowing administration of Moses "was added because of transgressions until the Seed to whom the promise had been made would come" (Gal 3:19; also Jer 11:7–8; Rom 5:20). Just prior to Israel's exodus from Egypt, God instructed Moses to reassure the captive people of their eventual inhabitation of the promised land according to the Abrahamic covenant (Exod 6:2–8). The subsequent necessity of the intervening Mosaic covenant was never intended to supersede or overshadow the promise. W. D. Davies incorrectly wrote, "In the Christological logic of Paul, the land, like the Law, particular and provisional, had become irrelevant."[7] The land was not promised to Abraham as a passing shadow, as something merely provisional. There is no such statement in the Bible. Rather, unlike the structure of the Mosaic economy, the land is perpetuated as a vital element of the new covenant (Jer 31:27–40; Ezek 11:14–21; 36:22–37:23). In other words, it is important to understand that the Abrahamic covenant finds its fulfillment in the new covenant, notwithstanding the intervening, temporal Mosaic covenant. The Abrahamic covenant promised the land, and the intervening Mosaic covenant involved temporal association with the land, yet the new covenant declares consummate fulfillment of that promise to Abraham with its specific references to the land, and not some extrapolated, abstract universalism. In particular, the new covenant describes Israel's return to the land from dispersion as "the land that I gave to your forefathers" (Jer 31:38–40; Ezek 11:17; 36:24,28).

---

[7] W. D. Davies, *The Gospel and the Land* (Berkeley: University of California, 1974), 179.

So in terms of *roots*, the OT as a whole always *originally* identifies the land with the Abrahamic covenant, but never the subsequent Mosaic covenant. Certainly the Mosaic covenant draws on the blessings of the Abrahamic covenant (Exod 3:6–8,15–17; 13:5; 33:1–3; Lev 20:24; Num 13:27), but the Mosaic covenant can never nullify that which was inaugurated with unilateral finality 430 years earlier (Gal 3:17). While the NT frequently describes the Mosaic old covenant as being comprised of shadows and types, this terminology is never directly applied to the promise character of the Abrahamic covenant, despite its sign of circumcision (Col 2:16–17; Heb 8:3–6; 10:1). Circumcision was the sign of the covenant that God made with Abraham, but the land was never regarded as a sign of the covenant; rather, it was intrinsic to that covenant, and this is a most vital distinction to keep in mind (Gen 12:1,7). This is the reason the land is distinguished from Mosaic typology—it is an abiding reality in itself.

By way of summary, we may understand the land from different perspectives according to the ways in which it is described.

1. The land as promise, according to God's irrevocable covenant, His sworn oath (Gen 50:24; Exod 12:25; Deut 6:3; 19:8)
2. The land as holy, that is, set apart by God who is holy, from other lands for inhabitation by His people (Exod 15:13; Zech 2:12–13)
3. The land as God's possession, so that the people of Israel, as His redeemed children, are tenants since "the land . . . is Mine" (Lev 25:23).
4. The land as God's gift, according to His gracious bestowal to Abraham and his descendants (Deut 1:20,25; 2:29).
5. The land as the fathers' possession, that is, Abraham, Isaac, and Jacob (Gen 31:3; 48:21; Exod 33:1).
6. The land as the Israelites' inheritance, possession, and permanent dwelling place, according to covenant promise (Gen 12:7; 15:7; 24:7; 28:4).
7. The land as security, blessing, and rest—a place flowing with milk and honey, that is, material and spiritual blessings (Exod 33:3; Lev 20:24).
8. The land as the center of the world, that is, its navel—the intention being that it will be a blessing to the world (Ezek 5:5; 38:12).
9. The land as God's dwelling place with His people, especially in holy and intimate union (Ps 37:9,11,22,29,34; 132:13–15; Isa 1:19).

The Land in the New Testament

The following compendium addresses the objection that the NT is silent about the land of Israel as a continuing divine heritage. During the formative years of the Christian Church, certainly no Jewish Christian, and especially the mother Church in Jerusalem, would have faintly considered the thought that the promise concerning the land was about to be rescinded or transcended. For that matter, it is just as unlikely that the Gentile Church at Antioch, having been granted great liberty by the Council of Jerusalem, would have concluded that the Jewish Church at Jerusalem had, by its decree in giving freedom to the Gentiles, at the same time established its own demise with regard to being distinctively Jewish. Surely this was never in the mind of Paul or Barnabas.

Some Biblical Indications

In the NT, "Israel" is used seventy-three times, eleven of which are found in Romans (9:6 [2x], 27 [2x], 31; 10:19,21; 11:2,7,25,26). "Israelite(s)" is used four times (John 1:47; Rom 9:4; 11:1; 2 Cor 11:22). Regarding the Synoptics, Mayer declares that "Israel stands for the people and the land (Matt 20:1; 21:1)."[8] Concerning Paul's overall usage, and after consideration of Rom 2:29; 9:6; 1 Cor 1:18; Phil 3:3, Burton concludes that, "there is, in fact, no instance of his using Ἰσραήλ [Israel], except of the Jewish nation or a part thereof."[9] Hence, to suggest that Paul the Israelite had nevertheless abdicated recognition of the legitimacy of the land is to impose on the apostle a Gentile perspective that he never remotely contemplated. In the light of the preceding, it is astonishing to consider once again a further aspect of Robert Strimple's earlier referenced definitive proposition concerning Israel (chapter 7):

> The true Israel is Christ: He is the suffering Servant of the Lord [Isa. 41:8–9; 42:1–7; 44:1–2,21; 45:4], this one who is—wonder of wonders—the Lord himself! . . . Yes, Israel was called to be God's servant, a light to enlighten the nations and to glorify God's name. But since Israel was unfaithful to her calling and failed to fulfill the purposes of her divine election, the Lord brought forth his Elect One, his Servant, his true Israel.[10]

---

[8] R. Mayer, "Israel," *Dictionary of New Testament Theology*, (Grand Rapids: Zondervan, 1999), 2.315.

[9] E. D. Burton, *Galatians* (Edinburgh: T&T Clark, 1968), 358.

[10] R. B. Strimple, "Amillennialism," *Three Views on the Millennium and Beyond* (ed. D. L. Bock; Grand Rapids: Zondervan, 1999), 87–88.

To begin with, here is a Reformed seminary professor describing Israel's election as lost through disobedience! Berkouwer rightly asked,

> Can a past that has been qualified by election ever come to naught? Can "election of God" as we usually understand it ever be changed into "rejection"? Can the Church inherit the place of the chosen people of Israel, so that election passes over to the church? Do we not usually consider God's election as something irrevocable, definitive, and all-powerful; and is it consequently meaningless to assume that the election of Israel could be negated by human reaction, even unbelief?[11]

The emphatic inference here that God's election of Israel is absolute leads us to consider the related fact that the land of Israel is part of that election, and as such it too is part of the inviolate character inherent in the Abrahamic covenant. Therefore, I believe the following references quite clearly give NT indications that the land of Israel has retained its validity during the Church age, particularly because "the *gifts* [emphasis added] and calling of God are irrevocable" (Rom 11:29).

Matthew 24:30; also Revelation 1:7. "Then the sign of the Son of Man will appear in the sky, and then all the peoples of the earth will mourn; and they will see the Son of Man coming on the clouds of heaven with power and great glory." In the phrase *hai phulai tēs gēs*, "the tribes of the earth," if *tēs gēs* is uniformly translated in the NT as "the earth," then the absence of any mention of the land of Israel there is virtually guaranteed. But the context suggests that Zech 12:10,14 is inferred by Matthew in this instance, in which case "the tribes of the land [of Israel]" is a more appropriate translation.[12] In that case, reference is being made to the conversion of national Israel at the Second Coming. Indeed the subsequent declaration that Christ "will gather His elect from the four winds" Matt 24:31), and the parable of the fig tree, would all support the focus here being on national Israel. The same translation option arises in Rev 1:7 where in view of Zech 12:10,14 the translation should probably read, "the tribes of the land [of Israel]," not "the families of the earth." Certainly reference to "the land" in Zech 12:11–12 offers further support to this interpretation.[13]

---

[11] G. C. Berkouwer, *The Return of Christ* (Grand Rapids: Eerdmans, 1972), 326–27.

[12] I owe this interpretation to D. Stern, *Restoring the Jewishness of the Gospel* (Gaithersburg, MD: Jewish New Testament Publications, 1988), 39; *Jewish New Testament Commentary* (Clarksville, MD: Jewish New Testament Publications, 1992), 74–75. Similarly, J. Gill; *The Collected Writings of John Gill* (Rio, WI: Ages Software, 2000), 767.

[13] Ibid., 788–90. Similarly J. A. Seiss, *Revelation*, I, (New York: Charles C. Cook, 1900), 57–58, on Rev 1:7. The attempt of G. K. Beale to disassociate "the earth" here from "the land" of Zech 12:12 is unconvincing, *The Book of Revelation* (Grand Rapids: Eerdmans, 1999), 25–27,

Luke 21:20–24, especially v. 24. "They [the Jerusalemites] will fall by the edge of the sword and be led captive into all the nations, and Jerusalem will be trampled by the Gentiles until [*achri hou*, as in Rom 11:25] the times of the Gentiles are fulfilled." Following the subjugation of Jerusalem and the land to Gentile dominion for many centuries, there will follow a reversal of this order in which the Jerusalemites, and hence the Jews, will regain dominion over the land and Jerusalem. Such a fulfillment would unquestionably validate Israel's covenant claim to the land at the close of this present dispensation. This restoration to tangible favor would include the climactic "fulfillment" experienced by Israel according to Rom 11:12. J. C. Ryle concluded,

> While the nations of Europe are absorbed in political conflicts and worldly business, the sands in their hour-glass are ebbing away. While governments are disputing about secular things, and Parliaments can hardly condescend to find a place for religion in their discussions, their days are numbered in the sight of God. Yet a few years and the "times of the Gentiles will be fulfilled." Their day of visitation will be past and gone. Their misused privileges will be taken away. The judgments of God shall fall on them. They shall be cast aside as vessels in which God has no pleasure. Their dominion shall crumble away, and their vaunted institutions shall fall to pieces. . . . When [the times of the Gentiles] do end, the conversion of the Jews and the restoration of Jerusalem will take place. . . . The Jews shall be restored. The Lord Jesus shall come again in power and great glory.[14]

John 1:11. "He came to his own [embassy, residence, inheritance], and his own people did not receive [welcome] him." That Christ came to his "own things/possessions" [*ta idia*] indicates his territory and all that it contains, that is, the land of Israel (2 Chr 7:20; Isa 14:24–25; Jer 16:18; Mal 3:1). The same expression is found in John 19:26–27: "Jesus saw His mother and the disciple He loved [John] standing there. . . . And from that hour the disciple took her into his home [*ta idia*, his own things/possessions]." In support of this territorial understanding, Westcott commented on John 1:11,

> There can be no reasonable doubt that this phrase [*ta idia*], and the corresponding masculine which follows, "his own" (οἱ ἴδιοι) i.e. "his own people", describe the land and the people of Israel as being, in a sense in which

---

especially because of the significant references to "tribe/s" in relation to Israel (Rev 5:5, 9; 7:4–8; 21:12) and the whole Hebrew underpinning of this Book.

[14] J. C. Ryle, *Luke* (Edinburgh: Banner of Truth Trust, 1986), 2.371, 374.

no other land and people were, the home and the people of God, of Jehovah (Lev. 25:23; Jer. 2:7; 14:18; Hos. 9:3; Zech. 2:12).[15]

Romans 9:26. Quoting Hosea 1:10, Paul wrote, "And it will be in the place where they were told, you are not My people, there [*ekei*] they will be called sons of the living God." Johannes Munck noted that "there" is "a natural designation for Palestine, in order to imply that the Gentile nations will gather in Jerusalem and the Messianic kingdom will be established there (cf. 11:26)."[16]

Romans 11:1. Here Paul is boasting that, "I too am an Israelite, a descendant of Abraham, from the tribe of Benjamin." The last expression, *phulēs Beniamin*, would, for a Hebrew Christian, undoubtedly include territorial meaning or divine land allocation. Tribal association for the Jews meant not only demographic personal identification, but also geographic territorial identification with a portion of the land. W. H. Bennett stated that "after the conquest [of the land] the tribes became essentially territorial."[17] So before King Agrippa, Paul declared, "And now I stand on trial for the hope of the promise made by God to our fathers, the promise our 12 tribes hope to attain as they earnestly serve Him night and day. Because of this hope I am being accused by the Jews, O king!" (Acts 26:6–7). Surely Paul not only had the Diaspora in mind but also the geographic portions and accompanying populace of the land as a whole. There is not the slightest intimation here that such territorial regions will be eliminated when the Jews were converted. James began his letter, "James, a slave of God and of the Lord Jesus Christ: To the twelve tribes in the Dispersion. Greetings." The attempts to spiritualize this reference are numerous and betray a Gentile bent, though it is not difficult to sense that such a conclusion is doctrinally rather than exegetically driven, especially in the light of the Jewishness that "Diaspora" in this same verse clearly indicates.[18] A similar problem is faced in Rev 7:4–7 where the 144,000 from the 12 tribes of Israel is commonly understood, according to frequent Gentile exegesis, as representing the Church, even though v. 9 describes a distinct Gentile assembly, as "a

[15] B. F. Westcott, *The Gospel According to St. John* (Grand Rapids: Michigan, 1967). Likewise Alford and Ryle.

[16] J. Munck, *Christ & Israel* (Philadelphia: Fortress, 1967), 12.

[17] W. H. Bennett, "Tribe," *Hasting's Dictionary of the Bible* (Edinburgh: T&T Clark, 1902), 4.810.

[18] According to D. A. Carson, D. J. Moo, and L. Morris, *An Introduction to the New Testament* (Grand Rapids: Zondervan, 1992), 415, "This designation [of 1:1] is so general as to be of little help in identifying the addressees." Then in conclusion there is the grudging confession: "Nevertheless, the early date and Jewishness of James favors the more literal meaning."

great multitude which no one could count, from every nation and all tribes and people and tongues."[19] Of course, all these references to the tribes of Israel, their demographic Hebrew identity, inevitably suggest a territorial association as well.

Romans 11:26. More recently, many commentators have expressed a belief that this passage does indeed refer to an eschatological national conversion of Jews toward the end of this age. More often than not in these expositions, there is no qualification as to whether such resultant Jewish Christians will retain national Jewish identity according to divine mandate. John Murray argued very persuasively for a future conversion of "the mass of Israel,"[20] according to covenantal promise. But he failed to explain the resultant status of converted Israel as a body, that is, whether Israel retains national distinction in the sight of God, which would then entail a relationship to the land.[21] Morris similarly opted for a future national conversion of Israel, though he less distinctly concluded, "Paul then is affirming that the nation of Israel as a whole will ultimately have its place in God's salvation."[22] A number of writers convey the idea that while there will be some future Jewish ingathering, no national identity on a covenantal basis is in view here. Rather, such a corporate conversion will result in incorporation into the people of God, that is, the church, which has no identification with national and geographic Israel. John Stott commented,

> The prophecy of Romans 11 is a prophecy that many Jews will return to Christ, but the land is not mentioned, nor is Israel mentioned as a political entity. . . . According to the apostles, the Old Testament promises are fulfilled in Christ and in the international community of Christ. A return to Jewish nationalism would seem incompatible with this New Testament perspective of the international community of Jesus.[23]

To begin with, Stott's reference to "many Jews" is nebulous since any definition he might offer disallows fundamental Jewishness. Again we have here a condescension to temporal, vague individuality that seems almost offended at the thought of prospective national expression. But further in-

---

[19] So J. A. Seiss wrote, "These 144,000 are just what John says they are—*Jews*, descendants of the sons of Israel—the first fruits of that new return of God to deal mercifully with the children of His ancient people for their father's sakes." *The Apocalypse*, I (New York: Charles C. Cook, 1900), 408.

[20] J. Murray, *Romans* (Grand Rapids: Eerdmans, 1965), 2.98.

[21] Ibid., 96–101.

[22] L. Morris, *The Epistle to the Romans* (Grand Rapids: Eerdmans, 1997), 421.

[23] J. Stott, "Foreword," *The Promised Land* (ed. P. Johnston & P. Walker; Downers Grove, Ill.: InterVarsity, 2000), 11.

consistency arises concerning this overall modern approach to Romans 11. By yielding to the obvious comprehensive meaning of references to "Israel" that are consistent throughout Romans 9–11 whereby some future form of national conversion is admitted, there is a reluctance to accept the obvious national associations that Paul makes with the term "Israelite" (11:1) as a converted Hebrew. Rather, the explicit boasting of Paul concerning his Jewishness in Rom 9:3–5; 11:1, particularly obvious territorial implications, must surely be associated with v. 26 and thus anticipate national conversion unto the land. However, a major problem arises at this point if a mere vague approach toward the future conversion of the Jews is concerned. If there is belief in some type of national conversion of Jews at the conclusion of the "times of the Gentiles," then what was their national status prior to this awakening, and what shall it be following their regeneration? Are they in every sense of the word national Jews according to the flesh, even though remaining in bondage to unbelief (Rom 11:28)? If so, then while their unbelief has resulted in dispersion from the land, yet their conversion would qualify them for inhabitation of that same land, especially since there is no biblical indication that the land has been *forever* taken from the Jews. In other words, to speak merely nominally of the Jews in Romans 9–11 is to fly in the face of the Jewishness that Paul there upholds, especially in Rom 9:1–5; 11:1–2,28–29. Paul's ongoing Jewishness would find it quite unthinkable for him to uphold his Jewish national status and at the same time deny continuity with its territorial foundation.

A final, conclusive proof in this regard concerns the eschatological hope of Israel because of "their forefathers" (Rom 11:28). Surely reference here to the Abrahamic covenant must include the essential component of the land, which, as Matt Waymeyer pointed out, exegetically leads us back to the "all Israel" of Rom 11:26.

> The antecedent of the supplied "they" in v. 28 is "them" (αὐτοῖς, *autois*) in v. 27, which refers back to "Jacob" (Ἰακώβ, *Iakōb*) in v. 26b, which in turn refers back to "all Israel" (πᾶς Ἰσραήλ, *pas Israēl*) in v. 26a. This is significant because it indicates that the group of individuals described in v. 28 describes the "all Israel of v. 26 and helps to establish its identity.[24]

Put another way, "all Israel" in Rom 11:26 refers to the unbelieving nation of Israel in v. 28 plus the remnant of v. 5 as it accumulates, which

---

[24] M. Waymeyer, "The Dual Status of Israel in Romans 11:28," *MSJ* (Spring 2005), 61–62. Also refer to M. J. Vlach, *The Church as a Replacement of Israel: An Analysis of Supercessionism* (Ph.D. diss. Southeastern Baptist Theological Seminary, 2004).

in total remains an heir of the Abrahamic covenant which is inclusive of the land.

Romans 11:26–27. This verse appears to incorporate quotations of both Isa 59:20 and Jer 31:33–34, which passages contextually include restoration to the land as part of Israel's redemptive blessings (see Isa 60:21; Jer 31:23).

Romans 11:29. "God's gracious gifts and calling are irrevocable." The plurality of the "gracious gifts" surely follows, by way of explication, that which is declared secure according to the Abrahamic covenant originating from "their [Israel's] forefathers" (v. 28). Of course, from a Hebrew perspective, the "gifts" include saving grace for Israel, yet surely more is included, such as the encompassing covenant blessings of Rom 9:4–5 that would unquestionably include the land.[25]

Galatians 3:16 (see v. 21). "Now the promises were spoken to Abraham and to his seed. He does not say, 'And to seeds,' as though referring to many, but and to your seed, referring to one, who is Christ." While the usual focus here falls on Paul's doctrinal understanding of the singular "seed," which is indicated to be Jesus Christ as the seed of Abraham, rarely is there any relating of this truth to the plurality of "the promises." What then were "the promises" that were spoken both to Abraham and consequently to Jesus Christ? Lacking specificity, Burton explained that "the promises here spoken of are those which accompanied the covenant and which constituted it on the side of divine grace."[26] Lightfoot appears to be closer to the truth in his comment,

> A question has been raised as to the particular passage to which Paul refers. In answering this question it should be observed, (1) That the words must be spoken to Abraham himself, and not to one of the later patriarchs; (2) That *kai* must be part of the quotation. These considerations restrict the reference to Gen 13:15; 17:8, either of which passages satisfies these conditions. It is true that in both alike the inheritance spoken of refers primarily to the possession of the land of Canaan, but the spiritual application here is only in accordance with the general analogy of New Testament interpretation.[27]

Aside from Lightfoot's dismissal of the literal primacy of the land here with regard to the details of "the promises," based on supercessionist pre-

---

[25] So H. C. G. Moule, *The Epistle to the Romans* (Cambridge: Cambridge University Press, 1903), 164; J. Shulam, *A Commentary on the Jewish Roots of Romans* (Baltimore, MD, 1998), 327.

[26] E. D. Burton, *The Epistle to the Galatians* (Edinburgh: T&T Clark, 1968), 181.

[27] J. B. Lightfoot, *The Epistle to the Galatians* (Grand Rapids: Zondervan, 1957), 142.

suppositions,[28] the parallel references to this covenantal term in Rom 9:4; 15:8 are instructive. Gentile commentators generally identify "the promises" as those made to the fathers and especially those that are Messianic, though without specific reference to the land. An exception is H. C. G. Moule who defined "the promises" as being "of the Land, and of the Messiah."[29] Jewish commentator Joseph Shulam provides the most comprehensive explanation of the plurality here that also includes the land:

> The "promises" are those God gave to Abraham, that his descendants would be as the sand and the stars (cf. Gen. 12:2; 15:5; 17:1f; 28:14); of the land (cf. Gen. 15:7; 17:8; 28:13; Exod. 12:25; 13:5; Deut. 1:11; 6:3; 19:8; Neh. 9:8; Rom. 11:29; Heb. 11:11–13,17); to the House of David and his messianic offspring (cf. 1 Kgs. 2:24; 8:20; 2 Kgs. 8:19; Isa. 7:13–16; 9:6–7; 11:1–5; Rom. 1:3; 2 Cor. 1:20; Gal. 3:16–22; 1 Pet. 1:10,12); of the Spirit and the new covenant (cf. Jer. 31:31; Ezek. 37:26; Joel 2:28; Acts 2:16–21,39; Gal. 3:8,15f; 4:24–28; Eph. 1:13; 2:12); and of life itself (cf. Deut. 8:3; 30:15–16; 32:39; Prov. 3:16; 8:35; Hab. 2:4; 1 Tim. 4:8; 2 Tim. 1:1; 2 Pet. 1:4).[30]

Of course "the promises" of Rom 9:4; 15:8 are rooted in the "forefathers . . . and from them, by physical descent, came the Messiah, who is God over all, blessed forever" (Rom 9:5). However, it is obvious from the preceding context that the plurality of "the promises" includes much more for Paul, who writes as presently being an "Israelite" (Rom 11:1), and thus in his terminology undoubtedly incorporates the land as part of the overall present inheritance.

Some Theological Indications

The argument from supposed silence put forward by Bavinck, Cranfield, Lloyd-Jones, Waltke, and others is based on the alleged absence of explicit and even implicit references to "the land" in the NT. The tone of these commentators is often quite categorical, and I suggest that such a response has Gentile undertones lacking the grace which Paul commends in Rom 11:18–20. Even if acknowledgment of the possibility of a national or mass conversion at the end of this age is granted on purely exegetical grounds,

---

[28] Lightfoot subsequently explained that "the Israel after the flesh becomes the Israel after the Spirit; the Jewish nation denotes the Christian Church," *Galatians*, 143. Concerning 6:16, the "Israel of God . . . stands here not for the faithful converts from the circumcision alone, but for the spiritual Israel generally, the whole body of believers whether Jew or Gentile" (*Galatians*, 225).

[29] Moule, *Romans*, 164.

[30] J. Shulam, *A Commentary on the Jewish Roots of Romans* (Baltimore, MD: Messianic Jewish Publishers, 1998), 27.

it remains a grudging admission that lacks Pauline enthusiasm. Few Jewish Christian commentators would support their reasoning. Rather I believe that the preceding biblical evidence, especially when viewed through a Jewish lens that most of the NT writers employed, provides both explicit and implicit references to the land which are intimately related to such expressions as "Israel" and "tribe," as well as "Jerusalem," "Zion," etc. But it could also be argued that since the land was undoubtedly a divine bestowal up to the NT era, then it is necessary that evidence be provided of explicit *land* disinheritance that is irrevocable. Such evidence is patently absent.

Reference has already been made in chapter 6 to Willem A. VanGemeren's important article on Israel and prophecy. With regard to infrequent references in the NT to the restoration of the Jewish people, he provides two significant reasons which also relate to the question of the sparseness of references to the land when compared with the OT:

> First, most of the NT writings were written before the events of A.D. 70. The judgment described by Jesus in the Mt. Olivet discourse pertains to Jerusalem and *not* the Jewish people. When Jerusalem was destroyed, the Jewish population remained in Judea and Galilee in large numbers. Most Jews voluntarily left the land during the subsequent centuries because of business opportunities elsewhere; however, a flourishing community continued in Palestine (Yabneh, Beth Shearim, and Tiberias). The excavation of ancient synagogues witnesses to a thriving and learned Jewish population in the land. All of this fulfilled God's promise given by Amos. Arguments against the future of Israel in the land, based on a naïve view of history, are not uncommon because most Christians do not know the history of Judaism post-A.D. 70. A study of the historical and theological development of Judaism would help Christians have a proper understanding of Jews and Judaism.
>
> Secondly, the apostolic concern is for the conversion of the Jewish people. The Gospels of Matthew (pre-A.D. 70) and John (post-A.D. 70) share this concern. The restoration of the land was never an issue because the Jews were in the land and remained in the land in large numbers for hundreds of years after the fall of Jerusalem (A.D. 70). They voluntarily left the land in large numbers over a period of hundreds of years, but returned before the founding of the State of Israel. Their return was not from exile but from the diaspora. They look on themselves as *'olim* (returnees), not *golim* (exiles).[31]

Baruch Maoz presented an insightful paper for the Lausanne Consultation on Jewish Evangelism in 1986. It was subsequently revised and included

---

[31] W. A. VanGemeren, "Israel As The Hermeneutical Crux In The Interpretation Of Prophecy (II)," *WTJ*, 46 (1984), 293–94.

in *The Land of Promise*, edited by Philip Johnson and Peter Walker. Four of his principles are summarized here that emphasize the significance of the land as well as its relationship to the New Testament.[32]

(1) The land is inseparable from God and His people. Israel as a people cannot truly fulfill its duties to God apart from the land. It is not "land" in general, nor even any land in particular, but only one certain and specific land. This is the land repeatedly designated in the Bible by way of its borders and its history. The land of Israel is not merely a piece of turf; it is God's blessing and God's presence. It is evidence of an ongoing relationship between God and the people of Israel. The land is the Abrahamic covenant made concrete.

(2) The land is intimately connected with God's people. The climax of blessing in the land is God's divine promise to His people: "I am the LORD your God" (Lev 25:17,55). The land is the epitome of God's promises to Israel and is an important part of the whole without which the remainder is incomplete. Nowhere in the Scriptures are the people of Israel considered to be blessed by God outside of the land. Nowhere is blessing promised by God to the people apart from the blessing of the land. Small wonder, then, that the people of Israel have come to love the land so vehemently.

(3) The land is the arena of salvation from covenant disloyalty. The people's right to enjoy the land of Israel is contingent on their covenant loyalty. Unfaithfulness results in stringent punishment. The people will be restored to the land if they repent, otherwise they will be brought back to the land and will there repent. Even then, the people and land will be inseparable. Spiritual restoration and a return to the land are linked so that the people are never considered blessed, forgiven, or redeemed except in the land promised to their fathers.

(4) The land is the arena of NT fulfillment. Israel as a people (and therefore in their divinely promised land) remains a focal point of NT expectation. This is not to say that OT expectations are now fully realized, or that whatever has not yet been fulfilled is now replaced with a different hope.

> The New Testament neither contradicts nor corrects what we have deduced from the Old Testament data. On the contrary, Old Testament expectations are heightened in the New Testament by the sheer fact that their fulfillment is described as having begun. After all, the New Testament claims to be a fulfillment of Old Testament promise, the reliable description of a climax of hope being realized and clarified by the coming of Messiah. Jesus is not

[32] Maoz, "People, Land and Torah," 188–200. Most of the voluminous supporting Scriptures are to be found in the original text.

a cancellation of the Old Testament hope but its unequivocal affirmation
(Luke 24:38–44; John 11:24; 20:24–27; Acts 24:15; Rom 8:18–24; Phil
3:21; Rev 21–22). . . . The New Testament makes it quite clear that the material [land] is the arena in which ultimate salvation is to take place (Rom
8:18–25), thus reconfirming Old Testament expectation. . . . Consequently,
Israel is not displaced by the church. Rather, the church enters into enjoy-
ment of Israel's blessings as a strange branch "grafted in . . . contrary to
nature", but never in place of the natural branches, who will be grafted in
again (Rom 11:23–24).[33]

The Land and Patrick Fairbairn

While Fairbairn's amillennial perspective has already been considered in
chapter 6, his discussions of the land in his volume on typology as well as
in his commentary on Ezekiel call for further comment. Anthony Hoekema
has indicated his reliance on Fairbairn,[34] and this in turn has influenced
Venema, Waldron, and others.

The Relationship between the Abrahamic and Mosaic Covenants.

It is not uncommon for amillennialists to associate the temporal nature
of the conditional Mosaic covenant with the abiding nature of the unconditional Abrahamic covenant, the result being that elements of the former are
imposed on the latter. The promise of the land to Abraham in Gen 12:13
thus becomes absorbed into a conditional, typological frame of reference.
As a result, this same land, having been forfeited through disobedience, is
merely regarded as a micro-earthly representation of future macro-heavenly
glory that the Church inherits on a universal scale. I have already addressed
Palmer Robertson's representation of this concept in chapter 3. He wrote,

> The land of the Bible served in a typological role as a model of the con-
> summate realization of the purposes of God for his redeemed people that
> encompasses the whole of the cosmos. Because of the inherently limited
> scope of the land of the Bible, it is not to be regarded as having continuing
> significance in the realm of redemption other than its function as a teach-
> ing model.[35]

[33] Ibid., 195–96, 198.
[34] A. A. Hoekema, *The Bible and the Future* (Grand Rapids: Eerdmans, 1979), 276n, 279. He
cites P. Fairbairn's *The Typology of Scripture* (Edinburgh: T&T Clark, 1882), 1.329–61; 2.3–4.
[35] O. P. Robertson, *The Israel of God* (Phillipsburg, New Jersey: 2000), 194.

Fairbairn expressed a similar approach, though over 150 years prior. He likewise wrote,

> The relations of the covenant people, as connected with the occupation of Canaan, leads naturally to the conclusion, that their peculiar connection with that territory has ceased with the other temporary expedients and shadows to which it belonged.[36]

In other words, the land is merely a basic type that projects through the Mosaic economy into the NT reality, and as such has no tangible relevance today. Hence one cannot but suspect that this association of the Abrahamic land promise with the Mosaic economy is most necessary, even if unbiblical, so that the former might, by association, be abrogated. For Fairbairn there is a necessary progression from Abraham to Moses:

> The Mosaic religion did not start into being as something original and independent; it grew out of the Patriarchal, and was just, indeed, the Patriarchal religion in a further state of progress and development. . . . We are not to imagine, however, that the additional religious truths and principles which were to be historically brought out at the commencement of the Mosaic dispensation, must have appeared there by themselves, distinct and apart from those which descended from Patriarchal times.[37]

This unsupported portrayal, however, is incorrect, and proof for what is a most necessary point to uphold this system that in fact would be difficult to produce. After all, if the land promised to Abraham remains as permanent for national Israel as the other terms of that covenant, then it radically interferes with supercessionist theology. The NT makes a clear distinction between the Abrahamic and Mosaic covenants, and especially their conditionality, along with the permanence of one and the abrogation of the other, as Gal 3:17 and Heb 8:13 make abundantly clear. Further, Paul's explanation concerning the purpose of the law, that it "was added because of transgressions" (Gal 3:19; see Jer 11:7–8; Rom 5:20), also conflicts with the idea of progression from Abraham.

Horatius Bonar Critical Analysis

Although we considered Bonar's general critical assessment of Fairbairn's eschatology in chapter 6, Bonar further challenged Fairbairn's amillennialism in a review article concerning *Typology of Scripture*. Bonar freely ac-

---

[36] P. Fairbairn, *The Typology of Scripture* (Edinburgh: T&T Clark, 1882), I, 497.

[37] Ibid., 2.2–3.

knowledged the author's dignified manner, learning, and lofty views, but commented,

> That with such powers and dispositions he has still so widely missed the truth, is owing, we think, to an undue influence by late German authors who have led him to mistake their false systems for the teachings of the word of God.[38]

What then is the essential problem with *Typology of Scripture*? It is reflected in Fairbairn's subtitle taken from the first edition: "The Doctrine of Types, investigated in its principles, and applied to the Explanation of the earlier Revelations of God considered as preparatory exhibitions of the leading truths of the Gospel. With an appendix on the Restoration of the Jews." Bonar summarized the fundamental problem as follows:

> He alleges that not only the principle things in the Mosaic ritual are types of corresponding things in the work of redemption as it is unfolded in the New Testament; but that all the chief personages, acts, and arrangements, that are recorded in the Old Testament, both in the histories and prophecies, are typical, in like manner, of other persons and events in the Christian church; and assumes and affirms that the very nature and design of the patriarchal and Mosaic dispensations, and actors, acts, and events that appear in their records, are such, that they are of necessity typical of things in the Christian church, and are to be taken, as far as they are prophetic, as exclusively predictive of them. No prophecy of the Old Testament, accordingly—if this scheme is adhered to—can by possibility relate in any degree to the real Israelites or Gentiles, Jerusalem or Palestine, or any other persons or places that are *literally* mentioned in them, and are philologically the subjects of their declarations.[39]

The Hermeneutic of Supercession

Fairbairn's subtitle alerts us to the fact that far more than a mere consideration of types in the Bible is the author's intention. Rather, we have the proposal of a whole hermeneutical system whereby the OT revelation, as a complete unit, is regarded as typological and as fulfilled and superseded by the NT. Bonar rightly complained that this work

> is nothing else than the theory of Origen reproduced under another name, and set off with much speciousness of learning and argument, but in fact without any ground for its support. . . . The supposition indeed which led to

---

[38] H. Bonar, "The Typology of Scripture," *The Theological and Literary Journal* (ed. D. N. Lord, January, 1852), 354.

[39] Ibid., 355.

the invention of the system, that the persons, transactions, and events of the Old Testament histories and predictions must be contemplated as types of answering things in the Christian system, in order that they may be the means to us of that instruction for which they were designed, is altogether mistaken. Mr. F. proceeds throughout his volumes on the assumption, that were it not for a typical office, the persons and occurrences of which the ancient Scriptures present a record would be almost wholly uninstructive to us.[40]

I believe this criticism to be especially true when it comes to the interpretation of OT prophecy. In this regard, it is fascinating to detect considerable correspondence here with the hermeneutic of "reinterpretation" that George Ladd advocated, whereby the OT has no independent, objective, prophetic significance except as expounded by the NT. Hence, we find ourselves in a period in which Fairbairn's considerable influence, especially as evidenced in the writings of Hoekema, Venema, Waldron, and others with regard to amillennialism, has led to a dominant typological hermeneutic. Since this in turn has resulted in objective textual and historic realities being subjected to NT categories, we need to reconsider Bonar's call for a return to one hermeneutic for the whole Bible and not two.[41] Further, that hermeneutic needs to return to the apostolic Judeo-centric hermeneutic that is not obscured by means of typological reinterpretation that focuses through a Gentile lens. Then Judeo-centric premillennialism will come into its rightful place once again.

The Land and W. D. Davies

The scholarly contribution of W. D. Davies toward a Christian understanding of the land is substantial indeed, though supercessionism is clearly fundamental to his thought. We may nevertheless appreciate his exegetical conclusions, especially because of their influence on Colin Chapman, David Holwerda (later reviewed in this chapter), and O. Palmer Robertson. On the issue of "Paul and the land," Davies summarized his conclusions as follows:

With the coming of Christ the wall of separation between Israel and the Gentiles was removed. This wall, usually interpreted of "the Law," or of "the veil in the Temple," in the passage in Ephesians 2:11–22, which here, whether written by him or by a member of his school or not, brings Paul's thought to its full expression, we may also interpret implicitly to

[40] Ibid., 392.
[41] Especially refer to Bonar's *Prophetical Landmarks*, the full text of which is available, via PDF files, at www.bunyanministries.org, under the new title of *Judeo-centric Premillennialism*.

include geographic separation between those in the land and those outside the land. Because the logic of Paul's understanding of Abraham and his personalization of the fulfillment of the promise "in Christ" demanded the deterritorializing of the promise, salvation was not now bound to the Jewish people centered in the land and living according to the Law: it was "located" not in a place, but in persons in whom grace and faith had their writ. By personalizing the promise "in Christ" Paul universalized it. For Paul, Christ had gathered up the promise into the singularity of his own person. In this way, "the territory" promised was transformed into and fulfilled by the life "in Christ." All this is not made explicit, because Paul did not directly apply himself to the question of the land, but it is implied. In the Christological logic of Paul, the land, like the Law, particular and provisional, had become irrelevant."[42]

To begin with, concerning Eph 2:11–12, the alienation of the Gentiles was from "the citizenship of Israel, and . . . the covenants of the promise," particularly as rooted in Abraham. But Christ knocked down "the dividing wall of hostility. In His flesh He did away with the law of the commandments in regulations" (Eph 2:14–15; see chapter 10). This abrogation by Christ was of the Mosaic economy (Rom 7:1–4), and not the covenants of promise in which the land is integral. Davies' incorporation of the land into the dissolution of the Law, with the use of terminology that speaks of "the land, like the Law," is a common but unwarranted association. I also suggest that it is logically *unnecessary* for the doctrine of both Jews and Gentiles, who are both "in Christ," to necessitate the "deterritorializing" of the original land promise. To similarly suggest that to be "in Christ" is consequently to "universalize" the land promise is to wrongly assume that within a universality there can be no diversity, which in fact the OT prophetically anticipates (e.g., Isa 60:1–4; 62:1–12; Mic. 4:1–5; Hag. 2:1–7; Zech 14:16–21). The same fallacy arises with regard to the frequent appeal to Gal 3:28 where in fact the unity incorporates a masculine and feminine diversity. The triunity of the only blessed God comprises the personal diversity of the Father, Son, and Holy Spirit. Jonathan Edwards described the unity of the coming kingdom of Christ on earth that comprises Israel in the land, under its Messiah, as having harmonious relations with the surrounding Gentile nations.[43] While it is comforting to read of Davies' acknowledgment that his conclusion here is at best implicit, it would undoubtedly be discomforting for contemporary Jews to be evangelized with the glorious

---

[42] W. D. Davies, *The Gospel and the Land* (Berkeley: University of California Press, 1974), 179.

[43] J. Edwards, Works, *Apocalyptic Writings*, v. 5 (New Haven: Yale University Press, 1977), 135.

good news that the land has become "irrelevant." Does anyone for a moment think that, as Paul witnessed from synagogue to synagogue, this was integral to his gospel message?

The Land and David E. Holwerda

The volume *Jesus and Israel: One Covenant or Two?* by David E. Holwerda of Calvin Theological Seminary is important particularly because it is a more recent Reformed estimate of Jewish national identity, especially in the light of Romans 11. He acknowledges God's present regard for unbelieving Jews as a whole, and not simply the Christian remnant. He also raises the question of nationality as well as the divine validity of the land. Nevertheless, it is this territorial aspect which is not answered with clarity. We now consider Holwerda's explanation, which certainly reflects sensitivity to a subject that is controversial within a Reformed environment. Clearly Holwerda was aware of criticism of much Reformed teaching in this regard when he commented,

> The faith of many Christians has been more heaven-oriented than land-oriented. The biblical themes of land and city have been spiritualized and focused elsewhere than on this earth. Is this the inevitable result of New Testament teaching? Is the land or this earth no longer important? Strikingly, since the return of the Jews to Palestine, the biblical theme of the land has caught the attention of Christian theologians.[44]

The land is identified in a subheading as "an irrevocable promise,"[45] though as with so many Reformed scholars, there is no interaction with the vital place of the unilateral signification of the Abrahamic covenant in Genesis 15.[46] However, the land is then qualified in the next subheading as "a conditional possession"[47] according to the covenant stipulations promising blessing or cursing in conjunction with obedience or disobedience. Consequently, in continually breaking the covenant Israel reaped judgment through exile. The land is then described in the next subheading as "lost and promised again."[48]

---

[44] D. E. Holwerda, *Jesus and Israel: One Covenant or Two?* (Grand Rapids: Eerdmans, 1995), 87.

[45] Ibid., 89–90.

[46] A classic instance of this omission is found in C. I. Crenshaw and G. E. Gunn III, *Dispensationalism Today, Yesterday, and Tomorrow* (Memphis, TN: Footstool Publications, 1985). In Appendix 3, "Conditional & Unconditional Covenants," 321–25, there is not so much as one reference to Genesis 15.

[47] Holwerda, *Jesus and Israel*, 90–93.

[48] Ibid., 93–96.

Concerning this Holwerda stated,

> The amazing message of the prophets is that in spite of the faithlessness
> of his people, God is faithful and will act in mercy to restore the covenant
> blessings. God's covenant with Israel is as certain as the order of creation.
> As long as the fixed order of creation continues, so will God's covenant with
> Israel continue (Jer. 31:35–37).[49]

Yet how strange that the author makes no mention here that his reference to Jeremiah 31 and Ezekiel 36 is in regard to the new covenant made
with "the house of Israel and with the house of Judah" (Jer 31:31) that
replaces the old covenant and incorporates repossession of the land (Ezek
36:24,28). However, concerning the tension that inevitably arises between
"an irrevocable promise" and "a conditional possession," the following
resolution is offered:

> Even when Israel failed and lost the land, the promise of possession did
> not cease. The promise that the land will be possessed is irrevocable. But
> if possession is to be maintained, God's people must become holy as God
> is holy.[50]

With this explanation we find ourselves in considerable agreement—that
is, if it is accepted that such holiness is to be accomplished according to
the eschatological promise concerning Israel's national regeneration (Ezek
36–37; Jer 31; see Matt 19:28; Acts 3:20–21). Furthermore, if the term
"land" here continued to be understood according to the exact territorial
meaning repeatedly invested within the OT, in the light of Holwerda's explanation here we might hope this understanding continued in the NT. But
such is not the case. Also, the land was never lost since it was rooted in the
unilateral, unconditional Abrahamic covenant. Though God's people were
exiled from the land, the promise of Jeremiah was that they would return
to it after 70 years (Jer 29:10). In the same way, the new covenant replaces
the Mosaic covenant and incorporates the promises of the Abrahamic covenant, including restoration to the land (Ezek 11:17; 36:24,28).

The most vital matter arises when we move on to consider Holwerda's
understanding of the land according to the NT and the closely related eschatological Jerusalem. With obvious sympathy for W. D. Davies' explanation whereby the promises concerning the land have been "personalized"
and "universalized" in Christ, Holwerda offers evidence from Eph 6:2–3.

[49] Ibid., 95.
[50] Ibid.

Here Paul's rendering of Deut 5:16 concerning the land is modified to "so that it may be well with you and you may live long on the earth."

> By omitting this specification [concerning the land], Paul declares that now in Christ the promise applies to any land. The promise has indeed been universalized, but it has been universalized precisely with reference to land. What was once a blessing promised to God's people in the particular land of Canaan, given by God as a gift, is now promised to God's people living anywhere on the earth, which was given by God as a gift. Thus, there is at least this one hint that Paul's relative silence about the land should not be construed as an implicit declaration that the land has become irrelevant and that the promise of the land should be forgotten. A universalized land is not an irrelevance.[51]

I would agree that at best we have a "hint" here of his proposal, especially since while Paul appears to adapt the Mosaic reference for the sake of his Gentile audience, he in no way denies the original territorial intent.[52] Of greater concern is the further malleable use of terminology employed to suggest that God's saving intent with regard to the whole earth is somehow an indication of how He continues to have continued interest in "the land." From a contemporary Reformed perspective, Robertson used the same hermeneutic.[53] To add some substance to his explanation, Holwerda refers to Paul's explanation in Gal 3:29 whereby

> Christ is the corporate embodiment of Abraham's seed, the One who represents and defines the authentic covenant lineage. In Christ it has been revealed that the inheritance of the promises is not by law but by promise, that the inheritance is a gift of God's grace (as was Canaan in the Old Testament) to those who believe. All those who have faith as Abraham had faith, who now believe in Jesus Christ, are "Abraham's offspring, heirs according to the promise" (Gal. 3:29).
>
> Heirs of what? Of "the promises," according to Galatians, and, according to Romans 4:13, these promises to Abraham and his descendants can be summarized in the promise "that he would inherit the world." For Paul, the

---

[51] Ibid., 102. Support is claimed from Calvin's exegesis at this point.

[52] Ibid., 98, concerning Paul's more likely employment of Exod 20:12 in Eph 6:2–3 according to a Judeo-centric hermeneutic.

[53] "In the process of redemptive history, a dramatic movement has taken place. The arena of redemption has shifted from type to reality, from shadow to substance. The land, which once was the specific place of God's redemptive work, served well in the realm of old covenant forms as a picture of paradise lost and promised. But in the realm of new covenant fulfillments, the land has expanded to encompass the whole world" (*The Israel Of God*, 30–31). Again I must point out that the land is grounded in the Abrahamic rather than the old Mosaic covenant. Further, the land is not represented as a shadow, but rather as part of the promise of the new covenant (Jer 31:31–40; Ezek 11:14–21; 36:22–32).

promise of Abraham has a cosmic sweep, including not just the territory of Canaan but the entire inhabited world.[54]

Granted that Abraham "would inherit the world," it is strange logic that concludes that this prospect would necessarily eliminate distinct national identity for Israel, especially since the original promise of Gen 12:1–3; 18:18; 22:18 indicated that Israel, as a nation and through its seed, would bring about blessing to the families of the earth, that is, to the Gentiles (Gal 3:8). This promise never indicated that there would be a final blending, an absorption whereby Israel would lose its identity, nor did subsequent confirmations of this promise. Thus Paul tells us "that Christ [the seed, Gal 3:16] has become a servant of the circumcised on behalf of the truth of God, to confirm the promises to the fathers, and so that Gentiles may glorify God for His mercy" (Rom 15:8–9). Here again we are faced with the same illogical, unbiblical suggestion that a universal truth cannot incorporate distinctive particulars, that oneness in Christ cannot incorporate distinctive maleness and femaleness, that the messianic kingdom of Christ cannot include Jewish and Gentile identity. Such a concept is quite fallacious. But we are further told,

> Has Paul rejected or even forgotten the promise of the land? By no means. Instead, the horizons of the land have been shaped by the revelation of Jesus Christ. His previous Jewish focus on a particularistic fulfillment has been transformed into a Christian universalism focused on the new creation.[55]

Yet again, Holwerda's definition of "the land" is linguistically reshaped whereby the land of the nations has both assimilated the land of the fathers and evacuated it of any distinctive Jewish heritage. Whether this process is called "transformational" or something else, what stands out here that is essentially replacement theology or supercessionism, is the eventual striping away of all things Judaic so that pure "Christian universalism" might remain. This does not appear to seriously heed Paul's warning to the Gentiles, "You do not sustain the root, but the root sustains you" (Rom 11:18). It will not do for Holwerda to identify the Jews as "all Israel," and not merely the remnant alone, according to Romans 11,[56] and then at the same time take away national and territorial identity. As W. D. Davies made plain, "The Land is so embedded in the heart of Judaism, the Torah,

---

[54] Holwerda, *Jesus and Israel*, 103.
[55] Ibid., 104.
[56] Ibid., 164.

that—so its sources, worship, theology, and often its history attest—it is finally inseparable from it."[57] But more importantly I suggest that this is so according to the terms of the new covenant, as Ezekiel explains"

> For I will take you from the nations and gather you from all the countries, and will bring you into your own land. I will also sprinkle clean water on you, and you will be clean. I will cleanse you from all your impurities and all your idols. I will give you a new heart and put a new spirit within you; I will remove your heart of stone and give you a heart of flesh. I will place My Spirit within you and cause you to follow My statutes and carefully observe My ordinances. Then you will live in the land that I gave your fathers; you will be My people, and I will be your God (Ezek. 36:24–28; see 11:14–21; Jer. 31:31–37).

The Land and the Heavenly Jerusalem

As noted in chapter 7, one major problem in the interpretation of the Letter to the Hebrews that looms larger than how to understand the warning passages is the manner in which a number of OT quotations and inferences appear to be related to the author's new covenant teaching. In this regard I repeat John Owen's warning, "There is not any thing in this Epistle that is attended with more difficulty than the *citation of the testimonies out of the Old Testament* that are made use of in it."[58] Let cavalier explanations of these OT references and intimations be shunned—those which simplistically suggest that the illustrative use of an OT passage in Hebrews automatically nullifies any original literal meaning. The truth is that the Hebrew author felt at liberty to quote with some variation in his hermeneutical methodology. I have referenced Kistemaker, Bonar, and Calvin in support of this contention (see chapter 7).

---

[57] W. D. Davies, *The Territorial Dimension Of Judaism* (Minneapolis, MN: Fortress, 1991) 85. It should be noted that this author adds the following qualification: "However, all this being recognized, it remains to emphasize one thing. If by a territorial religion is meant, as is usually the case, 'a cult whose constituency is a territorial group identified by common occupation of a particular land area, so that membership of the cult is in the final instance a consequence of residence and not kinship or ethnic designation' [quoting J. M. Schoffeleers], then Judaism is not a territorial religion: The Land is *not* the essence." Ibid. As far as it goes, this is true. Of course this would also be true of carnal, hence cultic Israel as Diaspora having longings for the land prior to 1948. But what stands is God's covenant promise to convert a carnal Israel into a spiritual Israel with the result that there *will* be kinship in the land (Ezek 36:22–28; 37:1–23). This being the case, then surely the land remains covenanted until that glorious day, intervening national conflict notwithstanding.

[58] J. Owen, *An Exposition of Hebrews*, I (Evansville, IN: Sovereign Grace Publishers, 1960), 106.

This leads to the suggestion that one of the most significant and yet neglected characteristics of this distinctive portion of Scripture is that the epistle was written by a Hebrew Christian for Hebrew Christians. This might seem an unnecessary comment except for the fact that problems can arise when a Gentile imposes his presuppositions on a text that only Hebrew presuppositions can illuminate. Whereas Paul's letters were all addressed to Gentiles in the main, the distinctive character of Hebrews (whoever wrote it) is due to the fact that Jewish Christians are addressed by a Jewish Christian who presumes a Jewish mindset.

With these thoughts in mind, we may consider the most common objection to national Israel having title to the land promised to Abraham, whether in the present or the future. Several NT texts are set forth as evidence that the earthly *ha'aretz* is indeed a former earthly hope that has been superseded by a more universal and heavenly one. These texts are Heb 11:10,16; 12:22, along with Gal 4:25–26. The proposal is that while Israel's land inheritance according to the OT economy was decidedly earthly, materialistic, and shadowy, the Christian's future, although rooted in the Abrahamic promise, is a more transcendently spiritual and heavenly hope. As an example of this popular understanding, especially where the repudiation of national Israel is concerned, consider Palmer Robertson's explanation:

> Just as the tabernacle was never intended to be a settled item in the plan of redemption but was to point to Christ's tabernacling among his people (cf. John 1:14), and just as the sacrificial system could never atone for sins but could only foreshadow the offering of the Son of God (Heb. 9:23–26), so in a similar manner Abraham received the promise of the land but never experienced the blessing of its full possession. In this way, the patriarch learned to look forward to "the city with foundations, whose architect and builder is God" (Heb. 11:10). . . . If the promised land of the old covenant becomes the blessed object to be achieved, then its tremendous fulfillment in the new covenant could be missed. To claim "the city with foundations, whose architect and builder is God" (Heb. 11:10), Abraham had to look beyond the shadowy form of the promise, which he never possessed, to the realities that could be perceived only by faith.[59]

Peter Walker's commentary is similar:

> [In Hebrews 11] positive descriptions of the physical land, however, are then immediately eclipsed by his [the author's] insistence that the real focus of the promise to which Abraham "looked forward" was the "city with foun-

---

[59] Robertson, *The Israel of God*, 13, 31.

dations, whose architect and builder is God" (v. 10). This eschatological focus is then repeated in verse 16: "Instead, they were looking for a better country—a heavenly one. Therefore God is not ashamed to be called their God, for he has prepared a city for them."

So the patriarchs were looking forward, not so much for the day when their descendants would inherit the physical land, but rather to the day when they would inherit the heavenly country (or city) which the physical land signified. In a sense they "saw through the promise of the land, looking beyond it to a deeper, spiritual reality.[60]

Several groups of contrasting expressions in Hebrews (and Galatians) are commonly understood as overlapping in meaning: "the present Jerusalem . . . the Jerusalem above" (Gal 4:25–26), "the city that has foundations, whose architect and builder is God" (Heb 11:10), "a better land—a heavenly one" (Heb 11:16), "Mount Zion . . . the city of the living God (the heavenly Jerusalem)" (Heb 12:22). These weighty expressions all relate to Abraham.

Abraham, summoned by God and converted from paganism in Ur of the Chaldeans, entered Canaan via Haran and was confronted with more paganism in the land of promise. He explored his inheritance from north to south as an unsettled nomadic tent-dweller and, it is reasonable to assume (Deut 18:9–14; 20:17–18), continued to be appalled at its pervasive unholiness that only the future leadership of Joshua could begin to cleanse. His search for "a better country, that is, a heavenly one" must be understood not according to a Gentile worldview, but the Hebrew worldview of the author. Franz Delitzsch's comment on Heb 11:16 is important in this regard:

It must be confessed that we nowhere read of the patriarchs, that they expressed a conscious desire for a home in heaven. The nearest approach to anything of the kind is in Jacob's vision of the angel-ladder, and his wondering exclamation, "this is the gate of heaven" (Gen. 28:17), but even there no desire is expressed for an entrance into the heavenly land, but the promise renewed of future possession of the earthly Canaan; "*The land whereon thou sleepest will I give to thee.*"[61]

Then Delitzsch adds concerning Heb 11:10,

Here the heavenly Jerusalem is not contrasted with the earthly city, but with the frail and moveable dwellings of the patriarchs in their nomad life.[62]

---

[60] P. Walker, "The Land in the Apostles' Writings," *The Land of Promise* (ed. P. Johnston and P. Walker; Downer's Grove, Ill.: InterVarsity), 90.

[61] F. Delitzsch, *Hebrews* (Edinburgh: T&T Clark, 1878), 2.246.

[62] Ibid., 238.

Abraham's hope was eschatological, but not in the sense of heaven's superiority to the earth, of the spiritual as superior to the material. Rather, his hope was of the future messianic age, the millennial kingdom in which heaven would be manifest on earth and residence there would be gloriously holy, permanent. George Peters explained this perspective as follows:

> Evidently that which misleads the multitude in this matter is the statement of the apostle (Heb. 11:16), that "they desire a better country, that is, a heavenly." Commentators, as Barnes, Bloomfield, etc., overlooking entirely *the Theocratic* relationship that this country (i.e. Palestine) is to occupy in the Kingdom of God, at once conclude that this "heavenly" country is the third heaven. They forget that this phraseology would not mislead a Hebrew, who was accustomed to designate the restored Davidic Kingdom a heavenly Kingdom, and the country enjoying its restoration and Theocratic blessings, a heavenly country. The expression does not mean "the third heaven," but something that pertains to, or partakes of, the heavenly, as heavenly vision, body, calling, etc.[63]

The hope of a "heavenly Jerusalem" was not a matter of a superior, exclusively spiritual or extraterrestrial location, but rather a fulfilled, holy, spiritually substantial regeneration of what was formerly polluted and imperfect. James Calvin De Young explained such a Hebrew hope:

> This eschatological liberation [of Jerusalem] is the antitype of the liberation of the Israelites from the bondage of Egypt, but is, of course, far greater and more glorious. Israel will at this time be gathered and re-established; Jerusalem will be rebuilt and her glory will last forever. Of all the apocalyptic literature, Tobit 13:8–18 paints the clearest and best picture of the future restored Jerusalem. . . . The clearest evidence that this renewed city is the earthly Jerusalem of Palestine is found in the numerous passages in Jewish literature where this renewal demands a great expansion in the city's territory.[64]

The challenge, then, as stated earlier, is to use a hermeneutical approach to these passages, especially in Hebrews, that relies on Hebrew perception. It is granted that rabbinical embellishment must be considered and purged. But C. K. Barrett, in making such an allowance, concluded that such eschatological language, as represented in Hebrews, looks forward to holy,

---

[63] G. N. H. Peters, *The Theocratic Kingdom*, I (Grand Rapids: Kregel, 1972), 295. J. B. Lightfoot confirmed this thought of Hebrew perception when, on Gal 4:26 concerning "the Jerusalem above," he commented. "St. Paul here uses an expression familiar to rabbinical teachers, but detaches it from those sensuous and material conceptions which they invested in it." *Galatians*, 182. Also see Alford, *The Greek Testament* (London: Rivingtons, 1856), 3.48.

[64] J. C. De Young, *Jerusalem in the New Testament* (N. V. Kampen: J. H. Kok, 1960), 113–14.

earthly glory, that is, a both/and resolution rather than one which takes us out of this world:

> The Rabbinic literature in general looks forward to a restored Jerusalem under earthly conditions. The new city is described in detail in terms which are often fantastic, but the welter of imagination bestowed upon the subject does not alter the fact that what the Rabbis hoped for, and described as "the Jerusalem of the age to come", was essentially the material capital of a material state.
>
> The heavenly tabernacle in Hebrews is not the product of Platonic idealism, but the eschatological temple of apocalyptic Judaism, the temple which is in heaven primarily in order that it may be manifested on earth.[65]

Such an approach to any supposed tension between the material and the spiritual, that is, between the material land and the heavenly Jerusalem, should be considered according to a both/and rather than an either/or resolution. Thus, Baruch Maoz wrote,

> Of course, salvation is not exclusively or primarily a matter of material realities (Heb. 4:8); nor are the Old Testament promises exhausted by exclusively material accomplishments as opposed to heavenly ones (Heb. 11:16). The contradictions found between 'heavenly' and 'earthly' lie not in terms of geography but in terms of the priority of things: Godward or otherwise, holy or sinful. The new heaven and new earth are said to 'descend'. There are spiritual bodies and natural ones (1 Cor. 15:36–44), and the New Testament doctrine of resurrection implies a spiritual kind of material existence rather than a non-material state of being (Exod. 3:6,8; Num. 32:11; Deut. 30:20; Neh. 9:7–8).[66]

Though amillennialist Samuel Waldron is not in the mainstream of Augustinian thought, I appreciate his confession of at this point:

> The heavenly country is not a country in heaven, but a country *from heaven*. The heavenly kingdom is the *kingdom from heaven* and not the kingdom in heaven. . . . Though heaven is the happy abode of the disembodied righteous during the present age, in the age to come heaven comes to earth.[67]

In conclusion, it is readily confessed once more that *some* manifestations of premillennialism are carnal with regard to a balanced or both/and comprehension of spiritual materiality. So with regard to national Israel, but

---

[65] C. K. Barrett, "The Eschatology of Hebrews," *The Background of the New Testament and its Eschatology* (ed. W. D. Davies and D. Daube; Cambridge: Cambridge University Press, 1956), 374, 389.

[66] Maoz, "People, Land and Torah," 192.

[67] S. E. Waldron, *The End Times Made Simple* (Amityville, New York: Calvary, 2003), 239–40.

especially the territorial factor, there are *some* manifestations of premillennialism that are carnal in their Zionist loyalty. Nevertheless, these deviant representations in no way nullify the essence of a biblical, Judeo-centric, premillennial eschatology. More specifically, this involves a future, holy, consummate messianic kingdom subsequent to the return of the Lord Jesus Christ and whose nature may be designated as spiritual materiality. It will be spiritually tangible. Even more specifically, this universal kingdom on a glorified earth will incorporate a blessed unity with diversity, that is, the regenerate nation of Israel will inhabit the fruitful promised land under the reign of Jesus Christ from Jerusalem surrounded by regenerate Gentile nations. In this setting of heaven come to earth, Israel and the Jewish people will be fulfilled (Rom 11:12), not superseded, and the Gentile nations will happily submit to this divine order as engrafted wild olive branches. To this end was the gospel sent forth (Zech 14:9; Acts 3:19–21; Rom 8:18–23).

Chapter 10
ISRAEL AND A ROMANS 11 SYNTHESIS

Romans 11 is, by common confession, the crucial passage with regard to the NT teaching concerning the present nature and destiny of national Israel. The following summary expositions of six key passages aim at establishing harmony with Paul's preeminent gospel teaching that I would define as vigorously Judeo-centric. Historic exegesis of these portions of Scripture, being predominantly Gentile in character, has tended to result in conclusions supportive of replacement, supercessionist, or fulfillment theology.

It should go without saying that all these passages of the Word of God were penned, humanly speaking, by Hebrew Christian authors. There needs to be recollection of Rom 1:16 where the gospel is to be offered "to everyone who believes, first [*prōtos*] to the Jew, and also to the Greek." The Lord Jesus revealed this principle to Ananias, namely, that Paul was "to carry My [Christ's] name before Gentiles, kings, and the sons of Israel" (Acts 9:15). As a result, Paul consistently witnessed to the Jews at every opportunity, even from the beginning at Damascus following his conversion (Acts 9:22). His first missionary journey saw initial synagogue witness at Salamis, Pisidian Antioch, and Iconium (Acts 13:5,14; 14:1). Acts 13:46 reveals, "It was necessary that God's message be spoken to you [Jews at Pisidian Antioch] first. But since you reject it, and consider yourselves unworthy of eternal life, we now turn to the Gentiles!" Nevertheless, at the next stop at Iconium, Paul first visits the synagogue (14:1). His second missionary journey finds him seeking the Jews first at Philippi, Thessalonica, Berea, Athens, Corinth and Ephesus (Acts 16:13; 17:1,10,17; 18:1–4,19). Acts 18:6 records, "Your blood [that of the Jews at Corinth] is on your own heads! I am clean. From now on I will go to the Gentiles." But at the next stop at Ephesus, Paul went first the synagogue. His third missionary journey found him returning to Ephesus, but first to the synagogue for three months (Acts 19:8). Paul's final journey, in which he was taken as a prisoner to Rome for trial, commenced in Jerusalem where he witnessed in the temple (Acts 21:26), then declared to the Jews that "I am a Jewish man" (Acts 22:3). Three days following his arrival at Rome, he "called together the leaders of the Jews" and declared, "It is for the hope of Israel that I'm wearing this chain" (Acts 28:17,20).

Paul's letter to the Romans was received in Rome from Corinth approximately three years before Paul's arrival in Rome. The apostle, though repeatedly scorned and assailed by the Jews, nevertheless manifested an indefatigable and gracious persistence with those to whom he continued to feel so indebted (Rom 9:1–5). Paul was relentlessly pro-Judaic, even when faced with the most stubborn unbelief and spiritual adultery (Rom 9:1–3; 10:1; 11:1,11; see Hos 11:8–9; 1 Thess 2:14–16). He manifested a degree of ongoing Jewishness that, while on occasion he used pragmatically (Acts 16:1–3), yet is reflective of deep love for "my countrymen by physical descent" (9:3). So no Christian should harbor any lesser attitude, though sad to say, many Christians have continued to be anti-Judaic both racially and theologically (see chapter 2).

With this in mind, a correct interpretation of the new covenant passages requires a hermeneutic that gives serious consideration to the Jewish presuppositions that are inherent in them. This approach was established in chapter 7. Such a Hebrew orientation results in agreement leading, by means of the progress of revelation, from the OT to the NT, from promise to fulfillment, that finds no necessity for the displacement of national Israel.

Romans 9–11 is not parenthetical, but continuative and climactic with chaps. 1–8. Many earlier references indicate an underlying interest in the destiny of God's covenant people (2:9–10,17–29; 3:1–2,9,29) and particularly the character of true Jewishness (2:28–29; see 9:6–8). Further, the theme of Romans is God's saving righteousness (1:16–17; 3:21–26; 5:17–21; 8:4,10), which highlights the integrity of God in saving sinners, whether Jews or Gentiles. God's righteousness is not to be questioned, even "if some [Jews] did not believe" (3:3). Therefore there is good reason for maintaining that v. 9:6a is of crucial importance when it declares, "But it is not as though the word of God has failed." John Piper rightly argues that v. 9:6a declares

> the main point which Romans 9–11 was written to prove, in view of Israel's unbelief and rejection. What is at stake *ultimately* in these chapters is not the fate of Israel; that is penultimate. Ultimately God's own trustworthiness is at stake. And if God's word of promise cannot be trusted to stand forever, then all our faith is in vain.[1]

Thus the Word of God has not failed, and so neither has its promised dealings with national Israel. In considering final proof of this fundamental truth, with Paul's close argument in mind, we proceed from the gospel and

---

[1] J. Piper, *The Justification of God* (Grand Rapids: Baker, 1993). 19.

Israel's *election* in Romans 9, to the gospel and Israel's *defection* in Romans 10, and now, ultimately, to the gospel and Israel's *salvation* in Romans 11.

Romans 11:1–32

If ever an opportunity presented itself for Paul to renounce unbelieving Israel once and for all, it would be here where the argument of chapter 10 has so conclusively demonstrated the accountability of the Jews for their blatant rebellion against the light of the gospel. A similar situation presented itself in 2:28–29 where we are told that "a person is not a Jew who is one outwardly, and true circumcision is not something visible in the flesh. On the contrary, a person is a Jew who is one inwardly, and circumcision is of the heart—by the Spirit, not the letter. His praise is not from men but from God." Surely at that point the extinction of national Judaism could have been affirmed once and for all. But Paul immediately says, "So what advantage does the Jew have? Or what is the benefit of circumcision? Considerable in every way" (3:1–2). So at the commencement of Romans 11 we find another passionate endorsement of the national descendents of Abraham. Hence Paul's subsequent dynamic argument calls for intense investigation since it best challenges anti-Judaism at its roots.

Israel Not Rejected by God, vv. 1–10

Even among Christians of this twentieth century who are indebted to the Reformation for the recovery of the gospel of the free grace of God, there has been vigorous disagreement with regard to the future destiny of Israel. My own strong commitment is to God's eschatological promise of a regenerated nation of Israel in the land under its acknowledged Messiah, the Lord Jesus Christ.[2] I believe that a *prima facie* reading of Romans 9–11 readily leads to this conclusion and that only a preconceived, dominant system of doctrine such as that of the Roman Catholic Church, or of entrenched Augustinianism, forces an alternative interpretation. Paul is adamant in this matter when, in reply to the question, "Has God rejected His people?" he vehemently responds, "Absolutely not!" (*mē genoito*, "perish the thought; it is unthinkable," Rom 11:1). Cranfield is right to designate Paul's dogmatic exclamation here as not only reflective of national Israel,

---

[2] The objection that the land has no place in Romans 11 is answered by evidence presented in chapter 9 of this book. Further, it would be nonsense for converted Rabbi Paul to reference the unbelieving Israelites' present investment in the promises of "their forefathers" (Rom 11:28; see 9:4) and then to suggest that the land is not included.

but also the theme of this chapter.[3] Horatius Bonar penned a hymn that is just as emphatic about this truth:

> Forgotten; no that cannot be;
> other names may pass away,
> But thine, MY ISRAEL, shall remain
> In everlasting memory.

> Forgotten! No, that cannot be;
> Inscribed upon My palms thou art,
> The name I gave in days of old
> Is graven still upon My heart.

> Forgotten! No, that cannot be;
> Beloved of thy God art thou
> His crown forever on thy head,
> His name forever on thy brow.

> Forgotten! No, that cannot be:
> Sun, moon, and stars may cease to shine,
> But thou shalt be remembered still,
> For thou art His and He is thine.[4]

Immediate proof that Israel has not been rejected is the biblical principle that there is "at the present time a remnant chosen by grace" (v. 5). This sovereign preservation is the guarantee of the preservation of the nation as a whole in the future. But it is vitally important to understand also that although a present remnant justifies God's ongoing faithfulness, the subsequent teaching here indicates that this is in no way meant to convey His final satisfaction with a remnant, even as v. 23 seems to suggest. Rather there will ultimately be Israel's "fulfillment" (v. 12), Israel's "resurrection" (v. 15), that is, the salvation of "all Israel" (v. 26).

Israel's Temporary Stumbling at Christ, vv. 11–24

The preceding stark definition of Israel's blindness, even as the church at Rome could so plainly observe, might lead to the belief that the nation as a whole had been finally abandoned by God. It would then be assumed that in the main the saved Gentiles now constituted the new spiritual nation comprised of all races, including a Jewish remnant. Sadly the early

---

[3] C. E. B. Cranfield, *The Epistle to the Romans* (Edinburgh: T&T Clark, 1979), 2:542, 574–77.

[4] H. Bonar, *Lamp and Light Hymn* (Hitchin, England: The Society for Distributing Hebrew Scriptures, 2000), 154.

Christian church, in embracing replacement or supercessionist theology, did eventually come to this conclusion, and with tragic consequences for the Jews.[5] But "No!" exclaims Paul. God's rejection of Israel is in no way final (v. 1); hence Israel's present stumbling is not irretrievable (v. 11).

God Blessing the Gentiles to Bless the Jews, vv. 11–15

While Paul's own distinctive Gentile ministry was significant in this divine saga, his ultimate vision concerned the saving of Israel, "their full number" (v. 12), and "life from the dead" (v. 15), through his distinctive vocation (vv. 13–15). But the interim bringing in of "the full number of the Gentiles" (v. 25), ought to provoke the Jews to jealousy, that is, make them desirous of God's evident outpoured blessing and so become, not Gentiles, but fulfilled Jews under their Messiah. David Larsen pointed out:

> Christian love, instead of arrogance [see vv. 18–20], ought to foster "envy or jealousy" among the Jews for what Christians possess in Christ (Rom 11:11). How frequently has this phenomenon been in evidence in Christian history or now?[6]

The answer is all too sadly obvious. Nevertheless, as Barrett stated, "Paul looks beyond the advantage conferred on the Gentiles by the unbelief of Israel to the far greater eschatological bliss which Israel's return will inaugurate."[7] While Israel's downside is its "rejection/being cast aside" (vv. 15,26–27; see Ezek 37:11), yet its greater upside is its eschatological resurrection (Ezek 37:7–10,12–14).

God Blessing the Jews through Wise Cultivation, vv. 16–24

While many a man quits a difficult task, the burden of Paul was to demonstrate that God's resolve in the saving of national Israel has never faded (Gen 18:14; see Phil 1:6), as is reflected by two OT images in vv. 16–24 that will stimulate the climactic declaration of vv. 25–32. Israel's Gomer-like

---

[5] The first century was dominated by the Jewish mother church at Jerusalem that acknowledged the inclusion of the Gentiles into the blessings of Abraham (Acts 15:1–35), But by the time of Constantine the Jews were believed to have forever forfeited the Abrahamic blessings. See H. W. House, "The Church's Appropriation Of Israel's Blessings," *Israel, the Land and the People* (ed. H. W. House; Grand Rapids: Kregel, 1998), 77–110; W. C. Kaiser Jr., "An Assessment Of 'Replacement Theology,'" *Mishkan* 21 (February 1994), 9–20; R. Pritz, "Replacing The Jews In Early Christian Theology," *Mishkan* 21 (February 1994) 21–27; J. S. Siker, *Disinheriting The Jews* (Louisville: Westminster, 1989).

[6] D. L. Larsen, "A Celebration of the Lord Our God's Role in the Future of Israel," in *Israel, the Land and the People* (ed. H. W. House; Grand Rapids: Kregel, 1998), 319.

[7] C. K. Barrett, *The Epistle to the Romans* (New York: Harper & Row, 1957), 214.

spiritual adultery (Hos 3:1) resulted in all the tawdry vicissitudes of human history, as with the conflict of the centuries in which the Jews have suffered unspeakable persecution, being "many days without king or prince, without sacrifice or sacred pillar and without ephod or household idols" (Hos 3:4). But "the people of Israel will return and seek the LORD their God and David their king. They will come with awe to the LORD and to His goodness in the last days" (Hos 3:5).

The Analogy of Israel as a Lump of Dough (v. 16a). According to Num 15:17–21, the first loaf resulting from a lump of dough was to be an offering of firstfruits or a consecrated offering to the Lord (cp. Lev. 6:14–18). So the holiness of the first part extends to the full lump of dough. Hence the salvation blessing of the Jewish "remnant" (v. 5) extends to the salvation blessing of the "full number" (v. 12) of all Israel (v. 26). The next analogy will clarify this point.

The Analogy of Israel as Natural Olive Branches (vv. 16b–24). By means of the olive tree analogy, Paul intends to provide his most compelling reasons as to why national Israel has glorious prospects in spite of ongoing obstinacy through unbelief resulting in dispersal. In a word, the reason is "grace" through unilateral, unconditional, covenantal promise (see 4:13–16; 9:8). However, while Gentile dominance continues, such privilege for saved barbarians should stimulate their humble gratitude and loving respect for the severed natural branches, rather than arrogance and conceit.

Moo comments that "Gentile believers [in Rome] were apparently convinced that they belonged to a new people of God that had simply replaced Israel,"[8] and consequently their derisive attitude was apparent. Haldane explained that Paul was describing "the [overbearing] spirit that has long prevailed among the Gentiles who profess Christianity. What marvelous ignorance, folly, and vanity, are often displayed even in God's people!"[9] However, while Israel is under discipline in the Lord's woodshed, Gentiles are to show them loving respect, even if the task is at times frustrating. But church history has not left an admirable record.[10] Paul's attitude (summarized in chapter 9) becomes a model in terms of what is here commended. Yet concerning the shameful record of many centuries, one scholar declared,

[8] D. Moo, *The Epistle to the Romans* (Grand Rapids: Eerdmans, 1996), 704.

[9] R. Haldane, *Commentary on Romans* (Grand Rapids: Kregel, 1988), 546.

[10] A study of church history regarding the treatment of the Jews by Christians is vital at this point. See chapter 10; also P. E. Grosser and E. Halperin, *The Causes and Effects of Anti-Semitism* (New York: Philosophical Library, 1978); D. L. Larsen, *Jews, Gentiles, and the Church* (Grand Rapids: Discovery House, 1995); D. Rausch, *A Legacy of Hatred* (Chicago: Moody, 1984); C. M. Williamson, *Has God Rejected His People?* (Nashville: Abingdon, 1982)

The Holocaust was, of course, the bitter fruit of long centuries of Christian teaching about the Jewish people. From the time of the gentile Church Fathers and the legal establishment of a triumphant ecclesiastical and philosophical control system with Constantine the Great, Christendom treated the Jewish people with contempt and taught contemptuously of them. . . . The baptized gentiles succumbed to that wrongheadedness against which Paul had warned: they turned in jealousy and envy against the very root that bore them (Rom. 11:18).[11]

Gentiles must not be arrogant but should "remain in His kindness" (v. 22) and allow grace to stimulate graciousness toward the unbelieving Jews, and thus promote jealousy in them (vv. 11,14). It is well worth contemplating here how a Christian, whose eschatological system denies the existence of Jews in the sight of God since AD 70, can adequately respond here in glad conformity with Paul's exhortation.

Israel's Temporary Hardening in Unbelief, vv. 25–32

From the beginning of Romans 9, Paul's overriding concern has been the justification of God in His covenant dealings with the nation of Israel. In vv. 25–32 a climactic thrust is reached that seals the dogmatic assertions of 11:1,11. The emphasis on the nation as a whole continues in large focus, especially since for Paul the OT manifestation has ongoing NT significance.

The End of Jewish Hardening, v. 25

Paul's remedy for the Gentiles' conceit, whereby they might esteem themselves singularly and forever favored by God to the exclusion of the Jews, is the revelation of Israel's future salvation. The present hardening of Israel will be "until" the mystery of the inclusion of the Gentiles within God's saving purpose has run its course and attained its "full number" (see also Luke 21:24). Moo rightly comments that Paul

leaves no doubt about what he wants his readers to learn from this mystery: to stop thinking so highly of themselves in comparison with Jews (v. 25a). We who are Gentiles should likewise take these verses as a reminder that we are only part of the great salvation-historical plan of God and that that plan has its climax in the salvation of Israel.[12]

---

[11] F. H. Littell, "Preface" to P. E. Grosser and E. G. Halperin, *The Causes and Effects of Anti-Semitism* (New York: Philosophical Library, 1978), xii.

[12] Moo, *The Epistle to the Romans*, 713. Also Barrett, Cranfield, Haldane, Hendriksen, Hodge, Morris, Murray, Shedd.

Gentiles are not to act with an "older brother" attitude (Luke 15:25–32). Trench, in expounding the parable of the Prodigal Son, explained,

> We Gentiles must not forget that at the end of the present dispensation all will be reversed, and that we shall be in danger of playing the part of the elder brother, and shall do so if we grudge at the largeness of the grace bestowed upon the Jew, who is now feeding upon the husks, far away from his Father's house.[13]

The Deliverer's Future Salvation of National Israel, vv. 26–27

"And in this way, all Israel will be saved" (v. 26). The controversy that surrounds this verse is closely related to systems of eschatology that have espoused three main perspectives. (1) "Israel" here refers to the redeemed of the NT era who constitute the church, whether converted Jews or Gentiles. Thus the Christian church has become the new Israel that has replaced the former OT nation. This view of Calvin has diminished in support because of obvious exegetical weaknesses. (2) "Israel" here refers to the accumulation over many centuries of the saved remnant of national Israel (11:5). While it is comprised of Jewish Christians, it merges with the church which is the new Israel. Both of the above views can admit to a larger number of Jews being converted at the end of this age, though without there being any national or territorial significance with regard to the future. Such an increase, again, merges with the church. This view is especially supported by English, Dutch, and Reformed scholars. (3) "Israel" here refers to a future national conversion of Israel, the larger unbelieving segment in particular, that results in Israel serving under Christ in the promised land with restored glory. This view, with variations, is most widely held today within evangelical Christendom, as N. T. Wright acknowledges.[14] It is the obvious meaning that is also in full harmony with a Judeo-centric eschatology.[15]

The National Salvation of All Israel (v. 26). There is clear chronological connection or "temporal reference," as Moo describes it, between vv. 25 and 26.[16] This is the case even when we translate, "in this way all Israel

---

[13] R. C. Trench, *Notes on the Parables of Our Lord* (Grand Rapids: Baker, 1948), 152. Cranfield makes a similar comment: "The order of salvation thus described marks significantly an inversion of the order in which the good news is preached according to 1:16 ('both for the Jew first and for the Greek'). *The Epistle to the Romans*, 2:572.

[14] N. T. Wright, *The Climax of the Covenant* (Edinburgh: T&T Clark, 1991), 246.

[15] For more conclusive proof in this regard, refer to M. Waymeyer, "The Dual Status of Israel in Romans 11:28," *MSJ* 16 (Spring 2005): 57–71.

[16] Moo, *The Epistle to the Romans*, 720.

[the same national Israel of v. 25, inclusive of the remnant of v. 5] will be saved." The agent of this salvation is "the Liberator . . . from Zion." Paul's flexible use of Isa 59:20 and Jer 31:33–34 probably incorporates Ps 14:7; 53:6 as well. The future tense here suggests the return of Jesus Christ, having come from the heavenly Zion and his throne of intercession (Heb 12:22–24) for the purpose of coming to earthly Zion in its present ungodly state; it complements the other future aspects of vv. 24,26. This is further indicated since this Liberator "will turn away [future tense] godlessness from Jacob" (see Isa 27:9; also vv. 6,12–13, which, according to Paul's reference here, must transcend the return from Babylon).

The National Covenant of Cleansing (v. 27). Paul's quotation of Isa 59:20–21 includes the thought of covenant cleansing from Isa 27:9; Jer 31:31–34. This indicates that the basis of the aforementioned salvation of Israel will be the atoning "Seed" of Abraham (Gal 3:16). The newness of this covenant (Heb 8:8–13; 12:18–24) is in relation to the old covenant made at Mt. Sinai, but it is the fulfillment of the Abrahamic covenant (v. 28). Cranfield rightly concluded that such unilateral deliverance "dashes Israel's self-centered hopes of establishing a claim on God, of putting Him under an obligation by its merits, making it clear that the nation's final salvation will be a matter of the forgiveness of its sins by the sheer mercy of its God."[17]

Comprehensive Salvation for Israel, vv. 28–32

The whole problem for the Gentiles has been misplaced focus, that is, self-centeredness. Paul's overriding purpose has been to correct this narrow vision so that it encompasses the broader perspective of Jews and Gentiles in God's plan of redemption. There is an emphatic contrast between "they" (Israelites) and "your" (Gentiles; v. 28), between "you" (Gentiles) and "their/these/they" (Israelites; vv. 30–31). Paul now continues to address the Gentiles in much the same way that God addressed and corrected the narrow focus of Peter (Acts 10:44–11:18).

According to Irrevocable Covenant (vv. 28–29). A more detailed study of v. 28 is found in chapter 11. Here biblical covenantalism with regard to God's saving purposes is brought to the forefront, enabling us to grasp that God's gospel is rooted in His sovereign will and purpose rather than human cooperation. Hence we are constrained to view God's dealings from His point of view rather than that of either Gentiles or Jews, and here this calls

---

[17] Cranfield, *Romans*, 2:579.

for continued emphasis on the Gentiles having their vision expanded, even as this thrust was introduced at v. 17. This necessity may also be due to the glorious deliverance of vv. 26–27 that could arouse Gentile discomfort, again after the manner of the "older brother" (Luke 15:25–32).

According to Universal Mercy (vv. 30–32). It is a common quirk of human nature, even among Christians, that we welcome grace bestowed on ourselves while at the same time being quick to mercilessly condemn sin in others (Matt 7:3–5). Likewise the Gentiles, particularly in their ascendancy, have tended to look with admiring exclusivity at themselves and with disparagement toward the Jews. But Paul is persistent in communicating God's inclusive, loftier perspective which, though nonetheless particular, intends that Gentiles and Jews should be accepting of each other even as He has been equally gracious in showing "mercy to all" (Rom 11:32). As Frederick W. Faber wrote,

> There's a wideness in God's mercy
>   Like the wideness of the sea;
> There's a kindness in His justice
>   Which is more than liberty.
> For the love of God is broader
>   Than the measure of man's mind,
> And the heart of the Eternal
>   Is most wonderfully kind.

The significance of Paul's continuing to exhort the Gentiles in particular throughout vv. 13–32 ought not to be missed. The point is that a wider perspective is necessary concerning God's design for human history. So often we are blinded by a narrow and exclusive frame of reference (v. 18), that requires divine enlightenment (vv. 24–29).

Conclusion

Paul obviously wrote Romans 11 with the passion of a Jewish Christian having unrelenting love for his Jewish brethren in the flesh. If some Gentiles in Rome had arrogantly followed a hermeneutic by which they asserted that historic Jewishness was absorbed within a homogenous Gentile identity, Paul would deem such a reinterpretation of the OT to be quite unnecessary, indeed unbiblical. Most Jewish Christians today readily empathize with the spiritual throb of the apostle's heart here, and especially his national and territorial hope. Unfortunately, for most Gentile Christians a mistaken Augustinian eschatology gets in the way of the text of Scripture here. Once this is jettisoned, then Romans 11 gloriously comes to life as never before.

Galatians 6:16

When apologists for Augustinian Reformed eschatology seek to biblically justify the identification of the Christian church as the new spiritual Israel of God, invariably Gal 6:16 is offered as the primary proof text.[18] Significantly, this is the *only explicit verse* in the NT that can reasonably be appealed to in this regard.

The Context

Paul was probably close to exasperation with the Jewish legalists who were so adamant in requiring that Gentile Christians be circumcised and then follow "the law of Moses" (Acts 15:5). So Gal 5:12 expresses, in a very down-to-earth manner, his desire that they "get themselves castrated." Again Gal 6:12–14 assails the carnality and hypocrisy of Paul's opponents, particularly their boasting in submission to circumcision. He responded with a different sort of boasting that is self-renouncing and exults in Jesus Christ's atonement alone. This proclamation of confidence in grace alone through Christ alone is antithetical to the formalistic religions of this world. And when all is said and done, what matters most is the sovereignty of grace that alone is able to convert a works-boasting sinner into "a new creation" [v. 15; see 2 Cor 5:17].

The Israel of God, v. 16

Paul exhorted the Galatians who were principally Gentiles to show discernment in this matter. "Peace" and "mercy," which are so central and resultant concerning a true experience of the gospel, is bestowed on those who are exclusively directed in their daily walk by grace and life in union with Christ. But for those who employ Moses along with Christ, as in a relationship that may be likened to spiritual bigamy (Rom 7:1–4), peace and mercy are impossible. Moses will only aggravate the problem (Rom 5:20; 7:7). Then Paul was reminded of a minority group in the church at Galatia, a small number of Jewish Christians. They were ethnically

---

[18] This is clearly evident in W. Hendriksen, *Israel and the Bible* (Grand Rapids: Baker, 1968), 33–34; O. P. Robertson, *The Israel of God* (Phillipsburg, New Jersey: P&R, 2000), 39–46; C. P. Venema, *The Promise of the Future* (Edinburgh: Banner of Truth Trust, 2000), 274–77. So H. LaRondelle commented, "Paul's Benediction in Galatians 6:16 becomes, then, the chief witness in the New Testament in declaring that the universal Church of Christ is the Israel of God, the seed of Abraham, the heir to Israel's covenant promise (see Gal. 3:29; 6:16)" (*The Israel of God in Prophecy* [Berrien Springs, Mich.: Andrews University Press, 1983], 110–11).

Jewish but different from "those who want to make a good showing in the flesh" (6:12). He included them as well in his exhortation since they, being authentic Jewish Christians, were "the Israel of God" and with the Gentiles were equally able to participate in the benediction of "peace" and "mercy" (6:16).

The Jewish Christian Interpretation

Considerable debate has surrounded the translation of this verse. The NASB, for example, reads, "And those who will walk by this rule, peace and mercy be upon them, *and* [emphasis added] upon the Israel of God." The HCSB reads similarly: "May peace be on all those who follow this standard, and mercy *also* [emphasis added] be on the Israel of God." But the NIV translates, "Peace and mercy to all who follow this rule, *even* [emphasis added] to the Israel of God."[19] This latter misinterpretation, wrote David Stern, a Jewish Christian, has caused

> immeasurable pain for the Jews. The conclusion was reached that the Church is now the "New Israel" and the Jews, the so-called "Old Israel," no longer God's people. If the Jews are no longer God's people, isn't it appropriate to persecute them? There are four reasons why this anti-Semitic conclusion is false and is not taught by this verse or any other: (1) the Greek grammar, (2) the Jewish background, (3) Sha'ul's [Paul's] purpose here, and (4) Sha'ul's teaching elsewhere.[20]

Stern's distress here is by no means unfounded. In John Gager's *The Origins of Anti-Semitism* is an honest reckoning with Gal 6:16 concerning the unfortunate neglect of certain historic doctrinal factors that conflict with the common association of Israel with the church. Having noted Peter Richardson's demonstration that "Israel" was first applied to the Christian Church by Justin Martyr c. 160,[21] Gager asserted,

> This is a sobering discovery. If language provides any clues to reality, we ought now to be more cautious when speaking about rejection-replacement views of Israel in the earliest stages of Christian development. Paul's writings come a full century before the time of Justin. They are certainly the

---

[19] The later TNIV (2005) has changed the rendering slightly: "Peace and mercy to all who follow this rule—to the Israel of God" and added an alternative translation of the final phrase in a note: "Or *rule and to.*"

[20] D. Stern, *Jewish New Testament Commentary* (Jewish New Testament Publications, Clarksville, MD), 574.

[21] P. Richardson, *Israel in the Apostolic Church* (London: Cambridge University Press, 1969), 1. He asserts that Justin's interpretation "is a symptom of the developing take-over by Christians of the prerogatives and privileges of Jews."

earliest Christian documents to have survived and perhaps even to have been written. If we knew nothing of their contents and were forced to hazard a guess based solely on an extrapolation from Richardson's observation about Justin, would we arrive at anything like the traditional interpretation of Paul on Israel and the Torah? In fact, Paul nowhere addresses his churches as Israel. Nor does he transfer to them Israel's distinctive attributes. The RSV translation of Philippians 3:3 ("We are the true circumcision. . . .") indicates such a transfer, but the RSV translation at this point must be seen as dependent on the rejection-replacement view of Israel, not the other way around.[22]

Gager rejected the identification of Israel with the church. He cited Ernest D. Burton's designation of "the Israel of God" as "the pious Israel, the remnant according to the election of grace (Rom 11:5)," but Gager apparently opted for Richardson's conclusion that "the blessing [of "peace and mercy"] falls on two separate groups: those who follow Paul's standard *and* the Israel to whom God will show his mercy, namely, 'all of Israel'" (see Rom 11:26).[23]

The Exegesis of Two Key Words

"Israel" According to Paul

There is no use of the term "Israel" in the NT that is an explicit equivalent to the Christian church. Regarding Paul's usage, Burton declared, "There is, in fact, no instance of his using Ἰσραήλ [*Israēl*], except of the Jewish nation or a part thereof."[24] Furthermore there is no evidence from history that the term "Israel" was synonymously used with regard to the church before AD 160 (see the previous section).

"And" Rather than "even"

The continuative "and" (*kai*) is not only contextually but also statistically preferable when compared with the ascensive "even." Most commonly, the translation is "and upon the Israel of God" (KJV, NKJV, NASB, ESV, NRSV, etc.), which shows Hebrew Christians retaining a distinct identity within the one people of God. The translation, "even upon the Israel

---

[22] J. G. Gager, *The Origins of Anti-Semitism* (New York: Oxford University Press, 1983), 228. He also notes that "there is no counterpart for 'true' in the Greek text" of Phil 3:3.

[23] Ibid., 228–29; E. D. Burton, *Galatians* (Edinburgh: T&T Clark, 1968), 358.

[24] E. D. Burton, *A Critical and Exegetical Commentary on The Epistle to the Galatians* (Edinburgh: T&T Clark, 1968), 358. In Rom 9:6, Paul writes of "an 'Israel' within ethnic Israel." J. Murray, *Epistle to the Romans* (Grand Rapids: Eerdmans, 1965), 2:9.

of God" (NIV), portrays the church, comprised of all the people of God, with a refined title, the "spiritual" Israel of God.[25] In the NT of the KJV the approximate usage is 97 percent for *kai* as "and" compared with 3 percent for *kai* as "even." The continuative use of *kai* has a far greater frequency than the ascensive use. Concerning the NIV's uncommon use of "even" in this regard, a degree of ambiguity remains. The ascensive use of *kai* could be correct, but the emphatic use is also possible: "Peace and mercy to all who follow this rule, even [by way of an adjunctive, emphatic thought] to the Israel of God." A. T. Robertson suggested that this may have been the original meaning of *kai*,[26] so that "also" here would seem to be a preferable translation, as with the HCSB (see above). In this instance the distinctive character of the Jewish Christian is retained. It is difficult not to suspect that the NIV translation was doctrinally driven so that the intention was to identify the church as the new Israel of God.

Compatibility with Romans 11:5,26

A broad Judeo-centric approach to Gal 6:16 is reflected in two interpretations related to Romans 11. First, some associate Gal 6:16 with the "remnant according to the election of grace" (Rom 11:5). These were authentic Jewish Christians at the time when Paul wrote Romans, and they parallel the remnant that Paul identified as "the Israel of God"—a minority within the Gentile churches of Galatia when Gal 6:16 was written. From this perspective, Burton supported

> the interpretation of the expression [*Israēl tou theou*] as applying not to the Christian community, but to Jews; yet, in view of τοῦ θεοῦ [*tou theou*], not to the whole Jewish nation, but to the pious Israel, the remnant according to the election of grace (Rom. 11:5).[27]

A considerable number of scholars has taken a similar exegetical path including G. C. Berkouwer, Hans Dieter Betz, F. F. Bruce, Walter Gutbrod, A. T. Hanson, S. Lewis Johnson, Jr., and Gottlob Schrenk.[28]

[25] Note the 2004 edition of the NLT renders the verse, "May God's peace and mercy be upon all who live by this principle; they are the new people of God."

[26] A. T. Robertson, *A Grammar of the Greek New Testament in the Light of Historical Research* (New York: Hodder & Stoughton, 1914), 1180.

[27] Burton, *Critical and Exegetical Commentary on the Epistle to the Galatians* (Edinburgh: T&T Clark, 1968), 358.

[28] See G. C. Berkouwer, *The Return of Christ* (Grand Rapids: Eerdmans, 1972), 344; H. D. Betz, *Galatians*, (Philadelphia: Fortress, 1979), 323; F. F. Bruce, *The Epistle to the Galatians: a Commentary on the Greek Text* (Grand Rapids: Eerdmans, 1982), 275; W. Gutbrod, "Ioudaios, Israel, Ebraios in the New Testament," *TDNT* (ed. G. Kittel; Grand Rapids: Eerdmans, 1965),

Second, it is difficult to ignore Paul's eschatological hope in a future conversion of national Israel, at which time "all Israel will be saved" (Rom 11:26). Hence this "full number" (Rom 11:12) parallels the consummation of "the Israel of God," as we have already seen with Richardson, along with the agreement of F. F. Bruce and Franz Mussner. Despite variations, both views provide a consensus that Gal 6:16 refers to Jewish Christians and therefore cannot be identified as a synonym for the homogenous people of God.

The Conflict between Exegesis and Doctrine

S. Lewis Johnson, formerly a NT professor at Dallas Theological Seminary and a strong Calvinist, wrote that in the interpretation of Gal 6:16 "dogmatic considerations loom large." He continued,

> The tenacity with which this application of "the Israel of God" to the church is held in spite of a mass of evidence to the contrary leads one to think that the supporters of the view believe their eschatological system, usually an amillennial scheme, hangs on the reference of the term to the people of God, composed of both believing Jews and Gentiles. Amillennialism does not hang on this interpretation, but the view does appear to have a treasured place in amillennial exegesis.[29]

Johnson claimed to have observed "a certain rigidity" in the viewpoint that identified Israel with the Church in this verse.

> Some amillennialists, however, think an ethnic future for Israel is compatible with their system. An example of this is found in the fine work of Anthony A. Hoekema on eschatology. He grants that an ethnic future for Israel would with certain strictures be compatible with his amillennial views, but he argues strongly against such an interpretation.[30]

He then raised the question, "Why, then are amillennialists so opposed generally to an ethnic future for Israel?" His suggested answer was that

> if such a normal interpretation of the language of the Old Testament is followed in this instance, it is difficult to see how one can then escape the seemingly plain teaching of many Old Testament prophecies that the nation of Israel shall enjoy a preeminence in certain aspects over the Gentiles in

---

3:387–88; A. T. Hanson, *The Pioneer Ministry* (London: SCM, 1961), 34–35; Gottlob Schrenk as referenced by S. Lewis Johnson, Jr., "Paul and 'The Israel of God': An Exegetical and Eschatological Case-Study," *Mishkan*, 6–7 (1987), 49–65.

[29] Johnson Jr., "Paul and 'The Israel of God'," 50.

[30] Ibid., 64.

the kingdom that follows our Lord's advent (cf. Isa. 60:1–4; 62:1–12; Mic. 4:1–5; Hag. 2:1–7; Zech. 14:16–21, etc).[31]

The Exegesis of Herman Bavinck and Geerhardus Vos

Herman Bavinck believed that the future salvation of Israel would only incorporate a remnant gleaned through the centuries, but Geerhardus Vos believed in a future mass conversion of Israel. In light of this, the preceding explanation of Gal 6:16 by S. Lewis Johnson is born out by the discussion in chapter 6 of Bavinck's anti-premillennial, eschatological understanding of Israel's future. As VanGemeren wrote,

> In the interest of polemic against premillennialism Bavinck sacrifices the OT prophetic hope to a harmonious understanding of the NT, in which the NT passages which hold out a hope for Israel and different exegetical options are either harmonized or not fully considered. The authority of the OT as well as of the NT seems to be sacrificed out of concern for unity, harmony, and systemization.[32]

VanGemeren also referenced Vos's similar anti-premillennial concern and why it was so difficult for him to enter into detail about his belief in the future conversion of Israel and its absorption into the Christian church. It was "because it had been connected on the one hand with the restoration of the Jews to the Holy Land and on the other hand with the millennial kingdom."[33]

Conclusion

The apostle Paul, who never repudiated his Jewishness, who always gave priority to Jewish evangelism, who continued to indicate the most tender love for his "countrymen by physical descent" (Rom 9:3), was not likely to be propounding here a vital truth through the use of ambiguous, even specious terminology. Surely he did not declare to the Galatian Jews that, through absorption among the Gentiles, they now had been racially disenfranchised by God. Upon his arrival at Rome several years after the letter to the Galatians had been penned, Paul first sought to witness to "the leaders of the Jews" concerning "the hope of Israel" (Acts 28:17,20). To suggest

[31] Ibid.

[32] W. VanGemeren, "Israel as the Hermeneutical Crux in the Interpretation of Prophecy," *WTJ*, 46 (1984), 263.

[33] Ibid., 263–64, with reference to G. Vos, "Eschatologie," *Dogmatiek* (Grand Rapids: 1910), 5:26. It was on exegetical grounds that Vos affirmed a hope in Israel's eventual conversion.

that in this situation he spoke deftly with his tongue, using an expression often employed before about a truth he believed would soon require divine "reinterpretation" is simply unthinkable. Certainly he would not have been declaring the demise of Judaism. Rather, in Rome he would have preached Christ to both Jews and Gentiles with the hope that unbelieving natural branches, through jealousy, might become part of the "remnant chosen by grace" (Rom 11:5), that is, the true "Israel of God" (Gal 6:16). In this way Paul would have heartily rejoiced in declaring, "I magnify my ministry" (Rom 11:13).

Ephesians 2:11–22

In churches of a Reformed persuasion, any eschatological distinction made between national Israel and the Church will often be challenged with the teaching of Paul in Eph 2:11–22. Here it is asserted that the apostle described Israel and the Church as having been uniformly joined together or amalgamated into one body, one new man, the new people of God that, nevertheless, retains the title of the Church of Jesus Christ. But it is further stressed that in such a unity God views the Jews as completely and covenantally divested of their Jewishness, even as Gentiles no longer retain any distinction. Martyn Lloyd-Jones, strongly influenced by Reformed theology, declared,

> The one new man here, the one body, is the Church, consisting of these various parts, all as a representation of the body of Christ. . . . The Jew has been done away with as such, even as the Gentile has been done away with, in Christ. If you believe in the new creation, you must realize that all else has been entirely done away with, put aside. "There is neither Jew nor Greek. . . for ye are all one in Christ Jesus" (Gal. 3:28). Another obvious principle is that nothing that belonged to the old state is of any value or has any relevance in the new state. If that seems startling to us we have but to read what Paul says in Galatians 6:15: "In Christ Jesus neither circumcision availeth anything, nor uncircumcision, but a new creature". . . . So the Jew has gone, Gentile has gone; all that belonged to the Jew, all that belonged to the Gentile, is irrelevant henceforward. It is the new creature that matters.[34]

Apart from the erroneous absolutist use of Gal 3:28; 6:15,[35] Lloyd-Jones believed, again in outright terms, that God has eliminated all racial

---

[34] M. Lloyd-Jones, *God's Way of Reconciliation: Ephesians 2*, (London: Evangelical Press, 1972), 216–17. G. Burge similarly aligns with the view that here: "In Christ the former categories of 'Jew' and 'Gentile' are abolished. . . . God has one people" (*Whose Land? Whose Promise?* [Cleveland, Ohio: The Pilgrim Press], 238).

[35] Obviously, Christian conversion does not eliminate racial, gender, and social distinctions.

distinctions, whether Jewish or Gentile. Hence there is no possibility of any divine future for national Israel or individual Jewish identity, though it is really not difficult to appreciate that this extreme egalitarian spirit has overstepped itself. The reason is that in Romans 9–11 the same author presents teaching that apparently is in direct conflict with Lloyd-Jones' exposition of Ephesians 2.

Of course, as already asserted, Romans is best understood from the Jewish perspective that so thoroughly permeates its doctrine, and not according to Gentile imposition upon this pivotal gospel account. Ephesians is similarly confronted with the same problem, especially in terms of centuries of Protestant exposition. In this regard Tet-Lim Yee expressed concern at

> the previous scholarship which has been hampered by too rigid an understanding of 'Pauline Christianity'. This can be attributed substantially to scholarly tradition whose hermeneutical 'grid' has been derived from the philosophy of dialectics or the Protestant Reformation. The 'new perspective(s) on Paul', however, shifts our perspective back to first-century Judaism and enables us to penetrate fully into the historical context of first-century Jews and Judaism.[36]

This preferred Judaic approach is not to be thought so surprising when one considers the conclusion of Yee's study of Ephesians overall:

> The reason for the heavy use of the Jewish Scripture in Ephesians is obvious enough: it shows the continuity of Ephesians with the Jewish tradition to such an extent that the Jewish scriptures had become part of the author's tacit dimension, forming the "grid" of his theological and ethical weaving.[37]

It is vital to note that the rapprochement presently under discussion here in Ephesians 2 is predicated on that period when Jesus declared to the chief priests and Pharisees that "the kingdom of God will be taken away from you [not eternally; see Matt 23:38–39] and given to a nation [mainly the Gentiles, the new people of God] producing its fruit" (Matt 21:43). This union instituted through the blood of Christ (vv. 13–16) commenced

---

They remain as diverse characteristics of Christian unity (Gal 3:28). Neither did Paul nullify circumcision for the Jewish Christian.

[36] T. N. Yee, *Jews, Gentiles and Ethnic Reconciliation: Paul's Jewish Identity and Ephesians* (Cambridge: Cambridge University Press, 2005), 213. As previously mentioned in chapter 6, we do not have to agree with all the conclusions that the "new perspective" presents via E. P. Sanders, James D. G. Dunn, and N. T. Wright to appreciate the significance of a heightened regard for the essential Jewish nature of biblical, indeed Second Temple Christianity, especially as reflected in Paul.

[37] Ibid., 43.

at the inauguration of the Church age, was signified at Pentecost, and thus progresses through the subsequent centuries and advances to the fullness of the Gentiles (Luke 21:24; Rom 11:25). In the language of Romans 11, we are at that point where "the [natural] branches were broken off, and you, though a wild olive branch [of Gentile stock], were grafted in among them [the Jewish remnant], and have come to share in the rich root of the cultivated olive tree" (v. 17).

Gentiles as the Main Subject of Discussion

As in Rom 11:11–32, in Ephesians 2 Paul addressed those formerly "Gentiles in the flesh—called 'the uncircumcised'" (v. 11), so that they might understand that they have been graciously engrafted into the root of Abraham as wild, uncultivated stock. Paul's language, though different from Romans, affirms the same truth—that Gentiles have been "brought near by the blood of the Messiah" (v. 13), having formerly been "without the Messiah, excluded from the citizenship of Israel, and foreigners to the covenants of the promise, with no hope and without God in the world" (v. 12).

Gentiles As "excluded from the citizenship of Israel," v. 12

At one time Gentiles were "excluded from the citizenship of Israel" (as a nation/state) and were "foreigners to the covenants of the promise."[38] That is, they were separate from "the rich root of the cultivated olive tree," the Abrahamic covenant and the "forefathers" (Rom 11:17,28). Such alienation was when Gentiles "were dead in [their] trespasses and sins in which [they] previously walked according to this worldly age. . . . We too all previously lived among them in our fleshly desires" (Eph 2:1–3). Thus the Gentiles were prodigals, "with no hope and without God in the world," (Eph 2:12).

Gentiles "brought near by the blood of the Messiah," vv. 13–19

Gentiles are not saved to constitute the Church, but are "brought near" to an unidentified entity by means of Christ's atonement. So in Rom 11:17 the wild olive branches are not independently saved to become the church, but are engrafted into "the rich [Abrahamic] root of the cultivated olive

---

[38] The plural "covenants" especially anticipates continuity with the original promise declared to Abraham on several occasions (Gen 12:1–3; 15:5–21; 17:7–8; 26:1–5; 28:10–17; 35:9–12), and by means of the subsequent Davidic covenant (2 Sam 7:8–17) and new covenant (Jer 31:31–37).

tree," that is, "brought near" to the Abrahamic covenant. As Carl Hoch Jr. described the connection, "The Gentiles are brought near to Israel in Christ to share with Israel in its covenants, promise, hope, and God. They do not become Israel; they *share* with Israel."[39]

Near to the Blessing of Abraham (v. 13). The context makes it clear that being "brought near" does not refer to union with or nearness to Christ. Rather it is by means of "the blood of the Messiah" that we are brought near to something else. In parallel with Rom 11:17 I suggest that Gentiles are certainly brought near to God, though more particularly through being engrafted into the Abrahamic covenant. Thus H. C. G. Moule explained,

> The thought of remoteness and nearness in respect of *God* is of course implied, and comes out clearly in v. 18; but it is not the immediate thought of this passage, which rather speaks of the incorporation of once heathen souls into the true *Israel*. But the two views cannot be quite separated.— "Nigh" and "far" were familiar terms with the Rabbis in the sense of having or not having part in the covenant.[40]

That is, by faith the Gentiles draw near to "the blessing of Abraham" (Gal 3:14); as uncultivated olive branches, they become engrafted into the "rich root of the cultivated olive tree" (Rom 11:17); they too become participants in "the covenants of the [Abrahamic] promise" (Eph 2:12), the sustaining root (Rom 11:18).

"Near" as "breaking down the barrier" Between Jew and Gentile (v. 14). Formerly there was a seemingly impenetrable fence or partition of animosity between Jews and Gentiles, especially on account of the law (v. 15). There may be an allusion to the temple wall that divided the Court of the Israelites from the Court of the Gentiles. Christ has established reconciliation and peace so that the two warring factions have become one, as in a marriage, even though the Jew and Gentile distinction is still present as with the male/female distinction within a Christian marriage (Gal 3:28). David Stern has suggested,

> Sha'ul's [Paul's] point is that Gentiles are no longer separated but can now join the Jewish people and be one with them as God's people through faith in the Jewish Messiah, Yeshua. The partition is down, the Gentiles can join us! The critics understand it the other way round: the partition is down, so that once Jews believe in their own Messiah they can no longer have the

---

[39] C. B. Hoch Jr. "The New Man of Ephesians 2," *Dispensationalism, Israel and the Church* (ed. C. A. Blaising and D. L. Bock; Grand Rapids: Zondervan, 1992), 125.

[40] H. C. G. Moule, *The Epistle to the Ephesians* (Cambridge: Cambridge University Press, 1891), 78.

right to maintain their Jewish identity but must conform to Gentile patterns. Amazing! And certainly not what Sha'ul himself did.[41]

Gentile alienation has been transformed through incorporation into the unity of "one new man" (Eph 2:15), but this does not result in the elimination of distinctions that concern sexuality, personality, giftedness, appearance, and ethnicity. Hence, with Romans 11 also in view, I reject the rather common Gentile understanding that this oneness results in a homogenous union which completely eliminates former Jew/Gentile distinctions, as Lloyd-Jones has represented. This "one new man" is identical with the "one body" of God (v. 16), which according to Paul's analogy comprises a diversity within a unity with regard to the church as the body of Christ (1 Cor 12:27; Eph 4:12; see Col 1:18). Similarly in marriage, a man and a woman, while retaining gender distinction, become "one flesh" (Gen 2:24). As Dan Gruber described this oneness,

> The church is composed of believers called out of the Gentiles to be joined to the faithful remnant of Israel. It is Israel's fruit. There is a distinction between Israel and the Church, not a separation. There is a union without a loss of identity. . . . Believers are not identically the same, but "Messiah is all, and in all." Messiah is the one new man, and we are all part of Him. There are many members of the body, with different appearances and functions, but only one body.[42]

"Near" as Making "one new man from the two," v. 15. After the fierce enmity between Jews and Gentiles was eliminated, the result is "one new man from the two." This is the church, "God's household" (v. 19), which is rooted in Abraham and presently comprises a growing fullness of Gentiles and a growing Jewish remnant that will attain to a climactic fullness (Rom 11:12,26); it is "a holy sanctuary in the Lord" (Eph 2:21) and "God's dwelling in the Spirit" (v. 22). A significant part of this "new man" is disassociation from "the law of the commandments in regulations" (v. 15), that is, the old covenant, "so that you may belong to another—to Him who was raised from the dead" (Rom 7:4). Thus, redeemed Jews and Gentiles are at peace with each other due to a better foundation. Yet the redeemed Gentiles "are no longer foreigners and strangers, but fellow citizens with the saints" (Eph 2:19). Such a united relationship does not invalidate a Jew/Gentile distinction within "God's household" any more than the male/

---

[41] Stern, *Jewish New Testament Commentary*, 584.
[42] D. Gruber, *The Church and the Jews* (Hanover, NH: Elijah Publishing, 1997), 331, 410.

female distinction is invalidated because they are "one in Christ Jesus" (Gal 3:28). David Stern commented,

> In this entire passage Sha'ul is writing to Gentiles, and his object is to reassure them that they are fully God's people, that because of their faith in the Messiah and his work no barrier exists between them and Jews—Gentiles are not second-class citizens of the Kingdom. His purpose is not to downplay Jewish distinctives, but to "up-play" what God has now done for Gentiles. To find in these verses grounds for opposing Messianic Judaism is simply to misappropriate them for a purpose Sha'ul never dreamed of.[43]

The "new man" then is the seed of Abraham brought to "new covenant" fulfillment; the newness here is not a replacement, as if brand new, but a fulfillment newness, a union through incorporation that involves the luster of grace and unity in the seed of Abraham which the OT people of God were never able to manifest. This household of God is essentially and foundationally Hebrew, with Zion as its headquarters (Rom 11:26; Rev 14:1), while the incorporated wild Gentile branches participate in a oneness that retains individuality.

"Near" as Reconciled "to God in one body," vv. 16–18. The church as "God's household" (v. 19), is established through reconciliation "to God in one body" (v. 16). Its foundation is "the rich root of the cultivated olive tree" (Rom 11:17), which supports the cultivated, along with the uncultivated branches that have been engrafted into the Abrahamic covenant. Through Christ, *the* seed of Abraham (Matt 1:1–17; Gal 3:16,29), peace, instead of former enmity between Jews and Gentiles, has been brought to those "who were far away" and "to those who were near" (Eph 2:17; see Isa 57:19). Further, "we both," Jews and Gentiles—as with the man and woman—through Christ the one Mediator have identical "access by one Spirit to the Father" (v. 18), while retaining Jew/Gentile distinctiveness.

"Near" as "fellow citizens with the saints" Comprising "God's household," v. 19. Here then is the resolution of the tension which Lloyd-Jones introduced. Here also is further explanation concerning the "one new man" (v. 15). While some interpret "the saints" as believers in general, for converted Rabbi Paul this term, in context here, would indicate Jewish Christians,[44] or the remnant of Rom 11:5, in parallel with Gal 6:16. Gentiles, through God's grace in Christ, now share with a remnant of Israel, resulting in coexistence as "the new man," the church, "the rich [Abrahamic/Hebrew]

---

[43] Stern, *Jewish New Testament Commentary*, 588.

[44] See C. B. Hoch Jr., *All Things New* (Grand Rapids: Baker, 1995), Similarly, John Gill.

root of the cultivated olive tree" (Rom 11:17).[45] The church is now "God's household" comprising Gentile Christians who are "fellow citizens with the saints [Jewish Christians]" (Eph 2:19). As another writer put it,

> The Church is not the people of God which has taken the place of Israel, the Old Testament people of God. Rather, according to Rom. 11:1, the Church is only "the participant in the root" (Israel) and its forefathers, the extended people of God who together with Israel form the one people of God.[46]

We must remember that Paul, who wrote Ephesians (1:1), continued to identify himself as an ethnic Jew (Acts 21:26,39; 22:3; Rom 9:3; 1 Cor 9:20) without any thought of a shallow fraternal acknowledgment or duplicity in his profession. So we have harmony with the eschatological prospect of Israel's national conversion and re-engrafting according to Ezekiel 36–37 and Rom 11:15,23–26. This great, distinctive ingathering (Rom 11:12,15,24–26) will become part of "God's household" (Eph 2:19).

Conclusion

The main point many Augustinian amillennialists attempt to derive from this passage is that the "one new man" and "God in one body" (Eph 2:15–16), evidence a homogenous unity that does not allow diversity, namely, divine recognition of Jewish and Gentile Christians. This I believe to be a fundamental error since the "one Spirit" and "one Lord" and "one God and Father" (Eph 4:4–6) constitute a personal diversity in the essential unity of the Godhead. In Eph 2:13–16, and in 1 Cor 12:12–30 where there is one body of Christ that is composed of distinctively gifted members, overall unity comprises a complementary diversity, as in the marriage union. Thus the "one new man" and the "God in one body"—indeed, "the whole building [is] a holy sanctuary in the Lord" (Eph 2:21)—represent a unity that incorporates Jewish and Gentile individuality ordained of God (Gal 3:28–29; 6:15–16).

Philippians 3:2–3

It has been common, especially among Gentile commentators, for Phil 3:2–3 to be understood as a clear indication that Paul believed all

---

[45] Hoch, "The New Man of Ephesians 2," 125. Also see W. H. Rader, *The Church and Racial Hostility* (Tübingen: Mohr, 1978), which traces the interpretation of Eph 2:11–22 throughout church history.

[46] F. Mussner, *Tractate on the Jews* (Philadelphia: Fortress, 1984), 9.

Christians constitute the circumcision of God. This new alleged identification, according to God's perspective, is in lieu of a now defunct physical rite that parallels an equally defunct nation of Israel. O. Palmer Robertson commented, "In Romans 2:29 and Philippians 3:3, Paul indicates that all believers in Christ, whether or not they are Jewish externally, are truly the Israel of God."[47] This I believe to be a mistaken understanding of Paul's overall teaching. According to Paul's own confession, he remained a distinctive, bona fide Jew after he became a Christian (Acts 16:1–3; 22:3; Rom 9:3–4; 11:1).

Warning against Carnal Signification, v. 2

In Philippians Paul wrote primarily to Gentiles with great concern about the "dogs" who were "evil workers" that "mutilate the flesh" (Phil 3:2). Whether these troublemakers were Gentiles who had been Judaized or Judaizing Jewish Christians, the apostle's concern was akin to that which he confronted in the churches of Galatia (Gal 5:12). Clearly these disturbers zealously attempted, as it were, to collect Gentile foreskins like scalps and then boast in their harvest for the cause of perpetuated Judaism (Gal 6:12–13; Phil 3:2).

Encouragement of Spiritual Signification, v. 3

In Phil 3:3 the HCSB says, "For we are the circumcision," but the NASB reads, "for we are the *true* circumcision," and the ESV, "For we are the real circumcision." The "we" here must be identified. Many have concluded that the general congregation at Philippi, along with Paul and his immediate entourage, is collectively indicated. But there is good reason for believing that a more exclusive reference is in mind—Paul himself and Timothy, both circumcised, as v. 17 would suggest. In a similar vein, there is a significant contrast in Galatians between "we [Jews]" (2:15–17; 3:23–25; 4:3–5) and "you [Galatian Gentiles]" (3:1–3,26–29). Carl Hoch Jr. has made a good case for the interpretation of "we" as equivalent to "we Jews." He references J. B. Lightfoot's comment that *latreuō* ("to worship, serve") was "used in a very special sense to denote the service rendered to Jehovah by the Israelite race, as His peculiar people."[48] Then Hoch added, "In every instance where

---

[47] O. P. Robertson, *The Israel of God* (Phillipsburg, New Jersey: 2000), 44n. This view follows a common Reformed perspective, as does R. Sibbes commenting on Phil 3:3 (*The Works of Richard Sibbes* [Edinburgh: James Nichol, 1863], 5.69).

[48] J. B. Lightfoot, *Philippians* (Grand Rapids: Zondervan, 1953), 145.

Paul uses this verb to describe service to God, he uses it of his own personal ministry (see also Acts 24:14; 26:7; 27:23; Rom 1:9; 2 Tim. 1:3)."[49] Hoch further commented,

> When Paul refers to possible confidence in the flesh in Philippians 3:5–6, he mentions, "circumcised on the eighth day, of the people of Israel, of the tribe of Benjamin, a Hebrew of the Hebrews; in regard to the law, a Pharisee; as for zeal, persecuting the church; as for legalistic righteousness, faultless." Paul is definitely contrasting his pre-Christian experience with his present Christian Jewish experience. Saying "we" are the circumcision may have been his way of anticipating the list of his pre-Christian credentials versus his new position in Christ.[50]

Hoch also quoted A. T. Hanson on this issue. While explaining that the prevailing interpretation of Phil 3:3 identifies the "we" as all true Christians, Hanson nevertheless declared that this understanding

> seems quite foreign to Paul's thought and means actually reading into Philippians ideas which seem to have originated at the time of the Reformation. . . . The Philippians, being Gentiles, would have no reason to boast in the flesh anyway. Paul goes on to describe what he means by this phrase in the ensuing verses: it is plain that he means boasting of the national and spiritual privileges peculiar to the Jews. This the Philippians could not do. . . . It is simpler to take "we" here as "we believing Jews", or even "we, Paul and Timothy", in whose name the letter is written. We know that Timothy was circumcised. So there is no good reason for maintaining that the use of "the circumcision" here suggests that Paul could apply the name Israel to Gentiles.[51]

Further, "true circumcision" (NASB) suggests a contrast with "false circumcision" in v. 2, but the latter is better translated "those who mutilate the flesh" (HCSB). Paul's intention here was not to contrast a false with a true circumcision so as to indicate that Jewish racial circumcision has been nullified and replaced with the true circumcision—whoever believes in Jesus Christ. Rather, while Paul did not reject the physical identification of a racial Jew by means of circumcision, he was certainly opposed to those who demand that circumcision is of such importance that it overshadows its significance, which is a representation of a truly circumcised heart. It seems Paul may have had the same thought in mind when, although believing in the significance of the two Christian ordinances, he could vigorously warn against their abuse (1 Cor 1:14–17; 11:20–22,29–30).

[49] Hoch, *All Things New*, 289.
[50] Ibid.
[51] A. T. Hanson, *The Pioneer Ministry* (London: SCM, 1961), 35.

Parallel with Romans 2:25–3:2; 4:11–12; 15:8–9

The definition of an authentic Jew for Paul the Jew, especially here in Romans, is a matter of disagreement among conservative Christians. Some suggest that in this church age it is the true Christian who is now the real and only spiritual Jew, and that since God has finished forever with Israel as a nation there is no such thing in His sight as a national or ethnic Jew. As already indicated, I believe this to be contrary to what Paul had in mind, not only with regard to Phil 3:3, but also in Rom 2:25–29 (especially in light of 3:1–2); 11:1–36; Acts 22:3; Gal 6:16. Paul had an opportunity to completely dismiss the Jews in the flesh at the end of Romans 2, but instead he enthusiastically vindicated them in Rom 3:1–2. The same surprise awaits the reader of Rom 10:18–21 where the opportunity was ripe for Paul to repudiate national Judaism. But in anticipating such a thought, Paul immediately responded that such an idea was unthinkable (Rom 11:1–2). Thus an unbelieving Jew is still a racial Jew, nevertheless with his soul in jeopardy (John 8:24); at the same time he is a beloved enemy of God (Rom 11:28). A Jewish Christian is an authentic, fulfilled Jew, one who has been circumcised both of the heart and of the flesh, as Paul described himself and Timothy in Phil 3:3. Likewise, Gentile Christians are in brotherhood with Jewish Christians, reckoned as spiritually circumcised in heart (Rom 2:26) and thus joined to Abraham through faith (Gal 3:29). Here then is racial diversity within spiritual unity, in the same way as a Christian man and wife are diverse in their spiritual unity (Gal 3:28). This same diversity in unity is strongly intimated in Rom 15:8–9 since "Christ has become a servant of the circumcised on behalf of the truth of God, to confirm the promises to the fathers, and so that Gentiles may glorify God for His mercy" because of their inclusion as Gentiles with the fathers.

Perpetuation of Distinctive Signification

Concerning the diversity in unity of Jews and Gentiles constituting the people of God rooted in the Abrahamic covenant, the Council at Jerusalem is of foundational significance. Surely Paul's contribution was substantial as a Jewish spokesman for the Gentile church at Antioch. Even so, it is Peter's testimony and conclusion, upheld by James, which is of supreme importance. Despite Peter's capitulation on another occasion (Gal 2:11–14), the declaration that "we [Jews] believe we are saved through the grace of the Lord Jesus, in the same way they [Gentiles] are" (Acts 15:11), was revolutionary to the common Jewish mind. Here is a definitive statement unambiguously pronouncing that physical circumcision was not salvific, and therefore neither was entrance into Judaism. Thus the Gentiles at that time well understood that the Council never for a moment demanded Jewish Christians to renounce circumcision. The uncultivated olive branches were not expected to become cultivated branches; neither were the cultivated branches expected to become uncultivated olive branches. However, by the time of the fourth century when Constantine converted to Christianity, Gentile assertiveness unbiblically required that Jews converting to Christianity should renounce their Jewishness.

Conclusion

For national Judaism, circumcision remains a valid signification of distinctive racial identity that was originally ordained to represent circumcision of the faithful, spiritually circumcised heart (Deut 30:6; Rom 2:25–29). There is no biblical indication that this outward right has been divinely disqualified for Jewish Christians. As Stern explained,

> Although Jews and Gentiles are equal as regards salvation, there are other distinctions between them, as Sha'ul acknowledges immediately (Rom. 3:1–2) and later (9:4–5, and especially 11:28–29). One distinctive (Sha'ul does not deal with it, but Yeshua does at Luke 21:20–24), for example, is that the Jewish people are to inherit the Land of Israel in perpetuity. This is a promise to physical or national Israel that has not yet been entirely fulfilled, but it will be. . . . The only real Jew is the born Jew who has been born again by trusting in Yeshua the Messiah, for only he lives up to what the name "Jew," conferred on him at birth and confirmed by physical circumcision, implies and demands.[52]

Hebrews 8:7–13; 10:15–18; Jeremiah 31:31–40

A common interpretation of Heb 8:7–13 has concluded that Jer 31:31–40 finds its fulfillment in the Christian church as the new Israel. For example, W. J. Grier wrote,

> In the Epistle to the Hebrews (chapters 8 and 10), we have the sacred writer claiming that the new covenant (of New Testament times) is the fulfillment of these words of Jeremiah: 'Behold, the days come, saith the Lord, when I will make a new covenant with the house of Israel and the

---

[52] Stern, *Jewish New Testament Commentary*, 339–40.

house of Judah.' Israel and Judah are evidently the Israel of God, the New Testament Church.[53]

Certainly this perspective has predominated through the centuries of the Christian church, which is very much in parallel with replacement theology and its derogation of national Judaism.

On the other hand, anyone who reads Jer 31:31–40, especially in its immediate context without any recollection of Hebrews 8 and 10, is unlikely to conclude that we are solely considering the NT church. According to Henry Alford (quoting F. Bleek),

> It belongs throughout to the cycle of Messianic prophecies, and is one of the most beautiful and sublime of them; and its true fulfillment can only be sought in the covenant brought in by the Savior, and in the salvation through Him imparted to mankind, and ever more and more unfolded and completed. This is the case, however this salvation, in the perception and declaration of the prophet, is bound up with the restoration of the ancient covenant people and their reunion in the land of their home.[54]

Background

The title, "To the Hebrews," traceable to the late second century, is a reasonable, long held, and prevailing suggestion, supported by considerable textual evidence, that the addressees were Jewish Christians,[55] that is, "a remnant chosen by grace" (Rom 11:5). No pagan background associated with Gentile converts is mentioned in this letter. The danger was that the recipients might "drift away" from sound teaching (2:1), "neglect such a great salvation" (2:3), develop "an evil, unbelieving heart that departs from the living God" (3:12), "become lazy" (6:12), stay "away from our meetings" (10:25), or be "led astray by various kinds of strange teachings" (13:9). But the author was especially concerned that his Jewish Christian audience might have an insufficient understanding of the superiority of Jesus Christ's priesthood over that of Moses and Aaron, who were ministers of the old covenant (Heb 3:1–6). Hence it is reasonable to expect that the Hebrew author had a decidedly Jewish appreciation of Jeremiah 31. Further, assuming that the date of composition was prior to AD 70, especially since there is no mention of the catastrophe that befell Jerusalem at

---

[53] W. J. Grier, *The Momentous Event* (London: Banner of Truth Trust, 1970), 47.

[54] H. Alford, *The Greek Testament*, IV, (London: Rivingtons, 1862), 152.

[55] D. A. Carson, D. J. Moo, and L. Morris, *An Introduction to the New Testament* (Grand Rapids: Zondervan, 1992), 401–404..

that time, we conclude that Hebrews was written during a period when there was no extra-biblical evidence of Israel being equated with the church, which happened about AD 160 when Justin Martyr's *Dialogue with Trypho* was published.[56]

Identity of "Old" and "New" Covenants?

The old covenant is the broken, bilateral Mosaic covenant established on tables of stone, mediated through Moses (Exod 19:1–9; 20:1–17), and affirmed by Israel with sacrificial offerings (Exod 24:1–8). It is different from the unilateral Abrahamic covenant (Gen 15:1–18) established 430 years earlier (Gal 3:17). The new covenant, according to its heart-renewing and cleansing ability, was designed by God to inaugurate His true worship by Israel (Jer 31:31–40; see Ezek 11:14–21; 36:22–32). The NT reveals that Jesus Christ initiated this divine contract in the very presence of Israel (Luke 22:20; 23:33–49; 1 Cor 11:25; 2 Cor 3:6).

According to Jeremiah 31:31–40

It is Jer 31:31 which anticipates that redemptive transaction made with the blood of Christ, "when I [the LORD] will make a new covenant with the house of Israel and with the house of Judah." Although the unilateral nature of this covenant is implicit at this stage, it becomes more explicit in v. 33 when "I will place My law within them and write it on their hearts." Both the nations of Israel and Judah, their unification also being implicit (see Ezek 37:15–23), are *here* the primary objects of the Lord's saving design, not the Gentile Christian church. With regard to its addressees, the new covenant is plainly established with the nation of Israel through its Messiah who was, in covenantal terms, "cut," that is, "pierced because of our transgressions, crushed because of our iniquities" (Isa 53:5). But through this new covenant "all the peoples [families] of the earth will be blessed" (Gen 12:3) as "wild olive branch[es]" that become engrafted into "the rich root of the cultivated olive tree" (Rom 11:17). Consequently, the new covenant communicates the new Torah of the God of Abraham, Isaac, and Jacob, which is incorporated in the new commandment (John 13:34–35; 1 John 2:7–8). Then the Gentiles will also enter into new covenant blessings. Similarly, Eph 2:13 describes this direction of reconciliation concerning

---

[56] Richardson, *Israel in the Apostolic Church*, 1.

the Gentiles "who were far away [but now] have been brought near by the blood of the Messiah [to the rich root of the cultivated olive tree]."[57] Subsequent blessing after Israel's national conversion will be the more glorious establishment of Jerusalem (vv. 38–40), so that

> this prophecy does not refer to the rebuilding of Jerusalem after the exile, but, under the figure of Jerusalem, as the center of the kingdom of God under the Old Testament, announces the erection of the more spiritual kingdom of God in the Messianic age.[58]

According to Hebrews 8:1–13 and 10:15–18

The Jewish recipients of this letter were well acquainted with Jeremiah 31, so that when the author writes of "the first [covenant]" (v. 7)—which is "the covenant that I made with their fathers" (the leaders of Israel at the Exodus)—and "a new covenant with the house of Israel and with the house of Judah" (v. 8), they are instantly in tune with the weeping prophet. There is not the slightest suggestion that the author of Hebrews had in mind "a new covenant" that is different or reconstituted from that which Jeremiah writes about. Nor is there here any mention of incorporation or engrafting of the Gentiles into this "new covenant" as Romans 11 and Ephesians 2 indicate. The reason is that this is not the author's concern here, but rather the very necessary comprehension by Hebrew Christians of the superiority of the new covenant over the old covenant (8:13–10:18). So Jer 31:33–34 is quoted again in Heb 10:16–17 to support the truth that "by one offering [not innumerable offerings] He [Christ, the Mediator of the new covenant] has perfected forever those who are sanctified" (10:14).

The New Covenant for Jewish and Gentile Christians

Judeo-centric eschatology embodies a unity which at the same time incorporates a functional diversity. Like the instrumentally diverse unity of a symphony orchestra that produces a glorious concerto, or the individual

---

[57] The common misunderstanding on the part of Christians is illustrated by a sermon of Charles Simeon on Jer 31:31–34 titled "The New Covenant." In the whole message there is not one reference to Israel or Judah while the new covenant is twice called the Christian covenant. The following sermon on Jer 31:35–37 is titled "The Church's Security." Nevertheless, Simeon's pro-Semitism is clearly indicated in the next sermon titled "The Future Conversion of the Jews," based on Jer 32:37–42, in which he expressed his belief in the restoration of Israel to the land. There is the specific qualification that "this diffusion of piety will not precede, but follow, their [Israel's] restoration to their own land." Then they will be "an holy people unto the Lord." *Horæ Homileticæ*, IX (London: Henry G. Bohn, 1847), 236–55.

[58] C. F. Keil, *The Prophecies of Jeremiah* (Grand Rapids: Eerdmans, 1968), 2:46.

notes that unite through chords to resound with harmonious melody, so the new covenant involves complementary diversity resulting in holy harmony. As Walter C. Kaiser Jr. put it,

> There is one people ("the people of God") with a number of discernible aspects within that one people (such as Israel and the church), and there is only one program of God (the "kingdom of God") with numerous aspects under that single program.[59]

The New Covenant and Jewish Christians (Luke 22:20)

As already indicated, the context of Jesus' declaration to the twelve disciples in the upper room, "This cup is the new covenant established by My blood" (Luke 22:20), is that of Messiah as "the King of the Jews" (John 19:19) addressing twelve believing Jews.[60] In a proleptic manner of speaking, the Son of God exclusively proclaimed to representatives of "the house of Israel and . . . the house of Judah" (Jer 31:31), direct benefactors of the new covenant, that He Himself was about to cut this new agreement by means of shedding His own blood. To point this out is in no way intended to stimulate Gentile discontent any more than the fact that the Abrahamic covenant was exclusively cut with Abraham (Gen 15:1–21) to the exclusion of Gentile participation. However, as the Abrahamic covenant was to result in blessing to "all the peoples on earth" (Gen 12:3), so the new covenant similarly is to result in the incorporation of "other sheep" (John 10:16). Nevertheless, this same new covenant was inaugurated in Jerusalem (Acts 1:8) with the Jews first (Rom 1:16; Acts 3:26).

The New Covenant and Gentile Christians (Acts 10–11; 15)

While Paul's conversion anticipated the proclamation of Christ "before Gentiles, kings, and the sons of Israel" (Acts 9:15), it was Peter's encounter with the converted household of Cornelius (Acts 10:1–48) that set the stage for the definitive proclamation from the Jewish church at Jerusalem that "God has granted repentance resulting in life to even the Gentiles. . . . that He made no distinction between us [Jews] and them [Gentiles], cleansing their hearts by faith" (Acts 11:18; 15:9). Hence the letter sent from the Jewish church in Jerusalem to the Gentile church in Antioch was an astonishing acknowledgment by Jewish Christians that there was no necessity for Gentile Christians to become Jewish Christians (Acts 15:22–30), and

---

[59] W. C. Kaiser Jr., "An Evangelical Response," in *Dispensationalism, Israel and the Church* (ed. C. A. Blaising and D. L. Bock; Grand Rapids: Zondervan, 1992), 367.

[60] Ibid., 366. Also Gruber, *The Church and the Jews*, 378–79.

the resultant rejoicing on the part of the Gentile Christians was demonstrative acknowledgment of this truth (Acts 15:31). However, the thought that while Gentile Christians were free to enjoy their liberty as Gentiles, the Jewish Christians should give up their Jewishness, would have been unthinkable at Antioch as well as Jerusalem. Yet such has been the sad historic development that, for centuries, Gentile Christians have been harshly enforcing their liberty on Jewish Christians and disenfranchising them of national and geographic identity. This ought not to be.

The New Covenant Celebrated by Jewish and Gentile Christians (1 Corinthians 11:25)

Paul stated that the ordinance of the Lord's Supper was "received from the Lord" (1 Cor 11:23). This means that these specific directions had been directly related to him by the Son of God, so connecting 1 Cor 11:25 with Luke 22:20. When Paul related the words of the Lord Jesus, "This cup is the new covenant in My blood. Do this, as often as you drink it, in remembrance of Me" (1 Cor 11:25), doubtless he was also referring to Jer 31:31. But the importance of this new covenant celebration was not only to Jews, but also to a preponderance of Gentiles among his audience at Corinth. Thus the Lord's Supper is for Jewish Christians as well as Gentile Christians.

The New Covenant Operative in Jewish and Gentile Christians (2 Cor 3:1–18)

Paul delighted to point out the intrinsic, distinctive character of the new covenant that Jesus Christ inaugurated. Like the author of Hebrews, he used *a fortiori* argumentation to stress the surpassing greatness of that which Jer 31:31 promised. Thus 2 Corinthians 3 contrasts the two covenants:

THE OLD COVENANT	THE NEW COVENANT
tablets of stone, v. 3	tablets of the human heart, v. 3
the letter kills, v. 6	the Spirit gives life, v. 6
the ministry of death, v. 7	the ministry of the Spirit, v. 8
the ministry of condemnation, v. 9	the ministry of righteousness, v. 9
the fading glory, vv. 10–11	the remaining glory, v. 11
veiled heart, vv. 13–15	unveiled heart, vv. 16–18

The resultant effect of the new covenant is heartwork on both Jews and Gentiles, whereby the formerly concealed glory of God is revealed to the children of God. So "we all, with unveiled faces, are reflecting the glory of the Lord and are being transformed into the same image from glory to glory; this is from the Lord who is the Spirit" (v. 18).

Conclusion

Hebrews 9:15; 12:24; 13:20 draw fulfillment from Jeremiah 31, as do Luke 22:20; 1 Cor 11:25; 2 Cor 3:6, but especially Romans 11. Here the Gentiles become invited guests with Abraham (Luke 14:16–24) and at the same time join in fellowship with the remnant of Christian Jews. However, when "the full number" of the Gentiles has come in," then will follow Israel's "full number" and consummate national salvation (Rom 11:12,25–26). As a result, in the consummate earthly kingdom there will be a unity under Christ that accommodates a functional difference between Jews and Gentiles, as Johnson indicated in his study of Gal 6:16.[61]

1 Peter 2:9–10

The assumption on the part of many is that 1 Peter addresses Christians in general throughout "Pontus, Galatia, Cappadocia, Asia, and Bithynia" (1:1). Hence, his designation of these same believers as "a chosen race, a royal priesthood [see 2:5], a holy nation, a people for His possession" (2:9–10) indicates that OT designations concerning Israel are now applied to Jews and Gentiles without distinction. The Church is now God's "chosen people," that is, the "new Israel." Richard J. Mouw, president of Fuller Theological Seminary, explained it this way:

> The church is, after all, in an important sense "the new Israel." I have been especially taken with the imagery employed in the First Epistle of Peter. The apostle is writing to a group of Christians that obviously includes Gentiles, but he begins his letter with Old Testament terminology, greeting his readers as the "exiles of the Dispersion" (1 Pet. 1:1, NRSV). Especially significant is the way, in the second chapter, he takes a series of images of Old Testament Israel and applies them to the New Testament church: "But you are a chosen race, a royal priesthood, a holy nation, God's own people." He then adds a quotation from one of the prophets: "Once you were not a people, but now you are God's people" (1 Pet. 2:9–10, NRSV). These verses helped clarify my own thinking about the nature of Christian community. . . . I realized the implications of 1 Pet. 2:9–10. God is putting together a new kind of "race," a new kind of "priesthood," and a new kind of "nation." Jesus is in the business of actively promoting a unity that he

---

[61] Johnson, "Paul and 'The Israel of God'," 49–65.

does not want us to define ourselves along artificial lines of what the sinful world sees as ethnic-racial or denominational or national identities. Through the blood of Jesus Christ we have been made into a new kind of people, in which "there is neither Jew nor Greek, slave not free, male nor female, for you are all one in Christ Jesus" (Gal. 3:28).[62]

Of crucial importance is the identification of the addressees, whether they are primarily Jewish or Gentile. E. G. Selwyn summarized the main conclusions over the centuries as follows:

> In the patristic age Origen, Eusebius, and the Greek fathers generally maintained that they [the addressees] had been Jews, while Augustine, Jerome, and other Latin writers held the opposite view. This divergence has continued almost to our own day, the Greek view on the whole prevailing under the weighty impetus given to it by Erasmus, Calvin, Bengel, and Grotius on the threshold of the modern age. Its doughtiest champion in more recent days has been Bernard Weiss, and the facts and arguments which he adduces deserve careful attention. Chief of them is what may be termed the Jewish character of the Epistle as seen in the O.T. quotations and allusions, which would hardly be familiar to Christians of Gentile origin, and in the conception of the Church which is markedly Levitical and suitable only to those who had been nurtured in Judaism.[63]

From a Reformed perspective, it is common to read of interpretations of which the following by Cornelius P. Venema is representative:

> In 1 Peter 2:9–10, the apostle gives a summary statement regarding the New Testament church. Writing to the scattered believers and churches throughout Asia Minor, Peter defines the new covenant church in terms drawn from the old covenant descriptions of the people of Israel. . . . What is so remarkable about this description of the church is that it identifies the church with the exact terminology used in the Old Testament to describe the people of Israel with whom the Lord covenanted. The best reading of this language takes it literally to mean that the new covenant church is altogether one with the old covenant church. The Lord does not have two peculiar peoples,

---

[62] R. J. Mouw, "The Chosen People Puzzle," *Christianity Today* (March 5, 2001), 45:4, 70. F. J. A. Hort similarly commented, with an extreme supercessionist view that seems almost blindly Gentile, "The truth is that St. Peter, as doubtless every other apostle, regarded the Christian Church as first and foremost the true Israel of God, the one legitimate heir of the promises made to Israel, the one community which by receiving Israel's Messiah had remained true to Israel's covenant, while the unbelieving Jews in refusing their Messiah had in effect apostatized from Israel." *The First Epistle of St. Peter*, I:1–II:17 (London: MacMillan, 1898), 7.

[63] E. G. Selwyn, *The First Epistle of St. Peter* (London: MacMillan, 1969), 42. While disagreeing with this author's inclusive view of Jew and Gentile audience, I would agree with his suggestion that the congregations would have included God-fearers and proselytes.

two holy nations, two royal priesthoods, two chosen races—he has only one, the church of Jesus Christ.[64]

Textual Indications of Jewish Addressees

First Peter is widely acknowledged to be addressed to Christians suffering intense persecution that does not appear to have the prospect of abating, that is, for pilgrims on earth (1:6; 2:20–21; 3:14; 4:1,12–19; 5:8–10). This being the case, it was especially the lot of Jews to have little rest from opposition to their racial distinctiveness at around the time of Peter's writing (c. AD 60), and particularly if they were Jewish Christians under the reign of Nero. We find much evidence that Peter, who we would expect to be writing to Jewish Christians, is indeed addressing, in the main, the Jewish Christian Dispersion (1:1). This is not to deny that Gentiles, engrafted into the stock of Abraham as wild olive branches (Rom 11:17), could read this passage and derive personal blessing and encouragement from it. They have been incorporated into this "chosen race, . . . royal priesthood, . . . holy nation" (1 Pet 2:9), the end result being both cultivated and uncultivated branches having diversity in unity. But I do deny that this passage establishes the Christian church as here designated the new Israel, supplanting any designation of historic, individual, national and territorial Jewishness.

1 Peter 1:1

On the Greek word for "Dispersion" in 1 Pet 1:1, Charles Bigg explained that "Diaspora, [is] a word which in its proper sense denotes those Jews who for one reason or another were domiciled in foreign countries."[65] Since the Jewish Christian apostle Peter was the author, Bigg is probably correct about Peter's use of the term. Further, a healthy interest in the doctrine of election according to Reformed standards should not be allowed to obscure the fact that for the apostle *eklektos* ("elect, chosen") focuses principally on Israel's national election in which Jewish Christians individually participated (LXX, Deut 14:2; Isa 41:8–9; 44:1–3; 45:4; 49:7; 65:9).

1 Peter 2:5–10

For the suffering Dispersion, here is comfort indeed that aims at a recollection of the OT revelation concerning "a holy priesthood" (2:5) that

---

[64] C. P. Venema, *The Promise of the Future* (Edinburgh: Banner of Truth Trust, 2000), 271–72.

[65] C. Bigg, *1 Peter* (Edinburgh: T&T Clark, 1969), 70.

has been established "through Jesus Christ" (Exod 19:5–6; Deut 4:20; 7:7; 10:15; 14:2; Ps 118:22; Isa 4:14; 28:16; 43:20; 61:6; 66:21). In Jesus Christ, "a chosen and valuable cornerstone" (2:6), "a stone that causes men to stumble, and a rock that trips them up," is fulfillment of the hope of the Dispersion truly becoming "a chosen race, a royal priesthood, a holy nation, a people for His possession, . . . God's people, . . . [who] have received mercy" (vv. 9–10). Thus John Calvin commented concerning v. 9:

> However, as the greater part of the nation was unbelieving, the Apostle indirectly sets the believing Jews in opposition to all the rest, though they exceeded them in number, as though he had said, that those only were the children of Abraham, who believed in Christ, and that they only retained possession of all the blessings which God had by a singular privilege bestowed on the whole nation. He calls them *a chosen race,* because God, passing by others, adopted them as it were in a special manner. They were also *a holy nation;* for God had consecrated them to himself, and destined that they should lead a pure and holy life. He further calls them *a peculiar people,* or, a people for acquisition, that they might be to him a peculiar possession or inheritance; for I take the words simply in this sense, that the Lord hath called us, that he might possess us as his own, and devoted to him. This meaning is proved by the words of Moses, "If ye keep my covenant, ye shall be to me a peculiar treasure beyond all other nations" (Exod. 19:5). There is in the *royal priesthood a* striking inversion of the words of Moses; for he says, "a priestly kingdom," but the same thing is meant. So what Peter intimated was this, "Moses called your fathers a sacred kingdom, because the whole people enjoyed as it were a royal liberty, and from their body were chosen the priests; both dignities were therefore joined together: but now ye are royal priests, and, indeed, in a more excellent way, because ye are, each of you, consecrated in Christ, that ye may be the associates of his kingdom, and partakers of his priesthood. Though, then, the fathers had something like to what you have, yet ye far excel them. For after the wall of partition has been pulled down by Christ, we are now gathered from every nation, and the Lord bestows these high titles on all whom he makes his people.[66]

The identification of the Dispersion as once being "not a people" who had "not received mercy" thus recollects, not some Gentile characteristic of alienation, but the declaration of Hosea concerning the house of Israel: "I will say to Not My people: You are My people, and he will say: You are My God" (2:23; see 1:10). From a Jewish Christian viewpoint, David Stern commented,

> Christians are indeed a chosen people set aside for God to possess—not by way of superceding the Jews as God's people, but by way of being joined

---

[66] J. Calvin, *The First Epistle of Peter* (Edinburgh: Calvin Translation Society, 1855), 74–75.

to them by faith in the same God and in the Jewish Messiah. A so-called 'Christian' who opposes or looks down on the Jews as merely God's 'former' people has missed the point altogether.[67]

1 Peter 2:11–12

First Peter 2:11–12 speaks of "aliens and temporary residents" who parallel those "not a people" (v. 10), the Jewish seed of Abraham (Hos 1:10; 2:23; Heb 11:9–10,13–16; see Lev 25:23), hence the Dispersion and not preeminently Gentiles. Thus "conduct yourselves honorably among the Gentiles" (v. 12), is a most natural exhortation to Jewish Christians who reside in Gentile Asia Minor. Calvin added concerning v. 12,

> And he [Peter] expressly says *among the Gentiles*; for the Jews were not only hated everywhere, but were also almost abhorred. The more carefully, therefore, ought they to have labored to wipe off the odium and infamy attached to their name by a holy life and a well-regulated conduct.[68]

And for Gentile Christians having union with the Dispersion as children of Abraham (Gal 3:29), this injunction would also have real personal meaning.

1 Peter 2:25

First Peter 2:25 would have brought to the Jewish Christian mind the OT representation of Yahweh as the Shepherd of Israel. This ancient imagery found messianic fulfillment in Jesus Christ (Ps 23:1; 78:52; 80:1; Isa 40:11; 53:6; Jer 31:10; Ezek 34:11–16). This is also a reminder of Peter's commission from Jesus: "Shepherd My sheep" (John 21:16) which the apostle later understood more specifically as a vocation directed toward the Jews (Gal 2:7–9). By way of contrast, Paul, the minister to the Gentiles (Gal 2:7–9), never used the shepherd metaphor except with reference to the Christian pastor, and that only twice (Acts 20:28; Eph 4:11).

1 Peter. 4:3

First Peter 4:3 refers to the former lifestyle of these Jewish Christians as one in which they lived in the midst of Gentile dominance, especially in Asia Minor. To their shame, there was capitulation to and lusting after aspects of Gentile paganism (see 2 Chr 36:14). Calvin explained,

> But instead of the *lusts* or covetings of men, he [Peter] now mentions *the will of the Gentiles*, by which he reproves the Jews for having mixed with

---

[67] Stern, *Jewish New Testament Commentary*, 747.
[68] Calvin, *The First Epistle of Peter*, 78–79.

the Gentiles in all their pollutions, though the Lord had separated them from the Gentiles.[69]

Conclusion

Why should it surprise us that Peter, the apostle to the Jews (Gal 2:7–9), would address Jewish Christians? Could it be that Gentiles, especially Gentile commentators, tend to find it difficult to appreciate that they are not always the center of new covenant focus (Rom 11:18)? Concerning the addressees of 1 Peter, amillennialist Patrick Fairbairn wrote that this epistle was "addressed, more immediately, to believing Israelites scattered throughout the cities of Asia Minor."[70] They were the remnant of Rom 11:5. It may also be significant in further considering the fact that the earliest interpreters of 1 Peter did indeed identify the addressees as predominantly Jewish Christians, and this was at a time of waning dominance for Jewish Christian leaders in Jerusalem. Subsequent Gentile identification of the addressees as being inclusive of Gentiles, who now collectively comprise the new Israel, parallels the surging dominance of the Gentile church that depreciated both Judaism as a whole and any Jewish Christian distinctiveness.

[69] Ibid., 123.

[70] P. Fairbairn, *The Prophetic Prospects of the Jews, or Fairbairn vs. Fairbairn* (Grand Rapids: Eerdmans, 1930), 106.

Chapter 11

ISRAEL AS GOD'S BELOVED ENEMY

Having considered the ongoing status of Jewish Christians in terms of their ethnic, national, and territorial identity, it is important now to consider the status of unbelieving Jews from a Christian perspective. In particular, we raise the question concerning the contemporary Jew who does not believe in Jesus of Nazareth as Israel's promised Messiah. While not circumcised in the heart through the Holy Spirit, that is, in Christian terms (Rom 2:29; Phil 3:3), nevertheless, is he still the object of any divine, covenantal regard according to the flesh? We would also press this question further by enquiring whether national, unbelieving Israel in this present age is the object of any divine recognition, especially in covenantal terms. In immediately responding positively to both questions, we realize that negative responses pose more than a doctrinal difference of opinion. Consider how today a Christian may propose that God has no covenantal interest whatsoever in unbelieving national Israel and the Jews, especially in the light of their strident opposition to biblical Christianity. In this case, for such a Christian, his eschatological belief raises the most profound ethical considerations with regard to his present treatment of Jews. He is forced to reckon with his covenantal repudiation of national Israel and the Jews while at the same time being confronted with Paul's contrasting recognition of and eschatological hope for national Israel, his personal identification with Judaism, his passionate pro-Semitism, and his lifestyle as a model for distinct, prioritized, persistent, loving Jewish evangelism.

Christians generally agree that in Rom 11:5 Paul distinguishes the Jewish Christian in terms of being part of "a remnant chosen by grace" (Rom 11:5). Even then, some will use the term "Jewish" here at best deferentially and nominally while at the same time rejecting any divine ethnic or covenantal meaning with regard to Jewishness. Nevertheless, the term "Jewish Christian" stands. But what is the ongoing status, if any, in the sight of God of the unbelieving Jews Paul describes in Rom 11:17 as branches "broken off . . . the rich root of the cultivated olive tree"? Some argue that the only authentic Jew, as part of the remnant in this Christian dispensation, is the Jewish Christian. But if this is so, then what does Paul mean in Rom 11:18 when he exhorts the Gentile Christian, "Do not brag that you are better than those [cultivated] branches" that were broken off—the unbelieving

Jews—and then contemplates that "God has the power to graft them in again" (Rom 11:23)? How could he speak this way if these severed cultivated branches had lost all Jewish identity in the sight of God forever? Does not the context of these branches that were broken off indicate that, for all their carnality, rebelliousness, and unbelief, God still retains a distinctive loving interest in them, as Rom 11:28 appears to indicate?

Carnal Israel as God's Beloved Enemy in Romans 11:28

For all the expressed good intentions of those with historic Reformed convictions who hold to an Augustinian, amillennial eschatology and at the same time abide by the unqualified authority of Scripture, it is not always easy, by way of the primacy of exegesis, to unreservedly adhere to a confessional standard. This is especially the case when one considers the commitment of these same people to an integrated system of doctrine that is linked to a historic creedal lineage. Thus when a Christian becomes convinced of this body of Reformed doctrine that is renowned for adhering to a logical and systematic body of truth, it is inevitable that he will also become immersed in the history of European Christianity, especially that of the sixteenth to eighteenth centuries. To be sure, no child of God is immune from pitfalls concerning the logic of his doctrinal system. But belief in Calvinism, often called the doctrines of grace—although closely rooted in one of the most esteemed expositors of all time—finds itself integrated within a historic and scholastic environment. We have already noted how, in varying degrees, much of historic Reformed Christianity has been influenced by shades of Platonic, Aristotelean, and Stoic thought as channeled through the scholasticism of Augustine, Aquinas, Calvin, Turretin, Bavinck, Fairbairn, and others. Hence many have developed a commitment to systematic Reformed theology that tends to assume that this faithful corpus of biblical truth, as an interlocking whole, directs us in our theological exegesis of major texts. In other words, the tendency is to assume that the exegesis has already been masterfully achieved by the Reformed fathers, and thus their eschatology is equally as dependable as their soteriology. But I believe this conclusion is exegetically, ethically, and thus doctrinally flawed.

So on account of the Reformation's rediscovery of the gospel, many heirs of this emancipating heritage have erroneously tended to assume that the eschatology emanating from that era must also have been an equally authentic recovery according to Scripture. For centuries it was the accepted belief of Roman Catholicism that as the true church of Jesus Christ it was the new Israel, and this teaching survived in the Reformed community (see chapter 6).

Thus the Reformation did not involve an eschatological, biblical recovery according to the first and early second century, but rather it embraced a medieval inheritance that has produced shameful consequences. This is abundantly evident, with some exceptions, in the ongoing exegesis of the most important passage in the NT concerning the status of national Israel, namely, Romans 11. Certainly John Murray's break with Calvin at this point is one of these exceptions. As a student at Westminster Theological Seminary in California, I recall one professor indicating that considerable time elapsed between Murray's release of his two volumes on Romans due to his wrestling with the exegesis of chaps. 9–11.[1] Nevertheless, in the area of eschatology, by and large Reformed exegesis has tended to be influenced by a systematic theological tradition that must uphold a certain understanding of a passage of Scripture—otherwise a crack in the dike would result in an overwhelming flood of inevitable millennial truth. S. Lewis Johnson came to this conclusion in his study of Gal 6:16 when he considered the reasons that those of Reformed conviction so strenuously defend their belief that "the Israel of God" here is identical with the Christian Church (see chapter 10). With this in mind, we now consider Rom 11:28, a critical passage concerning God's present regard for national Israel. This verse declares that God continues to have a loving covenant regard for rebellious, alienated national Israel, represented by the figure of disciplined, detached, cultivated olive branches.

The Interpretation of Romans 11:28

Having argued in Rom 11:11–27 for the interplay that God has sovereignly ordained in history between Jews and Gentiles, the apostle brings his thoughts to a summary conclusion in vv. 28–29. An especially literal translation may be helpful, followed by the HCSB:

> On the one hand, according to the gospel, [they, unbelieving Israel, are] enemies for your [Gentiles'] sake; on the other hand, according to the

[1] Murray's commentary on Romans was published in stages: chaps. 1–8 in 1959, then chaps. 9–16 in 1965. Whereas his eventual conclusion anticipated an eschatological "mass" conversion of Jews being "Israel as a whole," that is, "the theocratic election," he refrained from using the term "nation" and discussing the territorial implications of his conclusion. See J. Murray, *The Epistle to the Romans* (Grand Rapids: Eerdmans, 1965), 2:91–103.

election [they, unbelieving Israel, are] beloved for the sake of the fathers, for irrevocable [i.e., not to be regretted or repented of] are the gifts and the calling of God.

Regarding the gospel, they are enemies for your advantage, but regarding election, they are loved because of their forefathers, since God's gracious gifts and calling are irrevocable.

The antithetical parallelism in v. 28 is exact and instructive.

On the one hand	according to the gospel	enemies [they the Jews] are for you [Gentiles]
kata men	*to euangelion*	*echthroi di' humas*
on the other hand	according to the election	beloved [they the Jews] are for the fathers.
kata de	*tēn eklogēn*	*agapētoi dia tous pateras*

The absence of a connective with the preceding context only enhances the climactic nature of these verses. Behind all of Paul's argument in Romans 11 is God's "covenant with them [Israel], when I take away their sins" (v. 27; see vv. 1,17) which references the new covenant promise of Jer 31:33–34. Here is the fundamental reason "all Israel will be saved" (v. 26) *en masse*, nationally, eschatologically (see chapter 10 for the exegesis of Romans 11). As Matt Waymeyer points out, "It is difficult—if not impossible—to understand these two clauses as describing the church. In what sense can those of the Body of Christ be described as the "enemies" of God?"[2]

The historic tension between Gentiles and Jews will be wondrously resolved in the process that God has ordained. On the one hand, according to the present gospel dispensation, "they," the unbelieving Jews, corporate Israel, not the remnant, are "enemies" for the sake of the Gentiles, the main audience that Paul addresses. That is, unbelieving Jews are passively "enemies" of God, in parallel with passively being "beloved" of God.[3] On the other hand, from the standpoint of "the election," that is, God's original, irrevocable choice of national Israel by pure grace according to divine foreknowledge (vv. 1–2; see Ps. 33:11–12; Isa 41:8–9; 44:1–2; Amos 3:2),[4]

---

[2] M. Waymeyer, "The Dual Status of Israel in Romans 11:28," *MSJ* (Spring 2005): 63.

[3] So Cranfield, Morris, Murray, Schreiner, though Moo suggests that both an active and passive sense is intended.

[4] Here "the election" is descriptive of "they" and thus the nation rather than a reference to the "remnant according to God's gracious choice" (v. 5). So Barrett, Cranfield, Haldane, Hodge, Moo, Morris, Murray, Schreiner, against Lenski, O. P. Robertson.

unbelieving Jews, just designated as "enemies," hence not referring to the remnant, are *at the same time* "beloved" on account of the original, irrevocable promise made to "the fathers"—Abraham, Isaac, and Jacob.[5]

An expanded translation of Rom 11:28–29 might be useful at this point:

> From the perspective of the gospel of the righteousness of God that saves both Jew and Gentile, the bulk of national Israel presently remains an enemy of God for the sake of the salvation of Gentiles throughout the world. However, from the perspective of God's original election of national Israel, still remaining in unbelief, at the same time this Hebrew people continues to be beloved for the sake of the unconditional Abrahamic covenant ratified to Isaac and Jacob. Therefore because of God's covenant integrity, the gospel gifts and the saving call of God directed toward national Israel, through promise given to Abraham, will not be repealed.

Thus Ronald Diprose concluded his careful study:

> In the light of the conclusion in v. 28, we can safely say that Paul also is confirming the election of Israel despite the nation's failure to recognize Jesus as their Messiah. Nothing, not even their opposition to the gospel, could cancel the special love of God for his people. It is this election of Israel which makes her eschatological salvation certain. Likewise, her status as an elect people explains why, in the present time, even in her unbelief, Israel contributes to the enrichment and the reconciliation with God of the other nations of the world (vv. 11–15).[6]

If one is committed to the position that God is no longer covenantally related to national Israel in the present, then how is this verse to be interpreted? Palmer Robertson, as before, attempted to identify those "beloved for the sake of the fathers" as being elect Jews, not unbelieving Israel in a national sense.[7] Amillennialist Lenski followed a similar interpretation,[8] although the overwhelming opinion of most commentators is that, as Barrett concluded, "They [Israel] are the *race* [emphasis added] whom God elected to be his peculiar people, and their election rests in no way on their merits or achievements."[9] Moo also states,

[5] Waymeyer pointed out that "Paul's use of the correlative conjunctions *[men . . . de]* indicates that these individuals were simultaneously 'enemies' and 'beloved,' not enemies for a time and then later beloved." Ibid., 65.

[6] R. E. Diprose, *Israel and the Church* (Waynesboro, GA: Authentic Media, 2000), 20–21.

[7] O. P. Robertson, *The Israel of God* (Phillipsburg, NJ: P&R, 2000), 190.

[8] R. C. H. Lenski, *The Interpretation of St. Paul's Epistle to the Romans* (Peabody, MA: Hendrickson, 2001), 732–33.

[9] C. K. Barrett, *The Epistle to the Romans* (New York: Harper & Row, 1957), 225. Likewise, Cranfield, Hodge, Moo, Morris, Murray, Shedd, Schreiner.

Some think, because of the way that Paul describes election in 9:6b–13—an act by which God brings people into relationship with himself—that Paul must be referring here to the remnant. But a switch in subject in mid-verse, from the Jews who are God's enemies in the light of the gospel, to Jews who are beloved by God as elect members of the remnant, seems unwarranted.[10]

The Eschatological Significance of Romans 11:28

Murray concluded his discussion of Rom 11:28, "Unfaithful as Israel have been and broken off for that reason, yet God still sustains his peculiar relation of love to them, a relation that will be demonstrated and vindicated in the restoration (vv. 12,15,26)."[11] VanGemeren wrote similarly, "In the sense of historic and national continuity, Israel is still the people of God, even in their rejection of Messiah."[12] David Holwerda also declared,

> We err if we assume that the significance of the remnant pertains only to the elect individuals who constitute the remnant. Paul is not implying that the remnant alone is Israel and no one else. If we assume that the people of God in Romans 11:1 is now restricted to the elect remnant, we under-cut the rest of Paul's argument. Nowhere in Romans 11 does the apostle withdraw from unbelieving Jewish Israel the reality of being the people of God or the fact of their election. Instead, Paul points to himself and other Jewish Christians as evidence that God has not withdrawn his grace from Jewish Israel. The remnant is a sign that God is still faithful to his election of Jewish Israel.[13]

All these declarations are good as far as they go, but they do not go far enough. Indeed most commentators who agree with Murray, VanGemeren, and Holwerda fail to unpack the significance of national Israel being now a "beloved enemy," that is, covenantally in the sight of God. It is as if they sense what Paul is saying from an exegetical perspective, yet for various pre-suppositional reasons refrain from confessing the outcome of this truth in terms of the course of church history and the future. The truth is that while God was graciously dealing with the Gentiles, unbelieving Jews continued to retain an identity in His sight that in fact Gentiles have been loathe to confess, but especially in the national and territorial spheres. Again we are faced with this limited, temporal acknowledgement of Jewishness that contemporary Jewishness can in no way rightly endure. Granted that there

---

[10] D. Moo, *The Epistle to the Romans* (Grand Rapids: Eerdmans, 1996), 731.

[11] Murray, *Romans*, 2:101.

[12] W. VanGemeren, *The Progress of Redemption* (Grand Rapids: Baker, 1995), 400.

[13] D. E. Holwerda, *Jesus and Israel: One Covenant or Two?* (Grand Rapids: Eerdmans, 1995), 164.

is mystery here, yet the Christian, who should be a student of history, cannot easily deny the continuing evidence of God's hovering concern over the Hebrew people as a nation concerning which He is both offended and covenantally gracious. J. C. Ryle explained this inescapable truth as follows:

> I assert then that the Jews are at this moment a peculiar people, and utterly separate from all other people on the face of the earth. They fulfill the prophecy of Hosea: "The children of Israel shall bide many days without a king, and without a prince, and without a sacrifice" (Hos. 3:4). For eighteen hundred years they have been scattered over the globe, without a country, without a government, without a capital city, strangers and aliens everywhere, often fiercely persecuted and vilely treated. Yet to this moment they continue a distinct, isolated and separate nation, far more than any nation on the earth.
>
> Now how shall we account for this extraordinary state of things? How shall we explain the unique and peculiar position which the Jewish people occupies in the world? Why is it that, unlike Saxons, and Danes, and Normans, and Flemings, and French, this singular race still floats alone, though broken to pieces like a wreck, on the waters of the globe, amidst its 1500 million inhabitants, and after the lapse of eighteen hundred years is neither destroyed, nor crushed, nor evaporated, nor amalgamated, not lost sight of; but lives to this day as separate and distinct as it was when the arch of Titus was built in Rome?
>
> I have not the least idea how questions like these are answered by those who profess to deny the divine authority of Scripture. In all my reading I never met with an honest attempt to answer them from the unhappy camp of unbelievers. In fact it is my firm conviction that among the many difficulties of infidelity there is hardly any one more really insurmountable than the separate continuance of the Jewish nation. It is a burdensome stone which your modern skeptical writers may affect to despise, but cannot lift or remove out of their way. God has many witnesses to the truth of the Bible, if men would only examine them and listen to their evidence. But you may depend on it there is no witness so unanswerable as one who always keeps standing up and living, and moving before the eyes of mankind. That witness is the Jew.[14]

In the light of the Paul's explicit teaching in Rom 11:28 concerning the present status of unbelieving Israel, Colin Chapman's brief confession is significant. His book *Whose Promised Land?* advocates replacement theology and, therefore, is not appreciated in Jewish Christian circles.[15] Nevertheless, he stated,

---

[14] J. C. Ryle, *Are You Ready for the End of Time?* (Fearn, Scotland: Christian Focus, 2001), 148–150; previously published as *Coming Events And Present Duties, and Prophecy.*

[15] D. Stern wrote, "Let them [Christians] not be taken in by Colin Chapman's book, *Whose Promised Land?*, which uses replacement theology as its basis for denying that the Land of Israel

Unlike some of my Arab and Western Christian friends, I still believe there
is something special about the Jewish people. "They are loved on account
of the patriarchs" (Rom. 11:28). But I also believe that the fulfillment of all
that was promised to Abraham and his descendants is found in the kingdom
of God which came in Jesus.[16]

Unfortunately, "something special" is not only left undefined but also quite
inadequate in explaining Paul's meaning here. To a considerable degree,
Chapman's mystery is really of his own making. Such a concession is almost grudging since, in the bulk of this author's writing, he is quite adamant in his denial of Israel's national and territorial identity. We are grateful for Chapman's patronizing honesty in the face of such a crucial text of
Scripture. Nevertheless, as a whole, his book in its several editions remains
theologically anti-Judaic.

Carnal Israel and the Spiritual Remnant
in God's Dealing with His People in General

We have already considered the "remnant according to God's gracious
choice" in Rom 11:5 and identified it as those Jewish Christians who are
circumcised in both body and soul. We have also seen that the bulk of unbelieving national Israel, although carnal in their unbelief, retains national
Jewish identity in the sight of God (Rom 11:28). However, consideration of
the historic origins of this truth, with regard to a godly remnant, is necessary in relation to God's dealings with national Israel as a whole in the OT,
especially concerning persistence in unbelief. The reason for this is that
it is often claimed that the only Jews of the old covenant era were those
who were of faith. By extension it is also claimed that unbelieving Jews

is any longer promised by God to the Jews" (*Restoring The Jewishness Of The Gospel* [Gaithers-
burg, MD: Jewish New Testament Publications, 1988], 40). Chapman denied his use of "replacement theology," explaining that "Gentiles are grafted *into* Israel (Rom. 11:17–24), which
is thereby transformed to become the 'one new humanity' (Eph. 2:15)" ("Ten Questions for a
Theology of the Land," in *The Land of Promise* [ed. P. Johnston and P. Walker; Downers Grove,
Ill.: InterVarsity, 2000], 178). Apart from the subtlety here whereby Jewishness nevertheless
ceases, Stern's objection is quite valid in the light of Chapman's plain statement: "As a Christian,
I feel bound to conclude that the promise of the land to Abraham and his descendants 'as an
everlasting possession' does not give the Jews a divine right to possess the land for all time. . . .
Could it be that God is challenging the whole Jewish people to think again about their destiny as
a people? What is the whole enterprise of settling Jews in the land and setting up a Jewish state
doing to the soul of Judaism? Did God really intend that they should be 'a peculiar people' for
ever and ever?" (*Whose Promised Land?* [Tring, Herts, England: Lion, 1983], 226–28).

[16] Chapman, "Ten Questions for a Theology of the Land," 178. This book is heavily slanted
against any premillennial understanding of Israel and the Jews.

today, being wholly carnal, are not Jews in the sight of God in any sense whatsoever.

The doctrine of the remnant in OT Israel has its origin in the idea of something left over from a large corporate body, as is suggested in Deut 4:26–27. Whereas the Jews as a whole were subject to considerable destruction in the land, they were also told that "the LORD will scatter you among the peoples, and you will be reduced to a few survivors among the nations where the LORD your God will drive you" (v. 27). In this instance Israel, as a diminished, scattered nation, at the same time became a remnant. Furthermore, the remnant idea also has reference to part of national Israel, that is, a relative minority of exiles who survived judgment and captivity in Babylon. Following mourning and repentance, they joyfully became returnees to Jerusalem under Zerubbabel, Ezra and Nehemiah (Ezra 9:8,13–15; Neh. 1:3; Jer 42:2; 50:19–20; Isa 10:20–22; 11:11–16). In turn, this also anticipates an eschatological remnant with regard to the Dispersion that will be gathered from the four corners of the earth for the Messianic age (Jer 31:7–8; Mic. 5:7–8; 7:18; Zech 8:6–12). Hence, in the OT, a repentant remnant returned to Jerusalem from Babylon, contrasted with the larger part of national Israel that remained as the exiled dispersion. So in the present, according to Rom 11:5, a remnant, a relatively small number of Jewish Christians, contrasts with the larger part of unbelieving Israel that remains dispersed throughout the world. But the question that must now be asked concerns God's attitude toward the nation of Israel as a whole, from its very inception as a nation and onward to the Babylonian captivity, and particularly with regard to its division according to carnal and spiritual lines. The answer that becomes so clear is that while God did sharply distinguish between carnal and spiritual characteristics, He nevertheless regarded even the carnal constituency as retaining national status. Several OT passages support this truth, which is maintained as a principle in the NT.

God's Dealing with Carnal Israel
in the Wilderness and Today

Almost immediately after their redemption from Egypt, the children of Israel repeatedly murmured against God and sinned before they reached Mount Sinai (Exod 15:22–24; 16:1–3; 17:1–3). For this reason the law "was added because of transgressions" (Gal 3:19, see Jer 11:7–8; Rom 5:20). The complaining continued after they left Sinai (Num 11:1–12:16) and led to a point of crisis at Kadesh-barnea. There, despite God's wrath against their further unbelief and rebellion (Num 14:1–10), He heeded the intercession of Moses (Num 14:11–19) and declared, "I have pardoned them as you requested" (v. 20). However, the resultant discipline was banishment of the original redeemed generation from entrance into the promised land and consequent wandering in the Sinai wilderness (vv. 22–23,26–37). Even so, the "faithful remnant," namely, the households of Joshua and Caleb, as well as the new generation (v. 31), were assured of settlement in Canaan (vv. 24,38). All this transpired in under two years, that is, from Israel's departure from Egypt up to Kadesh Barnea. Hence the 38 years that followed saw the nation of Israel wandering in the wilderness, this period commencing with the rebellion of Korah and a resultant plague whereby over 14,700 of God's people perished (Num 16:1–50). The actual wilderness wanderings from Kadesh Barnea, and eventually back to that same location, are briefly recorded in Numbers 15–19. Israel proceeded north to the plains of Moab, though murmuring, unbelief, and rebellion continued (20:1–5; 21:5). Especially notable was the deceitfulness of Balaam that resulted in national apostasy and judgment once again, this time by plague and the death of 24,000 of God's people. It is hardly possible to say that the new generation proved to be much better than the preceding fathers. Nevertheless, they gained entrance into the promised land.

In this OT setting it is readily obvious that God esteemed Israel after the Spirit, the remnant, and was vexed by Israel after the flesh, or the bulk of Israel. We might further say that Israel after the Spirit was the true Israel having circumcision of the heart as well as the flesh. But Israel after the flesh had only circumcision of the flesh and was simply carnal Israel. It would be totally incorrect to say that Israel after the flesh had no national or territorial identity in the sight of God in that historic setting. During the 40-year wilderness period Israel had an overarching national identity granted by Yahweh which, from the very beginning of Israel's redemption was based, not on the Mosaic, but the Abrahamic covenant. To begin with, this was clearly established before Moses had even encountered God at the burning bush near Mount Horeb. Then "God heard their [the Israelites'] groaning, and He remembered His covenant with Abraham, Isaac, and Jacob" (Exod 2:24). Once Moses stood barefooted before God on holy ground, Yahweh identified Himself according to the covenant: "I am the God of your father, the God of Abraham, the God of Isaac, and the God of Jacob" (Exod 3:6, see vv. 15–16; 4:5; 6:3). In particular, Moses was instructed to pass this on to Israel,

> I will take you as My people, and I will be your God. You will know that
> I am Yahweh your God, who delivered you from the forced labor of the
> Egyptians. I will bring you to the land that I swore to give to Abraham,
> Isaac, and Jacob, and I will give it to you as a possession. I am Yahweh.
> (Exod 6:7–8)

Even after Israel sinned under the leadership of Aaron by worshipping the
golden calf, and Moses' intercession before God was accepted, we are told,
"The LORD spoke to Moses: 'Go, leave here, you and the people you brought
up from the land of Egypt, to the land I promised to Abraham, Isaac, and
Jacob, saying: 'I will give it to your offspring'" (Exod 33:1).

So when Israel was about to cross the Jordan into Canaan, God instructed His people,

> You are not going to take possession of their [the Canaanites'] land be-
> cause of your righteousness or your integrity. Instead, the LORD your God
> will drive out these nations before you because of their wickedness, in
> order to keep the promise He swore to your fathers, Abraham, Isaac, and
> Jacob. Understand that the LORD your God is not giving you this good land
> to posses because of your righteousness, for you are a stiff-necked people
> (Deut 9:5–6).

Israel's possession of the land was to be based, not on obedience but on covenant promise alone. Significantly, Moses did not inherit the land, though
upon viewing it from the heights of Mount Nebo, "The LORD then said to
him, 'This is the land I promised Abraham, Isaac, and Jacob, 'I will give it
to your descendants.' I have let you see it with your own eyes, but you will
not cross into it'" (Deut 34:4). This should be sufficient indication that
those who did not enter the land because of unbelief ought not be sharply
contrasted with those who did eventually cross over Jordan. Those who did
enter the land were virtually as carnal as their descendants. Even Moses
did not cross over on account of former disobedience, though of course he
would ultimately partake of God's promise in the Messianic kingdom. The
basis then of entrance into the promised land was solely God's covenant
faithfulness, that is sovereign grace.

However, the main point here is that God's dealing with the nation of
Israel is not merely with the Israel after the Spirit, with the remainder having no identity in the sight of God. Israel after the flesh was still the recipient of God's covenant interest. Granted it was of this world, so to speak. But
this in no way nullifies the fact that God in human history had a covenantal
interest in the earthly nation of Israel in total, both spiritual and carnal. We
are repeatedly told that God's persistence with national Israel, from the very

beginning of its redemption, is for the sake of "Abraham, Isaac, and Jacob."
So we would conclude that it ought not to surprise us that in this present
age, while there is a "[Jewish Christian] remnant according to grace" (Rom
11:5), this language of necessity demands that there is an unbelieving national Israel that still has God's offended yet loving and steadfast covenant
interest, "for the sake of the fathers" (Rom 11:28).

In further consideration of the fact that unbelieving national Israel today retains God's covenantal interest, Dan Gruber noted from Rom 10:21–
11:2 that when Paul called himself "an Israelite," that is, a descendant of
Abraham through Benjamin, "he was "identifying himself with his unfaithful, physical brethren."

> Paul is pointing to his own relationship with God as proof of the fact that
> God has not cast off unfaithful Israel. For indeed, Paul himself was part of
> unfaithful Israel.[17]

Gruber further observed that "Israel" in 10:21 and 11:2 refers to physical Israel and includes the "disobedient and defiant," that is, unbelievers.
Nevertheless, Paul called them "His [God's] people." And the believing remnant, of which Paul considered himself a part, was a subset of "His people."

> The fact that the faithful in Israel are a "remnant of Israel" indicates that
> there is much more of Israel that is not faithful. Paul makes this quite
> clear. Otherwise, there could not be a remnant. Had "Israel" signified only
> the faithful, God's continual call to Israel throughout the Bible would not
> have been to repentance, but to perseverance. Paul said, "I could pray that
> I myself were anathema, separated from Messiah for the sake of my breth-
> ren, *my kinsmen according to the flesh, who are Israelites,* to whom belongs
> the adoption as sons and the glory and the covenants and the giving of
> the Law and the service and the promises, whose are the fathers, and from
> whom is the Messiah according to the flesh, who is over all God blessed
> forever. Amen" (Rom. 9:3–5). It is clear that he is talking about physical,
> natural Israel. It is impossible to understand his words differently. It is for
> his unbelieving Jewish brethren that Paul is willing to be anathema. It is
> from them that Messiah came. It is to them that the adoption, glory, and
> covenants, etc. belong. It is they who are Israelites. Had "Israel" signified
> the faithful only, there would have been no need for, and no sense to, Paul's
> "unceasing grief and continual sorrow," nor to his willingness to be ac-
> cursed for their salvation.[18]

[17] D. Gruber, *The Church and The Jews* (Hagerstown, MD: Elijah, 1997), 365.
[18] Ibid., 365–66.

God's Dealing with Carnal Israel in Hosea

The appropriateness of Hosea for the subject of God's dealing with spiritual and carnal Israel is twofold. First, as a prophet to the northern kingdom, he ministered in times when, although God's people prospered, their religious devotion was at best external (6:4–6; 7:8–10; 8:14; 10:1–2; 12:8; 13:15) and at worst pagan (4:11–14; 6:7–10; 13:1–2). Second, in the light of spiritual declension and even adultery, God remained covenantally faithful in being wedded to Israel as a nation (1:10–11; 2:14–23; 3:1–5; 11:8–11; 14:4–8). The prospect was not merely the saving of a remnant, for nowhere in Hosea is a remnant mentioned. Rather it is the nation as a whole that is both an "enemy" of God and "beloved" by God, even as is the case in Rom 11:28. The triumph of pure grace is such that although God has become wedded to "an adulterous" people (3:1), the people of Israel will return and seek the LORD their God and David their king. They will come with awe to the LORD and to His goodness in the last days" (Hos. 3:4–5). The reason for this prophetic illustration of the truth that ultimately "all Israel will be saved" (Rom 11:26) concerns Hosea's closing declaration from the Lord: "I will heal their apostasy; I will freely love them, for My anger will have turned from him" (Hos. 14:4). This is really identical with Paul's declaration that unbelieving, adulterous Israel, is "loved because of their forefathers" (Rom 11:28), and for this reason, with absolute certainty, "the Liberator will come from Zion; He will turn away godlessness from Jacob" (v. 26).

God's Dealing with Carnal and Remnant Israel in Micah

Micah's appropriateness for the subject of God's dealing with spiritual and carnal Israel is threefold. First, as a prophet primarily ministering to the southern kingdom of Judah, he encountered times that saw the common people harassed by foreign enemies, impoverished, and insecure. While the wealthy class and religious establishment fostered carnal security, injustice, and oppression of the poor in particular, at the same time they continued to participate in mere formal religion (Mic 2:1–2,8–9; 3:1–12; 6:6–8,10–12; 7:1–6). Thus Micah declared that judgment was inevitable (1:5–7; 2:3–5; 6:13–16). Second, in the light of overall spiritual poverty, God remained covenantally faithful in view of his inevitable future triumph and redemption through the promised Messiah (5:1–5). Third, unlike Hosea, a distinction is made between a faithful remnant from the judgment of captivity (2:12–13; see Isa 10:20–22), and the nation of Israel as a whole that was exiled. Further, in the future there will be another "remnant of Jacob [that] will be among many peoples like dew from the LORD" (5:7; see Rom 11:5) having originated from the coming of Messiah (5:1–5). But for the present, Micah identified himself as part of the remnant in his time by means of the confession of sin and this confident assertion:

> But as for me, I will look to the LORD; I will wait for the God of my salvation. My God will hear me. . . . Because I have sinned against Him, I must endure the LORD's rage until He argues my case and establishes justice for me. He will bring me into the light; I will see His salvation (7:7,9).

Concerning the note of expectation here, Micah had earlier described the eschatological hope of national restoration (Mic. 2:12–13). But there is anticipation of the Messianic age incorporating a regenerate Israel who will "walk in the name of Yahweh our God" (4:5) and will be headquartered in restored Zion. Micah 4:1–5 describes the future distinctive glory of national Israel over against "peoples" and "nations" who will "stream" to "the house of the God of Jacob," and "instruction will go out of Zion and the word of the LORD from Jerusalem." This glory is further expounded at the close of Micah's prophecy. The prophet describes the reversal of circumstances with regard to the Gentiles and God's children of Jacob.

> Nations will see and be ashamed of all their power. They will put their hands over their mouths, and their ears will become deaf. They will lick the dust like a snake; they will come trembling out of their hiding places like reptiles slithering on the ground. They will tremble in the presence of Yahweh our God; they will stand in awe of You. Who is a God like You, removing iniquity and passing over rebellion for the remnant of His inheritance? He does not hold on to His anger forever, because He delights in faithful love. He will again have compassion on us; He will vanquish our iniquities. You will cast all our sins into the depths of the sea. You will show loyalty to Jacob and faithful love to Abraham, as You swore to our fathers from days long ago (7:16–20).

Clearly national Israel in these two passages in Micah has an identity that is distinct from the nations. It is the people of "Jacob" according to God's "faithful [covenant] love to Abraham" (7:20). While the spiritual remnant who eventually returned to Jerusalem continued as the perpetuated core of the nation, God will also continue to acknowledge the carnal remainder that would eventually be dispersed. Throughout the centuries subsequent to AD 70, there has always been a remnant of unbelieving Jews in the land, notwithstanding Arab dominion. But the Dispersion is also described as the remnant (Isa 11:11; Jer 23:3). As Scripture abundantly teaches, even the Dispersion is not to be spurned forever (Isa 11:11; 14:1; Jer 16:14; 23:3; 24:6–9; Ezek 37:21,25; 39:28; Amos 9:14–15; Zech 10:10). God promised the remnant, "Then I will pour out a spirit of grace and prayer on the house of David and the residents of Jerusalem, and they will look at Me whom they pierced. They will mourn for Him as one mourns for an only child and weep bitterly for Him as one weeps for a firstborn" (Zech 12:10). Then according to Rom 11:12, the remnant will eventually become part of the "full number" of Israel when "all Israel will be saved" (v. 26).

Carnal Israel as "Israel after the flesh"

In Rom 1:3 Paul referred to Jesus Christ as "a descendant of David according to the flesh." In 1 Cor 10:18 Paul declares, "Look at the people of Israel" (lit. "Look at Israel according to the flesh"). The HCSB correctly translates the phrase as designating the historic or physical nation of Israel. There is no intimation here concerning national Israel's lack of spiritual life. However, the physical Jewish emblem of circumcision is used in Scripture as a distinguishing feature in the contrasting realms of the flesh and the Spirit. God associated Israel's unfaithfulness with "their uncircumcised hearts" (Lev 26:41). To national Israel circumcised in the flesh, Moses declared

> And now, Israel, what does the LORD your God ask of you except to fear the LORD your God by waking in all His ways, to love Him, and to worship the LORD your God with all your heart and all your soul. . . . Therefore, circumcise your hearts and don't be stiff-necked any longer (Deut 10:12,16).

Jeremiah similarly exhorted the nation of Judah, "Circumcise yourselves to the LORD; remove the foreskin of your hearts, men of Judah and residents of Jerusalem. Otherwise, My wrath will break out like fire and burn with no one to extinguish it because of your evil deeds" (Jer 4:4). In all these instances, there is not the slightest intimation that God ceased to recognize Israel's national identity, notwithstanding carnality and consequent discipline. We will see Paul's use of the same dichotomy in Rom 2:25–29.

Circumcision—Significant, not Effectual
Romans 2:25

Having just argued in Rom 2:17–24 that possessing the law did not make someone righteous before God, in vv. 25–29 Paul argues the same point regarding circumcision. An observer of Paul's confrontation with the Jews in vv. 17–24 might well ask, "How is it possible for Jews to so shamelessly maintain their proud self-esteem and nationalism in the face of such deplorable condemnation by the Gentiles?" For example, in v. 24 Paul charges his countrymen, "The name of God is blasphemed among the Gentiles because of you." Our question may be answered in a word—circumcision. Whereas the current teaching was that "no person who is circumcised will go down to Gehenna [hell or the lake of fire]," [19] so Paul here commences to destroy the religious hypocrite's last bastion, namely, sacramental, ritual, covenantal regeneration. Paul commences with the bold statement, "For circumcision benefits you if you observe the law, but if you are a lawbreaker, your circumcision has become uncircumcision" (v. 25).

Some background on circumcision is called for here. According to Gen 17:9–14, circumcision was ordained by God as signification of the covenant He had made with Abraham and his subsequent *seed*. For this reason the *seed organ* was cut. At that same time, the name "Abram," meaning "exalted father," was appropriately changed to "Abraham," meaning "father of a multitude" (Gen 17:5). As a modern conservative Jew put it, "For Jews circumcision today, as in the past four thousand years, is not a detail of hygiene. It is the old seal of the pledge between Abraham and his Creator, a sign in the flesh, a mark at the source of life." [20] But even Jeremiah became aware that a physically circumcised Hebrew could still be "uncircumcised in heart" (Jer 9:25–26) and therefore be subject to punishment. [21]

Circumcision is "significant," that is, it is an authentic "sign" when it points to an authentic practicer of the Law. But for the lawless, circumcision has no significance and is invalidated; it is certainly not regenerative. In Rom 4:9–12 Paul explains that Abraham was justified through faith, and hence regenerated, before he was circumcised. So Paul is *not* repudiating circumcision as a sign of national Jewish identity, as 3:1–2 plainly indicates. Rather he is negating a delusive function of circumcision that never really existed.

Circumcision as Significant for Gentiles
Romans 2:26–27

The implications of this right teaching on circumcision are encouraging for Gentiles. The alternative is that uncircumcised Gentiles would be

---

[19] Moo, *Epistle to the Romans*, 167; also C. Hodge, *Epistle to the Romans* (Grand Rapids: Eerdmans, 1968), 63.

[20] H. Wouk, *This Is My God* (Garden City, NY: Doubleday, 1959), 140.

[21] See the argument of J. M. Hamilton Jr. that circumcision of the heart refers to regeneration (*God's Indwelling Presence*, NACSBT [Nashville, B&H Academic, 2006], esp. 41–54).

excluded from the favor and grace of God because of an absent physical qualification.

Gentile Obedience as Circumcision, v. 26.

"Therefore if an uncircumcised man keeps the law's requirements, will his uncircumcision not be counted as circumcision?" Paul hypothetically refers to a Gentile who keeps the law, an uncircumcised God-fearer who reveres and obeys the Mosaic law, such as Cornelius (Acts 10:1–2; see 13:26). How then is he to be regarded? God will credit circumcision to him, even as any fair minded observer ought to do, because God regards the doing of righteousness as the justifying evidence of his sonship. He may not have the fleshy circumcision of Abraham, but he is nevertheless a child of Abraham because he does "what Abraham did" (John 8:39) and therefore evidences circumcision of the heart.

Gentile Obedience Shaming the Transgressor, v. 27.

"A man who is physically uncircumcised, but who fulfills the Law, will judge you who are a lawbreaker in spite of having the letter of the law and circumcision." If a Gentile has a heart for God, a heart that is alive to God, that loves God, that yearns to please God with holy affections, then he is circumcised in heart even though he is physically uncircumcised. Consequently this man is the judge of the ungodly, circumcised Jew, since, by example, he reflects shame on him and lays bare the hypocrisy of mere legal conformity (Matt. 8:5–13, especially vv. 10–12).

The word "judge" is emphatic here and is in contrast with the Jew who has "the letter of the law" by which he is quick to judge. Such a circumcised religionist has the Bible in his hand and mind, intellectual proficiency, doctrinal comprehension, and an attitude that is quick to judge, yet his disgraceful godlessness will reap severe condemnation by the mere presence of the godly Gentile, without a word being spoken (see Phil 3:2–3). By way of illustration, in an office situation, the unbaptized member of The Salvation Army who manifests genuine graces of the Spirit will stand out in obvious silent judgment on the baptized Baptist who manifests the works of the flesh.

Circumcision as Significant for the Real Jew
Romans 2:28–29

The definition of an authentic Jew, especially for Paul here, is a matter of varying opinions according to conservative Christians. Some suggest that in this church age, it is the true Christian who is now the real and only spiritual Jew, and that since God has finished forever with Israel as a nation, there is no such thing in His sight as a national Jew. This is *not* what Paul had in mind in Rom 2:28–29, especially in the light of 3:1–2 (see 11:1–36; Acts 22:3; Gal 6:16). A genuine Jew is one who, having been circumcised in his heart, is also circumcised in his flesh, and he identifies geographically with those of the same commitment (see 9:6). In this respect circumcision has not been abrogated.

Circumcision Does not Signify a Real Jew (v. 28). "For a person is not a Jew who is one outwardly, and true circumcision is not something visible in the flesh." A more literal translation would be, "For not the one in the outward manifestation is [essentially] a Jew, neither is the one in the outward manifestation in fleshy circumcision." What is it that essentially identifies a Jew? Negatively, it is not any outward religious ceremony, not even the physical rite of circumcision. But this does not mean that formal circumcision itself has been eliminated (Rom 3:1–2; Acts 16:3). Such a rite identifies a profession, that is, the godly expression of the heart circumcised by the Holy Spirit, as v. 29 makes clear.

Circumcision Does Signify a Circumcised Jewish Heart (v. 29). "On the contrary, a person is a Jew who is one inwardly, and circumcision is of the heart—by [or "in"] the Spirit, not the [outwardly performed] letter. His praise is not from men, but from God [who knows his heart]." The *sine qua non* of true Jewishness is "heart circumcision," and its divine operation is "by the Spirit."[22] In such a case, the true Jew receives his affirmation of Jewishness from God, which for him is what really matters, and not as was commonly sought in Paul's time according to "the letter," the praise of man (John 5:41–44). Above all else, a true Jew has a heart that is made by God, owned of God, and consecrated to God.

Carnal Israel as a Present Reality in the Personal Testimony of Paul

On several occasions the apostle Paul declared himself to be a Jew. In the temple precincts of Jerusalem, the chained apostle implored a Roman commander, who had arrested him, that he be allowed to address an enraged Jewish crowd. He argued, "I am a Jewish man from Tarsus of Cilicia" (Acts

---

[22] This option is more probable than "in the spirit," though L. Morris considered that "either way gives good sense (see 7:6; 2 Cor. 3:6–7)" (*The Epistle to the Romans* [Grand Rapids: Eerdmans, 1988], 142). "Spirit" is supported by Calvin, Hodge, Moo, Morris, Murray, Schreiner; "spirit" by Barrett, Haldane, Lloyd-Jones, Shedd.

21:39). His request having been granted, Paul then addressed the crowd in Hebrew, but again declared, "I am a Jewish man, born in Tarsus of Cilicia" (Acts 22:3). Further, in Rom 11:1 Paul declared, "I am an Israelite." In all three instances the present tense of the verb *eimi*, "I am," is significant. In Rom 9:3–4 Paul lovingly wrote of "my brothers, my own flesh and blood. They are Israelites." Here again the present tense is used. Concerning this Schreiner commented that "the Jews still 'are' Israelites and that all the blessings named still belong to them."[23] Such a conclusion has profound ramifications with regard to the present validity of Jewish ethnicity, nationality, and territory.

Hence it is obvious that the apostle regarded his Jewishness as a continuing reality, both with regard to himself as a Jewish Christian as well as his kinship with unbelieving Jewish brethren. This was no mere token confession. Paul acknowledged that the unbelieving Jew has present authenticity with regard to the full meaning of Jewishness. He clearly upheld this vital truth, not merely for the cause of secular convenience, but because of his bona fide identification as a fellow Israelite with "the adoption, the glory, the covenants, the giving of the law, the temple service, and the promises" (Rom 9:4). This is not the language of superseded Judaism.

[23] T. R. Schreiner, *Romans* (Grand Rapids: Baker, 1998), 485.

Chapter 12

ISRAEL IN NEED OF THE PRODIGAL GENTILE'S LOVE

The parable of the Prodigal Son in Luke 15:11–32 is part of an illustrative trilogy that is based on Jesus Christ's confrontation with complaining Pharisees and scribes. These self-righteous Jewish zealots, having audited Jesus' teaching and social lifestyle, were complaining, "This man welcomes sinners and eats with them!" (Luke 15:1–2). In response, there follow three parables that all depict the Son of God's compassionate interest in the saving of the lost, they being represented by the Lost Sheep, the Lost Coin, and the Lost Sons. Obviously Jesus is not only justifying his ministry, but also indicating that both the leaders of Israel, as well as his disciples, should have the same merciful attitude. Therefore the interpretation of these three parables should be based on this one underlying theme. When the parable of the Prodigal Son is considered, though it is really concerned with two lost sons, two main approaches have been followed. First, there is simply the representation of God's fatherly love for a wayward member of His human family. Here an earthly father longs for the return of his rebellious son, and with largeness of heart is ready to forgive when eventually confronted with thoroughgoing contrition. But the father's eager desire to joyously celebrate such authentic repentance is especially noted. By way of contrast, the elder brother represents that hard-heartedness which self-righteousness engenders. He lacks God's tender concern for the lost and His readiness to forgive. Second, there is the more intriguing understanding of the prodigal son who, representing the Gentiles, sins with abandon in the world at large. However, the elder brother, depicting the Jews, is indignant that his younger brother's flagrant, persistent decadence should receive such an abundance of grace while he considers himself to have been consistently righteous. This latter view is presented by Richard C. Trench in his classic volume, *Notes on the Parables of Our Lord*, in which he provides a significant concluding application:

> We Gentiles must not forget that at the end of the present dispensation all will be reversed, and that we shall be in danger of playing the part of the elder brother, and shall do so if we grudge at the largeness of the grace bestowed upon the Jew, who is now feeding upon husks, far away from his Father's house.[1]

---

[1] R. C, Trench, *Notes on the Parables of Our Lord* (Grand Rapids: Baker, 1968), 152.

How appropriate is this comment in terms of the attitude of many conservative evangelicals today, especially of Reformed convictions, toward the ethnic Jew and national Israel. The disposition of the elder brother was not only one of contempt for his kinsman in the flesh, but he was also of the opinion that his brother was beyond redemption and thus permanently cast aside from his father's home. Certainly the Jews of Jesus' time were contemptuous in their regard for the Gentiles. But how strange it is that today so many Gentile Christians, and hardly any Jewish Christians, are of the opinion that now it is the Jews that are beyond redemption and forever cast aside by the Father in heaven. On the part of some Gentile Christians, their attitude toward ethnic Jews and national Israel is literally disgraceful. Like the elder brother, they are void of grace and full of condemnation toward their kinsmen in a spiritual sense (Gal 3:29), even to the degree where their theological anti-Judaism is in danger of becoming ethnic. As has already been demonstrated, much literature in this realm is, to say the least, offensive and utterly unchristian (see chapters 2, 3, and 4). Other Christians, less animated and vociferous in this regard, are nevertheless indifferent to ethnic Israel. There is no compassionate interest in the plight of the Jews, no inward sympathy for their historic tribulations, no admittance of widespread complicity on the part of Christianity with regard to these sufferings, no special interest in Jewish missions, but only a resignation that the judgment of God is rightly having its unwavering course.

The Admonition of Paul toward the Gentiles in Romans 11:17–21,31

In Romans 11 as a whole, the main thrust of the apostle's instruction concerning Israel is toward the Gentiles. The Gentile "wild olive branch" has been graciously grafted into "the rich root of the cultivated olive tree" (Rom 11:17) at the expense of disobedient Israel's temporal severance. Consequently the Gentile Christians are exhorted that they "do not brag" (v. 18) because they are better off than the cultivated branches that are presently scattered, that is, the unbelieving Jews as Dispersion. There is no place here for pride or arrogance because "[cultivated Jewish] branches were broken off [by unbelief] so that I [as a Gentile Christian] might be grafted in" (v. 19).[2] Commentators generally agree that here the Gentiles

[2] According to Moo, "these Gentile believers were apparently convinced that they belonged to a new people of God that had simply replaced Israel. . . . It is the egotism of Gentile Christians who present God's manifold plan as having the salvation of themselves as its focus that Paul wishes to expose and criticize" (*The Epistle to the Romans* [Grand Rapids: Eerdmans, 1996],

are encouraged to be compassionate toward the Jews while dispersed, notwithstanding their entrenched unbelief. So while in v. 30 the Gentile unbeliever has received gospel mercy at the expense of national Israel's unbelief, "now" (v. 31) the Gentile Christian is to show gospel mercy to unbelieving national Israel. However, the context of vv. 17–21 suggests that not only the primacy of evangelistic proclamation toward the Jews is involved, but also a comprehensive, loving attitude. In Rom 15:26–27 Paul encouraged the giving of material support for "the poor among the saints in Jerusalem" out of a sense of spiritual indebtedness. This would also suggest the related compassionate interest that Gentile Christians, after the manner of Cornelius (Acts 10:1–2), should spontaneously reflect toward the unbelieving, downtrodden Jews in their universal misery. Hence, although Jewish evangelism is to be of fundamental concern for the Christian, it is not to be at the neglect of material, social, and national support.

The Dilemma that Romans 11 Brings to Anti-Judaism

Is it possible for such compassionate concern about the Jews to be constrained by means of doctrine that regards Jewishness and national Judaism as passé? If a Christian's eschatology leads him to believe that Israel has been divinely, eternally disenfranchised, then is it possible for such teaching to engender a distinctive loving interest in the plight of the Jewish people as they presently exist? In this regard, history sadly witnesses to the fact that, in general, Gentile Christians have responded with shameful disdain that has included contempt, arrogant aloofness and even militant opposition to the Jew. Furthermore, the roots of this disregard for the mandate of Rom 11:17–21,31 have proved to be decidedly doctrinal. Melanie Phillips as a columnist for the London *Daily Mail* reported opposition to Israel being motivated by anti-Semitism that is deeply rooted in Christian replacement theology rather than economic and cultural factors (see appendix D). This is no mere isolated instance of eschatology effecting an unethical response, as Augustine's influence on subsequent centuries so well illustrates.

To clarify again, by "theological anti-Judaism" I mean that understanding of the present NT age in which the Christian Church is now alleged to have superseded or fulfilled the OT people of God. As a result, it is asserted

704–5). Murray similarly viewed Paul as admonishing the Gentiles since a "streak of contempt for the Jew may also be detected" (*The Epistle to the Romans* [Grand Rapids: Eerdmans, 1965], 2:87).

that covenantally, *in the sight of God*, there is now no such person as a "Jew" or "Hebrew" with distinctive national and territorial identity. This is true for many Christian writers who, while giving token recognition of Jews in contemporary society, as with Burge, Robertson, Chapman, and Sizer, nevertheless censure any who identify contemporary Israel with the biblical nation. Alternative expressions of "transference," "absorption," or "fulfillment" concerning Israel's lost national status still result in Jewish nullification. According to this anti-Judaic Augustinian perspective, although there are presently several million "Jews" in Israel—and for practical purposes only they are designated as "Jews," and we converse with them and witness to them in America and the United Kingdom—in theological reality and according to NT revelation their racial claim has no present or prospective divine validity. Rather, in a shadowy sense only, the Christian Church has inherited this past Jewish legacy including its terminology, so as to become the spiritual New Israel. As a result, every believer in Jesus as the Christ, of whatever nationality, is a spiritual Jew. The people of Christ throughout the world, void of ethnic distinctions, have become His new nation which, in inheriting the whole earth as the fulfilled land, is the truly ecumenical kingdom of God.

Yet how do the proponents of this supercessionist agenda respond toward the modern Jew who, in all honesty, is offended at this denial, indeed usurpation, of his Jewishness? It is rarely with the gracious, eschatological spirit of Paul's exhortation in Romans 11, especially vv. 17–21,31, according to careful, Judeo-centric exegesis which, as previously explained, resulted in a multitude of problems for the modern Augustinian. The humble confession of C. E. B. Cranfield, quoted at the beginning of this work (see "Personal Introduction") in relation to Romans 11, is especially pertinent here.

The Directional Challenge that Romans 11 Brings to Anti-Judaism

Such is the force of this key passage with regard to the future of Israel that many modern commentators have increasingly come to the opinion that Rom 11:26 does indeed refer to a future conversion of the Jews on a national, or at least a climactic, multitudinous scale.[3] Yet others of Reformed convictions have believed that the salvation of Israel here is merely the cumulative saving of a "Jewish" remnant over many centuries, though this interpretation, even if vociferously expressed, has not gained a broad fol-

---

[3] So Barrett, Hodge, Moo, Morris, Murray, and Schreiner.

lowing.[4] In this regard, there has also been a turning from Calvin's understanding of both saved Jews and Gentiles within the church who are designated as the "all Israel [that] will be saved" (see chapters 10 and 11 for a more detailed study). Yet having said this, at the same time many sense a dilemma that is not so readily clarified. With regard to Reformed convictions, there is often no indication whether this future *en masse* conversion of Jews, revealed in Romans 11, will incorporate divinely acknowledged individual, national, and territorial Jewishness. But denial of this is often intimated. Hence there is reluctance to admit that such an awakening will be nationally allied to the inhabitation of the land of Israel. One gains the impression that some scholars, their doctrine excluding the divine recognition of national and territorial Israel in the present or future Christian era, nevertheless sense being eschatologically driven in this direction through the plain meaning of Romans 11. They sense that the tendency here is to lead, as it were, down a slippery slope toward an acknowledgment of a distinct national and territorial destiny for Israel that is inevitably related to much that the OT has specifically promised. Consequently, while some attempt to allow a degree of temporary, vague corporateness in a future conversion of the "Jews," whatever this term may mean, nevertheless they put the brakes on when national and territorial identity seems to appear on the horizon as an inevitable consequence. And this restraint, I suggest, leads to some difficulty in spontaneous witnessing to Jews. The reason is that though a future climactic conversion of the "Jews" is anticipated, there is obfuscation with regard to affirming any specific eschatological future for the converted Jew, other than vague incorporation into the people of God. And the Jew who knows his OT well cannot be blamed for making reference to the prophets at this juncture. Having accepted the plain fulfillment of the numerous messianic prophecies, he then inquires as to why he ought not similarly accept the plain and obvious meaning of passages such as Ezekiel 36–37 and Zechariah 14 (see Horatius Bonar's response to this inquiry in chapter 8).

The Dynamic Challenge that Romans 11
Brings to Anti-Judaism

For the classic, theologically anti-Judaic Christian who places great store in his allegiance to Augustinianism with regard to the Jews, there is a

---

[4] So Bavinck, Berkhof, Hendriksen, and Hoekema, especially according to a Dutch Reformed lineage.

significant problem which he especially has to face in the light of Romans
11. He is ready to confess his responsibility for proclaiming Jesus as the
Messiah, even to those who mistakenly claim divine national identification as a Jew. After all, the exuberance and priority of Paul in this regard
is hard to avoid as a model for contemporary Christians. Hence he will
even declare that surely God has His people among unbelieving Jews, and
in designating them as the remnant of Rom 11:5, he then explains that for
this reason there must be evangelism directed toward the Jews. Ambrose,
Chrysostom, Augustine, and Luther were of a similar opinion! But in allowing the identification of resultant new converts as Jewish Christians in
a nominal sense, he is quick to deny them divine national and territorial
recognition. In fact, if pressed, he confesses that this new Jewish Christian
really has no distinctive Jewishness whatsoever, at least in connection with
divine OT terms.

In other words, this modern Augustinian speaks of these converted
Jews in an individual, token sense, but disallows historic Jewish corporate identity. He also believes that the non-Christian Jew has in fact no
real Jewishness, even in a carnal sense. Privately he believes that God has
abandoned Judaism so as never again to revive it. He is convinced that
the contemporary Jew is deceived, being a racial anachronism, though for
witnessing purposes, and at a strictly secular or social level, he ought to be
addressed as a "Jew." With this attitude in mind, the question then arises
as to what degree he really has a distinct passion for Jewish missions like
that of Paul (Rom 9:1–5; 10:1–2), who continued to identify himself, quite
unambiguously, as an Israelite (Acts 21:39; 22:3; Rom 11:1; 2 Cor 11:22)?
In fact, when it comes to a history of distinctive Jewish missions over the
last two hundred years, it stands out most plainly that agency after agency
has always doctrinally presupposed ongoing and eschatological Jewish
national, territorial identity according to God's covenant faithfulness. But
where has there been a similar burgeoning of evangelistic outreach toward
the Jews based on that contrasting Augustinian doctrine which upholds
Jewishness as a mere shadow that has been superseded by the substance of
Christianity? And which of these missionary scenarios most closely mir-
rors the missionary priority of Paul?[5] Of course there may be the response
by the Augustinian Christian that while he is second to none in concern for
evangelistic outreach, yet he believes it should be non-discriminatory—to
both Jew and Gentile without distinction. We would inquire what expla-

---

[5] For a more detailed consideration of this issue see B. E. Horner, "Evangelism and the Future of Israel," in a festschrift for Moise Rosen to be published in 2008.

nation is to be given for the fact that Paul's evangelistic thrust, Gentile by divine vocation, was always prioritized in terms of being "first to the Jew" (Rom 1:16; 2:9,10; see Acts 9:15)?[6]

As a representation of this problem with regard to formal expressions of interest in Jewish evangelism, consider the comments of Marten Woudstra of Calvin Theological Seminary who, in upholding continuity with regard to Israel and the subsequent Christian church, makes a number of comments that are quite representative of Augustinian, supercessionist eschatology. His words also reflect an essential detachment from divinely acknowledged, contemporary Jewishness. In consideration of Rom 11:25–26, he concluded,

> The apostle's emphasis is not upon some later point in time when there will be a reversal in the hardening in part of the Jews. Rather, the emphasis is upon the word "so" or "thus," "in this way." All Israel [the accumulating remnant] will be saved in the way of the bringing in of the fullness of the Gentiles. . . . As the fullness of the Gentiles is brought in and "until" this is finished, so, in this manner, "all Israel" [an accumulating remnant] will be saved. . . . There will be one body of the redeemed, Christ's flock, known to him by name and distinguished from those who are not his sheep. . . . The saving of "all Israel" is still going on, for the fullness of the Gentiles is also still being brought in. But at all events some of the Jews who are now hardened in part will be grafted into the one olive tree. They will not form a separate program or a separate entity next to the church.
>
> The question whether it is more proper to speak of a replacement of the Jews by the Christian church or of an extension (continuation) of the OT people of God into that of the NT church is variously answered. . . . What should be stated clearly, however, is that the idea of the church replacing Israel is not to be understood as a form of advanced anti-Semitism, as is done by some.[7]

There seems to be an underlying concern in Woudstra's final comment that betrays an inherent weakness of the doctrine being proposed. It could never be said that Paul's eschatological teaching in Romans concerning Israel might be misunderstood as having an anti-Judaic tone. Quite the contrary. Of course what Woudstra failed to make clear is the status of unbelieving Jews at the present time; one suspects it is not the covenantal regard of Rom 11:28 that inevitably calls for national and territorial recognition, even in unbelief. This being the case, any talk concerning "Jews" is simply

---

[6] See A. G. Fruchtenbaum, "Romans 1:16—To the Jew First," n.p. [cited July 2007]. Online: http://www.lcje.net/bulletins/2006/85/85_01.html.

[7] M. H. Woudstra, "Israel and the Church: A Case for Continuity," in *Continuity and Discontinuity* (ed. J. S. Feinberg; Westchester, Illinois: Crossway Books, 1988), 236–37.

with regard to a convenient term that in fact has no divine specificity or authentication. So the Jew, having become converted, loses all his Jewishness. Yet at the end of his explanation, Woudstra made a plea for Jewish evangelism: "The church-and-Israel question presents all evangelicals, regardless of where they stand with respect to any of the above questions, with the challenge to preach the gospel to the Jews."[8]

But is this expression driven by the same pro-Judaic passion of Paul, or a cool acknowledgment of the broad need of Jews and Gentiles to hear the gospel? What exactly, eschatologically and evangelistically, is Woudstra's meaning of "Jews" here? At best it would seem to have mere nominal, token meaning. His approach suggests that in witnessing to Jews, it is a most vital matter whether we tell them of the "good news" that they, in becoming a Christian, will lose their distinct Jewish identity, or whether we direct them to the King of the Jews as "the hope of Israel" (Acts 28:20). We suggest that the former approach will not gain much of a hearing, to say the least. But the latter method, far more akin to the eagerness of Paul in his missionary visits to innumerable synagogues, is much more likely to result in a respectful audience.

Two Analogies concerning Gentile Interest in the Unbelieving Jew

It is common for the Augustinian Christian to critically respond that the pro-Judaic Christian aligns himself with those who, in their "carnal Zionist zeal," neglect evangelism due to a preoccupation with Middle Eastern political affairs and prophetic speculation. After all, the Jew, in rejecting Jesus as the Messiah, is, according to that same Messiah, consigned to certain judgment (Luke 23:28). It was indeed Jesus who solemnly declared to the Jews of His day, "Unless you believe that I am [the Messiah/Son of God], you will die in your sins" (John 8:24). The Jew has to be warned concerning the grave danger that confronts his soul, and with this no evangelistic outreach worthy of the qualifying title of "Jewish" would disagree. But as Gentiles, how do we fulfill the burden of this responsibility for Jewish missions? Is it with the constraint of gratitude for the legacy that the Jew represents (Rom 9:4–5)? Is it with appreciation that the Savior is fully Jewish? Is it with respect for the truth that the Christian Bible is mostly Jewish? Or is it with a more dispassionate attitude that merely includes "Jewishness" as a temporary accommodating term within one's Augustinian eschatology?

[8] Ibid.

The Analogy of the Christian and the Family Unbeliever

By way of illustration, suppose as a Christian we have unbelieving loved ones and family members to whom we have witnessed on numerous occasions. Our soul aches with concern for a mother, father, sister, or brother who with stubborn unbelief does not hesitate to scoff at our faith, caricaturing it as a religious crutch and an anachronism. Such reproach within the family circle may persist for many years. Do we likewise believe in this situation that such relatives will "die in their sins" if they don't believe that Jesus Christ is their Savior? Yes, we do believe this with both love and fear. But how do we continue to relate to these beloved relatives? After such a long time of rejection, is it with eventual abandonment since they have become so hard-hearted? Having prayed for them, do we then eventually give up on them before God's throne of grace? No, such a limitation of our patience is unthinkable when we contemplate God's great forbearance toward us. While we have life in our bodies, we will continue to hope and pray for our loved ones, and at the same time take every opportunity to reflect graciousness through life and lip in the face of unremitting hard-heartedness. It is the fact that we are related through the flesh to our loved ones that constrains us to persevere with renewed effort, endeavoring to commend Christ by a godly lifestyle, even while our verbal witness continues to be spurned. In the same vein then, ought we not also lovingly persevere in witnessing to the Jewish people, our relatives through saving faith in the God of Abraham?

To take the analogy further, is our witness to unsaved loved ones strictly in the realm of literature distribution, conversation about the Bible, and invitations to hear the gospel preached? Surely not! There is also enjoyable social intercourse, sharing on a host of topics, genuine interest when family difficulties arise, and a readiness to offer practical help whenever trouble looms on the horizon. Then how is it that some convey the idea that to help the Jew is simply to expose him to the gospel, but any other more secular assistance is to be discarded as carnal, even inappropriate Zionism? Surely such an attitude is to be thoroughly condemned. The Christian should be concerned for the Jew in matters individual, national, and territorial. Yes, he should be, like Paul, enthusiastically pro-Judaic, ever supportive of the cause of Israel, its great failings and carnality notwithstanding.

Hence our attitude toward the Jew to whom, through faith in Christ, we are related according to the flesh (Gal 3:29), should be one of loving, unfailing, apostolic persistence (Rom 9:3). And this same undying concern is precisely what Paul seems to have in mind in Rom 11:17–21,31 with regard to the proper attitude of Gentile Christians toward unbelieving Jews. The fact that the apostle exhorts us to have this loving family regard is surely further proof that the Jewish ethnic status he wrote about is not null and void. Rather, it will eventually blossom into a "full number" of unimaginable proportions for the glory of God (Rom. 11:12,33–36).

The Analogy of Ruth and Orpah concerning Naomi

In Dan Gruber's book, *The Church and The Jews*, he makes an application from the book of Ruth. He contrasts the Gentile attitudes of Ruth and Orpah with the Jewishness of Naomi so as to illustrate how a Gentile Christian should respond to the Jews. Then he makes a parallel application concerning Cornelius in the NT.

While both Ruth and Orpah were Gentile Moabites, there was a stark contrast between their attitudes as widows toward their widowed and deprived Jewish mother-in-law, Naomi. Returning from desolate Moab to Bethlehem, Naomi believed herself to be oppressed by the Lord, as was the case with the Jews down through the centuries. However,

> God was not against Naomi, Job, or Paul. Despite what people think, God is not against the Jewish people. God intends to do something more wonderful for all Israel than what He did for Naomi, Job, or Paul. Though His hand may sometimes be against His first-born son, His heart never is. Naomi is a type of the Jewish people. She was bereaved, bitter, and angry at God. She had no hope. In that condition, she came back to her own land. Ruth saw that, but she saw something more. There was something that she had seen in her mother-in-law and in her own [late] husband, that was more precious to her than life. She saw something invisible that Orpah could not see.
>
> "But Ruth said [to Naomi], 'Do not urge me to leave you or turn back from following you; for where you go, I will go, and where you lodge, I will lodge. Your people shall be my people, and your God, my God'" (Ruth 1:16). Ruth said, "I will be joined to the Jewish people, and I will serve the God of Israel." She knew that He, and He alone, is the only God. She made that choice before she ever met Boaz.
>
> Ruth made the same choice that Abraham made. She left her family, her people, and her land behind. She lost her life in order to find it. Orpah said good-bye to Naomi and then went to reclaim her old life. She found her life in order to lose it. Naomi's Gentile daughter-in-law, Ruth, was to be the means of her greatest blessing. God planned it that way. Ruth embraced the Jewish people, and God blessed her eternally.
>
> What did Cornelius see? He was a military man, and Rome ruled over Jerusalem. Jerusalem itself, as a city of the first-century world, could not

compare to "the glory that was Rome." Cornelius was assigned to a backward, troublesome, superstitious province and people. At least that was the Roman view. They believed that Rome had better ways, more might, and greater gods. What did Cornelius see in Israel that is described in the gospels? He saw everything. He saw the corruption, the legalism, the brutality, and the hypocrisy. But he also saw the invisible hand of God, the only God, upon His people Israel.

Cornelius made a choice which would have made him the laughingstock of all his family, friends, and neighbors back home. He started to pray to the God of Israel, and he started to give his money to help the Jewish people. He made that choice before he ever met Peter. And the angel said, "Your prayers and alms have ascended as a memorial before God" (Acts 10:4). Cornelius embraced the Jewish people, and God blessed him eternally. "Now faith is . . . the conviction of things not seen" (Heb 11:1). Gentiles who are believers need to look at the Jewish people and see the invisible. They need to choose as Ruth and Cornelius did: "Your people will be my people; your God will be my God."[9]

The Discouragement of Jewish Evangelism

The mere justification of a distinctive prophetic cause has not been the main purpose of this defense of a pro-Judaic eschatology. To be sure, the repudiation of theological anti-Judaism has been vigorous. Nevertheless the singular intent has been the vindication of the cause of the Jewish people according to the mind of God even as has been portrayed in the whole of Scripture. The perspective upheld here might be broadly identified as premillennial. Even so, if necessary, let such a title perish. But never let perish the biblical indications of God's sovereign grace that will supremely triumph in the salvation of Israel as a nation through the mediation of its Messiah, Jesus, the Son of God, and His consummate reign from Jerusalem. Israel's original election was according to the purest grace, and so will be the climactic salvation of national Israel unto holiness as God's people.

In a sizeable part of contemporary Reformed Christianity, an eschatological perspective on Israel often results in anti-Judaism of varying shades, even if more kindly defined as theological rather than racial, and progressive or fulfilling rather than the replacement variety. In reality, many who confess faith in the doctrines of grace or historic Calvinism have acted both neglectfully and shamefully with regard to their consideration of

---

[9] D. Gruber, *The Church and the Jews* (Hanover, NH: Elijah Publishing, 1997), 401–2. W. C. Kaiser Jr.'s back cover commendation declares this book to be "thoroughly biblical. I have never seen things stated so courageously and forthrightly. . . . I think you have a breakthrough. . . . This is a very, very important book."

and association with Jews, the present nation of Israel, and even Jewish Christians. Conversation with those holding to this modern supercessionist eschatology usually reveals that such belief is doctrinally driven. Of course exceptions have been referenced. Nevertheless, they remain only exceptions to the overwhelming, unseemly, abiding general rule. So over the centuries, indications of belief in national Israel's everlasting disenfranchisement have not been difficult to discover. And not surprisingly, in parallel with this has been a dearth of biblical evangelistic outreach to the Jews as God's beloved enemy (Rom 11:28). Further, those of Jewish extraction have found it easy to notice this attitude which, I have been told by Jewish Christians, does not commend Christ.

The Experience of the Church of Scotland and Jewish Missions

Following the visit of Andrew Bonar, Robert Murray M'Cheyne, Alexander Keith, and Alexander Black to Palestine in 1839 under the auspices of the Church of Scotland, a full account of this investigative journey—which was concerned with missionary outreach to the Jews—was published with the title, *A Narrative of a Visit to the Holy Land*. Of particular significance are the following extracts that indicate the deplorable attitude of Christians toward Jews in Jerusalem at that time:

> On another occasion, passing by the Church of the Holy Sepulcher, the monks mistaking him [a Mr. Nicolayson, a Christian resident in Jerusalem dressed in an eastern manner] for a Jew, rushed out upon him, and pursued him through the streets, into a house where he took refuge, threatening to kill him, unless he kissed a picture of the Virgin, in a New Testament which they held out to him. This he did, and saved his life.
>
> The professing Christians here [in the holy land]—Greeks, Armenians, and Roman Catholics—are even more bitter enemies to Jews than Mahometans; so that in time of danger, a Jew would betake himself to the house of a Turk for refuge, in preference to that of a Christian. How little have these Christians the mind of Christ![10]

How shameful this is, not only because of the way this behavior is so antithetical to that of the apostle Paul, but supremely because of the way in which Jesus Christ is unnecessarily blasphemed before His brethren in the flesh. The *Narrative* goes on to describe that, when the Jews recognized the more genuine loving interest of the delegation from Scotland, there was a contrast-

---

[10] A. A. Bonar, *A Narrative of a Mission of Inquiry to the Jews from the Church of Scotland in 1839* (Philadelphia: Presbyterian Board of Publications, 1845), 146–47, 149.

ing response of desire for cordial fellowship. It also needs to be pointed out that the eschatological doctrine of this delegation, in the main, recognized the ongoing national and territorial status of the Jews at that time, notwithstanding their unbelief. Their eschatology was decidedly not Augustinian.

Yes, for those Christians upholding a Judeo-centric eschatology, the tension that daily confronts them does not presently abate. On the one hand, the Jewish people in general reject Christ and are as carnal as the rest of western society; on the other hand, there is a relentless loving concern for them that Paul so passionately modeled. In other words, for the Christian the modern Jew remains a beloved enemy. No matter how intensely the Christian's testimony to Jesus as the Christ is scorned and vilified, his loving interest in the Israelis and Israel is indefatigable. In this regard, the Jews' greatest friends are evangelical Christians because they will never turn against their elder brother relatives in the flesh. And this ought to be so because such an attitude is in reality derived from the attitude of the God of Israel, who through Paul declared them to be "enemies for your [the Gentiles'] advantage, but regarding election, they are loved because of their forefathers" (Rom 11:28).

The Challenge of Benjamin Netanyahu

Concerning present tensions in the Middle East, *A Durable Peace* by Benjamin Netanyahu, prime minister of Israel from 1996 to 1999, is essential reading. He provides an erudite and informed explanation of events which the modern media rarely reports. My own conservative perspective resonated with this enlightened understanding of current tensions. But one paragraph caused me considerable distress. Netanyahu wrote,

> The final guarantor of the viability of a small nation [such as Israel] in times of turbulence is its capacity to direct its own destiny, something that has eluded the Jewish people during its long centuries of exile. Restoring that capacity is the central task of the Jewish people today.[11]

One is immediately moved to respond, *Why has the stateless Jew endured such a desolate existence around the world for centuries?* Surely Netanyahu's declaration, all too true, that the Jews thus far have failed to direct their own destiny leads us to the obvious answer if we consider the root of Judaism. For in the face of overwhelming biblical testimony from the beginning of Israel's history in Abraham, the existence and perpetuity

---

[11] B. Netanyahu, *A Durable Peace: Israel and its Place Among the Nations* (New York: Warner Books, 2000), xxiii.

of God's people was revealed to be grounded in divine election by Yahweh, that is, pure grace, not ethnic or national merit (Deut 7:6–8; Amos 3:2). They do not have a self-generated destiny. Hence the suggestion that secular Israel should again attempt to "direct its own destiny" is fraught with fearful prospects (Hos 8:14). It is God who must intervene, as promised, and fulfill His purposes in grace (Ezek 36–37; Hos 3:4–5; Zech 14). Furthermore, Netanyahu refers to the prophets Isaiah, Jeremiah, Ezekiel and Amos, as well as to Joseph, Abraham, Sarah, Jacob, Rachel, Moses, Joshua, Naomi, David, and Lazarus. Yet no mention is made of the God of Israel, apart from whom these individuals have no significance whatsoever, as all of them would readily agree. Surely the leaders of Muslim nations would never refrain from the mention of Allah in such a situation.

In light of this great void, shall I as a Christian abandon prayerful and active support for the likes of such present leaders of Israel? Such a thought ought to be unthinkable because the God of Abraham has not given up on the Jews, as He did not give up on me, a great sinner redeemed by grace alone. Hence, in our concerns and dealings with both the Dispersion and modern Israel we shall persist in unfailing love as did the God of Hosea for His adulterous people, and as did the father of the prodigal son.

Christian Responsibility toward the Jew with Encouragement from Horatius Bonar

The present need for awakened Christian interest in Jewish evangelism requires not so much a contemporary methodology as a fervent, passionate spiritual interest in the Jewish people according to biblical, theological and eschatological stimulation. Once such an arousal takes place, the *modus operandi* will tend to burst forth with suitable variety that focuses on making Jesus the Messiah's redemption known to His ethnic people. While expanding on this principle, we also turn to the stimulation that Horatius Bonar provided when he wrote in 1855 on "The Responsibilities of Christians as Regards the Jews."[12] Today, over one hundred and fifty years later, his insights remain timeless, choice and necessary.

The Arid History of Jewish Evangelism

The Reformation brought spiritual awakening, gospel illumination, and social improvement from the sixteenth to the seventeenth centuries. But

---

[12] H. Bonar, "The Responsibilities of Christians as Regards the Jews," *The Quarterly Journal of Prophecy* (October, 1855), 347–52.

millions of unbelievers beyond Europe were neglected until the commencement of the eighteenth century when a slumbering church awoke to the broader dimensions of its gospel mandate (Mark 16:15; see Luke 14:23). This arousal to missionary outreach resulted in a fruitful spiritual harvest outside Europe through the formation of numerous missionary agencies in Britain and beyond. Notable among these was the Church Missionary Society, the London Missionary Society, and the Baptist Missionary Society. Nevertheless, this zealous evangelistic advance of international proportions passed by the poor abandoned Jew. Serious missionary outreach toward him did not commence until the nineteenth century. Bonar pointed to the analogous plight of the assaulted but neglected Jew on the Jericho road, lovingly cared for by the good Samaritan (Luke 10:30–37). He described

> the poor neglected Jew, torn and bleeding at every pore, trodden down and despised, a proverb and a byword. And who cared for him? . . . But "God had not rejected his people whom He foreknew" [Rom 11:2]; he still has wondrous thoughts of lingering love toward them, and it became a sight well-pleasing in his eyes when, in the spirit of the Samaritan, the Church directed her steps towards the plundered and wounded traveler, and sought to "pour oil and wine into his bleeding wounds." Surely those missionary agencies which seek the spiritual and eternal welfare of the scattered and long-injured children of Abraham richly deserve the name of "Good Samaritan Societies;" and surely all Christians who now observe these efforts would do well to give heed to the application which the Great Teacher and Pattern of Love makes of his own beautiful parable, *"Go thou and do likewise."* Yes, Christian; if you would be in *full sympathy with God*, you must not only trust the cross, love holiness, and send the gospel to the heathen; but you must love the Jew, pity and pray for the Jew, and be willing to lay out personal investment and energy so as to send the good tidings that Jesus of Nazareth "came into the world to save sinners" [1 Tim 1:15], to the Jew, to whom he came "preaching peace" [Acts 10:36].[13]

The Constraint of Jewish Evangelism

Acknowledgment of the biblical mandate for Jewish evangelism is one thing (Rom 1:16; 2:9); the enthusiastic, eager fulfillment of this mandate is quite another. But where do we start in the pursuit of a right biblical attitude in this regard, even as we contemplate the ardent concern of Paul, his "heart's desire and prayer to God concerning . . . [the Jews'] salvation" (Rom 10:1)? We commence then, as did Paul, with God as the object of his

---

[13] Ibid., 348.

prayer, the God of Abraham, whose glorious attributes are seen, not only in the priority of His Son's ministry toward lost Jews (Matt 10:5–6; 15:24; John 1:11), but also the Father's overall revelation of personal, multi-faceted concern for the nation of Israel.

The Knowledge of God concerning His love for Israel

As we have seen earlier in chapter 10, Romans 9–11, particularly 9:6, is ultimately concerned with the justification of God's covenant faithfulness, preeminently as is evident in His dealings with the Jews. How significant it is that in the whole compass of this Scriptural trilogy concerning God's unrelenting covenant love for Israel, Paul concludes with such a theocentric symphony of praise that is born of God's saving interest in the Gentile, but especially the Jew (Rom 11:33–36). However, on a wider scale this knowledge of God is also made known by means of His dealings with the Jewish people since the call of Abraham and throughout subsequent centuries.

> Here God has written out his glorious name. In this Jewish people we see every divine perfection in act and operation. *Omnipotence* raised them up at first. . . . *Wisdom* watched over, led, and guided them unerringly. *Faithfulness* fulfilled every promise uttered by the lip of Truth. *Goodness* established them in a noble land, gave them holy laws, divine and instructive institutions, sent among them prophets to teach and priests to minister. *Holiness* warned, cautioned, and exhorted them, and when they rebelliously spurned the gentle tones of love, how long did *Patience* bear with them; how often did God return and have mercy on them! When they had sinned "till there was no more remedy" [2 Chr 36:16], when they had consummated the rebellions of fifteen hundred years by that unparalleled deed of blood, the murder of the Son of God, then, after some yet further lingerings and invitations of insulted *Mercy*, did awful *Justice* arise, bare his arm for the battle, and strike down the terrible and crushing blows. Now, in what state do we behold them? Even as they have been for the last eighteen hundred years, like a burnt mountain on the plains of Time, scorched and splintered by the lightnings of divine wrath.
>
> Yes! still preserved in all their woe, still unconsumed by all these penal fires! Preserved! And for what? Let a thousand glorious prophecies answer! That burnt mountain shall yet be clothed with lovely foliage; down its sides shall streams of living water gush; and the nation that now witnesses to the *truth, justice,* and *power* of God, shall sing till the ends of the earth shall hear and echo back the song, "Who is a God like You, who pardons iniquity, and passes over the rebellious act of the remnant of His possession? He does not retain His anger forever, because He delights in unchanging love" (Mic 7:18). Then shall the Lord be glorified in Israel, and all his attributes displayed in full-orbed glory, when he shall "call her Hephzibah, and her

land Beulah" [Isa 62:4]. What a glorious Jehovah is the LORD God of Israel! With what awe, what love, what fear, what hope, should this character, as exhibited towards Israel, inspire *us*![14]

The Obligation of the Christian toward Israel

Surely it is this particular, steadfast, indomitable love of God for national Israel that ought to stir the Christian heart today toward Jewish evangelism. Since "the LORD became zealous for His land and spared His people" (Joel 2:18), then it is incumbent upon the child of God today to be constrained similarly toward the Jewish people. Since God continues to love the nation of Israel with such loyal love that the centuries cannot diminish, we as Christians, claiming to be children of this same God, ought to be spontaneously directed according to our heavenly Father's divine animus, His persistence in fervent concern and unquenchable loving-kindness.

> How great, then, are our obligations to a nation, from whose history we learn so much of God, and so much of ourselves! They encourage us to hope in God, they warn us against tempting him. Their very failure is for our profit; "by their stumbling, salvation has come to the Gentiles" (Rom 11:11). We "Gentiles have shared in their spiritual benefits" (Rom 15:27) and have been "grafted in . . . the rich root of the cultivated olive tree" (Rom 11:17), from which, for a time, they are broken off. Surely we are responsible, as regards the Jew, to a very large amount. Have we felt this? Have we so acted as to show that, like the apostle, we feel that "we are indebted to them"? [Rom 15:27]. Do our prayers on their behalf prove this? Are they not too much forgotten, both in public and private, by many of God's people? We must feel that we are verily guilty concerning our brethren. Israel's past we cannot remedy; their future, as a nation, is with God, and is safe in his omnipotent and faithful hands; but let men speak or think as they will, Israel in the *present* is with us; God in a measure casts it upon us, and calls upon us to care for their souls, and he will work by the means which he has put in our hands, and will be pleased if these means are used diligently in faith, and with prayer.[15]

The Exhortation to Jewish Evangelism

For those who deny any covenantal future for the Jews and national Israel, the continuing cry of Bonar in what follows has no deep meaning; it cannot be appreciated from the heart. Spiritual rapport with the unity of his thought

[14] Ibid., 349–50.
[15] Ibid., 350.

here is simply impossible, though sadly such a condition is doctrinally self-inflicted. How can any Christian who claims that the modern Jew is ethnically *persona non grata* in the mind of God yet genuinely confess his love for the "Jew" when his meaning here is necessarily so obscure, even duplicitous? If someone of an Augustinian persuasion should respond, "But I can enter into the essential gospel exhortation here," then let him consider why it would be preferable that he be quiet about the Jewish prospect of nullification within an Augustinian legacy, otherwise this integral part of his witness would tend to subtract from the attractiveness of the evangel. It is unlikely that such a proclamation would make the Jew jealous. On the other hand, let such a person ponder why Paul is far more likely to be in full and hearty agreement here with Bonar's impassioned plea!

> Israel has been a long time neglected, persecuted, and grievously wronged. Let us go, like Jeremiah, and sit down with them amidst their ruins, and in a sympathetic spirit tell them of the Restorer of Israel—the Almighty Repairer of the great breach—the true Antitype of their own Zerubbabel, who can yet build them up "an holy temple, an habitation of God through the Spirit" (Eph 2:21–22). While we mourn over their great griefs, their mighty wrongs, and their yet mightier sins, let us gently tell them of "the Man of sorrows," who is the all-sufficient "consolation of Israel" (Luke 2:25). We carry God's own message, prepared by the hand of mercy for the heart of the miserable, and which can, by the blessing of the Holy Spirit, win its way through a mountain of stone and a heart of stubbornly resolute hardness. Go, Christian, to thy wandering and fugitive brother, tell him of Blood "which speaks better than the blood of Abel" (Heb 12:24)—Blood which can cleanse even those who have "gone in the way of Cain" (Jude 11). Go, in the spirit of Paul, "with our hearts desire and prayer to God, that Israel may be saved" (Rom 10:1). Go, "praying in the Holy Spirit" (Jude 20); and you will give no heed to those who say that "it is of no use preaching the gospel to the Jew." *It is of use*; facts abundantly prove it; God has owned his own word, and is still blessing his servants. "Many of the sons of Israel have been turned to the Lord their God" (Luke 1:16); several of them are now the ministers of Christ to the Gentiles or to their own countrymen; and "how welcome are the feet of those who announce the gospel of good things!" . . . We should pray earnestly for Israel's final restoration, even for her national glory and spiritual salvation. In so doing we pray for the blessedness of the earth, and the life of the world, which God is pleased to conjointly establish. But believing that God has at the present time "a remnant chosen by grace" (Rom 11:5), we should give, pray, and labor, if we can "somehow make [the Jew] jealous and save some of them" (Rom 11:14).[16]

[16] Ibid., 351–52.

The Future of Jewish Evangelism

Ultimately our hope is in the God of Israel, and especially the sovereignty of His grace with regard to the salvation of the Jews, both individually and nationally. This is the same sovereign grace in which the modern Gentile Christian readily boasts. All of our human efforts in Jewish evangelism pale before the vision of His certain promises, and it is for this reason that the vision of Romans 11 is so ultimately glorious. With this vista before us, no matter how gloomy the approaching cloud and thunder may appear on the world stage, yet at the same time God is pleased to use the "weak things to shame the strong" so that no one can boast in His presence" (1 Cor 1:27,29). In this regard consider Bonar's closing realism, honesty, and triumphant hope:

> Their "*future!*" Ah! There is a dark cloud resting over the years that are fast hastening on; but beyond, what brightness! what glory! and both prompt us to pray. Prophecy tells us that beyond the fiery trials, "a nation [will] be born in one day" (Isa 66:8), and that nation will be "the perfection of beauty" (Ps 50:2), "joy, praise and glory before all the nations of the earth" (Jer 33:9), "dew from the LORD" (Mic 5:7), "life from the dead" (Rom 11:15); and all of their eventual faith and national glory will be God's answer to the prayers of those who "find pleasure in the [Zion's] stones, and favor its dust" (Ps 102:14).
>
> Compassion for Israel must be of great pleasure to God. . . . [With] "Beginning in Jerusalem" (Acts 1:8) resounding in our ears, we cannot be indifferent to the spiritual welfare of a people so useful to ourselves, so dear to God, and with whose future blessedness the full salvation of a ruined world is connected. "Oh, that Israel's deliverance would come from Zion!" (Ps 14:7). Soon may the day dawn when Israel, brought through her great tribulation, shall as the priestly nation breathe forth the acceptable prayer, "May God be gracious to us and bless us; look upon us with favor so that Your way may be known on earth, Your salvation among all nations. God will bless us, and all the ends of the earth will fear him" (Ps 67:1–2, 7).[17]

From whence then comes this compassionate concern that so fervently drives Bonar and at the same time warmly commends that which he writes? Surely this enthusiasm is inevitably born of a distinct eschatological perspective. Certainly biblical, Pauline missionary interest in the Jews has never blossomed from the roots of theological anti-Judaism, notwithstanding cool, token confessions of interest. Love for the heritage of the Jew—past, present, and future—cannot erupt from a well that is declared to be dry and sealed with the notice of a divine, irreversible embargo. Rather

---

[17] Ibid., 352.

Bonar's indomitable regard for the people of Israel, so passionate, while all too well aware of the present parched status of the Jews, is yet convinced of the gospel principle on a broader scale, "that He who started a good work in you will carry it on to completion until the day of Christ Jesus" (Phil 1:6). So God, having begun a good work with the promised seed of Abraham, will certainly complete what He has covenanted to establish. He will not fail. He may have changed a "fruitful land into salty wasteland, because of the wickedness of its inhabitants"; nevertheless, "He [the LORD] turns a desert into a pool of water, dry land into springs of water. He causes the hungry to settle there, and they establish a city where they can live" (Ps 107:34–36). So God has promised Israel,

> Say to the faint-hearted: "Be strong; do not fear! Here is your God; vengeance is coming. God's retribution is coming; He will save you." Then the eyes of the blind will be opened, and the ears of the deaf unstopped. Then the lame will leap like a deer, and the tongue of the mute will sing for joy, for water will gush in the wilderness, and streams in the desert; . . . and the ransomed of the LORD will return and come to Zion with singing, crowned with unending joy. Joy and gladness will overtake [them], and sorrow and sighing will flee" (Isa 35:4–6,10).

Conclusion

As was stated in the introduction to this volume, in the field of eschatology there are matters of lesser significance that concern the antichrist, the great tribulation, the rapture, etc. But the issue of the place of Israel in the Bible, and especially in relation to the NT, is a transcendently important one. With regard to this vital matter of national Israel's present existence or nonexistence according to divine covenant, history plainly leads us to an unavoidable conclusion: profound ethical and practical consequences are involved here—even issues of life and death. It is for this reason, among other lesser matters, that I have felt compelled not only to make such a vital distinction in the field of what is really important in eschatology, but also to vigorously defend that doctrine which tends to rectify such an appalling anti-Judaic heritage. Here we are not dealing with an eschatological refinement concerning which we can agree to disagree. If the Christian Church in general over the centuries had followed Paul's exhortation in Romans 11:17–24,31, it is not unreasonable to conceive that the tragic treatment of the Jews during the twentieth century that resulted in the ashes of nearly a whole nation might have been replaced with the fruit of a great harvest of Jewish souls saved because they had been lovingly provoked to jealousy

(Rom 11:11), to the glory of God (Rom 11:36). With this in mind we are moved to prayerfully sing,

> Wake, harp of Zion, wake again,
> Upon thine ancient hill,
> On Jordan's long deserted plain,
> By Kedron's lowly rill.
> The hymn shall yet in Zion swell
> That sounds Messiah's praise,
> And Thy loved name, Immanuel!
> As once in ancient days.
> For Israel yet shall own her King,
> For her salvation waits,
> And hill and dale shall sweetly sing
> With praise in all her gates.
> Hasten, O Lord, these promised days,
> When Israel shall rejoice;
> And Jew and Gentile join in praise,
> With one united voice.
>
> *James Edmeston, 1846*

In conclusion, we return to a most vital matter in the current debate over the future destiny of national Israel. It is the question of "tone" or "attitude" with regard to the Jewish people. Sadly it needs to be pointed out that much of the literature which continues in the Augustinian eschatological tradition is fatally flawed at this most vital juncture (see chapters 3 and 4). This anti-Judaic genre resounds with an unsavory character that most Jewish Christians and unbelieving Jews will quickly identify with a sense of revulsion. The result is that a basic defect in the whole system is discovered. By contrast, consider the preceding brief article by Horatius Bonar which throbs and breathes with a gospel that generates a loving regard for the Jewish people and that speaks for itself as being essentially Pauline. If this chord does not resonate in the biblical Christian, then without apology it is maintained that the fundamental, doctrinal, eschatological root here is unsound. It is the right theological, eschatological root which produces from the likes of Bonar such a sweet resonance that both the Jewish Christian and the Gentile Christian will delight in and spontaneously, fervently act upon.

APPENDIX A

JONATHAN EDWARDS
AND THE FUTURE OF ISRAEL

Jonathan Edwards (1703–1758) is arguably the most significant and influential evangelical Christian in the history of the United States. He is frequently identified with a sober Puritan image that characterized Massachusetts during the eighteenth century. Although a leading figure throughout the Great Awakening of that period, his most notable writings have tended to identify him as a Calvinist theologian and philosopher, though certainly not in any mere academic or detached sense. His volume on *Freedom of the Will* is a profound study of a much debated vital point of doctrine, and his *Treatise Concerning Religious Affections* penetrates to the very heart of experiential Christianity.

However, the more recent and comprehensive publication of Edwards' writings by Yale University Press has provided an expanded vision of what this man of God regarded as important. Notably, among many other matters, Edwards was a decided millennialist, somewhat following a revival of interest in this aspect of biblical eschatology that erupted in England during the middle of the seventeenth century. Stephen J. Stein, editor of the Yale Edition, Volume 5, *Apocalyptic Writings*, explained,

> The millennium remained a matter of consuming private interest for
> him. . . . During the millennium kings will be like the judges who ruled
> ancient Israel before the monarchy was established—a form of government
> that pleased God greatly. . . . In that glorious day, Edwards conjectured,
> a variety of forms of government may prevail, but none shall be contrary
> to "true liberty." . . . The geography of the millennium, another issue that
> divided commentators, attracted his exegetical attention. Edwards found
> scriptural warrant for placing the land of Canaan at the center of the com-
> ing kingdom of Christ. . . . In like manner, he speculated that the return
> of the Jews to their homeland is inevitable because of the promises of land
> made to them have been only partially fulfilled. God intends the Jews to be
> "a visible monument" of his grace and power. The return to their traditional
> homeland, however, was premised by Edwards upon a conversion of the
> Jews to Christianity. . . . [Then] Canaan will be the spiritual center of the
> coming kingdom, and Israel will again be a truly distinct nation.[1]

[1] S. J. Stein, ed., "Introduction," *Jonathan Edwards, Works, Apocalyptic Writings*, vol. 5 (New Haven: Yale University Press, 1977), 17–19.

Although Edwards' perspective differs somewhat from the premillennialism that this volume upholds, with regard to the issue of the Jews, the land of Israel, and the millennium, we can largely agree with his attitude and expectations. Edwards was a postmillennialist, believing that authentic Christian expansion through evangelism would effectively sweep the world to such an extent that a largely Christianized, millennial world would result.[2] Only then, at such a triumphant world climax, would Jesus Christ return in universally acknowledged glory. Stein further explained the historic setting of Edwards' prophetic optimism:

> Since the Reformation, God has reversed the fortunes of the church by pouring out the vials of wrath upon his enemies. The memory of persecution and martyrdom will fade in the future as the knowledge of divinity spreads, injustices are rectified, the saints and martyrs vindicated, and men stimulated to greater holiness during the millennium. The promised triumph of the saints is the hope and encouragement of the church on earth.[3]

Who among us, if living in America during the eighteenth century, could avoid the encouraging force of circumstances in the world at that time, especially with regard to the stimulus of revival and the effective expansion of evangelical missionary endeavors. But if Edwards were alive today, most likely he would write with a more disturbing prospect in mind. However, since our focus is chiefly on his regard for the Jews and Israel, we will consider several significant excerpts from Edwards' writings. The first is from *A History of the Work of Redemption*, posthumously published in 1773. Edwards concluded that as the millennium is inaugurated, following the overthrow of the Mohammedan kingdom, there will be gradual conversion of the Diaspora.

> Jewish infidelity shall then be overthrown. However obstinate they have now been for above seventeen hundred years in their rejecting Christ, and instances of conversion of any of that nation have been so very rare ever since the destruction of Jerusalem, but they have against the plain teachings of their own prophets continued to approve of the cruelty of their forefathers in crucifying [Christ]; yet when this day comes the thick veil that

---

[2] At the urging of many for a Second American Bible and Prophetic Conference (premillennial) in Chicago in 1886, following the immensely successful first conference in New York in 1878, the organizing secretary, George C. Needham, commented, "Many of postmillennial faith ratified the call, and were present at every session as interested listeners" (*Prophetic Studies of the International Prophetic Conference* [Chicago: F. H. Revell, 1886], 1). Classic postmillennialism is in mind here, not the more recent revisionist, reconstructionist variety. Of course, nonmillennialists would sense relatively little affinity in such a setting.

[3] Edwards, *Works, Apocalyptic Writings*, vol. 5, 11.

blinds their eyes shall be removed (2 Cor. 3:16), and divine grace shall melt and renew their hard hearts, "And they shall look on him whom they [have pierced, and they shall mourn for him, as one mourneth for his only son, and shall be in bitterness for him, as one that is in bitterness for his first-born]" (Zech. 12:10, etc.). And then shall all Israel be saved [Rom. 11:26]. The Jews in all their dispersions shall cast away their old infidelity, and shall wonderfully have their hearts changed, and abhor themselves for their past unbelief and obstinacy; and shall flow together to the blessed Jesus, penitently, humbly, and joyfully owning him as their glorious king and only savior, and shall with all their hearts as with one heart and voice declare his praises unto other nations [Isa. 66:20; Jer. 50:4].[4]

It is quite clear that Edwards regarded this as conversion of the Jewish nation. He considered it virtually indisputable that the Jews have been miraculously preserved over many centuries for this divine purpose.

Nothing is more certainly foretold than this national conversion of the Jews is in the eleventh chapter of Romans. And there are also many passages of the Old Testament that can't be interpreted in any other sense, that I can't now stand to mention. Besides the prophecies of the calling of the Jews, we have a remarkable seal of the fulfillment of this great event in providence by a thing that is a kind of continual miracle, viz. the preserving them a distinct [nation] when in such a dispersed condition for above sixteen hundred years. The world affords nothing else like it—a remarkable hand of providence. When they shall be called, then shall that ancient people that were alone God's people for so long a time be God's people again, never to be rejected more, one fold with the Gentiles; and then also shall the remains of the ten tribes wherever they are, and though they have been rejected much longer than [the Jews], be brought in with their brethren, the Jews. The prophecies of Hosea especially seem to hold this forth, and that in the future glorious times of the church both Judah and Ephraim, or Judah and the ten tribes, shall be brought in together, and shall be united as one people as they formerly were under David and Solomon (Hos. 1:11), and so in the last chapter of Hosea, and other parts of his prophecy.[5]

Surely the references here to the kingdoms of David and Solomon are meant to include the territory of Israel, even as Hosea 1:11 explicitly declares.

We further assert from other writings of Edwards that the conversion of ethnic Israel was related to the nation's promised return to the material land of Israel. This man of acknowledged, profound spirituality was wholly at rest with such a substantial triumph; to charge him with carnality would be absurd. Further, while Israel and the church compose the people of God,

---

[4] Jonathan Edwards, *Works, A History of the Work of Redemption*, vol. 9, ed. John F. Wilson (New Haven: Yale University Press, 1989), 469.

[5] Ibid. 469–70.

there is national distinction within this unity, as Gal 3:28 well illustrates. Hence, we will consider Edwards' more detailed description of the millennial economy, both with regard to geography and the diversity within unity that will incorporate Jews and Gentiles.

That the land of Israel has distinct eschatological importance is indicated by Edwards' consideration of its strategic location:

> The land of Canaan is the most advantageously posited of any spot of ground on the face [of the earth], to be the place from whence the truth should shine forth, and true religion spread around into all parts of the world. There are three continents of the earth: the old continent, America and Terra Australis. This land is right in the center of the old and principle continent, between Europe, Asia and Africa, but most in Asia, because it is abundantly the largest. And [it is] lying at the end of the Mediterranean Sea, which opens the way from Canaan directly to America, and having the Red Sea and Persian Gulf touching its borders as much as the Mediterranean, according to Exodus 23:31 and other places, opening the way straight to Terra Australis, the third continent. . . .
>
> That God did take care of the situation of his people Israel, upon their account, for the advantage of spreading the truth and diffusing the influences of religion, I think is evident from Deuteronomy 32:8–9, and from Acts 17:26–27 and from Habakkuk 3:6. . . .
>
> And it is the more evident, that the Jews will return to their own land again, because they never have yet possessed one quarter of that land, which was so often promised them, from the Red Sea to the river Euphrates (Exod. 23:31; Gen. 15:18; Deut. 11:24; Josh. 1:4). Indeed, it was partly fulfilled in Solomon's time, when he governed all within those bounds for a short time; but so short, that it is not to be thought that this is all the fulfillment of the promise that is to be. And besides, that was not a fulfillment of the promise, because they did not possess it, though they made the nations of it tributary.[6]

So both the Jew in the land of Israel and the Gentile in surrounding regions shall enjoy distinct yet harmonious relations:

> We are not to suppose but that when the nation of the Jews are converted, other Christians will be as much God's Israel as they, and will have in every respect the same privileges. Neither can we suppose, that their church will have any manner of superiority over other parts of Christ's church, any otherwise than as that part of the church will be more glorious. Religion and learning will be there at the highest; more excellent books will be there written, etc. Without doubt, they will return to their own land; because when their unbelief ceases, their dispersion, the dreadful and signal punishment of their unbelief, will cease too. As they have continued hitherto,

[6] Edwards, Works, *Apocalyptic Writings*, vol. 5, 133–34.

with one consent, to dishonor Christ by rejecting the gospel, so shall they meet together to honor him, by openly professing of it with one mouth, and practice it with one heart and one soul, together lamenting their obstinacy, as it is said they shall (Zech. 12:11–12), and together praising God for his grace in enlightening them. And as they have hitherto continued a distinct nation, that they might continue a visible monument of his displeasure, for their rejecting and crucifying their Messiah, so after their conversion will they still be a distinct nation, that they may be a visible monument of God's wonderful grace and power in their calling and conversion. But we cannot suppose they will remain a distinct nation, any more than the primitive Jewish Christians, if they continue dispersed among other nations.

But yet, we are not to imagine that the old walls of separation will be set up again. But all nations will be as free to come to Judea, or to dwell in Jerusalem, as into any other city or country, and may have the same privilege there as they themselves. For they shall look upon all the world to be their brethren, as much as the Christians in Boston and the Christians in other parts of New England look on each other as brethren.[7]

According to Edwards' postmillennial expectations, the definitive biblical account of this future state in Revelation 20 will be accomplished gradually, and not in an apocalyptic fashion.

The ruin of the popish interest is but a small part of what is requisite, in order to introduce and settle such a state of things, as the world is represented as being in, in that millennium that is described in Revelation 20, wherein Satan's visible kingdom is everywhere totally extirpated, and a perfect end put to all heresies, delusions and false religions whatsoever, through the whole earth, and Satan thence-forward "deceives the nations no more" [v. 3], and has no place anywhere but in hell. This is the sabbatism of the world; when all shall be in a holy rest, when the wolf shall dwell with the lamb, and there shall be nothing to hurt or offend, and there shall be abundance of peace, and 'the earth shall be full of the knowledge of the Lord as the waters covers the seas" [Isa. 11:9], and God's people shall dwell in quiet resting places. There is not the least reason to think, that all this will be brought to pass as it were in one stroke, or that from the present lamentable state of things, there should be brought about and completed the destruction of the Church of Rome, the entire extirpation of all infidelity, heresies, superstitions and schisms, through all Christendom, and the conversion of all the Jews, and the full enlightening and conversion of all Mahometan and heathen nations, through the whole earth, on every side of the globe, and from the north to the south pole, and the full settlement of all in the pure Christian faith and order, all as it were in the issue of one great battle, and by means of the victory of the church in one great conflict with her enemies . . . If the Spirit of God should be immediately poured out,

---

[7] Ibid., 135.

and that great work of God's power and grace should now begin, which in its progress and issue should complete this glorious effect; there must be an amazing and unparalleled progress of the work and manifestation of divine power to bring so much to pass, by the year 2000.[8]

As earlier indicated, surely if it were possible now for Edwards to survey this present turbulent, unspeakably decadent world in the year 2007, how likely it is that, while his basic expectations concerning the Jews and the land of Israel would indicate little fundamental change, yet his optimistic gradualism would be discarded. In its place there would be optimistic hope in God's apocalyptic intervention, that is, "the great day of Their wrath," the wrath of God the Father and His Son, "the Lamb" (see Rev 6:12–17), and the subsequent establishment of "new heavens and a new earth, where righteousness will dwell" (2 Pet 3:13).

---

[8] Ibid., 410–11.

APPENDIX B

J. C. RYLE AND THE FUTURE OF ISRAEL

John Charles Ryle (1816–1900), the first Bishop of Liverpool, was, according to C. H. Spurgeon's consideration of that period, "the best man in the Church of England." Near Macclesfield, Cheshire County, where he was born there remains today at the church of St. Michael and All Angels a memorial plaque rightly describing him as, "A Man of Granite, with the Heart of a Little Child." Anticipating a wealthy inheritance, the bankruptcy of his father was a crushing blow for this young man. He was well educated at Eton and completed studies at Oxford. Then thoughts of entering Parliament were abandoned upon Ryle's conversion in 1837. As a result he was ordained as a minister of the Church of England in 1841 and became a bishop in 1880. His whole ministry was marked by a singular devotion to the evangelical reformed faith, especially as confessed in the Thirty-nine Articles of Religion of the Anglican Church. His vigorous, uncompromising, and yet kindly manner lives on in the books and tracts he authored that have continued to go through numerous reprints.

In 1879 a collection of sermons by Ryle was published under the title, *Coming Events and Present Duties*, in which his clear yet carefully stated premillennial convictions are expressed. As with Horatius Bonar's *Prophetical Landmarks*, which Ryle highly recommended,[1] here the dominant subject is Israel. The following excerpts express Ryle's firm convictions regarding the future of the Hebrew people and the regathering of the Jews to the promised land.

By way of introduction, Ryle set forth his prophetic creed in eleven sections, three of which are especially pertinent here:

6. I believe that after our Lord Jesus Christ comes again, the earth shall be renewed, and the curse removed; the devil shall be bound, the godly shall be rewarded, the wicked shall be punished; and that before He comes there shall be neither resurrection, judgment, not millennium, and that not till after He comes shall the earth be filled with the knowledge of the glory of the Lord (Acts 3:21; Isa. 25:6–9; 1 Thess. 4:14–18; Rev. 20:1; etc.).

7. I believe that the Jews shall ultimately be gathered again as a separate nation, restored to their own land, and converted to the faith of Christ, after going through great tribulation (Jer. 30:10–11; 31:10; Rom. 11:25–26; Dan. 12:1; Zech. 13:8–9).

[1] J. C. Ryle, *Are You Ready For The End Of Time?* (Fearn, Scotland: Christian Focus, 2001) 183; repr. of *Coming Events and Present Duties*.

8. I believe that the literal sense of the Old Testament prophecies has been far too much neglected by the Churches, and is far too much neglected at the present day, and that under the mistaken system of spiritualizing and accommodating Bible language, Christians have too often completely missed its meaning (Luke 24:25–26).[2]

Watch!

In the first chapter, titled "Watch," Ryle expounded Matt 25:1–13, especially the example of the five wise virgins whose eager expectation prepared them for the Bridegroom's coming. Here is Ryle's description of what is to be anticipated:

> When the number of the elect is accomplished, Christ will come again to this world with power and great glory. He will raise His saints, and gather them to himself. He will punish with fearful judgments all who are found His enemies, and reward all His believing people. He will take to Himself His great power and reign, and establish an universal kingdom. He will gather the scattered tribes of Israel, and place them once more in their own land. As He came the first time in person, so He will come the second time in person. As He went away from earth visibly, so He will return visibly. As He literally rode upon an ass, was literally sold for thirty pieces of silver, had His hands and feet literally pierced, was numbered literally with the transgressors and had lots literally cast upon His raiment, and all that Scripture might be fulfilled so also will He come, literally set up a kingdom and literally reign over the earth, because the very same Scripture has said it shall be so (Acts 1:11; 3:19–21; Ps. 102:16; Zech. 14:5; Isa. 24:23; Jer. 30:3,18; Dan. 7:13–14).[3]

Occupy Till I Come

The next chapter, "Occupy Till I Come," is concerned with those who declare on the one hand that God has left Israel with no national identity, especially concerning the promised land, yet on the other hand they profess some vague necessity for the "Jews" to hear the gospel. Some believe a remnant of the Jews will be saved through the centuries, while others expect the conversion of a large number of them toward the end of this age. In either case, Jewish identity will be lost since there will result an engrafting within Christendom that completes the people of God, the church, also being known as the new supplanting, spiritual Israel. To this Ryle re-

[2] Ibid., 9.
[3] Ibid., 22–24.

sponded, concerning Luke 19:11–13, where the twelve disciples erroneously "thought the kingdom of God was going to appear right away":

> I believe we have fallen into an error parallel with that of our Jewish breth-
> ren, an error less fatal in its consequences than theirs, but an error far
> more inexcusable, because we have had more light. If the Jew thought too
> exclusively of Christ *reigning*, has not the Gentile thought to exclusively of
> Christ *suffering*? If the Jew could see nothing in Old Testament prophecy
> but Christ's exaltation and final power, has not the Gentile often seen noth-
> ing but Christ's humiliation and the preaching of the gospel? If the Jew
> dwelt too much on Christ's *second* advent, has not the Gentile dwelt too
> exclusively on the *first*? If the Jew ignored the *cross*, has not the Gentile
> ignored the *crown*? I believe there can be but one answer to these questions.
> I believe that we Gentiles till lately have been very guilty concerning a large
> portion of God's truth. I believe that we have cherished an arbitrary, reck-
> less habit of interpreting first advent texts *literally*, and second advent texts
> *spiritually*. I believe we have not rightly understood "all that the prophets
> have spoken" about the second personal advent of Christ, any more than
> the Jews did about the first. And because we have done this, I say that we
> should speak of such mistakes as that referred to in our text with much ten-
> derness and compassion.[4]

Then in a manner so representative of Ryle's "child like" gentleness that
combines with his "granite like" firmness, he presses home the importance
of a correct hermeneutic upon which rests the likelihood of a Christian gain-
ing, through the employment of Scripture, the sustained interest of a Jew.

> Reader, I earnestly invite your special attention to the point on which I am
> now dwelling. I know not what your opinions may be about the fulfillment
> of the prophetical parts of Scripture. I approach the subject with fear and
> trembling, lest I should hurt the feelings of any dear brother in the Lord.
> But I ask you in all affection to examine your own views about prophecy.
> I entreat you to consider calmly whether your opinions about Christ's sec-
> ond advent and kingdom are as sound and scriptural as those of His first
> disciples. I entreat you to take heed, lest insensibly you commit as great an
> error about Christ's second coming and glory as they did about Christ's first
> coming and cross.
>
> I beseech you not to dismiss the subject which I now press upon your
> attention, as a matter of curious speculation, and one of no practical impor-
> tance. Believe me, it effects the whole question between yourself and the un-
> converted Jew. I warn you that, unless you interpret the prophetical portion
> of the Old Testament in the simple literal meaning of its words, you will find
> it no easy matter to carry on an argument with an unconverted Jew.[5]

---

[4] Ibid., 46.
[5] Ibid., 46–47.

Should a Christian holding to an Augustinian, supercessionist eschatology witness to an unbelieving Jew concerning the gospel as revealed in the Old Testament, he may find himself confronted with questions that draw forth exposure of hermeneutical inconsistency with regard to Israel's prophesied future. At this point the Jew may then consider the commended good news to be less appealing.

> You would probably tell the Jew that Jesus of Nazareth was the Messiah promised in the Old Testament Scriptures. To those Scriptures you would refer him to for proof. You would show him Psalm 22, Isaiah 53, Daniel 9:26, Micah 5:2, Zechariah 9:9 and 11:13. You would tell him that in Jesus of Nazareth those Scriptures were literally fulfilled. You would urge upon him that he ought to believe these Scriptures, and receive Christ as the Messiah. All this is very good. So far you would do well.
>
> But suppose the Jew asks you if you take *all* the prophecies of the Old Testament in their simple literal meaning. Suppose he asks you if you believe in a literal personal advent of Messiah to reign over the earth in glory, a literal restoration of Judah and Israel to Palestine, a literal rebuilding and restoration of Zion and Jerusalem. Suppose the unconverted Jew puts these questions to you, what answer are you prepared to make?
>
> Will you dare to tell him that Old Testament prophecies of this kind are not to be taken in their plain literal sense? Will you dare to tell him that the words Zion, Jerusalem, Jacob, Judah, Ephraim, Israel, do not mean what they seem to mean, but mean the *Church of Christ*? Will you dare to tell him that the glorious kingdom and future blessedness of Zion, so often dwelt upon in prophecy, mean nothing more than the gradual Christianizing of the world by missionaries and gospel preaching? Will you dare to tell him that you think it "carnal" to expect a literal rebuilding of Jerusalem, "carnal" to expect a literal coming of Messiah to reign? Oh, reader, if you are a man of this mind, take care what you are doing! I say again, take care.[6]

How timely is this analysis that those involved in missionary outreach to the Jews will readily confirm. The Bible calls for one consistent hermeneutic with regard to the interpretation of both the Old Testament and the New Testament. Ought not this to be expected when we consider that most of the books of the Bible are of Hebrew origin? To suggest two hermeneutics is to introduce a stumbling block.

> Do you not see that you are putting a weapon in the hand of the unconverted Jew, which he will probably use with irresistible power? Do you not see that you are cutting the ground from under your own feet, and supplying the Jew with a strong argument for not believing your own interpretation of Scripture? Do you not see that the Jew will reply, that it is "carnal"

---

[6] Ibid., 47.

to tell him that the Messiah *has* come literally to *suffer*, if you tell him that it is "carnal" to expect Messiah *will* come literally to reign? Do you not see that the Jew will tell you, that it is far more "carnal" in you to believe that Messiah could come into a world as a despised, crucified Man of sorrows, than it is in him to believe that He will come into the world as a glorious King? Beyond doubt he will do so, and you will find no answer to give.

Reader, I commend these things to your serious attention. I entreat you to throw aside all prejudice, and to view the subject I am dwelling upon with calm and dispassionate thought. I beseech you to take up anew the prophetical Scriptures, and to pray that you may not err in interpreting their meaning. Read them in the light of those two great polestars, the first and second advents of Jesus Christ. Bind up with the *first advent* the rejection of the Jews, the calling of the Gentiles, the preaching of the gospel as a witness to the world and gathering out of the election of grace. Bind up with the second advent the restoration of the Jews, the pouring out of judgments on unbelieving Christians, the conversion of the world and the establishment of Christ's kingdom upon earth. Do this and you will see a meaning and fullness in prophecy which perhaps you have never yet discovered.[7]

So Ryle, having such a deep regard for the writings of the Reformed and Puritan heritage, yet is bold in making his point concerning the decided fallibility of many of this lineage with regard to prophecy, and especially concerning the future restoration of Israel.

I am quite aware that many good men do not see the subject of unfulfilled prophecy as I do. I am painfully sensible that I seem presumptuous in differing from them. But I dare not refuse anything which appears to me plainly written in Scripture. I consider the best of men are not infallible. I think we should remember that we must reject Protestant traditions which are not according to the Bible, as much as the traditions of the Church of Rome.

I believe it is high time for the Church of Christ to awake out of its sleep about Old Testament prophecy. From the time of the old fathers, Jerome and Origen, down to the present day, men have gone on in a pernicious habit of "spiritualizing" the words of the Prophets, until their true meaning has been well nigh buried. It is high time to lay aside traditional methods of interpretation, and to give up our blind obedience to the opinions of such writers as Poole, Henry, Scott and Clarke, upon unfulfilled prophecy. It is high time to fall back on the good old principle that Scripture generally means what it seems to mean, and to beware of that semi-skeptical argument, "*Such and such an interpretation cannot be correct, because it seems to us 'carnal'*"!

It is high time for Christians to interpret unfulfilled prophecy by the light of prophecies already fulfilled. The curses of the Jews were brought to pass literally: so also will be the blessings. The scattering was literal: so

[7] Ibid., 47–48.

also will be the gathering. The pulling down of Zion was literal: so also will be the building up. The rejection of Israel was literal: so also will be the restoration.[8]

Scattered to be Gathered

The chapter titled "Scattered Israel to be Gathered," is based on Jer 31:10: "Nations, hear the word of the LORD, and tell it among the far off coastlands! Say: The One who scattered Israel will gather him. He will watch over him as a shepherd guards his flock." Ryle maintained that the Gentiles are told here to make known God's will with regard to the nation of Israel. In particular this means the inevitable future restoration of the Jews to the land, following a prolonged scattering, that far exceeds in wonder the return that immediately followed the Babylonian captivity. To this end, Ryle vigorously upheld a consistent meaning with regard to the term "Israel" referring to the nation:

> For many centuries there has prevailed in the Churches of Christ a strange, and to my mind, an unwarrantable mode of dealing with this word "Israel". It has been interpreted in many passages of the Psalms and Prophets, as if it meant nothing more than Christian believers. Have promises been held out to Israel? Men have been told continually that they are addressed to Gentile saints. Have glorious things been described as laid up in store for Israel? Men have been incessantly told that they describe the victories and triumphs of the gospel in Christian churches. The proofs of these things are too many to require quotation. No man can read the immense majority of commentaries and popular hymns without seeing this system of interpretation to which I now refer.[9] Against that system I have long protested, and I hope I shall always protest as long as I live.
>
> I do not deny that Israel was a peculiar typical people, and that God's relations to Israel were meant to be a type of His relations to His believing people all over the world.
>
> I would have it most distinctly understood that God's dealings with individual Jews and Gentiles are precisely one and the same. Without repentance, faith in Christ and holiness of heart, no individual Jew or Gentile shall ever be saved.
>
> What I protest against is, the habit of allegorizing plain sayings of the Word of God concerning the future history of the *nation* of Israel, and explaining away the fullness of their contents in order to accommodate them to the Gentile Church. I believe the habit to be unwarranted by anything in

[8] Ibid., 48–49.

[9] It hardly needs mentioning that these volumes are almost exclusively Gentile in authorship.

Scripture, and to draw after it a long train of evil consequences.

Where, I would venture to ask, in the whole New Testament, shall we find any plain authority for applying the word "Israel" to anyone but the nation of Israel? On the contrary, I observe that when the Apostle Paul quotes Old Testament prophecies about the privileges of the Gentiles in gospel times, he is careful to quote texts which specifically mention the "Gentiles" by name. The fifteenth chapter of the Epistle to the Romans is a striking illustration of what I mean. We are often told in the New Testament that, under the gospel, believing Gentiles are "fellow heirs and partakers of the same hope" with believing Jews (Eph. 3:6). But that believing Gentiles may be called "Israelites", I cannot see anywhere at all.[10]

Concerning the future of national Israel, Ryle was emphatic about the eventual return of the Hebrew people to the promised land. He provided supportive quotes from the prophets (Isa 11:11–12; Jer 30:3,11; Ezek 37:21; Hos 1:11; 3:4–5; Joel 3:20; Amos 9:14–15; Obad 1:17; Mic 4:6–7; Zeph 3:14–20; Zech 10:6–10), and explained,

Reader, however great the difficulties surrounding many parts of unfilled prophecy, two points appear to my own mind to stand out as plainly as if written by a sunbeam. One of these points is the second personal advent of our Lord Jesus Christ before the Millennium. The other of these events is the future literal gathering of the Jewish nation, and their restoration to their own land. I tell no man that these two truths are essential to salvation, and that he cannot be saved except he sees them with my eyes. But I tell any man that these truths appear to me distinctly set down in holy Scripture and that the denial of them is as astonishing and incomprehensible to my own mind as the denial of the divinity of Christ.[11]

In relation to this matter of Israel's return to the land, Ryle made a further qualification:

I might show you by scriptural evidence that the Jews will probably first be gathered in an unconverted state, though humbled, and will afterwards be taught to look to Him whom they have pierced [Zech 12:10–14], through much tribulation.[12]

And So All Israel Shall Be Saved

Ryle understood the crucial text of Rom 11:26 in a manner consistent with the earlier definition of "Israel" as the nation identified with Judaism:

[10] Ryle, *Are You Ready*, 107–8.
[11] Ibid., 112–15.
[12] Ibid., 115.

To a plain man, untrammeled by traditional interpretation, the words of this prophecy appear very simple.

Israel shall be saved: that means the Jewish nation and people. It cannot possibly mean the Gentiles, because they are mentioned in the verse which directly precedes our text, in direct contrast to the Jews. "Blindness in part is happened to Israel, until; the fullness of the Gentiles be come in" (Rom. 11:25).

All Israel: that means the whole people or nation of the Jews. It cannot possibly mean a small elect remnant. In this very chapter the Israelitish nation and the *election* out of Israel are mentioned in contradistinction to one another. "Israel hath not obtained that which he seeketh for; but the election hath obtained it; and rest were blinded" (Rom. 11:7).[13]

Despite centuries of oppression under "the just displeasure of God," and at the same time preservation unlike any other racial group,

the history of Israel then has not yet come to an end. There is another wonderful chapter yet to be unfolded to mankind. The Scripture tells us expressly that a time is coming when the position of Israel may be entirely changed, and they shall be once more restored to the favor of God.[14]

Ryle cited several supporting passages of Scripture (Zech 12:10; 13:1; 2 Cor 3:16) but gave special attention to Ezek 36:24–38:

Once more I remind you that this wonderful passage *primarily* belongs to the Jews. No doubt the Church of Christ may *secondarily* make spiritual use of it. But let us never forget that the Holy Ghost first caused it to be written concerning Israel.

But time would fail me, if I attempted to quote all the passages of Scripture in which the future history of Israel is revealed. Isaiah, Jeremiah, Ezekiel, Hosea, Joel, Amos, Obadiah, Micah, Zephaniah, Zechariah all declare the same thing. All predict, with more or less particularity, that in the end of this dispensation the Jews are to be restored to their own land and to the favor of God. I lay no claim to infallibility in the interpretation of Scripture in this matter. I am well aware that many excellent Christians cannot see the subject as I do. I can only say, that to my eyes, the future *salvation* of Israel as a people, their *return* to Palestine and their national conversion to God, appear as clearly and plainly revealed as any prophecy in God's Word.

But I freely confess that these are deep things. Enough for you and me to know that Israel shall be restored to their own land, and shall be converted and saved, without entering too minutely into particulars. Let me close this branch of my subject with the Apostle's words: "O the depth of the riches

---

[13] Ibid., 145–46.

[14] Ibid., 151. See also Ryle's comment on Luke 21:24, *Expository Thoughts on Luke*, 2 (Edinburgh: Banner of Truth Trust, 1986), 371.

both of the wisdom and knowledge of God. How unsearchable are His judgments, and His ways past finding out" (Rom. 11:33).[15]

For Ryle such a perspective concerning God's ongoing regard for national Israel brings with it a responsibility toward this distinctive people. From Israel came our Bible, the first preaching of the Bible, the mother of Jesus and her Son. Although the Jews presently remain in unbelief concerning their Messiah, Jesus Christ, it should be incumbent upon Gentiles to do all they can to show kindness to their spiritual benefactors, as Ryle stated:

> We may all pay our debts *indirectly* by striving to remove stumbling-blocks which now lie between the Jews and Christianity. It is a sorrowful confession to make, but it must be made, that nothing perhaps so hardens Israel in unbelief as the sins and inconsistencies of professing Christians. The name of Christ is too often blasphemed among Jews, by reason of the conduct of many who call themselves Christians. We repel Israel from the door of life, and disgust them by our behavior. Idolatry among Roman Catholics, skepticism among Protestants, neglect of the Old Testament, contempt for the doctrine of the atonement, shameless Sabbath breaking, widespread immorality, all these things, we may depend upon it, have a deep effect on the Jews. They have eyes and they can see. The name of Christ is discredited and dishonored among them by the practice of those who have been baptized in Christ's name. The more boldly and decidedly all true Christians set their faces against the things I have just named, and wash their hands of any complicity with them, the more likely are they to find their efforts to promote Christianity among the Jews prosperous and successful.[16]

More directly, Ryle concluded with the following recommendations concerning this vital subject of the destiny of Israel in Scripture:

> 1. Take up the subject because of the *important position which it occupies in Scripture.* Cultivate the habit of reading prophecy with a single eye to the literal meaning of its proper names. Cast aside the old traditional idea that Jacob, and Israel, and Judah, and Jerusalem, and Zion must always mean the Gentile Church, and that predictions about the second Advent are to be taken spiritually, and first Advent predictions literally. Be just, and honest, and fair. If you expect the Jews to take the 53rd of Isaiah literally, be sure you take the 54th and 60th and 62nd literally also. The Protestant Reformers were not perfect. On no point, I venture to say, were they so much in the wrong as in the interpretation of Old Testament prophecy. Even our venerable Authorized Version of the Bible has many "tables of contents" which are sadly calculated to mislead, in the prophetical books. When the Revised Version comes out, I trust we shall see a great improvement in this respect.

[15] Ibid., 152–54.
[16] Ibid., 157.

2. In the next place, take up the Jewish subject because of the times in which we live. That man must be blind indeed who does not observe how much the attention of politicians and statesmen in these days is concentrating on the countries around Palestine. The strange position of things in Egypt, the formation of the Suez Canal, the occupation of Cyprus, the project of the Euphrates railway, the drying up of the Turkish empire, the trigonometrical survey of Palestine, what curious phenomena these are![17] What do they mean? What is going to happen next? He that believeth will not make haste. I will not pretend to decide. But I think I hear the voice of God saying, "Remember the Jews, look to Jerusalem."

3. In the next place, take up the Jewish subject *because of the special blessing* which seems to be given to those who care for Israel. I challenge anyone to deny that few ministers of Christ have been so useful of late years and made a greater mark on the world than the following well-known men, Charles Simeon, Edward Bickersteth, Haldane Stewart, Dr. Marsh, Robert M'Cheyne and, though last not least, Hugh McNeile. They were men of very different gifts and minds; but they had one common feature in their religion. They loved the cause of the Jews. In them was the promise fulfilled. "They shall prosper that love thee" (Ps. 122:6).

4. In the next place, take up the Jewish subject because of its *close connection with the second Advent of Christ and the close of this dispensation.* Is it not written, "When the Lord shall build up Zion, He shall appear in His glory"? (Ps. 102:16). "If the casting away of Israel be the reconciling of the world, what shall the receiving of them be, but life from the dead?" (Rom. 11:15). The words which the angel Gabriel addressed to the Virgin Mary have never yet been fulfilled: "He shall reign over the house of Jacob forever; and of His kingdom there shall be no end" (Luke 1:33).

5. Last of all, let us annually support that great and good institution, the Jews' Society, by our money and our prayers. Our money will be bestowed on an old and faithful servant of Christ, which does Christ's work in Christ's own way. Our prayers are well bestowed if given for a cause which is so near our Master's heart. The time is short. The night of the world is drawing near. If ever there is a "nation born in a day", that nation will be Israel. Let us pray for that blessed consummation, and give habitually as if we really believed the words, "All Israel shall be saved."[18]

---

[17] Ryle was referring to the decline of the Ottoman Empire from its climactic vastness during the seventeenth century to its eventual dissolution in 1922. As Ryle wrote, he had just witnessed the defeat of the Ottoman Empire in the Russo-Turkish War of 1877–1878. He seemingly anticipated Britain's significant role in the Jews' repossession of the land of Israel. See D. L. Larsen, *Jews, Gentiles and the Church: A New Perspective on History and Prophecy* (Grand Rapids: Discovery House, 1955), 135–221.

[18] Ibid., 157–59.

Appendix C

GOD'S DEALINGS WITH ISRAEL—
BY GRACE OR LAW?

I t is usual for those writers who declare that God has irrevocably abandoned national Israel to propose that the basis of this divine disenfranchisement was the Hebrews' violation of the Mosaic covenant.
Philip Mauro, for example, maintained that according to Deut 28:63–64
("Just as the LORD was glad to cause you to prosper and to multiply you,
so He will also be glad to cause you to perish and to destroy you. You will
be deported from the land you are entering to possess. Then the LORD will
scatter you among all peoples from one end of the earth to the other, and
there you will worship other gods, of wood and stone, which neither you
nor your fathers have known"), the disobedience of this "odious kingdom"
was to result in a destruction that would be "the end of their history as
a nation." This national destruction, he wrote, came at the hands of the
Romans in AD 70, from which "there was to be no recovery."[1] Further, in
classic Augustinian style we are told, "Romans 11 contains proof of the
most conclusive sort that there is *no future in the purposes of God for the
natural seed of Jacob as a nation*, but that there is the hope and promise of
personal salvation for individual Israelites if they abide not still in unbelief"
(see Rom 11:23).[2]

Samuel Hinds Wilkinson, late director of the Mildmay Mission to the
Jews, England, published a response to this ardent upholder of replacement theology.[3] Chapter 15, titled "Grace and the Rainbow," presents a
moving apologetic for the sovereignty of grace toward national Israel, even
as the church has likewise been a recipient.[4]

> The root of the solemn consideration raised by Mr. Philip Mauro's book, in
> and by which he challenges the assurance to God's chosen people Israel of a
> national restoration, conversion and beneficent mission, will be exposed if
> we ask the question: Did Law precede Grace of Grace precede Law?
> This is indeed a vital question: for indisputably the original promises to
> Abraham, recorded in Genesis 12, were given *unconditionally*. No one was
> bound by those promises but the One Who made them. No terms were

---

[1] P. Mauro, *The Hope of Israel* (Boston: Hamilton Bros., 1929) 57, 61.

[2] Ibid., 238. The fallacy of this selective regard for the Israelites has been dealt with in chapters 2 and 3 (emphasis original).

[3] S. H. Wilkinson, *The Israel Promises and their Fulfilment* (London: John Bale, Sons, 1936).

[4] Ibid., 115–20.

imposed. No mediator was present (Gal. 3:20). Whatever those promises were, whatever kind of fulfillment they required, those promises and that Covenant which ratified them, in particular the grant of a specific territory as an everlasting possession, were unconditional and undeserved.[5] We are told that Israel was not thus chosen for Divine love and favor because they were more numerous than other peoples: for they were "the fewest of all peoples" (Deut. 7:7–8): nor was the territory granted to them because of their righteousness, for they were "a stiff-necked people" (Deut. 9:4–6). And this unconditional Covenant and all that it included and involved ante-dated the Covenant of the law by 430 years. And the legal Covenant "which was four hundred and thirty years after, cannot disannul it, that it should make the promise of none effect" (Gal. 3:17).[6]

When "the God of glory" revealed Himself to Abram (Acts 7:2), it was due to no discovery by Abram. Rather, it involved a divine "call" (Heb 11:8) according to God's gracious, sovereign initiative, beginning only with "the LORD said to Abram" (Gen 12:1) and "the LORD appeared to Abram" (Gen 12:7). Abram was the first of the prospective elect nation, and through him, notwithstanding the preceding defilement of the human race, there was covenantally guaranteed the prospect of God's new Hebrew nation. To infer ultimate defeat because of unconquerable human rebellion is simply to deny the principle of Phil 1:6 that God completes what He starts, and of Rom 11:29 that "God's gracious gifts and calling are irrevocable."

Philip Mauro argued from Deut 4:1 that Israel was to "hearken always to God's statutes and judgments: and *upon that express condition*, they were to go in and possess the land. Every blessing mentioned in this book is made to depend upon that same condition."[7] But Wilkinson responded,

Then in that case, Mr. Mauro, the original Covenant of grace *could* be disannulled by the terms of the legal Covenant, made 430 years after. In that case, temporary deprivation of privilege or delay in its realization con-notes absolute and final cancellation of a Divine promise. In that case, the Scriptures you quote (Deut. 4:1,15–24,26–30) are of private or individual or isolated *(idias)* interpretation [see 2 Pet 1:20], and not to be understood as in harmony with the whole body of prophetic Scripture. In that case, the law was *not* "added because of transgressions till *(archi)* the seed should come to whom the promise was made" [Gal 3:19]; but it was introduced

---

[5] This is even more certainly established in Gen 15:1–21 where the unilateral nature of the Abrahamic covenant is signified by God's passing between the severed portions of animals while Abraham was deep in a divinely imposed sleep. For this reason, God declared that Abraham would "know . . . for certain" that the covenant is sure (vv. 13–16).

[6] Wilkinson, *The Israel Promises and their Fulfilment*, 115–16.

[7] Mauro, *Hope of Israel*, 42.

to impose new terms and conditions by means of which promises already freely given and confirmed might be annulled and superseded.[8]

Everything necessary for the redeemed nation of Israel was in the Abrahamic covenant, including the promise of the land and the Redeemer seed (Gal 3:16). The law was an interim administrator "added" until that Redeemer seed should come (Gal 3:19,25–29; see Jer 11:7–8; Rom 5:20). To suggest that the conditionality of the Mosaic covenant introduced conditionality into the Abrahamic covenant is ultimately to challenge the integrity of God.

Wilkinson continued to declare the priority and superiority of grace over law, especially in that grace will "outlast all legal enactments and all covenants based upon them." He then asked some probing questions:

Was not the Church, was not every member of it, whose standing is on the ground of grace alone, chosen in Christ Jesus before the foundation of the world? Were not the tables of the law shut within the ark and placed in the Holiest apartment of all in the temple of God and made thus to rest *beneath* the mercy seat? Is not judgment God's *strange* work? Does He not *delight* in mercy? Where sin abounds, does not grace *much more* abound? Does He forsake Israel for a small moment, will He not gather Israel with great mercies? If He hides His face in a little wrath for a moment on account of broken law, will He not have mercy with everlasting kindness on the same people who have been the subjects of His wrath? When God saved His people Israel over and over again from oppressive enemies was it not because He "remembered His covenant with Abraham, with Isaac and with Jacob (Exod. 2:24; cf. Ps. 115:8,42; 116:45; &c.)"? Was He in such cases remembering the broken and unrenewable Covenant of Sinai or the everlasting covenant of grace made with Abraham 430 years earlier? If the law, even to the believer, was a schoolmaster, having done his work, to be for ever intruding? When faith is come are we longer under a schoolmaster? Is Israel as a nation *always* to be unbelieving? Is the new covenant not to be made with the same people as were under the old covenant (Jer. 31:31–34)? And if so, does it not guarantee individual and national repentance, faith and regeneration to the same people?[9] And if the legal Covenant of Sinai could not disannul the Covenant and promises made with Abraham, Isaac and Jacob, can it do so *now* or *ever*? Can grace be tied by conditions? Can out-and-out gifts be withdrawn? Can God repent of gifts or calling or grants or

---

[8] Wilkinson, *The Israel Promises and their Fulfilment*, 116.

[9] It is simply astonishing that those who so fervently proclaim the sovereignty of God in this realm with regard to new covenant conversion should so adamantly deny this same effectual grace to the nation of God's old covenant people. In other words, during the church age there is belief in the sovereignty of grace by which the Church has been established, never to finally fall, that is, from a Reformed perspective. But only conditionality of an Arminian style is permitted for Israel.

promises, unconditionally made? Is not God able to graft Israel again into its own olive tree? Shall they not be grafted in, if they abide not in unbelief? Will the time limit of Israel's blindness never be reached and passed?[10]

This is the reason both Jewish and Gentile Christians should delight to sing,

> Grace! 'tis a charming sound,
>   Harmonious to mine ear;
> Heav'n with the echo shall resound,
>   And all the earth shall hear.

Philip Doddridge, 1702–51

Wilkinson pointed out the contrasting conditionality that Mauro upheld because he imposed the Mosaic terms of blessing for obedience and cursing for disobedience on the unconditional Abrahamic Covenant. Thus, as indicated at the beginning of this chapter, Mauro considered Deut 28:63–64 to prophesy "the end of their [Israel's] history as a nation."[11] In other words, persistent disobedience supposedly resulted in the Jews being cast aside forever. Mauro's breathtaking finality is indicated when, with necessary qualification, he pushed aside the plain understanding of subsequent prophets:

> Nor is there any promise of God, by any later prophet [after Moses], of recovery for the earthly nation from this final destruction and dispersion at the hands of the Romans. For an attentive reading of the prophecies concerning "Israel," "Zion," and "Jerusalem," leads to the conclusions that such as are yet to be fulfilled relate to the heavenly people, country, and city, to which respectively those names properly belong; and that all prophecies of recovery intended for "Israel after the flesh" (I Cor. 10:18) were completely fulfilled in and after the return from the Babylonian captivity.[12]

In itself this claim is sufficiently demeaning of God's gospel workings through the priority of sovereign grace and is open to serious challenge hermeneutically according to chapters 6 and 7. I am sorry to say that many of Reformed convictions also adhere to this same defective teaching that has resulted in tragic consequences throughout church history. Mauro's tart attitude in general toward the Jews throughout his writings is no exception. We have already seen the same conflict evident in modern scholars when the conditionality of the Mosaic order is imposed on the Abrahamic

---

[10] Wilkinson, *The Israel Promises and their Fulfilment*, 116–18.

[11] Ibid., 57.

[12] Mauro, *The Hope of Israel*, 57–58.

covenant, especially with regard to the land, even when there is the agreement concerning the unconditional nature of the new covenant.[13]

Furthermore, Wilkinson charges that Mauro's interpretation of Scripture at this point "causes him to divert the clear promises of God from the parties to whom they were given and to confine them to a new constitution." Such a diversion, he says, defames the divine character, "for it leaves no scope for grace, no credit for inviolability of oath, nor for continuity of purpose, nor for overcoming of set-backs and resistances and failures, no place for pardon, no delight in store for the Father's heart when the repentant prodigal returns (Jer. 31:18–20)."[14] One wonders if Mauro's denial of the sovereignty of grace for national Israel could be the cause of his graceless attitude toward the Jews in general. In *The Gospel of the Kingdom*, Mauro wrote that

> of all the as yet unfulfilled promises of God, whatsoever and how many soever they be, *nothing remains for the natural Israel.* . . . The sober facts are that *Zionism* has been a pitiful failure almost from the beginning; and that in the period of its greatest success the volume of immigrants constituted but a trickling stream, and they were of the most undesirable sort. The movement reached its peak in 1926; and from that time to the present *Zionism* has been palpably a dying enterprise. . . . Subsequent reports show that conditions have not improved; that the state of the Jews in Palestine is wretched in the extreme, and that the attitude of the great mass of Jews throughout the world towards the Zionistic project is that of complete apathy and indifference."[15]

Surely an impoverished eschatology, as reflected here, leads to such impoverished and inaccurate conclusions. So Wilkinson asked in conclusion,

> Then if Mr. Mauro be right, *what* is grace and *where* is it? Better, far better, is the great vision of John the Divine while in the Isle that is called Patmos: "And immediately I was in the Spirit; and behold a throne was set in heaven, and One sat on a throne. And He that sat was to look upon like a jasper and a sardine stone: and there was a rainbow about the throne, in sight like unto an emerald" (Rev. 4:2–3).
>
> Are the colors significant? . . . Surely then the encircling rainbow, enclosing all with its endless line of radiant green, speaks of grace and abiding. For was not the first exhibition of a rainbow the token of God's first Covenant with all flesh, "between Me and you and every living creature that

[13] See the discussion of Robertson and Burge in chapter 3, Chapman and Sizer in chapter 5, Fairbairn, Hoekema, Venema, and Waldron in chapter 6, and Davies in chapter 9.

[14] Wilkinson, *The Israel Promises and their Fulfilment*, 118–19.

[15] P. Mauro, "The Hope of Israel," in *The Gospel of the Kingdom*, [cited July 2007]. Online: http://www.preteristarchive.com/Books/1927_mauro_gospel-kingdom.html (emphasis his).

is with you for perpetual generations (Gen. 9:12)." Was not that Covenant made independently of all future human resistance and apostasy and guilt—was not the rainbow the token, "of a covenant between Me and the earth (Gen. 9:13)?" Surely the rainbow symbolizes and represents grace—the grace of benevolent purpose, the grace of changeless attitude, the grace of persistent long-suffering and patience, the grace which is endless, all-inclusive, all conquering.[16] [Quotes Rom 11:6 and Mal 3:6] No other reason but that of changeless grace could have spared Israel the complete annihilation they deserved. And shall the original purpose fail, the original declaration be falsified or even modified, shall works be substituted for grace or any kind of transference of specific promise take place? Shall not the whole purpose come to final achievement as with Zerubbabel, who after gazing on the desolations of Jerusalem, desertion, rubbish, silence, defilement and ashes, after confronting opposition and apathy, yet saw in vision and by promise the work of the new temple completed and the headstone thereof brought forth with shoutings of "Grace, grace unto it" (Zech. 4:7).[17]

---

[16] John Gill commented concerning the rainbow around God's throne, "The rainbow is of various colors and fitly expresses the various promises and blessings, in the covenant of grace, and the various providences, both prosperous and adverse, with respect to soul and body; and as the rainbow was an emblem of mercy, peace, and reconciliation in God to man, after he had destroyed the world by a flood, so the covenant is a covenant of grace and mercy; it springs from it, and is full of it, and provides for the peace and reconciliation of the people of God, by the blood of Christ; whence it is called a covenant of peace: and as the rainbow is a security to the world, and the inhabitants of it, from a destruction by a flood any more, so the covenant is a security to those who are interested in it, from eternal destruction, and wrath to come; herein lies all their salvation, and this is the security of it: to which may be added, that God calls it my bow, as he often calls the covenant of grace my covenant, in distinction from man's." J. Gill, "Exposition of the Old and New Testaments," *The Collected Writings of John Gill*, Rev. 4:3 (Albany, Oregon: Ages Software, 1998).

[17] Wilkinson, *The Israel Promises and their Fulfilment*, 119–20.

Appendix D

MELANIE PHILLIPS ON REPLACEMENT THEOLOGY

Anyone who doubts a cause and effect relationship between Christian replacement theology and Christian anti-Judaism will find the writings of Melanie Phillips to be illuminating, challenging and distressing, especially for the Christian. As a British journalist, author, social commentator, and graduate in English from Oxford University, her regular column in the *Daily Mail* has forthrightly addressed many political and social issues. Other writings have also appeared in the *Guardian, Observer, Sunday Times*, and *Spectator*. She received the Orwell Prize for journalism in 1996. Her Jewish perspective is particularly relevant with regard to the topic at hand.

More recently Phillips has authored *Londonistan* through a New York publisher. Although she had previously published in the United Kingdom, like D. Selbourne's *The Losing Battle with Islam* (New York: Prometheus, 2005), the political climate of British publishing made it necessary to publish her work in the United States.[1] The coining of the title *Londonistan* is described with chilling clarity.

> The London bombings [of July 2005] revealed a terrible truth about Britain, something even more alarming and dangerous to America's long-term future than the fact that foreign terrorists had been able to carry out the 9/11 attacks on U.S. soil in 2001. They finally lifted the veil on Britain's dirty secret in the war on terrorism—that for more than a decade, London had been the epicenter of Islamic militancy in Europe. Under the noses of successive British governments, Britain's capital had been turned into "Londonistan"—a mocking play on the names of such state sponsors of terrorism as Afghanistan—and become the major European center for the promotion, recruitment and financing of Islamic terror and extremism. Indeed it could be argued that it was in London that al-Qaeda was first forged from disparate radical groups into a global terrorist phenomenon. During the 1980s and 1990s, despite repeated protests from other countries around the world, Londonistan flourished virtually without public comment at home—and, most remarkably of all, with no attempt at all to combat it by the governmental and intelligence agencies that were all too aware of what

---

[1] "Terrified publishers won't print truth about Islam, says author [Selbourne]," *London Daily Telegraph*, 12/13/2005.

was happening. Incredibly, London has become the hub of European terror networks.[2]

The author goes on to document the cowering response of the United Kingdom to the modern invasion of Islamic culture. Through intimidation, such as with the complaint of giving religious offence to Muslims and the threat of being charged with Islamophobia, multicultural paralysis has resulted, especially within governmental and educational agencies. This has led to a related rise in open anti-Semitism, but especially within the Muslim community.

> Walk down the Edgware Road, in the heart of London's Arab district, and you will find on open display in bookshop after bookshop copies of *The Protocols of the Elders of Zion* and *Mein Kampf*, books devoted to Holocaust denial and vilification of Israel, cartoons depicting George W. Bush wearing a skullcap with the Star of David on it, and countless other texts and images defaming both Israel and the Jewish people.[3]

Yet is not this merely the reflection of a small extremist minority? If this were so, then why is there such a wide distribution of this racist slander within Muslim communities? And why is there no outrage from an offended nation? Why is there mainly silence from the wider religious non-Muslim and Muslim communities? In the heart of England,

> the murderous rage against Israel, expressed by one Muslim organization after another, is greeted with indifference. Despite the plethora of antisemitic materials on sale in bookshops, there are virtually no prosecutions because the prosecuting authorities believe these would not be "in the public interest"—in other words, they are afraid of a Muslim backlash.[4]

The reaction of the mainstream Christian community and even many evangelicals, but especially within the Church of England, has been one of increasingly vociferous anti-Judaism that at the same time has been cringing, almost servile, in its accommodation of Muslim influence. So Phillips included a chapter aptly titled, "On Their Knees before Terror." It is especially concerned with the response of the Church of England that partly stems from the effects of social liberalism on Christianity.

> The Church stopped trying to save people's souls and started trying instead to change society. It signed up to the prevailing doctrine of the progressive class that the world's troubles were caused by poverty, oppression and dis-

---

[2] M. Phillips, *Londonistan* (New York: Encounter Books, 2006), x-xi.
[3] Ibid., 114.
[4] Ibid., 115.

crimination. Miracles were replaced by Marx. . . . Absorbing the prevailing utilitarianism which preached the creed of lifestyle choice, the Church came to believe that it too was in the business of delivering the greatest happiness to the greatest number. So it went with the flow of permissiveness, supporting the liberalizing of abortion, homosexuality and divorce.[5]

As a result, multiculturalism moved into the religious arena, resulting in the naive, welcome embrace of animated Islam by means of the ecumenical cliché of interfaith relations in company with ready Christian self-abasement. As a result,

> It is, perhaps, no surprise therefore that the Church [of England] should have taken the side of the Palestinian Arabs in the Israel/Arab impasse. A letter to the prime minister about the Iraq war, from the archbishops of Canterbury and York backed by every diocesan, suffragan and assistant bishop in the Church of England, showed how deeply the Church's views about Iraq were dominated by the issue of Israel, which they approached solely from the perspective of Arab and Muslim opinion. There was no mention in this letter of the rights of Israel or the Jews as the principal victims of annihilatory aggression and prejudice.[6]

With this development of Muslim and Palestinian sympathies in mind, at the expense of former historic loyalties with Israel, Phillips recounted her surprising discovery of the essential reasons for the heightening of tensions between Jews and Christian in Britain. At that time (February 16, 2002), she wrote an article in the *Spectator* with the justifiably provocative title, "Christians who hate the Jews." Here we are not dealing merely with a theological, or even an eschatological, nuance that readily admits the legitimacy of opposing opinions. There is, rather, an impending unethical maelstrom of growing proportions that threatens to transfer shame from the twentieth to the twenty-first century. Perhaps the most incredible feature of this movement, known for its replacement theology or supercessionism, which disgraces the Jewish people and thus generates Christian anti-Judaism, is the claim that its theology is based on the person of Jesus Christ, the quintessential Jew. However, let us now consider the circumstances whereby Phillips was quite shocked to be advised as to the essential roots of the escalating conflict between Christianity and Israel:

> It was one of those sickening moments when an illusion is shattered and an ominous reality laid bare. I was among a group of Jews and Christians who met recently to discuss the churches' increasing public hostility to

[5] Ibid., 140.
[6] Ibid., 147-48.

Israel. The Jews were braced for a difficult encounter. After all, many British Jews (of whom I am one) are themselves appalled by the destruction of Palestinian villages, targeted assassinations and other apparent Israeli over-reactions to the Middle East conflict. But this debate never took place. For the Christians said that the churches' hostility had nothing to do with Israel's behavior towards the Palestinians. This was merely an excuse. The real reason for the growing antipathy, according to the Christians at that meeting, was the ancient hatred of Jews rooted deep in Christian theology and now on widespread display once again.

A doctrine going back to the early Church fathers, suppressed after the Holocaust, had been revived under the influence of the Middle East conflict. This doctrine is called replacement theology. In essence, it says that the Jews have been replaced by the Christians in God's favor, and so all God's promises to the Jews, including the land of Israel, have been inherited by Christianity. Some evangelicals, by contrast, are 'Christian Zionists' who passionately support the State of Israel as the fulfillment of God's Biblical promise to the Jews. But to the majority who have absorbed replacement theology, Zionism is racism and the Jewish state is illegitimate.[7]

So when she heard with frightening honesty such a revelation, this Jewish writer learned that the spirit of Augustine lives on. And well might a Christian seriously consider attempting to place himself in her shoes and contemplate the shuddering distress that such an awakening might bring about. Phillips then explained how she and her Jewish companions inquired whether they may possibly have misunderstood what they had been told:

> The Jews at the meeting were incredulous and aghast. Surely the Christians were exaggerating. Surely the Churches' dislike of Israel was rooted instead in the settlements, the occupied territories and Prime Minister Ariel Sharon. But the Christians were adamant. The hostility to Israel within the Church is rooted in a dislike of the Jews. Church newspaper editors say they are intimidated by the overwhelming hostility to Israel and to the Jews from influential Christian figures, which makes balanced coverage of the middle east impossible. Clerics and lay people alike are saying openly that Israel should never have been founded at all. One church source said what he was hearing was a "throwback" to the visceral anti-judaism of the middle ages.[8]

As further proof of this insidious development, Phillips related a conversation she had with Andrew White, canon of Coventry cathedral and the Archbishop of Canterbury's representative in the Middle East who is

---

[7] M. Phillips, "Christians who hate the Jews," *Spectator* (Feb 16 2002): 1. Cited July 2007. Online: http://www.spectator.co,uk.
[8] Ibid., 1.

heavily engaged in trying to promote dialogue and peace between Israelis and Palestinians.

> He says of attitudes in the church: "These go beyond legitimate criticism of Israel into hatred of the Jews. I get hate mail calling me a Jew-lover and saying my work is evil." The reason, he says, is that Palestinian Christian revisionism has revived replacement theology. "This doctrine was key in fanning the flames of the Holocaust, which could not have happened without 2,000 years of anti-Jewish polemic", he says. After the Holocaust the Vatican officially buried the doctrine, the current Pope affirming the integrity of the Jewish people and recognizing the State of Israel. But according to White, the doctrine is "still vibrant" within Roman Catholic and Anglican pews. "Almost all the churches hold to replacement theology", he says. The catalyst for its re-emergence has been the attempt by Arab Christians to reinterpret Scripture in order to de-legitimize the Jews' claim to the land of Israel. This has had a powerful effect upon the churches.[9]

As corroboration of what had been told to her by Christians, Phillips cited the writings of Naim Ateek and Stephen Sizer, variously mentioned in chapters 3-7. She provides even more detail in this regard in *Londonistan*, including the following assessment of Colin Chapman's *Whose Promised Land?*

> His version of replacement theology is based on the premise that the existence of Israel has to be justified. It does not. To single out Israel's existence in this way is without precedent in the world and is itself evidence of prejudice. Moreover, replacement theology is not just a form of anti-Zionism; it directly attacks Jewish religion, history and identity. At the same time, Chapman's history grossly downplays the extent of Arab violence against the Jews in the decades of Jewish immigration to Palestine before the State of Israel was created. His conclusion that Zionism was an innate deception and that violence was always implicit is a baseless slur, as is the confusion of Jewish self-determination with racism.[10]

Overall, the implications here for Christians who take their Bible authoritatively and seriously are enormous. Here is plainly exposed regression into a shameful past that might well foreshadow similar tragic results in the future. Just suppose the surrounding Arab nations were eventually successful, with the subtle nod of approval from Europe and indirect assistance from Christian sympathizers, in their quest for pushing the Jewish population into the Mediterranean and the elimination of the State of Israel. What crocodile tears would then be expressed among the forums of

---

[9] Ibid., 2.
[10] Phillips, *Londonistan*, 155.

the nations, including formal international declarations of disapproval? It would probably then be suggested that any Jewish remnant either be treated as *dhimmis* under domination within a new Muslim state, or that they be transported to a remote part of Africa. What joy would also be celebrated among the Arab conquerors! Would not there also be heightened hope for the acceleration of Muslim expansionism? But what of the Christian advocates of replacement theology, with all of its subtle variations? What would they say? While deploring another Holocaust, yet inwardly there would be feelings that their supercessionist eschatology had been vindicated. Surely once again God had spoken in judgment! And there would also be suggestions as to how another future State of Israel, certainly within the Middle East, might be avoided, and that with supposed biblical justification. What a bitter, anti-Judaic prospect this whole scenario presents.

But I am persuaded of something far better, and this I believe to be explicitly declared throughout the panorama of Scripture. At its root will be the constraint of love for the Jews, in all their distress, much of which is the fruit of their own disobedient ways. Nevertheless, we remain debtors to the Hebrew race because of the legacy of the Scriptures, Jesus the Son of God, and the Christian church. Consequently, like Paul, while regarding them as "enemies" because of their aversion to Jesus as the Christ, yet they remain "loved" for the sake of God's irrevocable promise made to them through Abraham (Rom 11:28). Until the end of this age when the Lord Jesus will return, we are to offer the Jews unrelenting love and support, including the use of every opportunity to commend to them Jesus as the Jewish Savior. We look forward to the glorious day when the Jews shall ultimately inherit because God promised, "I will pour out a spirit of grace and prayer on the house of David and the residents of Jerusalem, and they will look at Me whom they pierced" (Zech 12:10) and "On that day Yahweh will become king over all the earth—Yahweh alone, and His name alone" (Zech 14:9).

Appendix E

ANNOTATED BIBLIOGRAPHY OF JEWISH-CHRISTIAN RELATIONS IN CHURCH HISTORY

A high proportion of conservative evangelical Christians, including those of a Reformed persuasion, are unaware of the historic roots underlying the eschatological concept of the Christian Church, as the new people of God, that has superseded the nation of Israel, and ethnic Jews in particular. This concept of dismissal or transference, in which God has supposedly forever disenfranchised national Israel, indeed Judaism as a whole, is better known as replacement or supercessionist theology. The revelation from church history of the outworking of this doctrine is one which Gentile Christians will find painful to digest, despite its undeniable truth. Unless they are prepared to read of this shameful legacy, the agony of these centuries, it will be difficult to make headway in dealing with doctrinal anti-Semitism as it manifests itself today among Christians who profess a serious biblical faith.

This annotated bibliography is offered as an introduction for those who will not retreat from the truth about centuries of unsavory Christian behavior derived from Augustinian eschatology. Time and time again this writer has met sincere Christians who simply were ignorant of the following testimony. Regardless of whether these historic accounts are Jewish, Roman Catholic, evangelical, or secular, the conclusions are in general agreement.

Baron, David. *The Shepherd Of Israel and His Scattered Flock.* London: Morgan and Scott, 1910. This author, born in a strict orthodox Jewish home in Russia, converted to Christianity and founded the *Hebrew Christian Testimony to Israel*, based in London, England. His commentary on Zechariah is a classic. Here is an exposition of Psalm 80, of which vv. 4–7 are seen as a summary description of Jewish travail during this Christian dispensation. Thus pages 25–79 present a discerning panorama of this same period according to the actual events of Jewish history as they merge with Christian church history.

Brown, Michael L. *Our Hands Are Stained with Blood: The Tragic Story of the "Church" and the Jewish People.* Shippensburg, PA: Destiny Image, 1992. While written in a popular and animated style, this book by a Hebrew

Christian provides extensive documentation, including a comprehensive Bibliographical Supplement, that demands consultation. He states, for example (pp. 125–26),

> It is a fundamental tenet of the Koran that both Israel and the Church failed. Moses was a prophet. Jesus was a prophet. But Muhammad was the seal of the prophets, the messenger of the final revelation. The Jews are not the people of God—they failed! The Christians are not the people of God—they failed! It is the Muslims who are the people of God. Of course this is preposterous. But, in the event that you are still uncertain about the calling of Israel, consider this simple truth: If God could *forsake* Israel, in spite of His unconditional, everlasting promises, then He could forsake the Church! If God could *replace* Israel, in spite of His unconditional, everlasting promises, then He could replace the Church! So, if you hold to a theology that says, "God has forsaken physical Israel," or "The Church has replaced Israel," you had better be extremely careful. Maybe the Koran is right!

Also refer to this author's three volumes on *Answering Jewish Objections to Jesus*, recommended by Moishe Rosen of *Jews for Jesus*. Volume 1 deals with general and historical objections; volume 2 deals with theological objections; volume 3 deals with objections to Messianic prophecy.

Callan, Terrance. *Forgetting the Root, the Emergence of Christianity from Judaism*. Mahwah, NJ: Paulist, 1986. As the title suggests, Rom 11:13,17–24 describes the birth of Gentile Christianity and the apostle Paul's warning that this engrafting of wild olive branches into the rich root of the olive tree should not lead to arrogance. This author concludes (pp. 107–8),

> The liberal Gentile Christians forgot that they had been grafted into the root of Judaism. This forgetfulness is strikingly illustrated by a comment made by Clement of Alexandria (died c. 215). . . . [He] interprets Romans 11:17 as a reference to the grafting of converts to Christianity into the Word. . . . Clement's interpretation of the cultivated olive tree as the Word, and the wild olive tree as including Jews who need to be grafted into the Word, reverses Paul's use of the metaphor and shows to what extent the Jewish roots of Christianity have been forgotten. This is precisely what Paul was trying to prevent by using the image. . . . To have retained this positive appreciation of Israel might have prevented much Christian anti-Semitism in the past; to retrieve it for our time might put relations between Christians and Jews on a much better foundation than otherwise supports them.

Carroll, James. *Constantine's Sword*. Boston: Houghton Mifflin, 2001. A former Roman Catholic priest of the Paulist order, Carroll's traumatic discovery of the substantial anti-Semitic legacy of the Roman Catholic Church led him to delve into this matter with great thoroughness while employing a style that constantly interacts with the churnings of his soul. While not conservative in his biblical presuppositions, this revelation of the unending abuse of Jews over the centuries by professing Christians is a tragic yet necessary record. Consider the significance of the following analysis (pp. 102–3, 142, 176, 368):

> If the death camps [of Nazi Europe] are causally linked through two millennia to mistakes made by the first generation of Christians—and I believe they are—can they still not be acknowledged as mistakes? What difference does it make whether two years have passed or two thousand if the causal link can be made? . . . Paul knew nothing of supercessionism. He remained a Jew. Indeed, his faith in Jesus was, to him, a way of being more Jewish than ever. . . . For Christians, the dramatic and unexpected conversion of Constantine was a proof of the Church's proclamation, but the change of fortune it led to was proof of even more. "The creation of the Christian state," Neusner says, "claiming to carry forward the ancient Israelite state, and to appeal to its precedents, brought to a critical stage the long-term Christian claim that Christians formed the new Israel."[1] . . . The basis of Luther's anti-Judaism, as the historian Heiko Oberman sums it up [see this volume referenced below], was the conviction that ever since Christ's appearance on earth, the Jews have had no more future as Jews.

Cohn-Sherbok, Dan. *The Crucified Jew: Twenty Centuries of Christian Anti-Semitism.* Grand Rapids: Eerdmans, 1997. A professor of Jewish theology at the University of Kent, Canterbury, England, this author provides a readable yet scholarly account of Judaism suffering under centuries of Christian malice (pp. 240–41).

> For twenty centuries, then, Jews have suffered at the hands of anti-Semites. The injustices and pogroms inflicted on the Jewish community have been to a large degree the result of Christian contempt. Anti-Jewish attitudes in the history of the Church were not accidental—rather they were the direct consequence of Christian teaching about Judaism and the Jewish nation. . . . Anti-Semitism has thus been a constant feature of the history of

---

[1] J. Neusner, *Judaism and Christianity: the New Relationship* (New York: Garland, 1993), 58. Martyn Lloyd-Jones made a significant and related comment concerning the Puritans: "Were they not too much influenced by the analogy of the Old Testament and of Israel? Here, it seems to me, was the source of the trouble, that they would persist in taking the analogy of Israel in the Old Testament and applying it to England. Was not that the real error? In the Old Testament and under that Dispensation of the State (of Israel) was the church (Acts 7:38), but the State of England in the sixteenth century was not the church. In the Old Testament the two were one and identical. But surely in the New Testament we have the exact opposite. The church consists of the 'called out' ones, not the total State." (*The Puritans: Their Origins And Successors* [Edinburgh: Banner of Truth Trust, 1987], 64-65).

Christendom. As we reach the end of the second millennium of this era, it is vital that both Christians and Jews affirm that they are heirs of a fearful tradition. . . . Only then will Christians and Jews fully appreciate the promise in the Psalmist's words: [Psalm 133:1–3].

Also refer to his edited volume, *Holocaust Theology: A Reader* (New York: New York University Press, 2002). The contributions to this volume include the writings of Edward Flannery, Graham Keith, Franklin Littell, Jacob Neusner, and David Rausch who are referenced in this bibliography. More recently Cohn-Sherbok published *AntiSemitism: A History* (Stroud, Gloucestershire: Sutton, 2002), concerning which he stated, "In an earlier study, *The Crucified Jew*, I focused on the Christian roots of anti-Semitism. The aim of this volume is to answer this question by surveying the history of anti-Semitism from a more global perspective" (p. vii).

Diprose, Ronald E. *Israel and the Church.* Waynesboro, GA: Authentic Media, 2000. This doctoral thesis presented to the Evangelische Theologische Faculteit, Louvain, Belgium, is a patristic and exegetical study of the origin and effects of replacement theology. Following careful analysis, the author declares (p. 168),

> It is a fact of history that the Augustinian concept of a Christian theocracy is closely linked with the anti-Semitic attitudes of the medieval church and unbelievably harsh treatment of the Jewish people. Thus it is not surprising that the traditional claim of Christendom to embody the promised messianic kingdom is an embarrassment to Christians involved in dialogue with Jewish people.

The exegetical highlight may well be his study of Israel's uniqueness according to God's election in Romans 9–11, especially 11:28 (pp. 171–72):

> Failure to reflect seriously on Israel in light of all the relevant biblical data has serious consequences for the entire enterprise of Christian theology. It was the neglect of relevant biblical data concerning the place of Israel in God's plan which permitted replacement theology to develop during the early centuries of the Christian era. Once replacement theology became a presupposition of theological reflection, it required that much of the Old Testament be interpreted allegorically. This involved the loss of the Hebrew world view and influenced the direction of theological reflection in areas such as ecclesiology and eschatology. Christian theology must be based on sound hermeneutical principles which presuppose the Church's essential relationship with Israel. These include taking into account the whole of the biblical Canon, taking seriously the Jewishness of Jesus and of much of the New Testament, recognizing the institutional distinctions between Israel and the Church, avoiding gratuitous allegorization of Scripture, and giving

normative value to what the New Testament teaches concerning both the first and second advents of Christ.

Ellison, Stanley A. *Who Owns The Land?* Portland: Multnomah, 1991. From a conservative evangelical perspective, here is one of the better assessments of the biblical, historical, and political issues that arise from the ongoing tensions which are endemic concerning the Middle East. Though supportive of the biblical grounds of Israel's present and future claims upon the land, it is not without reasonable consideration of opposing opinions and the opponents of Israel. He concludes (p. 186),

> Israel's basic need today is not peace with the Arabs; it is peace with God. The national turmoil and heartache of both clans is spiritual in nature rather than merely racial. Israel's deepest need is not economic, political, or military, but one she yet firmly resists—a historic tryst with her covenant Lord, similar to that of Jacob returning from exile [Gen 32–33]. That meeting will do what no military victory could accomplish—inaugurate permanent peace with good will toward all.

Flannery, Edward H. *The Anguish of the Jews.* New York: Macmillan, 1965. As a Roman Catholic priest, Flannery provides a helpful overview of the relationship between Christianity and Judaism over the centuries. He commences his study by recounting (p. xi),

> One evening several years ago, I walked north on Park Avenue in New York City in the company of a young Jewish couple. Behind us shone the huge illuminated cross the Grand Central Building displays each year at Christmas time. Glancing over her shoulder, the young lady—ordinarily well disposed toward Christians—declared: "That cross makes me shudder. It is like an evil presence." This disturbing comment evoked many questions in me, not least of which was: How did the cross, the supreme symbol of universal love, become a sign of fear, or evil for this young Jewess? It soon became clear that her fearful reaction to it was the fruit of a knowledge which she, but not I, had—a knowledge of the immense suffering undergone by her people at the hands of Christians for many centuries. It was my first introduction to the problem of anti-Semitism. Later discussions of the incident with both Jewish and Christian friends led me to a further discovery. Jews generally are acutely aware of the history of anti-Semitism, simply because it comprises so large a portion of Jewish history. Christians, on the contrary, even highly educated ones, are all but totally ignorant of it—except for contemporary developments. They are ignorant of it for the simple reason that anti-Semitism does not appear in their history books. Histories of the Middle Ages—and even of the Crusades—can be found in which the word "Jew" does not appear, and there are Catholic dictionaries and encyclopedias in which the term "anti-Semitism" is not listed.

Gager, John G. *The Origins Of Anti-Semitism.* New York: Oxford University Press, 1983. This scholarly work proposes that anti-Semitism surged following the birth of Christianity, principally because of conflict among Christians with the result that the opponents of Judaism triumphed. Thus modern anti-Semitism is not a uniquely modern phenomenon; it is not paganism in a modern dress or that pagan anti-Semitism which influenced early Christianity. Furthermore, Paul was totally outside the mainstream of early Christian anti-Judaism. He viewed Christ as the fulfillment of God's promise to redeem the Gentiles. In Paul's thinking, Christ represents neither an abrogation of God's covenant with Israel nor the replacement of Jews by Christians as the chosen people of God.

Goldhagen, Daniel Jonah. *Hitler's Willing Executioners.* New York: Random House, 1997. This Harvard University professor brings to the public the fruits of his acclaimed doctoral dissertation. In simple terms, with regard to responsibility for the Holocaust, Germans in general were culpable, especially in the light of exposed myths such as supposed ignorance and reluctance. While German nationalism, which mushroomed from the nineteenth century onward, was the distinctive incubator for "eliminationist antisemitism" of the twentieth century, the antecedents of this historic atrocity streamed forward from the early centuries of Christianity (pp. 49, 51, 53, 72, 74, 79):

> From the earliest days of Christianity's consolidation of its hold over the Roman Empire, its leaders preached against the Jews, employing explicit, powerfully worded, emotionally charged condemnations. . . . From the time of John Chrysostom until the modern period, the attitudes and treatment of Jews in the Christian world underwent frequent adjustment, as did Christian doctrine and practice. Yet while all the changes in Christians' theology and practice were taking place, the underlying belief in the divinity of Jesus remained firm. So too was anti-Semitism. . . . The medieval European hatred of Jews was so intense and so divorced from reality that all calamities in society could be and were attributed to the Jews' malfeasance. The Jews stood for everything that was awry, so that the reflexive reaction to a natural or social ill was to look to its supposed Jewish sources. Martin Luther's anti-Semitism was ferocious and influential enough to have earned him a place in the pantheon of anti-Semites. This did not matter to the Church that Luther was fighting, for the Church denounced him and his followers as heretics and Jews. The ubiquitous anti-Semitism that existed in 1800 and in 1850 became, if anything, more intense and certainly more deadly as the century was drawing to a close, as Germany became more economically and technologically advanced. . . . By the end of the nineteenth century, the view that the Jews posed extreme danger to Germany and that the source of their perniciousness was immutable, namely their race, and the consequential belief that the Jews

had to be *eliminated* from Germany were extremely widespread in German society. The tendency to consider and propose the most radical form of elimination—that is, extermination—was already strong and had been given much voice. . . . The fact was that as the 1920s and then the Nazi takeover approached, the German people were more dangerously oriented towards Jews than they had been during any other time since the dawn of modernity.

Gorday, Peter. *Principles Of Patristic Exegesis: Romans 9–11 in Origen, John Chrysostom, and Augustine.* New York: E. Mellen Press, 1983. How did these three influential church fathers understand the most important passage in the New Testament concerning the relationship between Christianity and Judaism? Insofar as disregard for national Israel in the Christian dispensation is concerned, there was unanimity of opinion.

Concerning Origen he states (pp. 91, 100),

Origen's summary statement [in his exegesis of Romans] is ". . . through the whole text of the epistle . . . the Apostle has taught how the highest religion has been transferred from the Jews to the Gentiles, from circumcision to faith, from the letter to the spirit, from shadow to truth, from carnal observance to spiritual observance." . . . The "letter" of the Old Testament text is always for Origen pointing in some way to its "spirit," i.e. the specifically Christian transformation of the Old Testament content. This may take the form of a Christological application or of a refining in some way of the ethical and inner-spiritual horizon of the text by means of a New Testament reference. Along the way a fair amount of anti-Jewish polemic takes place as Origen reflects on the relation of the church and the synagogue.

Concerning Chrysostom he states (pp. 129–30),

The event of Christ and the New Covenant for the Gentiles have divested the Jews as a people of any special standing before God. But finally it is the unbelief of the Jews and their rejection of Christ that constitute their supreme offense; for these there is no forgiveness, only the hope that God in his providential mercy will one day move their hearts to conversion. Thus Chrysostom finds consistent denunciation of the Jews in chapters 2, 3, 4 and 9–11 of Romans, as he senses in Paul's polemic a fundamental critique of the privileges and prerogatives of Judaism. This perspective on the Jews is held consistently throughout Chrysostom's writings, and down to the present day has been one of his best known and most ignominious characteristics. He frequently polemicized against "Judaizing" and freely encouraged repressive measures against the synagogues.

Concerning Augustine he states (pp. 171, 333),

[In Romans 11] some Jews have believed in Christ, and they are the remnant of the natural olive and fulfillment of the divine promises to historical

Israel. . . . The "Israel" that will ultimately be saved are the predestined elect, drawn into a unity out of Jews and Gentiles. . . . Judaism is simply relegated to the latter [non-elect] category, and its status in salvation-history assigned to the pre-Christian past.

Grosser, E and Edwin Halperin. *The Causes and Effects of Antisemitism: The Dimensions of Prejudice.* Secaucus, NJ: Citadel, 1979. This account of 1900 years of anti-Semitic attitudes and practices includes a preface by F. H. Littell. The authors' declared purpose is to increase awareness and understanding of anti-Semitism's historical magnitude and continuity, and its deep infection of the Western world. The method involved the concise listing, in chronological order, of anti-Semitic incidents. There is also a compilation, analysis, and synthesis of the causes and theories of anti-Semitism that are apparent from the catalogue. The authors explain (p. 3),

> The extent of anti-Semitism in Western history has never, to say the least, been common knowledge. And today there is a tendency to assume that the problem of Jewish security and the attitudes of Jews toward their survival grow from the experience of the Holocaust alone. The actions of the Nazis and their collaborators are of such a scale and horror as to obscure the long history of anti-Semitism. Often lost in appraisals of anti-Semitism is the fact that the underlying spirit of the Holocaust is almost 2,000 years old. The genocide carried out by a civilized and cultured nation in the mid-twentieth century was an extreme manifestation of this spirit, but not an isolated one.

Gruber, Dan. *The Church and the Jews: The Biblical Relationship.* Hagerstown, MD: Serenity, 1997. This significant book is highly commended as seminal by Walter C. Kaiser Jr. The unveiling from history concerning how the Christian church has mistreated Israel is comprehensive and compelling. Particularly enlightening is the comfortable relationship that existed between the historian Eusebius and the Emperor Constantine by means of which state sanctioned anti-Judaism came to the fore. It emphasizes that God made the new covenant with the house of Judah and the house of Israel; the Church does not have its own covenant with God. The Bible does not mention any covenant that God has made with the Church, though according to Romans 11, the Church is incorporated into the new covenant that God made with Israel. The author concludes (p. 324),

> The greatest obstacle to the salvation of the Jewish people is the Church designed by men. The greatest means of bringing salvation to the Jewish people is the church designed by God. Paul warned the Gentile believers not to be arrogant towards the Jewish people, nor ignorant of God's faithful-

ness to them. Yet it is this very arrogance that generally characterizes the Church's traditional theology and behavior.

Hay, Malcolm. *Thy Brother's Blood.* New York: Hart, 1975. This Roman Catholic historian was commended by Walter Kaufmann for his intellectual honesty. This concerns the author's unveiling of the dishonesty of great religious figures, that is, their disdainful regard for and mistreatment of the Jews over the centuries of church history. For example (p. 27),

> The violence of the language used by St. John Chrysostom in his homilies against the Jews has never been exceeded by any preacher whose sermons have been recorded. Allowances must, no doubt, be made for the custom of the times, for passionate zeal, and for the fear that some tender shoots of Christian faith might be chilled by too much contact with Jews. But no amount of allowance can alter the fact that these homilies filled the minds of Christian congregations with a hatred which was transmitted to their children, and to their children's children, for many generations. These homilies, moreover, were used for centuries, in schools and in seminaries where priests were taught to preach, with St. John Chrysostom as their model—where priests were taught to hate, with St. John Chrysostom as their model.

Heer, Friedrich. *God's First Love: Christians and Jews over Two Thousand Years.* London: Phoenix Giant, 1970. The author, a professor at the University of Vienna, explains that this book, "by an Austrian Catholic, is dedicated to the Jewish, Christian and non-Christian victims of the Austrian Catholic, Adolf Hitler." In raising the question of the positive guilt of Christianity in fostering anti-Semitism throughout its history, Heer shows that the concepts of Jew-hating and Jew-killing were based on Christian theology, taught by the most eminent fathers of the church.

Keith, Graham. *Hated Without A Cause? A Survey of Anti-Semitism.* Carlisle, Cumbria: Paternoster, 1997. This is a serious study of Israel in relation to the Christian Church written by a conservative evangelical with a British touch. Less disturbance about the fruit of supercessionism concerning heirs of the Reformation appears in the comment that "most churches have acknowledged that Christians bear some responsibility for anti-Semitism" (p. 279). He writes of "eminent Christians like John Chrysostom or Martin Luther, whose piety is unquestioned and whose opposition to the Jews clearly derived from their piety" (p. 268). He supports John Murray's exegesis of Romans 11. The issue of the return to and repossession of the land of Israel, from a biblical perspective, is skirted. Though quite erroneously, according to history, it is in the main identified with

Zionism, dispensationalism, and the uncritical support of Americans. He concludes (p. 283),

> Clearly it is as difficult today as at any time for the Gentile churches to hold in balance the two elements of Paul's perspective in Romans 11:28. Yet, they must strive to do so. If they forget that the Jewish people are beloved of God and their election is irrevocable, inevitably they will slip into anti-Semitic attitudes and practices. On the other side of the coin, to ignore the reality of Jewish unbelief and the fact that it makes them enemies of God means that the Jewish people will be deprived of the greatest service the Gentile Christians can give them—the testimony to Jesus of Nazareth as the Savior of Israel.

Larsen, David. *Jews, Gentiles and the Church: A New Perspective on History and Prophecy.* Grand Rapids: Discovery House, 1955. The author, a professor at Trinity Evangelical Divinity School, is unabashedly pro-Semitic and has provided a very readable yet comprehensive record of the relationship between Israel and Judaism over the past two millennia. As such, it is one of the best introductions to this subject. Larsen comments (pp. 84–85),

> the 'displacement theory' by which Israel is totally and finally replaced by the church in the plan and purpose of God . . . may lurch dangerously toward anti-Semitism. Any careless implication that the Jews are superfluous or unrelated to the divine scheme of things is dangerous."

Lindsey, Hal. *The Everlasting Hatred: The Roots of Jihad.* Murieta: Oracle House, 2002. As a prolific and popular writer and commentator on eschatology from a dispensational perspective, this volume is especially relevant. The easy reading style does not cloud an enlightening exposé of the contemporary conflict between Jews and Muslims that reaches back over 4,000 years and yet is presently attaining white-heat proportions. The following excerpt gets to the heart of the matter and at the same time calls upon the western world, Christians in particular, to wake up to the imminent threat that such tensions present (pp. 129–30):

> Israel's victories over the "armies of Allah" in five wars have placed the Koran in jeopardy, for it promises the forces of Islam victory in "holy wars." Devout Muslims fervently believe this is something that must be rectified. Nothing can remove this insult to Allah but a final military defeat of Israel. . . . As Mohammad said, "War is deception." He set the example for negotiating peace with an enemy until you are strong enough to annihilate him. It is called "the Quraysh Model." This was the ten-year peace treaty Mohammad signed with the Quraysh tribe of Mecca, which within a year he broke by destroying them. This is how he conquered Mecca and made it the holiest site in Islam—through treachery.

Littell, Franklin. *The Crucifixion of the Jews.* New York: Harper, 1975. A United Methodist Church minister, Littell is also an ecumenicist, a former professor at Temple University, a Holocaust scholar, and a friend of Israel. This volume is a vigorous polemic that calls Gentile Christians to honestly face the shameful legacy of theological anti-Semitism which cannot be divorced from the fact of the Holocaust. He begins by explaining (p. 2),

> The cornerstone of Christian anti-Semitism is the superseding or displacement myth, which already rings with the genocidal note. This is the myth that the mission of the Jewish people was finished with the coming of Jesus Christ, that "the old Israel" was written off with the appearance of "the new Israel." To teach that a people's mission in God's providence is finished, that they have been relegated to the limbo of history, has murderous implications which murderers will in time spell out. The murder of six million Jews by baptized Christians, from whom membership in good standing was not (and has not yet been) withdrawn, raises the most insistent question about the credibility of Christianity. The existence of a restored Israel, proof positive that the Jewish people is not annihilated, assimilated, or otherwise withering away, is substantial refutation of the traditional myth about their end in the historic process. And this is precisely why Israel is a challenge, a crisis for much contemporary Christian theology.

Mussner, Franz. *Tractate on the Jews: The Significance of Judaism for Christian Faith.* Philadelphia: Fortress, 1984. This Roman Catholic NT theologian confesses that, regarding his relationship to Judaism, he was no different from the vast majority of Christian scholars, filled with undisturbed prejudices against Judaism. Then, with Vatican II and its aftermath, he underwent a *metanoia* (repentance) and ventured forth on the rereading of the Scriptures with new eyes as far as Judaism is concerned (p. xi):

> "Tractates *against* the Jews" were written in the time of the church fathers, and the anti-Jewish spirit of these tractates has its effect even in our own times; thus, as the churches undertake a comprehensive rethinking of their relationship to Judaism, it is appropriate and timely for us to produce a "tractate *for* the Jews." . . . Behind this book lies a learning process of many years, a true changing of the mind, and I would like to invite the reader to enter into this learning process and to think newly and differently about Israel, the elder brother and the "root" of the Church.

Oberman, Heiko. *The Roots of Anti-Semitism in the Age of Renaissance and Reformation.* Philadelphia: Fortress, 1984. This recognized work is by a former professor at Harvard University and the University of Tübingen, West Germany. Focusing on the founders of modern Europe (Reuchlin, Erasmus, Luther, and Calvin), he concludes that their achievements, at

best ambiguous in contemporary Jewish eyes, did little to make the six-
teenth century anything more for the Jews than a bleak extension of the
Middle Ages. Hence, the roots of anti-Semitism were laid long before the
Reformation (p. xi):

> Hatred of the Jews was not an invention of the sixteenth century. It was
> an inherited assumption. Far from acquitting the age of Renaissance and
> Reformation, we should recognize that this same age which so consciously
> scrutinized the medieval traditions simultaneously passed on, with new
> strength, whatever withstood the test of inspection. This is what stamps the
> character of the age and determines its significance for the modern era.

Parkes, James. *The Conflict of the Church and the Synagogue: A Study in
the Origins of Antisemitism.* New York: Athaneum, 1969. This Ph.D. thesis
submitted to Oxford University by a Church of England clergyman is an
exhaustive study of the roots of anti-Semitism in the first eight centuries of
the Christian era. Convinced that the hostility of the Roman world to the
Jew offers no explanation of the creation and survival of this scourge, the
author was persuaded that it was in the conflict of church with synagogue
that the real roots of the problem lay. Parkes explains (pp. 371, 373),

> In the passage of the eight centuries reviewed in the previous chapters
> of this book we have seen the laying of the foundations of modern anti-
> Semitism. At times the ancient legislation itself has an appallingly modern
> ring in its very phraseology. With Leo and Charlemagne the curtain rings
> down upon the first act. The second act takes us up to the Reformation:
> the third act is still upon the stage. But it is an act of the same play, and
> can be explained only in the light of what has preceded it. Our interpreta-
> tion of the first act is, therefore, no academic question, but the means by
> which we can understand what is passing before our eyes. . . . At the end
> of the [first] century the leadership of the Church was already passing into
> Gentile hands. Gentile congregations were powerful and numerous. Any
> compromise on the ceremonial law had been completely rejected. . . . The
> hardening of Judaism is a result, not a cause, of the separation. But whether
> through the influence of Paul, or, more likely, through the misunderstand-
> ing of him by Gentile successors, the issue had gone much deeper, and the
> entirety of the religious conceptions of Judaism as proclaimed in the Old
> Testament was rejected as superseded by the Church.

A companion volume is Parkes' *Whose Land? A History of the Peoples of
Palestine* (Harmondsworth: Penguin, 1971). Also refer to the more recent
edition of *End of an Exile: Israel, The Jews and the Gentile World* (Marblehead,
MA: Micah, 1982). For a consideration of anti-Semitism as it relates to

the past one hundred and fifty years, consult the author's *Antisemitism* (Chicago: Quadrangle, 1969).

Peters, Joan. *From Time Immemorial: The Origins of the Arab–Jewish Conflict over Palestine.* London: JKAP, 1993. Differing claims amidst conflict between Arabs and Jews call for a studied response. Historian and journalist Joan Peters has provided such a book that both the *Christian Century* and *National Review* acknowledged as providing unrivaled clarifying thoroughness. Fierce criticism of this book by Noam Chomsky and Norman Finkelstein has not greatly subtracted from the essential challenge that it presents to Palestinian claims, which Alan Dershowitz cautiously referenced in *The Case for Israel* (Hoboken, NJ: John Wiley, 2003).

Phillips, Melanie. *Londonistan.* New York: Encounter, 2006. As a columnist for London's *Daily Mail*, this author lays bare the threat that resurgent Islam presents to the United Kingdom. However, special focus is brought upon London as the hub of Muslim extremism. From here we learn how Britain sleepwalks toward cultural oblivion by means of multicultural paralysis. Even Christian leaders, by buying into replacement theology, aid the advance of Islam while at the same time expressing support for anti-Judaism and anti-Zionism. This book is an excellent supplement to Bat Ye'or's *Eurabia.*

Rausch, David A. *Fundamentalist-Evangelicals and Anti-Semitism.* Valley Forge: Trinity Press International, 1993. Rausch is a conservative evangelical historian whose writings dispel numerous fallacies concerning the mischaracterization of "fundamentalist-evangelicals," especially in America. In particular, premillennial eschatology and its sympathy for national Israel and secular Zionism have frequently come under fire, such as from amillennialists who tilt toward an anti-Judaic eschatology (p. 206):

> In spite of scholarly perceptions to the contrary, the prophetically minded fundamentalist-evangelical has been (and currently is) a firm supporter of the Jewish state. And, in an age when anti-Zionism is often indistinguishable from anti-Semitism, this fact is crucial to our study. As we have seen throughout this study, the fundamentalist-evangelical was long a supporter of Jewish restoration to the Holy Land and, to this day, has received ridicule and scorn from other Christians for pro-Israel views. In spite of numerous liberal and conservative Christian cries to the contrary, this Christian Zionism has been a positive factor in combating any anti-Semitism within the fundamentalist-evangelical community.

See also Rausch's *A Legacy Of Hatred: Why Christians Must Not Forget the Holocaust* (Grand Rapids: Baker, 1990).

Remaud, Michel. *Israel, Servant of God.* London: T&T Clark, 2003. Here is another Roman Catholic, indebted to Franz Mussner, who challenges the established supercessionism of centuries while attempting to better reconcile the present reality of elect Israel and the Church, especially in the light of the Vatican II declaration, *Nostra Aetate.* For example (pp. 5–6, 19, 36–37),

> It is well known that the [Roman Catholic] Church calls herself the 'New Israel', and it is regrettable that Vatican II itself made use of this expression. Now traditional in theology but nowhere to be found in the New Testament, it gives the impression that the Church has taken the place of Israel, so that from the theological point of view Israel no longer exists. Such a simplistic position, pushed to extremes, contradicts more balanced texts found in the New Testament (Rom. 9–11; Eph. 2–3). . . . Of all the theological documents promulgated by the Second Vatican Council, only the text on the Jews *[Nostra Aetate]* is without a single reference to any of the teachings of the Church, whether patristic, conciliar or pontifical. As is usual for all the declarations of the Magisterium, documents of Vatican II include references to former tradition. . . . The text on the Jews is the sole exception to this rule in that it refers exclusively to Scripture. . . . To study the horrendous history of anti-Semitism, overwhelming for us, is to perceive that nowhere did the Jews suffer more than within the Christian world. No theology of history can spare itself from deep reflection on this fact.

Sachar, Howard M. *A History of Israel, from the Rise of Zionism to Our Time.* New York: Alfred A. Knopf, 1979. This is an outstanding work. Especially relevant is chapter 9, "Britain Repudiates the Jewish National Home." Sachar is also the author of *A History of the Jews in America, Israel and Europe,* and editor of *The Rise of Israel: A Documentary History* (39 vols.). He serves as Professor of Modern History at George Washington University, is a consultant and lecturer on Middle Eastern affairs for numerous governmental bodies, and lectures widely in the United States and abroad.

Siker, Jeffrey S. *Disinheriting the Jews.* Louisville: Westminster/John Knox, 1991. This revision of a doctoral thesis presented to Princeton Theological Seminary was originally titled "Disinheriting the Jews: The Use of Abraham in Early Christian Controversy with Judaism from Paul Through Justin Martyr." This is the work of a recognized authority. The author's conclusion is that (pp. 195–97) the various uses of Abraham from Paul through Justin Martyr show a shift in focus from Gentile inclusion to Jewish exclusion. However: Was this move theologically necessary or defensible? . . . Does Gentile inclusion in God's promises necessitate Jewish exclusion? Justin Martyr, Marcion, Heracleon, Barnabas, and Ignatius apparently did equate Gentile inclusion with Jewish exclusion. . . . Only Paul seems clearly to have had problems with such an equation, in fact rejecting it implicitly in Romans 4 and explicitly in Romans 9–11. . . . Paul did not equate Jewish rejection of the gospel with God's rejection of the Jews. Nor would he allow such an equation to be inferred. Rather, Jewish rejection of the gospel served God's purpose of Gentile inclusion within the gospel. The Jews became enemies of the gospel so that Gentiles might be included within the gospel. Thus the Gentiles were saved by their enemies. This situation is the utter paradox and mystery of the gospel for Paul. . . . For Paul, non-Christian Jews continue to be included within God's promises simply because of God's covenant faithfulness to Abraham and other patriarchs. . . . Paul would not affirm the theological doctrine that became entrenched among later generations of Christians, namely, that Gentile inclusion necessitates Jewish exclusion.

Vlach, Michael J. *The Church as a Replacement of Israel: An Analysis of Supersessionism.* This doctoral dissertation was presented to Southeastern Baptist Theological Seminary in Wake Forest, North Carolina. Included are assessments of Justin Martyr, Origen, Augustine, Thomas Aquinas, Martin Luther, John Calvin, Immanuel Kant, Friederich Schliermacher, and Karl Barth. He argues that although supercessionism was the dominant view of the church throughout most of its history (pp. xv–xvi), "the Scriptures do not support the view that the New Testament church is the new Israel that has forever superseded national Israel as the people of God."

White, Derek C. *Replacement Theology, Its Origin, History, and Theology.* Teddington, Middlesex: Christian Friends of Israel, 1997. This booklet of only 30 pages is an excellent introduction to and summary of the nature and role of replacement theology in church history. White states (p. 2),

One of the greatest tragedies to befall the Church was the severance from her Jewish roots, a rift which has been a cause of many heresies, of monasticism and departures from Biblical truth and lifestyle. The very descent of the Western Church into the dark middle ages—the period of intellectual and spiritual darkness in Europe from the fifth to the (possibly) fifteenth centuries—was almost certainly the result of this separation, not the least as a divine judgment on the Church for the anti-Semitism which was part of this severance.

Williamson, Clark M. *Has God Rejected His People?* Nashville: Abingdon, 1982. Designed as an introduction to the history of the relationship between Judaism and Christianity, this author provides an excellent resource, although lacking expression of conservative evangelical views. As to the roots of anti-Semitism that pervaded Hitler's Germany, the author concludes (p. 134),

> All the literature one reads on the final solution leaves the clear impression that the pervasiveness of classical Christian anti-Jewish theology was a significant factor in the success of Hitler's program. Where it did not directly contribute to support for Hitler's policies—and it often did—it created an apathy toward Jews that was equally decisive in permitting the Holocaust. The great majority of the German people did not actively support or actively oppose Hitler: they were merely indifferent.

Wilson, Marvin R. *Our Father Abraham: Jewish Roots of the Christian Faith.* Grand Rapids: Eerdmans, 2000. This is an excellent corrective to the widespread ignorance that pervades Christendom concerning its Jewish heritage. The author concludes (pp. 84, 101),

> Though the break between Synagogue and Church had now essentially been made, the struggle between the two was far from over. A triumphalist and arrogant Church, largely Gentile in makeup, would now become more and more de-Judaized—severed from its Jewish roots. This de-Judaizing developed into a history of anti-Judaism, a travesty which has extended from the second century to the present day. . . . We must emphasize in conclusion that the Holocaust did not happen in a vacuum. Though it was devised in a country with an enviable reputation for brilliant culture and intellectual sophistication, the seeds of anti-Semitism had been planted much earlier. The Holocaust represents the tragic culmination of anti-Jewish attitudes and practices which had been allowed to manifest themselves—largely unchecked—in or nearby the Church for nearly two thousand years. Perhaps the most important reason the Holocaust happened is that the Church had forgotten its Jewish roots.

Wistrich, Robert S. *Antisemitism, The Longest Hatred.* New York: Pantheon, 1991. This is a companion volume to the excellent Thames Television video production *The Longest Hatred*, 150 minutes, also released in 1991. With the encouragement of Simon Wiesenthal, Wistrich has provided a broad, scholarly sweep of anti-Semitism from a Jewish perspective that is approvingly referenced in Graham Keith's *Hated Without A Cause?* Of particular interest is "Part 1, From the Cross to the Swastika."

Yee, Tet-Lim N. *Jews, Gentiles and Ethnic Reconciliation: Paul's Jewish Identity and Ephesians.* Cambridge: Cambridge University Press, 2005. This revised doctoral thesis presented to Durham University, with James Dunn as advisor, provides a detailed study of Eph 2:1–22 from the "new perspective" which reconsiders the epistles of Paul through the distinctive focus of first century Judaism. Although Yee does not assume Pauline authorship of Ephesians, he does not deny it. He concludes that the author of Ephesians "is at heart a (Christian) Jew," who "never ceased to be a Jew" (pp. 33, 70). He concludes a detailed exegesis of Ephesians 2 with some important results for the issue of Jewish-Christian relations. For instance (pp. 217, 221–222, 228),

> It may be fairly claimed that the 'Christianity' represented by the author of Ephesians is a movement of renewal breaking through the boundaries within one Judaism (not all) of the first century which is marked characteristically by covenantal ethnocentrism. That being said, it would be wrong to suggest that Ephesians represents the abandonment of Judaism in favor of Greek triumphalism over ethnic Israel. Rather, we should speak of a Jewish messianic inclusivistic movement which transcends covenantal ethnocentrism: the Messiah Jesus, who is portrayed as a peace-maker in Ephesians, has come to preach peace to the 'far off' *and* the 'near.' He has surmounted the social distance between Jew and Gentile so that 'both' can gain access to the God of Israel in a common spirit.

This well represents the essential thrust of Judeo-centric eschatology.

Ye'or, Bat. *Eurabia: The Euro-Arab Axis.* Madison: Fairleigh Dickinson University Press, 2005. The Arabic word *dhimmi* refers to a non-Muslim who is under harsh terms of subjection within a Muslim society. Particularly since the defeat of the combined Arab military by Israel during the 1967 Six Day War and the 1973 Yom Kippur War, the Muslim states, especially those with substantial petroleum resources, have focused upon a different strategy. The exchange of European technology, both economic and military, for Middle Eastern oil, has come with the added price of recognition of the Palestinian Liberation Organization's territorial claims as well as an anti-American and anti-Israel and anti-Christian and anti-Western agenda. Hence, for over 30 years, European capitulation to these demands has resulted in "Eurabia: The Land of Dhimmitude," that is, the gradual subjection of Europe in general to spreading Muslim influence without ideological capitulation to the West in return, as well as increasing anti-Judaism. In parallel with this intended penetration of western society, there has also come about an increase in the influence of strident Christian anti-Judaic supercessionism as represented by Anglican Stephen Sizer and Islamophile literature represented by Anglican Bishop Kenneth Cragg. Ye'or's book is essential reading for those who would better understand the present Muslim resurgence along with, especially in Europe, the increase in anti-Judaism.

Author Index

Subject Index

Scripture Index